VOICE, WORD, AND SPIRIT

Rickie D. Moore and
Brian Neil Peterson

VOICE, WORD, AND SPIRIT

A Pentecostal Old Testament Survey

Abingdon Press

Nashville

VOICE, WORD, AND SPIRIT:
A PENTECOSTAL OLD TESTAMENT SURVEY
Copyright © 2017 by Abingdon Press

Library of Congress Cataloging-in-Publication Data has been requested.

ISBN 978-1-5018-1516-4

17 18 19 20 21 22 23 24 25 26—10 9 8 7 6 5 4 3 2 1

MANUFACTURED IN THE UNITED STATES OF AMERICA

*"One generation will praise your works to the next one,
proclaiming your mighty acts."*
(Psalm 145:4)

This book is dedicated to our children:
Emily and Hannah (Rickie Moore)
and Madeline, Mark, and Kevin (Brian Peterson).
May God's Voice, Word, and Spirit
ever be a vital part of your lives.

*"For the promise is unto you, and to your children
and to all that are afar off, even as many
as the Lord our God shall call."*
(Acts 2:39 KJV)

CONTENTS

LIST OF ABBREVIATIONS

ANE	ancient Near East
Ant	*Antiquities of the Jews* (by Flavius Josephus)
Dtr	Deuteronomist
DtrH	Deuteronomistic History
JPTSup	Journal for the Study of the Old Testament Supplement Series
Jwr	*The Jewish War* (or *Flavius Josephus's Books of the History of the Jewish War against the Romans*)
LXX	the Septuagint
MT	Masoretic Text
NT	New Testament
OT	Old Testament

INTRODUCTION

The first introduction to the Bible for many of us was the children's Sunday School song "The B-I-B-L-E." Perhaps it is time for a new verse to this song—one that calls us to a deeper engagement with Scripture:[1]

The B-I-B-L-E.
The Book that's reading me,
The Voice that's heard is Spirit-Word,
The B-I-B-L-E.
BIBLE!

As the authors of this textbook, we believe it is time for a new introduction to the Old Testament (OT). Recognizing that every such textbook has its own slant, we want to be up front about the approach we are taking in this survey. The first thing to be said is that, as a college-level introduction, this book presents an overview of the OT that engages with current academic scholarship. Thus, we will provide a basic orientation to the major issues, debates, methods, discoveries, and directions of OT scholarship today.

For many and probably most readers of this book, this will be your first time to approach the Bible in terms of academic scholarship. Having experienced the Bible up to this point only in the context of church life and devotional settings, you may find this encounter a bit like being thrust into a foreign country. Such an experience is well illustrated in the story that begins the OT book of Daniel (Dan 1). Here we see Daniel and his three young Hebrew friends taken into captivity by the Babylonian Empire and subjected to a three-year educational program to learn the Babylonian "language and literature" (Dan 1:4)—a curriculum that exposed them (as our study will surely expose our readers) to subject matter far outside and at many points at odds with the Hebrew faith tradition being brought to the encounter.

The way this story of Daniel unfolds also illustrates the second major aspect of the approach being taken in this textbook. As Daniel and his three friends (Shadrach, Meshach, and Abednego) took care not to swallow (both literally and figuratively) everything the Babylonians were trying to feed them (1:8-16), the story takes note of a remarkable development: "God gave knowledge, mastery of all literature, and wisdom to these four men. Daniel himself gained understanding of every type of vision and dream" (1:17). This verse has a couple of key things to show us. First, the Hebrew faith of these young people did not keep

---

1. Rickie D. Moore, "Altar Hermeneutics: Reflections on Pentecostal Biblical Interpretation," *Pnuema* 38 (2016): 1–12.

them from learning scholarship from "outside" sources. On the contrary, God was the source behind this learning, even their learning of the Babylonian curriculum, all the way to the point of enabling them to master it and to graduate at the top of their class (1:18-20)! Yet verse 17 points to something else that goes far beyond scholarly knowledge. It attests to Daniel being given a supernatural or spiritual knowledge—the kind that involves perceiving and interpreting prophetic revelations. As the subsequent chapters of the book of Daniel proceed to show, this second kind of knowledge opens Daniel and his people to seeing more than just a series of specific revelations; it opens them to an entire worldview—a way of seeing and interpreting *everything*, including Scripture, in the light of spiritual revelation (chs. 2; 7; 9).

Thus, like this opening story of Daniel, this textbook is coming from a perspective that affirms the integration of what could be described as academic scholarship and charismatic spirituality. Accordingly, we will present an overview of the OT that is explicitly engaged with the faith and practice of the Pentecostal movement and the recent scholarship that has been generated by this contemporary, global, Christian movement, especially as it bears upon biblical interpretation.[2] In line with this, we have chosen as the title of this survey the phrase, *Voice, Word, and Spirit*. These three terms highlight the conviction that the Holy Word cannot be fully comprehended apart from the Holy Spirit. Thus, to approach the Holy Scripture is to do so in expectation of being encountered and addressed by a Living Voice. As the song above puts it, "The Voice that's heard is Spirit-Word." Taking this seriously cannot help but expand and sometimes even flip the goal of biblical study from us interpreting Scripture to Scripture interpreting us. In other words, this survey is committed to fostering an approach to reading the Bible as "The Book that's reading me"—an approach that promises to be much more critical than what usually goes under the name of "critical academic study of the Bible."[3]

In the following chapters, each OT book (in the "Protestant Bible" sequence) is surveyed in a seven-part format: (1) The "Hook," a point of contact or personal story (by Peterson) designed to hook (i.e., engage) the reader; (2) "Quick Facts," basic information about the book's title, date, authorship, audience, purpose, genre, and so forth ("what you need to know for the exam"); (3) "Structure," the organization and arrangement of the book's main sections; (4) "Summary," a brief overview of the content of each biblical book; (5) "Debated Issues," a list of questions arising from scholarly debate on the book that make great paper topics; (6) "The Message of the Book," a succinct statement that identifies the book's essential meaning; and (7) "Closing the Loop," a concluding section (by Moore) that addresses key points of intersection between the given OT book and Pentecostal faith and practice.

In addition to treating each OT book individually, this textbook provides a brief chapter to introduce each of the four major book collections, as standardized in the Protestant Bible's arrangement of OT Scriptures: (1) Pentateuch; (2) Historical Books; (3) Poetical Books; and (4) Prophets.

---

2. See John Christopher Thomas, "Where the Spirit Leads: The Development of Pentecostal Hermeneutics," *Journal of Beliefs & Values: Studies in Religion & Education* 30, no. 3 (December 2009): 289–302; John Christopher Thomas, "Pentecostal Biblical Interpretation," *Oxford Encyclopedia of Biblical Interpretation*, ed. S. L. McKenzie (Oxford: Oxford University Press, 2013), 2:89–97.

3. Rickie D. Moore, *The Spirit of the Old Testament*, JPTS 35 (Blandford Forum, UK: Deo, 2011): 1–18; Moore, "Altar Hermeneutics."

This raises the issue of *canonization*, or the process by which individual books of Scripture were collected, arranged, and settled on to become the Bible; that is, the accepted body of writings regarded as the unalterable and authoritative divine word for God's people. The term *Bible* comes from a word simply meaning "books." The term *canonization* comes from an ancient word that means a "reed" or "cane" used for measuring (like a yardstick). Thus, the books that have been canonized—that is, have become the canon of Scripture—have been measured and have become the authoritative standard of measurement for everything else.

Today there are four major faith traditions (Protestant, Catholic, Orthodox, and Jewish) that have OT canons that differ from one another. A brief sketch of the canonization process that yielded these variations is in order. The process began, of course, with the Hebrews, the ancient Jewish people, who wrote, preserved, collected, and canonized the OT books over a very long span of time, possibly a millennium or more. There is much about this process that remains hidden, but a few things are fairly clear. The Hebrew canon formed in terms of three major collections. The first of these was the **Torah** (from the Hebrew term for "law" or "instruction"), which Christians know as the Pentateuch or the Five Books of Moses (Gen, Exod, Lev, Num, and Deut). The second Hebrew canonical section to form was the **Prophets** (Heb *Nevi'im*), which had two subdivisions: the Former Prophets (Josh, Judg, Sam, and Kgs) and the Latter Prophets (Isa, Jer, Ezek, and the Twelve [originally the 12 Minor Prophets combined as a single scroll]). The final Hebrew canonical division to form was the **Writings** (Heb *Ketuvim*), which included the rest of the books we know as the Hebrew Scriptures, ordered in various ways until finally arriving in the following order: Psalms, Proverbs, Job, the Five Scrolls (Song of Songs, Ruth, Lamentations, Ecclesiastes, and Esther), Daniel, Ezra–Nehemiah, and Chronicles. This three-part canon of Hebrew Scripture (Torah, *Nevi'im*, and *Ketuvim*) accounts for the Hebrew term *TaNaK* (or *Tanak*), which is the Jewish people's primary term for their Scripture. They don't use the term *Old Testament*, since that's a Christian term that presupposes the New Testament.

There is no certainty about when this threefold canon reached its final fixation. One prominent theory is that this took place near the end of the first century CE at the so-called Council of Jamnia (a center of Jewish scribal activity about 30 miles west of Jerusalem, after it was destroyed by the Romans in 70 CE). This theory speculates that the Jews at this time and place were trying to come to terms with their canon in response to the competing authority claims posed by the rise of Christianity. Other scholars believe the Hebrew canon formed much earlier, sometime near the middle of the Intertestamental Period (the four centuries between the end of the OT and the beginning of the NT). This was when the Jewish people were responding to the threat of being assimilated to the Greek culture, or Hellenized, after having been subjected to dispersion (i.e., the Diaspora) throughout the Mediterranean world. This scattering of the Jews took place at the hands of a series of ancient empires that took turns conquering this region (viz., Assyria, Babylon, Persia, Greece, and finally Rome).

This latter view sees the finalizing of the Hebrew canon taking place somewhere around the time that the Hebrew Scriptures were being translated from the original Hebrew into another language for the first time. This first Bible translation effort produced a Greek translation of the Hebrew Scriptures known as the "Septuagint"—a title based on the Greek word for 70 (abbrev. LXX), which points to an intertestamental legend that 70 Jewish scholars in Alexandria, Egypt, working independently of one another, produced 70 identical copies of the Torah. Alexandria became the center for Diaspora Jews of the time alongside the older, more conservative center for Jewish life in Palestine. In addition to the bold step of translating the Hebrew Scriptures into Greek, the Jewish tradition of Alexandria is also known for propagating a number of intertestamental writings that eventually came to be counted as "deuterocanonical books," books of *secondary* canonical status, as the name implies (e.g., Tobit, Judith, Sirach, Baruch, 1–2 Maccabees, etc.). These books were included in the larger Greek canon of Scripture that came to constitute the Bible of early Christianity. Thus, early Christianity enlarged the canon of Scripture beyond that of the Hebrew canon (the *Tanak*) by including not only the NT but also the deuterocanonical books, which came to be known as the "Apocrypha" (i.e., "hidden" writings). Early Christianity moved beyond the Hebrew canon in still another significant manner, namely, by rearranging the Hebrew order of the biblical materials in several ways, which included the previously mentioned scheme of Pentateuch-Historical Books-Poetical Books-Prophets. We will give further details on this as we come to these different canonical sections.

The East–West schism of the Christian church in 1054 CE produced little difference between the canon of Scripture of the Orthodox Church in the East and that of Roman Catholicism in the West, except for the former's inclusion of a few additional apocryphal books. However, the division with Roman Catholicism that came with the Protestant Reformation about five centuries later yielded a very significant change. The Protestant Bible removed the apocryphal books entirely and returned to the more restricted contents of the Hebrew *Tanak*. Yet, the Protestant canon retained the Catholic and Orthodox ordering of these materials rather than returning to the original Hebrew order. Here again, we will note these differences between our Protestant canon and the Hebrew canonical arrangement as we go.

As noted earlier, there is much that remains hidden in the lengthy process by which the Hebrew canon was first formed. The same can be said of the even shorter processes involved in the forming of the Christian canon of Orthodox and Catholic traditions and then in the "reforming" effort that brought about the Protestant Bible. All of these processes obviously have a human dimension that is open to being excavated through academic scholarship, although this gets harder the farther one goes back in time. Yet there are those of us who believe that these processes involve a dimension that goes beyond a merely human level to a divine dimension—one that academic scholarship by itself may not be fully equipped to appreciate. This would be a dimension that charismatic spirituality might have a much better vantage point for discerning. Doesn't the process of canonization, much like the process of interpretation as discussed earlier, ultimately come down to a spiritual discernment by the people of God—a discernment that certain human words that have been written and then passed down by human hands are not merely human words but words that embody the word of God for the people of God? If one has ever experienced something akin to this inspiration in a spoken word, then it is probably easier to grasp the notion of the divine inspiration of inscripturated, or written, words. The experience in view here does not necessarily entail the context of a charismatic worship event. One might try watching a video of Martin Luther King Jr.'s "I Have a Dream Speech" as a segue to thinking further about the processes by which human words might come to be discerned as inspired words.

In addition to the canonization process that brought us the books of Scripture, there is the textual transmission process that brought us the specific wording of the biblical books. The study of this latter process for the purpose of determining the most likely original wording is called *text criticism*. It begins with the recognition that we do not have access to any original documents (often called "original autographs") of any biblical books. Instead we have Scriptures that have been transmitted to us through many generations of copies of copies of copies—most of these generated through copying done by hand long before the invention of the printing press. Obviously, such copying is tedious work subject to human error. Through centuries of textual transmission, the evidence of human error crops up in the many (mostly small) textual variants that appear among the most ancient manuscripts that scholars have found and are still discovering today. Of all of these discoveries, none has been more significant than the Dead Sea Scrolls, found half a century ago in caves at ancient Qumran near the Dead Sea. In the extremely dry conditions of this place, hundreds of texts dating back to the Intertestamental Period (as early as the third century BCE) were preserved in clay pots on leather parchment and papyrus (along with one copper scroll). Among the hundreds of texts found, close to half of the scroll manuscripts and fragments are texts of Hebrew Scripture, representing at least some portion of every book of the Hebrew Bible except Esther. The overall significance of this discovery is that it gives scholars a treasure trove of biblical manuscript evidence that is more than 1,000 years older than the oldest complete manuscripts of Hebrew Scripture that scholars previously had available for the work of text criticism and Bible translation. What's more, the Dead Sea Scrolls have overwhelmingly confirmed that, despite the many textual variants that crop up in the details of ancient Hebrew manuscripts, including the Dead Sea Scrolls, the Hebrew textual transmission process, undertaken across centuries of time by Hebrew scribal scholars known as the Masoretes, is remarkable in its overall meticulous preservation of the exact wording of the Hebrew text of Scripture (often referred to as the Masoretic Text, or MT). This amazingly careful work of the ancient scholars comes together with the painstaking work of text-critical scholars of today to ensure the trustworthy rendering of the wording of the texts and translations of Scripture, one verse at a time. Text criticism is a very important branch of academic biblical scholarship (among other branches that will be described in later chapters). It focuses on the human dimension of how the Scriptures have come down to us. Yet one might be permitted to see the preserving hand of God even in the mundane work of making copies of Scripture. The ancient Masoretes certainly thought so.

The work of Bible translation is the culminating step in the process that puts Scripture into our hands. In our contemporary English-speaking world, there has been a proliferation of different English Bible translations. As each attempts to span the gap between the ancient language and contemporary expression, some are more inclined to aim for "formal correspondence" with the ancient words and word order (e.g., RSV, NKJV, ESV, NASB, et al.), whereas others strive for "dynamic equivalence" of impact in the

One of the Dead Sea Scrolls. Photo courtesy of Michael Luddeni.

contemporary language (e.g., NEB, GNB, NLT, et al.).[4] Some even pursue this latter goal to the point of moving beyond translation to paraphrase (e.g., *The Living Bible*, *The Message*). Then there are English Bible translations that seek more of a middle course between formal correspondence and dynamic equivalence (e.g., NIV, CEB, et al.). All of these translations have their place and have been useful at various points to us as the authors of this textbook. Yet for our purposes here, we have quoted from the Common English Bible (CEB) unless otherwise noted.

In the end, for people of faith, there is an unavoidable tension between the human and divine dimensions of Scripture—one that is part of the human-divine tension in the life of faith itself. In 2 Cor 4:7, the Apostle Paul addresses all this when he says, "We have this treasure in clay pots so that the awesome power belongs to God and doesn't come from us." Academic scholarship provides an important tool that can help us open up those "clay pots," and charismatic theology and spirituality can offer special help in opening us to the "treasure" hidden inside—the untold riches that bear witness to the "awesome power" of God. So let's get started.

4. Eugene A. Nida and Charles R. Taber, *The Theory and Practice of Translation* (Leiden, NL: E. J. Brill, 1982).

INTRODUCTION TO THE PENTATEUCH

The first five books of our Bible—Genesis, Exodus, Leviticus, Numbers, and Deuteronomy—compose a sequential grouping of books called the Pentateuch, a term derived from the Greek Septuagint title, meaning "five books." The Hebrew Bible first gathered and named this collection "Torah." This term is usually translated as "law," drawing attention to the great volume of material devoted to God's revelation of the law at Mount Sinai that appears from the middle of Exodus to the end of Deuteronomy. Yet the Pentateuch is about much more than "law," and so is the term *Torah*. In fact, most Jewish scholars today prefer to translate *Torah* as "Instruction," pointing to how the term derives from a common noun referring simply to teaching. Because *Torah* has become such a theologically loaded title it would take something closer to a term like "Revelation" to convey its present weight.

While the law looms large in Torah, its overarching genre is *story*. It presents a grand story line that starts with the beginning of the whole world and its peoples (Gen 1–11) and then narrows to focus on the beginnings of Israel—both the people of Israel and the land of Israel (Gen 12–Deut). The shift in focus comes in Gen 12:1-3, where God calls Abraham to leave his people and his land and go to a land that God would show him. In this new land, God would make out of him a great people for the purpose of bringing blessing upon all the peoples of the world. Thus, Torah here, at this pivot point, ties together the beginning of the world and the beginning of Israel with the good promise of God's end goal and purpose for Israel and for the world.

This transition is punctuated by a shift in the usage of the Hebrew term *eretz,* which is used primarily to refer to the "earth" in Genesis 1–11, but from Genesis 12 onward it will be the primary term for the "land." This pivot in focus from the whole earth to the promised land sets the geographical stage for the grand story of Torah and also for the even larger story (or metanarrative) that frames the rest of the OT. In other words, Torah puts the land of Israel at the geographical center of the Bible (cf. Ezek 38:12). Indeed, Israel is in the middle of the so-called Fertile Crescent of what we still today call the *Middle* East and what OT scholars prefer to call the "ancient Near East" (ANE). Israel is situated between Mesopotamia to the northeast (the continent of Asia) and Egypt to the southwest (the continent of Africa), thus making it a land bridge between the regions where the great ANE empires arose in the fertile valleys of the Tigris-Euphrates rivers and the Nile River, respectively. Israel's own geography is made fertile by the more modest Jordan River flowing from Lake Chinnereth in the north (called the Sea of Galilee in the NT and Lake

Tiberias today) to the Dead Sea in the south. Israel is bordered on the west by the Mediterranean Sea and on the east by the Arabian Desert.

The story that Torah tells does indeed have all the elements of an epic drama, which we will sketch here with the broadest of brushstrokes. There can be no drama without a plot and no plot without a crisis. So Torah has a vibrant plot driven by some crises of major proportions. This is indeed the case, both in the first part, which narrates the beginning of the world (Gen 1–11), and in the second part, which unfolds the beginning of Israel (Gen 12–Deut). God creates a good earth and human beings in God's own divine image to fill it, but from the start things begin to go violently bad to the point of God sending a destructive flood, making it necessary to start the world all over again with Noah and his family. After this second beginning falls short at the Tower of Babel, God begins yet again with Abraham. God gradually makes good on his promise to make a great people out of Abraham, but not before they spend a period of time in slavery in Egypt (Gen 15:13-16). In a mighty act, God saves his people and leads them back toward the land of Israel. The Torah epic ends with the people of Israel looking across the Jordan River, still waiting just outside the promised land. There are, of course, many more problems along the way to thicken the plot and to generate subplots. We will have much more to say about the details as we go. And as the plot develops, so do the main characters: there are the peoples of the world (esp. the ANE world), the people of Israel, and most important, God, in the leading role—as the creator and re-creator of both the world and Israel. Thus, the story of Torah shows God to be the ultimate source of life for Israel and for the world. Yet God is a creator who has created enough space so that *all* people, made in God's own image as they are, can choose either to live from the Source or to turn from the Source—that is, to look exclusively to their *own* resources, which, apart from the Source, can sustain life for only so long.

Ironically enough, modern academic study of the Bible began with a branch of Old Testament study called *source criticism*. Developed by a school of German scholarship that emerged in the rise of the Western Enlightenment, it was the first of what became a cluster of branches that together came to be called *biblical historical criticism*—all devoted to understanding the historical background and history of the composition of the biblical books. It sought to determine who composed the biblical books and when, where, and how they were composed. Source criticism focused on identifying the original author(s). Other branches of the historical-critical method that followed included *form criticism* and *redaction/tradition criticism*. The former looked for the "forms" (i.e., genres) or patterns and pieces of literary material that the authors used to compose a given text and the possible "setting in life" (German *Sitz im Leben*) that spawned them. The latter looked at how all the literary pieces and traditions were put together and edited in stages over time to develop the larger compositions. These historical-critical methods were thus used together to get at the *history behind the text*.

This entire historical-critical approach arose during a time of questioning older traditions and systems of authority. The Protestant Reformation had challenged the authority of the Catholic Church by means of the authority of Scripture alone (*sola scriptura*). Yet the Western Enlightenment (and rise of the scientific worldview) that soon followed questioned all supernaturally grounded authority, including that of Scripture, on the basis of human reason alone. To their credit, these developments pushed back against ways that the older systems of authority, secured by their supernatural claims, had too often pushed down the human spirit and had not done justice generally to the human dimension of life, even the human dimension of the Bible. Yet once this revolution of humanism got going, the pendulum of the Enlightenment worldview swung to the other extreme, granting no place whatsoever for the validity of the supernatural. This naturalistic perspective was applied across the entire spectrum of human learning, including study of the Bible. Scripture would now be viewed as nothing more than a human book, to be explained only in terms of its human dimensions and sources.

This new approach to Bible study was applied first to the Pentateuch. The traditional belief that God was its ultimate source had been tied to the tradition of Moses's inspired authorship of the entire Pentateuch. This tradition went beyond what the Pentateuch itself claimed in the matter of Moses's authorship. A few verses in Deuteronomy speak of Moses's writing down (at God's direction) certain portions of this final book of the Pentateuch (27:3, 8; 31:19), but no such claim is made for Mosaic authorship of the Pentateuch as a whole. This more expanded claim for Moses's authorship was thus overreaching and made an easy target when the practitioners of modern source criticism turned their attention to the matter. Starting with the observation that Moses surely could not have written his own death story (Deut 34), they proceeded to search for all the many other details from the biblical text that could be used to challenge the tradition of Mosaic authorship. Beyond merely modifying or revising this tradition, many scholars instead aimed to demolish it entirely, together with its tandem claim for Scripture's divine inspiration.

Yet if Moses was not the author of the Pentateuch, then who was? The work of several generations of German scholarship throughout the 18th and 19th centuries led to the development of a comprehensive theory for the authorship of the Pentateuch that came to be known as the *documentary hypothesis* or the *Wellhausen hypothesis*, named after Julius Wellhausen, the scholar who gave the theory its classic formulation in 1878. The theory argued that the Pentateuch is a composite of four source documents written by different authors at different times and then layered or combined together to form the whole. The source documents were identified in terms of their respective differences in literary styles, themes, traditions, vocabulary, concerns, and so forth, as well as the historical time periods and contexts from which the documents were thought to have originated. The four source documents were designated as follows:

- **J or Jahwist (or Yahwist):** Named for its use of "Jahweh" (German spelling of Yahweh, the Hebrew personal name of God, which we will hereafter render YHWH). Reflects theological traditions of the southern kingdom of Judah. Alleged to be written in mid-900s BCE.

- **E or Elohist:** Named for its use of "Elohim" to refer to God. Reflects traditions of the northern kingdom of Israel. Alleged to be written in mid-800s BCE.

- **D or Deuteronomist:** Named as the source document for Deuteronomy. Alleged to be written in the 600s BCE in connection with the 2 Kgs 22–23 story about the finding of "the book of the Torah" in the Jerusalem Temple.

- **P or Priestly Source:** Named for its focus on priestly concerns. Alleged to be written in the 500s BCE by priests reflecting the Jewish context after the Babylonian Exile.

This JEDP hypothesis (as it is also commonly called) swept the field of academic biblical studies and became what is arguably the single most influential theory in biblical scholarship throughout the 20th century. Not only did it dominate academic study of the Pentateuch, but it also led the way for source criticism and the other historical-critical methods to dominate the academic study of the rest of the biblical writings, both OT and NT. Biblical historical criticism's lasting success, which lingers to this day, is its meticulous scrutiny of textual details that has compellingly raised awareness of the human dimensions of the biblical text. Yet seeing the traces of different human hands and historical contexts does not provide conclusive evidence for reconstructing the specific dates and stages of compositional history. Consequently, the JEDP hypothesis and other theories of historical criticism have splintered into so many variations by subsequent scholars that the very methods have lost more and more of their authority for recovering the history behind the text. This is undoubtedly one of the reasons why academic biblical scholarship since the last quarter of the 20th century has turned more and more from historical criticism to *literary criticism*; that is, from focusing on the history behind the text to focusing on *the text in front of the reader*, particularly in terms of the literary artistry of the final form of the biblical text.

Biblical literary criticism has also developed its own cluster of branches (e.g., canonical criticism, rhetorical criticism, narrative criticism, aesthetic criticism, etc.) that have similarly spread like a wave across the study of the Bible in its entirety, both OT and NT. Its stunning success has been to discover the sophisticated literary features by which the ancient biblical authors skillfully designed and unified their compositions—features mostly overlooked by historical criticism's exclusive focus on diverse details in the text in order to argue for diverse sources.

Applied to the Pentateuch, literary criticism has effectively shown how this entire body of literature is tied together by a single, overarching theme, namely: *God's promise to the patriarchs concerning children, covenant relationship, and land*.[1] In the following chapters we will see how this threefold theme, first introduced in God's promise to Abraham in Gen 12:1-3, moves forward in each individual book of the Pentateuch.

Yet there is still another, more recent wave of biblical scholarship that has come in the wake of literary criticism, namely, postmodern approaches to biblical study—approaches that focus on *the reader in front of the text*. These approaches go by many names (e.g., reader-response criticism, contextual hermeneutics, post-critical hermeneutics, and deconstruction, to name a few), but they have one thing in common. They all emphasize that where readers "are coming from" and what they are bringing to the biblical text make

---

1. David J. A. Clines, *The Theme of the Pentateuch*, 2nd ed. JSOTSup 10 (Sheffield, UK: JSOT Press, 1997).

a decisive difference in what they find there. This postmodern turn in academic biblical study comes, of course, as a part of the massive worldview shift away from the Western Enlightenment worldview to what we all now know as postmodern culture. The end of the absolute reign of the Enlightenment, with its naturalistic perspective, has had the positive benefit of granting space for many new perspectives and voices to be heard, even those who would affirm supernatural dimensions of existence. Indeed, this is the very space that now makes possible this OT survey textbook from a Pentecostal perspective! Yet on the down side there is the threat that all this openness to a multitude of new perspectives and new voices will result in nothing more than a chaotic mass of peoples speaking in different tongues!

So, where do we go from here in view of the foregoing sketch of the history of how academic biblical scholarship, over the last few centuries, has read the Bible, and the Pentateuch in particular? Perhaps we could consider turning this question around and asking how the Pentateuch might "read" the history of academic biblical scholarship. Just maybe it would look something like the story of the Tower of Babel in Gen 11:1-9, in which a new human project was proposed that ruled out any foundation upon a divine source (source criticism), then conceived a construction process of entirely human formulation (form criticism), with self-assured confidence of knowing how the project pieces would all be put together (redaction criticism). Yet no sooner than attention could turn to the final form of the project (literary criticism), the whole project disintegrated in the face of a breakdown in communication with a mass of people groups speaking, each from their own perspective, in diverse tongues (reader response, postmodern criticism, and deconstruction).

The story could end here. However, the story of Genesis at this very point offers a new beginning that comes in God's call to Abraham in Gen 12:1-3—a threefold promise of children, covenant relationship, and land. Perhaps it is enough to give us hope that our own story in these very unsettling postmodern times could have a new beginning—hope that we, too, amid the clamor and confusion of so many voices, could hear a Voice much better than our own—one that would reveal the very Source of life for us and for all the peoples of every tribe and tongue in all the earth.

The Torah story itself ends with such a hope only partially fulfilled. When we come to the last verse of Deuteronomy, God's people have become a great nation with many children, but they still find themselves outside the promised land. Thus, it is a story with an open ending—one that just might be open enough to make room for our own story. So let's take a closer look.

GENESIS

In the beginning . . .
        —Genesis 1:1 (KJV)

When I think about the book of Genesis,

the classic Star Trek II movie, *The Wrath of Khan* (followed up by the sequel, *The Search for Spock*) comes to mind. In this movie scientists create a "Genesis Device" that, in theory, can make an uninhabitable planet livable by taking existing matter and rearranging it into a life-sustaining utopia. A dead moon is turned into an inhabitable planet in a little over one minute. When Spock (played by Jewish actor Leonard Nimoy) sees the theoretical application of the device, he concludes that it "literally is Genesis," to which Captain James Kirk (played by William Shatner) adds, "power of creation." The irony in the depiction of this imaginary device is that science fiction has actually taken the premise of Genesis 1 and condensed the six days of creation into a few seconds. While modern people have often argued that God could never create the world in six days, the characters of this movie are quick to accept the possibility of an even more condensed time frame for creation to occur—only this time devoid of God.

As interesting as the "Genesis Device" is for our science fiction-enhanced thinking, the biblical account of Genesis is so much more than a mere creating of a space for life to exist. What the book of Genesis depicts is nothing less than the desire of the creator God to establish relationship with creation—in this case especially with the highest form of creation—humankind. From the opening chapter of the Bible, we are introduced to a God who creates and oversees the created order for the greater good of eventually bringing about the plan of salvation through Jesus, who was "slain from the foundation of the world" (Rev 13:8 KJV; cf. Rev 17:8; 1 Pet 1:20). Indeed, for the reader, Genesis becomes an introduction to the God whose Spirit first hovered over the waters of creation and now dwells within each and every believer today!

Quick Facts

Title: In our English Bibles, the word *Genesis* comes from the Greek LXX title meaning "beginnings." The title for the first book of the Hebrew canon comes from the first Hebrew word in the text, *bᵉreshith*, which means "in the beginning."

Date: The dating of Genesis is a somewhat complex issue depending on one's theory of how the final form of the book came into existence (see the introduction, on source theory and Wellhausen's JEDP hypothesis). Those holding to source-critical theory insist that Genesis is an amalgam of different traditions woven into a final form during the sixth century BCE or later. Those holding to Mosaic authorship (i.e., ca. 1446–1406 BCE or the 13th century if one adopts a late date for the Exodus) assert that Moses contributed a large portion of the material found in Genesis with only minor editing of the content during the monarchy or exilic period. This, it is argued, can be seen in the proposed anachronisms in the text (cf. kingship intimated—Gen 36:31; Philistines appear—21:32; 26:1, 8, 14, 18; place names are updated—14:14; 28:19; 35:6; Rameses is mentioned—47:11; the tribe of Judah is elevated—49:10, etc.).

Authorship: Closely associated with the dating of the book is the question of authorship. Unlike the prophetic texts where authorship is attested usually in the opening verses of a given book (Isa 1:1; Jer 1:1; Ezek 1:3; Hos 1:1, et al.), nowhere in Genesis do we find a direct attribution of authorship to Moses. Source theorists have proposed that later editors combined the Yahwist (southern/Judah perspective) and the Elohist (northern/Israel perspective) authors' work with the Priestly writers, adding an editorial layer as well (e.g., Gen 1 and portions of the flood narrative). Whatever position one takes on authorship, the thing to remember is that the final form is all that we presently have. Any theory about authorship and origins remains just that—a theory.

Audience: As with the entire OT, Genesis had a Jewish/Israelite audience in view. One can easily see that the message of Genesis (see below) would have served a Hebrew audience in almost any historical time frame. What must be kept in mind is that Genesis is in fact Torah (instruction) for the nation. And as such, this instruction becomes timeless.

Genre: On the micro level, Genesis contains a variety of genres, as noted by critical scholarship. These include, but are not limited to: poetry (e.g., chs. 1; 49); genealogies (e.g., chs. 4; 5; 10; 11; 25; 36); ancestral epics (11:26–25:11—Abraham; 21:3–35:29—Isaac; 25:26–37:34 and 42:1–50:24—Jacob; and 30:24–50:26—Joseph; note that these accounts overlap significantly); dream accounts (28:12-15; 37:5-10; 40:5-22; 41:1-32); mythology (e.g., 2:4–4:16; 6:1-4); and etiologies (that is, narratives that account for the origin of something: e.g., 2:20-25—the origins of woman; 3:15-17—pain in childbearing and the curse on the ground; 4:20-24—the origins of nomadic life and farming, music, metalworking; 14:20; 28:22—tithing; 32:32—food practices).

On the macro level, as the first book of a five-book block, Genesis is a story, and yet a story that falls within the genre of instruction called Torah (and the concern specifically for legal instruction can be found at a number of points: sacrifice—8:20; 12:7-8; 13:18; 26:25; 31:54; 33:20; 35:7; clean and unclean animals—7:2, 8; 8:20; tithing—14:20; 28:22, etc.). As Torah, certain passages of Genesis clearly reflect larger theological and practical truths. For example, the garden of Eden with the tree of the knowledge of good and evil represents instruction to obey God's laws so that the nation could stay in the land (Eden➔Canaan); that is, choose life (i.e., the tree of life) and not death! (i.e., the tree of the knowledge of good and evil; cf. Deut 30:15, 19; 1:35, 39). Also, the cryptic account of Gen 6:1-4 could have been a warning that indiscriminate marriage between the holy and the profane brings the destruction of people and land (cf. Judg 3:6—intermarriage with the Canaanites set the stage for Israel's expulsion from the land; see also 2 Cor 6:14). When viewed from this larger perspective, Genesis indeed fits this genre classification.

Purpose: In light of the discussion immediately above, the foremost purpose of Genesis is to offer instruction in the ways of God. Moreover, the book is powerfully instructional in a more implicit way by giving an account of God's creation of the universe and a prehistory of Israel's ancestors—Abraham, Sarah, Isaac, Rebekah, Jacob, and Rachel—while giving a record of the election of Abraham, and by extension, Israel. Introducing a plethora of theological themes (soteriology, anthropology, angelology, pneumatology, hamartiology, etc.), Genesis establishes a monotheistic worldview (Gen 1); reveals the need for the sacrificial system (Gen 3–4); initiates the promise of the land (Gen 12:1); records the institution of the Abrahamic covenant (Gen 15) and circumcision (Gen 17); and gives the reason for the Egyptian sojourn (Gen 45–47). One can clearly see why this introductory OT book is rightly called Genesis ("beginnings").

Structure

While a number of structural patterns have been recognized for Genesis, there are two dominant views. The first is based on what is known as the *toledoth* formula (*toledoth* is the Hebrew term for "generations" in the KJV's recurring phrase "these are the generations of"). The 11 appearances of the *toledoth* formula serve as a linking device that is frequently seen as evidence for the unity of the book (2:4; 5:1; 6:9; 10:1; 11:10, 27; 25:12, 19; 36:1, 9; 37:2; cf. also Num 3:1; Ruth 4:18). The second major view of the structure of Genesis relates to the content of the book. Genesis 1–11 presents what is often called the *primeval history*, with chapters 12–50 being labeled the *patriarchal* or *ancestral history*. The former presents the universal scope of God's creation and plan for humanity, whereas the latter presents God's plan for Israel through the ancestral promise and lineage.

Through these structural segments of the book, one can also see a fluctuation between the focus on an individual to the focus on a group. For example, Genesis begins with Adam (and Eve—chs. 2–3) and moves to a family (ch. 4) and then to the larger populace (5:1–6:7). At this point the author narrows his focus to one man, Noah (Gen 6:8–9:29), then to his family and then to the nations (10:1–11:9). Again, the focus thereafter narrows to one man, Shem, and his larger family and descendants (11:10-32), only to narrow once again to one man—Abraham (12:1–21:2)—and his family (21:3–46:27) and his people as a nation (46:2; Exod 1:7). Exodus extends this pattern with a narrowed focus on Moses.

Summary

The Primeval History: 1–11

Over the past decade or so, an increasing number of evangelical scholars have labeled the first 11 chapters of Genesis as "mythology." However, for the ancient audience, these chapters would have been read as history. The structural indicators noted above as well as the inclusion of genealogies and the references to Adam and Noah in other parts of the Bible lead naturally to this conclusion (e.g., 1 Chron 1:1-4; Job 31:33; Isa 54:9; Ezek 14:14, 20; Luke 3:38; Rom 5:14; 1 Cor 15:22, 45;1 Tim 2:13-14; Heb 11:7; 1 Peter 3:20; 2 Peter 2:5; Jude 14).

Creation: Genesis 1–2

Genesis begins with what could be called the "grand overture" to the Bible. Much like Tchaikovsky's grand 1812 Overture, Genesis 1 gives the reader an introduction to the God who created the cosmos and to God's character (e.g., God is the creator of good things, God is ordered, relational, and is outside of creation). God is therefore not a "force" (as in the *Star Wars* movies), but is an individual, personal, albeit utterly transcendent, being. What's more, human beings are created by God in the "image" of God (Gen 1:26), and this establishes the dignity, significance, and worth of humanity as the crown of all God's creation. By contrast, all other ANE creation accounts see creation as the work of a number of deities, in some cases at war with one another (e.g., Marduk and Tiamat in the Babylonian creation story, *Enuma Elish*), with human beings originating as mere by-products of these cosmic conflicts. Genesis 2 picks up similar themes from chapter 1 only in a slightly rearranged order for the purpose of emphasizing the creation of humanity and the establishment of the garden of Eden as a place of relationship with the Divine. The altered order and overlapping nature of these accounts could serve to remind us that ancient authors were not as concerned about chronology as we are today.

Cosmogonies: A number of theories of origins have been put forward to help explain the significance of these opening chapters of Genesis. Some seek to harmonize science and the Bible while others seek to situate the modern reader in the world of the ancient authors. Seven theories have come to prominence over the past century and a half.

1) Those holding to a literal six-day creation (also known as the "young-earth theory") suggest that God created the world in six 24-hour days. Any apparent indications of age in the earth (e.g., billions of years as evidenced in geology and cosmology) were placed there by God, according to this view, during creation *ex nihilo* ("out of nothing"). This, it is argued, is exemplified in a mature creation (trees, mountains, humans). This is further supported by the argument that when Jesus—God incarnate—created in the New Testament, he did so *ex nihilo* with age (turning water into aged wine and creating full-grown fish and bread; cf. John 2:1-10 and Matt 14:13-21; Mark 6:34-44; John 6:1-15 respectively).

2) Proponents of the "gap theory" hold that there is a temporal gap between Gen 1:1 and 1:2, during which time there was a pre-Adamic flood/destruction, thus explaining why there was already water on the earth in verse 2. According to this theory, in Gen 1:1 God created everything as a tropical paradise, including the dinosaurs and all creeping things. The gap between verses 1 and 2 (perhaps accounting for millions or even billions of years) explains why there is

a fossil record, and the extreme age of the earth. It was during this time, proponents argue, that Satan rebelled against God and fell from heaven, causing a mass destruction that left the earth as a "formless and void" watery chaos (v. 1 NASB; cf. Luke 10:18; Isa 14:12-14). From verse 2 onward, so the theory goes, God re-created the earth in a literal six-day span.

3) Those holding to a theory of "theistic evolution" seek to wed science and the Bible by postulating that the evolutionary processes embraced within the sciences are God's way of creating. In turn they argue that Genesis 1 is mythology (although they would insist that there is a nugget of truth in the account, namely, that God is behind creation). They argue that God used the evolutionary process to bring forth all living things. In the beginning, God created the first life form with the "fully gifted" potential to bring forth humanity at the end of the long evolutionary process.

4) Within evangelical circles, "the temple theory" has become very popular in recent years. Proponents argue that Genesis 1 must be read from an ancient perspective of temple building. The basic premise behind this theory is that the author of Gen 1:1–2:4 was not so much concerned about material creation as he was with explaining the functions of creation in a temple context. In Genesis 1, God is therefore arranging an abode; that is, the cosmos, as a place for his dwelling. The establishment of the Sabbath rest is the moment when God takes up his place in the cosmic temple.

5) Advocates of the "framework theory" suggest that Genesis 1 is a poetic literary construct and is not to be taken in a literal sense. Days 1–3 become the time when the *spaces* are created, whereas days 4–6 present the *filling* of those spaces. The framework theory thus accounts for why there are evenings and mornings before the creation of the sun on the fourth day. Those holding to this theory would not necessarily deny God's involvement in creation, but rather would insist that the author did not intend a literal understanding of Genesis 1.

6) Several variations of the "day-age theory" have been proposed. The simplest version is that each day does not equal a 24-hour period but rather 1,000 or more years (cf. 2 Pet 3:8). Thus, the earth is much older than 6,000 years. One variation of this theory sees the six days as literally 24-hour periods, but does not see the days in a consecutive, one-week sequence. In between these 24-hour days are eons of various lengths during which time God allowed evolutionary processes to take their course. At select moments in this process, it is proposed, God stepped in and worked during a 24-hour span, tweaking creation and setting it on its way until the next intervention was needed to keep things running smoothly.

7) The "revelatory theory" sees the six days of creation not so much as the time it took God to create certain parts of the created order, but rather as representing six literal days on Sinai when Moses received his revelations about creation from God. In this scenario, for example, on "day

one" Moses saw, through the spiritual mind's eye, God's process of dividing the light from the darkness.

All of these theories have been proposed by believers seeking to explain the origins of creation. While some insist that following any theory other than a literal six-day creation is spiritually dangerous, this insistence tends to disregard how others have attempted to honor God in their interpretive theories. Whatever view one follows, keep in mind that all of these theories are just that—*theories*—speculative interpretations that, in one way or the other, read between or behind the lines of the Genesis account. Genesis simply does not provide conclusive answers to all the questions we might have about the origins of life and the universe. In this light, one could say that the Genesis account of creation *creates space for multiple views* on these matters—views that we should not be quick to disparage as either unbiblical on the one hand or unscientific or unscholarly on the other. Finally, for those of us who believe God is the ultimate source behind not only the universe but also the book of Genesis, we would do well not to "shout," as the saying goes, "where God is whispering."

Cosmology: Before leaving Genesis 1 and 2, it is important to point out that the language used within the OT is often confusing for the modern reader. Terms such as the following, from the KJV, are foreign to our modern ear.

- "windows of heaven" (Gen 7:11; 8:2; 2 Kgs 7:2, 19; Mal 3:10)

- the "fountains" of the deep (Gen 7:11; 8:2; Prov 8:28)

- the "pillars"/"roots" of the earth/mountains (1 Sam 2:8; Job 9:6; 28:9; Ps 75:3)

- the "pit," (Num 16:30, 33; Job 17:16; 33:24; Pss 28:1; 30:3, 9; 71:20; 88:4; 139:8; 143:7; Prov 1:12; Isa 14:15; Ezek 26:20), the "depths of the pit" (Isa 14:15 CEB), or "Sheol" (NASB)

This language must be understood within the context of a pre-scientific audience. Israel had, as did many other ancient peoples, a certain perspective of their cosmology whereby their land and temple served as the center of their cosmos. That is not to say that this perspective was divinely endorsed, but rather that scripture used language to which Israel could relate. However, even though Israel may have taken part in this cosmological outlook, God's law for Israel denounced any ritualistic embrace of it. For example, the ancients believed that the mountains held up the firmament of heaven (much like a dome). The mountains also were seen to have roots that extended into the bowels of the earth and Sheol; that is, the "grave" (Gen 37:35) or the "underworld" (Isa 14:15). Many ancient people believed that worshipping the gods on the mountains connected them to the three tiers of the cosmos: heaven, earth, and Sheol. With this in view, God forbade Israel to practice cultic worship on what the KJV translates as "high places" (cf. Lev 26:30;

Num 33:52; Deut 12:2; 1 Kgs 3:2, 3; 12:31, 32; Jer 7:31; 19:5; 32:35; 48:35; Ezek 6:3, 6; Hos 10:8).

Finally, because Israel's neighbors equated many of the natural phenomena with the gods, something forbidden by God (Exod 20:4), the author of Genesis went out of his way to make sure that no connection was made between the created order and God. For example, Shamash and Yareach were names of sun and moon deities in the ancient world. In Genesis 1, the author does not use the Hebrew terms for the sun (*shemesh*) and the moon (*yareach*) but rather calls them the "larger" and "smaller" lights. Israel was not to think that God created Shamash and Yareach. On the contrary, these are mere cosmological realities subject to God's will!

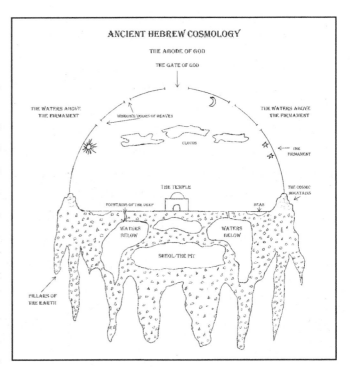

Drawing by Brian Peterson

The Fall: Genesis 3–4

Here Genesis presents the downfall of the first couple through disobedience, followed by the downfall of their son Cain through fratricide. The general effect of these two narratives is to show that sin is systemic and in need of an answer. In this regard, many see in God's words to Eve in Gen 3:15 the *protoevangelium* ("first gospel"), which constitutes Scripture's first foreshadowing of the work of Jesus. Another important factor related to the fall of Adam and Eve is the curse God pronounced over them. Eve would have increased emotional pain in childbearing, attended by a "desire" for her husband, who would "rule over" her (3:16), whereas Adam would have increased emotional and physical pain in bringing forth the fruit of the ground (3:17). An ironic parallel in the curse is that the metaphorical ground of Eve's womb (*beten*) would no longer bear "fruit" the way it was intended—barrenness would abound. Similarly, the literal ground (*adamah*) would not yield to Adam its fruit without toil.[2]

In the unfolding context of Genesis, this plays out in that all the major matriarchs in Genesis suffered from barrenness (Eve—4:1; Sarah—11:30; Rebekah—25:21; Rachel—29:31b and perhaps Leah—29:31a; note also the complications in conception for Lot's daughters [19:31-38] and Tamar [38:6-30]), while all the patriarchs struggled with famines and the accompanying difficulty in providing for their families (Abraham—12:10-21; Isaac—26:1; Jacob—42:1-5). This twofold theme plays a key and unifying role in

---

2. See more in Curley and Peterson, "Eve's Curse Revisited: An Increase of 'Sorrowful Conceptions,'" *Bulletin of Biblical Research* 26, no. 2 (2016): 1–16.

the book of Genesis. Finally, an additional connection that might be made is that, because women now would struggle to get pregnant, their "desire" (sexually) would be for their husband in order to become pregnant and alleviate this emotional pain (3:16b; see Rachel's words in 30:1). Sadly, this becomes the breeding ground for oppressive patriarchy. Before the fall, the man and the woman were created equal before God (1:26-28)—indeed both in the very "image" of God—but now the *shared dominion* of the man and woman gives way to the *one-sided domination* of the man over the woman.

Before leaving the concept of God's judgment on Adam and Eve, note that translators have often missed the awesome dimension of God's appearance in Genesis 3. Most translations present God strolling in the garden in the cool of the evening, looking for his old friends. However, the scene is one of judgment—when God shows up in the OT, it is typically a frightful event (e.g., Exod 19:18; 1 Kgs 19:11-12; Isa 29:4; Ezek 1). Four words in verse 8 might suggest this: (1) in this context, the word rendered "cool . . . breeze" (*l'ruach*) might better be rendered "wind"; (2) another translation for the Hebrew word for "day" (*yom*) is "storm"; (3) "voice" (KJV)/"sound" (*qol*) can mean "thunder"; and (4) "walking" (*mithallek*) appears in a verbal form (the *hithpael* stem) in Hebrew that registers intensity. Therefore, a better translation of verse 8 might be: "They heard the *thunder* of the LORD God *coming* in the *wind of the storm*." That is why Adam says, "I heard your *sound* [i.e., "your thunder"] . . . and I hid myself" (Gen 3:10). This scene depicts God coming in judgment! The next time in Genesis that God sends judgment will be in the form of actual storm clouds accompanying the Flood.

The Flood to the Tower of Babel: Genesis 6–11

As one of the first stories we learn in Sunday school, the Flood narrative is perhaps one of the best-known stories of the OT. The cause of the flood is addressed in 6:1-5. Here the reader finds that the indiscriminate marriage of "the sons of God" (KJV, a phrase that, while debated by scholars, might refer to human rulers) along with increased violence led to the deluge, which lasted for forty days and nights. Beyond the question of mythology versus history, today scholars also question whether the flood was global or local.[3] Regardless of these debates, the most important message to take away from the flood account is that God will tolerate sin only so long. Yet, God eventually set his rainbow in the cloud as a promise not to destroy the earth by a flood again (however, see 2 Pet 3:12). Interestingly, the Hebrew word for rainbow (*qesheth*) is the term employed for a "bow" used for shooting arrows. What the Israelites probably would have heard is that God had hung his bow in the cloud, thus signifying that he was at peace with humanity. This image of the inverted bow in the clouds was a powerful symbol of peace in the ancient word.

The Flood also brought several changes for humans. God established basic rules for humanity: animals will fear people (9:2); all animals and plants can serve as food for people (9:3); blood is not to be eaten (9:4; cf. Acts 15:29; 21:25); and capital punishment is to be instituted for murder in order to uphold the sanctity of human life, created in the image of God (9:5-6). The author also wants the reader to see Noah

---

3. See the work of Robert Ballard, the man who discovered the *Titanic,* at Ballard & the Search for Noah's Flood (© 1999 National Geographic Society), at http://www.nationalgeographic.com/blacksea/ax/frame.html.

as a second Adam. Noah is told to be fruitful and multiply and fill the earth just as Adam was told (cf. 1:28; 9:1); both have three sons—one of whom is cursed (Cain and Ham); and they both commit a fateful sin that involves an act by eating/drinking. Structurally what plays out through Genesis 1–9 is a pattern of creation—de-creation—and re-creation; from a watery chaos to a created order—back to a watery chaos—to a re-created order.

The Tower of Babel: Genesis 11

God's general command to spread out and fill the land was the next great challenge for Noah's descendants (note that chapter 10 is not in chronological order with 11:1-9). Instead of following God's command, they sought to build for themselves a city on the plains of Shinar (i.e., Babylon) with a tower up to heaven (11:1-9). Medieval artists often portrayed this as a European-styled tower much like the leaning Tower of Pisa; however, the tower in Genesis 11 was no doubt a ziggurat, common in the region of ancient Babylonia. Even to this day the ziggurat of Ur (ca. 3rd millennium BCE) still stands as a testimony to the building prowess of the ancients. In a region that had few natural mountains, the ziggurat was a human-made "mountain" on which the people could meet with their gods (see discussion on cosmology above). They would take a human-made image of their god up the ziggurat and place the image in a shelter erected at its top. They believed their god would then come down from heaven and indwell the image. The priests would then carry the image down the steps of the ziggurat and place it in the temple at the base of the ziggurat.

The builders of Babel (in ancient Akkadian *Babel* = "gate of god"; in Hebrew = "confusion"; whence comes our English verb "to babble") sought to make a name for themselves (11:4). Ironically, before the account of the Tower of Babel, the mighty men of the pre-Flood era also were men of "a name" and yet had suffered destruction (6:4). Immediately following the Babel account, in Genesis 12, God promises to make a "name" for Abraham if he obeys (12:1). The message is clear: when humans seek to make a name for themselves it usually ends poorly; when God makes someone's name great, it endures! To this day three world religions (Judaism, Christianity, and Islam) know Abraham's name; no one knows the name of the builders of Babel!

Ziggurat of Ur from ancient Babylon. Photo courtesy of Michael Luddeni.

As punishment for their disobedience, God confused the language of the people of Babel. It is not surprising that archaeologists have found a parallel account to that of Gen 11:1-7. In this account from ancient Sumer (southern Babylon), the ancient gods also confuse the language of humans.[4] Today language is a natural social barrier between civilizations. Nevertheless, the work of the Spirit on the day of Pentecost (Acts 2), in a way, served as a reversal of the curse in Genesis 11. Ironically God used an effusion of diverse languages in Genesis 11 to induce a scattering of human discord, then used an outpouring of different languages in Acts 2 to produce a human gathering of "one accord" (v. 1 KJV). Indeed, Pentecost is a foretaste of the ultimate reunion and communion between saints of every language in the eschaton (Rev 5:9; 14:6).

The Ancestral Narrative: Genesis 12–50 and the Call of Abraham

As noted in our discussion of Genesis' structure, even though there is a level of overlap between the ancestors' lives, Genesis 12–50 can be properly subdivided according to each major patriarch. Before chapter 12 begins, Abram (who is eventually renamed Abraham) is introduced as one of the descendants of Shem (11:10, 26-27). Within this context, God calls Abraham to leave his homeland of Ur of the Chaldeans (i.e., ancient Babylon) and travel to a land that God would show him. The distance from Ur to Canaan is roughly 950 miles (imagine traveling from Chattanooga, Tennessee, to Hartford, Connecticut, by camel!). In 12:1-3, God makes a promise to Abraham that he would give him a land, make his progeny into a nation, make his name great, and make him a blessing. With this promise, Abraham sets out with his immediate family to Canaan.

After a period of time in Haran in northern Mesopotamia, Abraham finally completes his journey to Canaan, taking his nephew Lot with him. Once there, he is faced with a famine. Abraham decides to travel down to Egypt (12:10-20). The account of Abraham's sojourn in Egypt can be read as a foreshadowing of the Exodus event. Abraham goes down to Egypt (12:10), Sarah is taken into the service of Pharaoh (12:15), Pharaoh gives material wealth to Abraham (12:16), God sends plagues upon Pharaoh (12:17), and Pharaoh expels Abraham from Egypt (12:20). Gen 12:10-20 serves to show the reader the potency of God's promise in 12:1-3. Despite Abraham's duplicitous actions with Pharaoh, God still protects Abraham and curses those who attempt to undermine the promise to Abraham, even though they appear innocent. Once back in Canaan, Abraham and Lot are forced to part company, due to tensions generated by their excessive wealth (13:6-12), no doubt given to them in part by Pharaoh (12:16). At this time Abraham receives a promise that the land of Canaan will be his—a promise that will be repeated later to his son Isaac and his grandson Jacob (Gen 13:14-17; 28:12-15; 35:9-12).

Promise, Covenant, and Circumcision

As certification of the previous promises, God enters into a unilateral covenant with Abraham (ch. 15), instituting circumcision as the sign of the covenant (cf. 17). It was common in the ANE for covenanting partners to literally "cut a covenant" by killing an animal or animals, often cutting them in half and walking

---

4. Bill Arnold and Bryan Beyer, *Readings from the Ancient Near East*, Primary Sources for Old Testament Study (Grand Rapids: Baker Academic, 2002), 71.

together between the two halves while repeating their oaths and self-imprecations to each other. Curses may have sounded something like this: "So may I be cut in two pieces if I break my covenant with you." For Abraham, God alone makes these oaths, revealing to Abraham that God alone would see to fulfilling the promises of chapter 12. One must keep in mind that the promises of Gen 12:1-3 did not constitute the covenant alone. The covenant ceremony of chapter 15 served as the framework in which God would now fulfill the promises he made with Abraham. This reflects something very similar to the relationship between a modern engagement and a wedding ceremony. A man can make all the promises he wants to his future bride when they get engaged, but until the marriage covenant is complete, these promises are not fully and publicly sanctioned. The only thing that was required of Abraham was to undergo the sign of the covenant, namely, circumcision (circumcision is still practiced among Jews and in several other cultures even today, e.g., in parts of Africa and in many Muslim countries). From this point onward, circumcision was required of all Hebrew males in order to be connected to the Abrahamic covenant—failure to do so caused one to be cut off from his people (17:14). It was also at this time that God changed Abram's name to Abraham ("father of many peoples") and Sarai's to Sarah ("noblewoman"), changes that reflected the promises of God.

Hagar, Ishmael, and Isaac

God's promises to Abraham could be fulfilled only if Abraham had a son. Because of Abraham's and Sarah's advanced ages (86 and 75 respectively), they assumed that God meant for them to use the ancient customs of adopting a child that would be born to Hagar, Sarah's Egyptian handmaiden (as found in the laws from Mari, Code of Hammurabi 170, Nuzi HSS 5:67, and Lipit-Ishtar). Genesis 16 and 21 record the fiasco that their "intervention" caused in their lives. Ishmael was the child born of the union of Hagar and Abraham—he became the father of many of the Arab nations. Because Abraham was a righteous man and was unwilling to break the laws of his people and region, it would take God's intervention to get Abraham to send Ishmael and Hagar away (Gen 21:10-14). Due to Ishmael's connection to Abraham, Ishmael was promised to be a great people as well (17:20; 21:13, 18); however, Isaac would be the son of the promise (17:20)—born to Sarah when Abraham was 100 years old!

Several years later, God asked Abraham to sacrifice his son Isaac on a mountain that God would show to Abraham (Gen 22 is known by the Jewish people as the *Akedah*, "the binding" of Isaac). While this request creates both ethical and theological issues for the modern reader, it should be noted that this is presented as only a test (22:1). This could be seen as the narrator using finite language to present the thoughts and motives of an infinite God (22:12; cf. Gen 6:6; Exod 32:14; Judg 2:18; 1 Sam 15:35; 2 Sam 24:16). Some may suggest that God needed *to know* if Abraham trusted him (22:12), but the primary point is that this is a test for Abraham, not God.

In many parts of the ANE, child sacrifice was the highest form of worshipping one's deity (cf. 2 Kgs 3:27). When God asked Abraham to sacrifice Isaac, Abraham did not resist—perhaps thinking, in line with the religious milieu of the time, that this was what the gods required. However, God surely wanted

Abraham to know that the God who called him out of Ur was not like the gods of the nations, especially the nation of Babylon from whence he came. The message for Abraham, and by extension, for Israel, was that God did not require such a sacrifice (Exod 13:13, 15; Jer 19:5).

The Sin of Sodom and Gomorrah

As early as Genesis 13, the narrative notes that the men of Sodom were extremely wicked (13:13). In chapter 18, during Abraham's encounter with three heavenly guests, he is told of God's intent to destroy the city (18:16-33). After a series of negotiations, God agrees not to destroy the city if ten righteous people can be found there—sadly only four righteous people could be identified, thus sealing its fate. Chapter 19 picks up the story of two angels coming to remove Lot and his family and to effect the destruction. During their stay overnight in Lot's house, all the men of the city surrounded the house, insisting that he send out his guests so they could "know" them (9:5 KJV).

Scholars have long argued about what actually is the sin of Sodom. Some propound that the men were upset that Lot, a foreigner, brought men into his house without the proper introductions. The men thus are there to (literally) get to know the new men. Others insist

Dome of the Rock on the temple mount/Mount Moriah, the third holiest site in Islam. Photo courtesy Christine Curley.

that this is a case of rape and violence and has nothing to do with modern same-sex issues. Others, by focusing on a later reference to Sodom in Ezek 16:49-50, propose that the sin of Sodom was inhospitality. Finally, a number of scholars hold to a more traditional interpretation and conclude that same-sex acts, whether rape or not, is at the heart of Sodom's sin.

A few points need to be made about these positions: (1) Seeing inhospitality as the only sin of Sodom is questionable; the larger context suggests that Sodom's breach of hospitality was a part of greater sin. After all, God had already determined to destroy the city (Gen 18:23) before the act of inhospitality recorded in Genesis 19 had taken place. (2) Ezekiel's comments in 16:49-50 appear in the context of a chapter in which Jerusalem's sins against God are presented in sexual terms. Moreover, Ezekiel actually notes that the sin of Sodom included "abomination" (KJV; *to'evah* in the singular), the term used in reference to same-sex acts in Lev 18:22 (Ezekiel is a priest who uses the Levitical law throughout his book). (3) The sin of

Sodom appears in the larger context of Genesis 19, in which Lot's two daughters are seen committing incest with their father (19:30-38)—an act that represents one of the other major concerns of Lev 18:5-17. These connections make it hard to avoid seeing this story in Genesis 19 as one that is intentionally drawing attention to the magnitude of Sodom's wickedness by focusing on violence, same-sex acts, and incest. (4) Inhospitality is the symptom of careless ease and abundance. One can easily conclude that with this carefree lifestyle came sexual deviance.[5] This is no different in today's society where careless ease has opened the door for numerous sexual sins.

The Life of Isaac: Genesis 21:1–28:9

While Isaac appears in a number of chapters, the narrative content dealing with his life is much shorter than that of Abraham and Jacob. After the death of Isaac's mother, Sarah, Abraham secures Rebekah as a wife for his son. Just like his father, Isaac is given the promise of the land (26:2-5) and tries to save his own life by telling a powerful leader who is attracted to his wife that she is his sister (26:7; cf. 12:10-20). Even though Rebekah struggles with barrenness, she and Isaac eventually have twin sons— Jacob and Esau. The most memorable event in the life of Isaac is that of the treachery of Jacob when Jacob steals the blessing from his brother, Esau, by pretending to be Esau in the presence of an aged and blind Isaac (ch. 27). Jacob's duplicity would come back to haunt him in his interactions with his father-in-law, Laban.

Jacob and Joseph: Genesis 28:10–50:26

As with Isaac, the life of Jacob, and his son Joseph, is intertwined with the narrative of the previous generation/patriarch. After Jacob's deception of Isaac, Esau seeks to kill Jacob. This forces Jacob to flee to Haran, the birthplace of his mother. On his way there, during a night dream of a ladder extending from earth to heaven, Jacob encounters God, who in turn extends the covenant of Abraham and Isaac to Jacob, prompting Jacob to name the place of this encounter Bethel, which means "house of God" (28:10-20). From this point onward, God works, often behind the scenes, to protect and direct Jacob's life.

This is exemplified in the narratives of chapters 29–31, which tell of Jacob's sojourn in Haran with Laban and his eventual return to Canaan. Throughout the narrative, it is evident that God blesses and preserves Jacob (31:5, 12, 24, 29, 42). Nevertheless, through the duplicitous actions of Laban against Jacob, which are reminiscent of Jacob's treatment of Esau, he also has the chance to learn the hard lesson about the repercussions of his earlier treatment of his brother (29:23-25; 31:41). Despite the actions of Laban, God blesses Jacob with twelve sons and vast herds of livestock—a clear connection to the promises of Gen 12:1-3. At the end of 20 years of service (31:38), Jacob and his wives, Rachel and Leah (along with their handmaids, Bilhah and Zilpah), flee to Canaan without telling Laban. After a seven-day

---

5. For more on this, see Brian Peterson, *What Was the Sin of Sodom: Homosexuality, Inhospitality, or Something Else* (Eugene, OR: Resource Publications, 2016).

pursuit, Laban finally catches up to Jacob in the mountains of Gilead in the Transjordan. There, in a tense meeting, Jacob and Laban part ways after entering into a covenant by which they promise never to cross the boundary marker that they have set up (31:45). In the ANE, boundary stones served as ter-

ritory markers and often had curses inscribed on them. There can be no doubt that this is the picture being presented in 31:44-55.

Jacob still faces one obstacle in his return to Canaan—Esau. Chapters 32 and 33 tell of this encounter. Once again God protects Jacob, even though Jacob gives Esau much of what he had taken from him 20 years before (32:13-20). Also, the night before his reunion with Esau, Jacob "wrestle[s]" with a man (32:24-32). While the exact identity of the divine figure is debated, within this account Jacob's name is changed to Israel, which means something along the lines of "he struggles and prevails with God"—a name that will eventually be used for the nation.

Genesis 34–50 focuses on Jacob and his sons' interaction with each other and the local

Ancient Mesopotamian boundary stone marker with curses. Jacob and Laban also set up stones as a type of "boundary marker" (Gen 31:46). Photo by Brian Peterson.

population (e.g., Shechem in ch. 34). Here the narrative comes to a special focus on Jacob's next-to-youngest son, Joseph, the dreamer (37:5-10), who eventually, and in fulfillment of his childhood dreams, will be blessed by God with promotion to the second position in Egypt (41:40). Jacob shows extreme favoritism to his young son, Joseph, the firstborn son of Rachel, Jacob's beloved wife. In giving his son the "coat of many colors" (37:3 KJV, no doubt representative of the promise to give him the double portion of the inheritance as firstborn), Jacob sets Joseph above his older brothers, creating a breeding ground for envy. At the opportune moment, Joseph's brothers seize Joseph and throw him into a pit and scheme about how they might kill him. Many people fail to recognize that the actions of the brothers when they immediately sit down for a meal (37:25) no doubt had covenantal significance, as the brothers covenanted not to tell anyone about their actions. When given the opportunity to make some money from their actions, the brothers sell Joseph into slavery, where he ends up in Egypt.

Next, the actions of Judah and Joseph recorded in chapters 38 and 39 must be read together and juxtaposed. On the one hand, in chapter 38, we find the account of Judah, the future leader of his people, marrying a Canaanite woman and sleeping with a prostitute. On the other hand, Joseph finds himself in slavery in Egypt, being tempted to sleep with his master's wife but refusing to do so—a decision that leads to a false accusation that costs him his freedom (39:20). The implied message in this contrast is clear: Judah, the heir to the inheritance (cf. 49:3-7), surrounded by the support system of family, culture, and home influences, behaved in an ungodly manner; conversely, Joseph, away from family, cultural familiarity, and the influence of home followed his God with integrity.

The final portion of Genesis (chs. 40–50) interweaves the experiences of Joseph in Egypt with the hardships of famine faced by his family back in Canaan. Through a series of providential events, Joseph is promoted to the second position in the kingdom of Egypt in order to prepare Egypt for seven years of famine. When the effects of the famine finally reach Canaan, Jacob sends his ten sons (all but Benjamin) to Egypt to buy grain. Once Joseph recognizes his brothers, who do not recognize him, he sets a trap for them, apparently for the purpose of testing them to see whether or not they have changed since they sold him into slavery. These final chapters of Genesis serve to answer this question as the reader realizes that the selfish actions of Joseph's brothers in selling him into slavery are now transformed as they try to protect their youngest brother, Benjamin (44:16-34). The tension of the narrative builds until Joseph finally reveals himself to his brothers in a tearful and joyful reunion (45:1-5). Genesis draws to a close with the happy reunion of Jacob and his presumed-dead son, Joseph (46:29-30); Jacob adopting Joseph's two sons, Ephraim and Manasseh (48:1-20); Jacob's blessings of his sons (Gen 49:1-28); and the deaths of Jacob (49:33) and Joseph (50:26).

There are numerous parallels between Joseph and the life of Jesus that seem to go beyond mere coincidence. One could see in them the overarching influence of the divine Author, indeed the Spirit's imprint on the biblical trajectory that leads fully and finally to Christ. For the human author of Genesis, the promise of Genesis 12:3 had been fulfilled, in part, by Joseph's salvation/blessing of not only his family, but Egypt as well. The promise of progeny had a level of fulfillment in Abraham's descendants who traveled to Egypt, numbering just under 80 (cf. 12:2). However, Genesis closes with the land promise yet to be fulfilled (12:1)—a fulfillment that will be realized only later, in the days of Joshua (cf. Gen 50:26// Josh 24:32).

Debated Issues (aka Great Paper Topics)

1) Who are the "sons of God" in 6:1-4 (KJV)?

2) Was the flood of Genesis global or local?

3) What was the sin of Sodom in chapter 19?

4) With whom did Jacob wrestle in 32:24-32?

5) How do scholars handle the similarities between the Joseph account and the Egyptian myth, the *Tale of Two Brothers*?

The Message of the Book

While a number of themes and messages could be gleaned from Genesis, the overarching message appears to be that God desires relationship with creation and is determined to bless and protect those who follow him. Throughout the lives of Israel's ancestors, God is active both overtly and behind the scenes to foster relationship and to offer blessings to those who fear God. Of course, one could press more narrowly to the heart of this by pointing to God's ultimate plan to bring about salvation for a fallen world through a coming Seed—a "Seed" that would come through the lineage of Adam, Seth, Shem, and Abraham—namely, Jesus.

Closing the Loop

Genesis, the Bible's book of beginnings, addresses a primal question that arises sooner or later for all of us as human beings: "Where did we come from?" We have what appears to be an innate drive to know the significance of our origin *and the origin of our significance*. We often see this desire played out in the life of an adopted child who, upon reaching a certain age, becomes suddenly and intensely motivated to track down and meet his or her biological parents. And this desire does not stop at the level of our origin as individuals, but extends to the level of the origin of our family, our nation, and even our species.

Genesis tells a sweeping story that is structured, as was previously noted, in two major parts: the first part (chs. 1–11) focusing upon the origin of the world, and the second part (chs. 12–50) narrowing to a focus upon the origin of God's people, Israel. In this way, Genesis binds together the origin of the world and the origin of the people of God, seeing them both in terms of the same single ultimate source—God.

Yet Genesis tells a story that clearly wants to offer more specific elaboration about how our origins issue from our ultimate source. In the origin of the world, the first verses of Genesis show God's creative work initiated ("In the beginning God created the heavens and the earth," 1:1 KJV) and then enacted by *God's Spirit and God's word*: "And the Spirit of God was moving upon the face of the waters, and God said, 'Let there be light,' and there was light" (1:2-3 RSV). In the rest of the first chapter of Genesis, the phrase "and God said, 'Let there be x,' and there was x" becomes the repeated refrain that constitutes and carries out the creative acts of God. In Genesis 2 we again see God's Spirit (or breath) and word generating God's creation, this time in relation to the specific creation of human beings when God creates the first human out of dust and breathes into this special creature the breath of life (2:7; cf. 2:18-22).

Other creation stories, both ancient and modern, have other views of the ultimate source of the cosmos and the human species, whether a battle among the gods or a big bang among the atoms of the universe, but Genesis makes the emphatic and wondrous claim that all things and all human beings have their beginning in the personal, purposeful word of the creator God. No creation story in all of creation has ever provided a stronger grounding for the origin of our significance than this.

In the second part of Genesis, which presents the origin of God's people, we find something similar. The first verses of this second part mark a new beginning that can be seen to parallel the first verses of the first part:

> The LORD said to Abram, "Leave your land, your family, and your father's household for the land that I will show you. I will make of you a great nation and will bless you. I will make your name respected, and you will be a blessing . . . all the families of the earth will be blessed because of you." (12:1-3)

Once again, God's spoken word generates a new beginning—in Genesis 1 God creates the world, and in Genesis 12 God makes a people. In both cases, God's word by itself is the generating source; God does not rely on and work with preexistent resources. This is somewhat different from what we see in the rest of Genesis. There God is shown to be fully committed to a covenant relationship with his creation that welcomes and works in continuing partnership with his creatures' own generative activities—with plants bearing seed after their kind, animals birthing offspring after their kind, and humans reproducing children after their kind. The God of creation is *pro*-creation and, in the covenant with humanity throughout Genesis, this is registered by his being "pro" *procreation*! Indeed, God's first word and blessing to humankind in Genesis is "Be fertile and multiply; fill the earth" (1:28). God, as the ultimate generator of all things, calls for humankind to continue his generating work *from generation to generation*. In fact, Genesis makes this a key theme by using the previously mentioned *toledoth* formula ("These are the generations of x," KJV) as the introductory phrase that signals the beginning of every section of Genesis, that is, all but two. Genesis 1:1 and 12:1 do not use the *toledoth* phrase, and perhaps now we can see the reason why. As elaborated recently by OT scholar L. R. Martin, these two Genesis passages represent the two new beginnings in the book that are *absolute beginnings*—beginnings that do not come from human generations but from nothing other than *the word of God*. This divine word, all by itself, is enough to generate a world or a people. God can make anything and everything *out of nothing*.[6]

Thus, God speaks to Abram, "Go from your country *and your kindred*" (12:1 RSV); the Hebrew term for "kindred" is *moledoth*, from the same word root as *toledoth*. God's word here is emphasizing to Abram that he must leave behind the *resources* of human generativity in order to find in God's word alone the true *source* of his life, of his generativity.[7] This is the call, the word that, when followed, makes Abram into a great people and makes Abram's name great, indeed makes it "*Abraham*," which literally means, "the father of many peoples." And it is, in its essential character, the same call and the same word that, when followed, make *us* the *children* of Abraham!

Genesis, then, calls us to see God's Spirit and word as the originating source of the universe, of all life, and of our life as the people of God. We see this call renewed time and again throughout the book of

6. Lee Roy Martin, "Where Are the Descendants of Abraham: Finding the Source of a Missing Link in Genesis," in *The Spirit and the Mind: Essays in Informed Pentecostalism*, ed. Terry L. Cross and Emerson Powery (Lanham, MD: University Press of America, 2000), 23–34.

7. Ibid.

Genesis and throughout the Scriptures that flow from it, whether through a spoken word (as in the case of Abraham—Gen 15), a miraculous manifestation (as in the case of Jacob—Gen 32) or a supernatural dream (as in the case of Joseph—Gen 36). It is a call that has been renewed throughout the world in recent times by the global Spirit movement associated with Pentecostalism—a movement that has borne fresh witness to the in-breaking of the God who spoke the world into existence and spoke to Abraham, and is now speaking a new and renewing word to those who have ears to hear among "all the families of the earth" today (12:3).

EXODUS

"I am the LORD your God who brought you out . . ."
    —Exodus 20:2

When I think about the book of Exodus,

a most unlikely picture comes to mind: the story of the comic book and movie hero Superman. Let me explain.

Common to several ancient cultures is the abandonment motif whereby a child, generally a boy, is abandoned by his parents (usually due to some uncontrollable event) with the hope that the gods will take care of him and make him a great leader. In the case of Superman, Jor-El, the father of the young Kal-El (aka Clark Kent) sends his son from the distant planet of Krypton to earth to save Kal-El from the impending destruction of Krypton. The hope of Kal-El's parents is that he will become a great leader/savior of earth. Kal-El is rescued by lowly farmers, Martha and Jonathan Kent, and eventually fulfills the hope of his Kryptonian parents.

A similar scenario plays itself out in the Sumerian Legend of Sargon (ca. late 3rd millennium BCE). According to the legend, Sargon I's priestess mother places him in a reed basket and sets him adrift on the Euphrates River. A lowly gardener named Akki, who worked for the king of Kish in ancient Sumer, finds and raises Sargon. Sargon goes on to become a great leader of ancient Akkad. Similarly, in Rome's foundational legend the mother of the twins Romulus and Remus is forced to abandon her sons on the river Tiber. A female wolf finds the boys and suckles them. Later, a shepherd and his wife raise them to adulthood. The two boys become the founders of Rome.

All of these stories have a similar theme—a theme that also finds parallels with Moses and the nation of Israel. For Moses, in order to avoid certain death as decreed by the Egyptian pharaoh (Exod 1:22), his parents abandon him by setting him adrift in a reed basket on the Nile River (2:3). Their hope is that God will take care of him. Pharaoh's daughter finds Moses and rears him in the very house of Pharaoh; he receives the best education and is even nursed by Moses's own mother (2:5-10). While most people are familiar with this account of Moses, few know about the similar motif present in Ezek 16:3-6, which metaphorically tells of the beginning of Israel in the wilderness era (i.e., Exodus). Israel was a newborn baby girl who was abandoned by her parents (a Hittite mother and an Amorite father, 16:3) and left to die. YHWH (God of Israel) finds her in the wilderness, adopts her, and then enters into a marriage covenant with her. The hope is that this "child" would become a great nation/leader. The Israelite people did in fact become a nation, but they failed in their role as a kingdom of priests to be a leader/example to the nations (19:6; cf. Isa 42:6; 49:6; 60:3). The book of Exodus thus presents the early years of Israel becoming a nation and being led by their great leader, Moses; both nation and leader had a shared experience of being delivered from impossible circumstances to become great before God.

Quick Facts

Title: *Exodus* comes from the Septuagint title meaning "to depart." In Hebrew the title is *Shemoth* ("Names"), which appears in the first phrase in the book (*weʾelleh sheʾmoth*) and is translated: "Now these are the *names* of."

Date: As with the book of Genesis, views on the date of Exodus vary depending on a given scholar's presuppositions. Most agree that the final form of Exodus dates to the exilic or postexilic period. However, if one opts for Mosaic authorship, then a 15th or 13th century BCE date obtains for large portions of the book. The Book of the Covenant/Covenant Code (chs. 20–23) is deemed to be the oldest written portion of the book (perhaps with the exception of Miriam's Song of the Sea in Exod 15) arising early in the monarchy or before (ca. 1000 BCE). The Covenant Code also has parallels with older ANE codes, such as the Babylonian Law of Hammurabi (ca. 18th century BCE).

Authorship: Exodus makes no direct claim about authorship, although we do see references in the book where God commands Moses to write what God tells him (Exod 17:14; 20:22–23:33; 24:4; 34:27). New Testament authors also ascribe portions of Exodus to Moses (Mark 7:10; 12:26; Luke 2:22-23; 24:44; John 7:19, 22; etc.). Source-critical scholars suggest Exodus is an amalgam of sources written by the Yahwist, Elohist, and the Priestly authors (see "Introduction to the Pentateuch").

Audience: The audience implied by the book is the nation of Israel before the death of Moses. However, generally speaking, the audience is Israel at any time, from the period of Moses onward.

Genre: Exodus contains a number of genres: biography (e.g., chs. 2–4); genealogies (6:14-25); travelogues (13:18–14:2; 17:1); a song (ch. 15); battle reports (17:8-14); law (chs. 20–23); and building instructions (chs. 25–31; 35–40). As history, the book records the events of Israel's beginnings, starting with the birth of Moses until the nation left Sinai. It is also possible to view Exodus as biography. Moses is the key character throughout the book. Eyewitness-type content can easily lead one to conclude that Moses wrote at least portions of the book.

Purpose: The purpose for the book is to give a history of the Hebrews from their time in Egypt until their departure from Sinai. It also serves as a record of legal codes. Theologically it teaches the reader about the redemptive, holy, and protective nature of God.

Structure

Very few scholars agree on the structure of Exodus when based on thematic content. Geographically the structure could be arranged as follows: in Egypt 1:1–12:36; the journey to Sinai 12:37–18:27; at Sinai 19–40. This structure will be followed in the summary below, even though Moses's travels to Midian and back to Egypt in 2:15–4:28 forms a brief break in this tidy geographical sequence.

Summary

In Egypt: Exodus 1:1–12:36

The book of Exodus begins where Genesis ends. Comments such as those found in 1:5-8 and 13:19 dealing with Joseph clearly reference the book of Genesis. However, the focus in Genesis on Joseph shifts in Exodus to the line of Levi, Moses in particular. The fulfillment of the promises to Abraham in Gen 12:2 has come to fruition (1:7) as the size of the nation of Israel now threatens the very existence of the governing powers in Egypt (1:9). The new king "who didn't know Joseph" decrees that all the male children are to be thrown into the Nile (1:22). Moses's parents put him in a reed basket and set him adrift on the Nile. Pharaoh's daughter finds and adopts Moses (2:1-10). The narrative then jumps to Moses as an adult (about 40 years old). In attempting to rescue one of the Israelites being beaten by an Egyptian taskmaster, Moses kills the Egyptian and is forced to leave Egypt for fear of Pharaoh (2:11-15). Moses flees to Midian on the opposite side of the Sinai Peninsula, where he meets and marries Zipporah, the daughter of Jethro (2:15-22).

Chapters 3–4 cover Moses's time in Midian and his eventual return to Egypt at age 80. In chapter 3, Moses encounters God at the burning bush, where God reveals to Moses both his covenantal name (YHWH: "he will be what he will be"—translated "I Am Who I Am" in 3:13-15; cf. 6:3) and his desire for Moses to return to Egypt to deliver Israel from bondage (cf. Jer 1:5-10 and Josh 5:13-15), because, God says, "I've heard their cry of injustice because of their slave masters. I know about their pain. I've come down to rescue them" (3:7b-8a). After some negotiation, Moses agrees to return to Egypt. On the way, the Lord confronts Moses concerning his failure to circumcise his son. The quick action of compliance by his wife, Zipporah, preserves Moses's life (4:24-26).

The text of 5:1–7:16 records Moses's attempts to negotiate with Pharaoh a suitable solution whereby Israel can leave Egypt without causing harm to the Egyptian people. However, Pharaoh refuses to acquiesce to Moses's requests. Instead, the pharaoh makes the Israelites' work even more severe, insisting that they are lazy (5:8, 17). The pharaoh thinks that he is dealing with a bunch of slaves, but he soon finds out that he is confronting the creator of the universe! Pharaoh sees himself as a god—the sun god Ra incarnate. For this reason, God touches the very thing over which a "god" is supposed to have control—his heart/mind.

Indeed, Pharaoh may have hardened his own heart (8:15, 32; 9:34), but God aids in the process so that he might show his power (9:12; 10:1, 20, 27; 11:10; 14:8). A similar scenario plays itself out many years later in Israel's history in the events of 1 Sam 5:1-5, where the Philistine god Dagon has his hands and head knocked off when he falls before Israel's ark of the covenant (i.e., representative of YHWH), also known as God's chest. The imagery is clear: like Pharaoh, Dagon could neither act nor think; he was not God (cf. 1 Sam 4:8).

A popular view today is that the plagues can be explained away in terms of natural phenomena germane to the region of Egypt. However, if the plagues can be explained "naturally," how does one account for the fact that none of the plagues affected the land of Goshen, where Israel lived (9:6, 26; 10:23; 11:7)? Also, the timing and the beginning and end of each plague were according to Moses's command (8:6, 8-13, 16, 29-31; 9:5, 10, 18, 22-23, 29, 33; 10:4, 12, 18-19, 21). Naturalistic explanations run counter to the

The 10 Plagues: An Attack Against the Gods of Egypt*			
Plague	Reference	**Egyptian Deity	Deity of
Nile Turned to Blood	Exodus 7:14-25	Hopi, Khnum	the Nile river
Frogs	Exodus 8:1-15	Heket	fertility, water, renewal
Gnats/Lice/Mosquitos	Exodus 8:16-19	Geb	dust and earth
Flies	Exodus 8:20-32	Khepri	rebirth
Plague on Livestock	Exodus 9:1-7	Apis, Mnevis, Khnum	bulls and rams
Boils	Exodus 9:8-12	Isis	well-being
Hail	Exodus 9:13-35	Nut	the sky
Locusts	Exodus 10:1-20	Set	storms, darkness, chaos
Darkness	Exodus 10:21-29	Ra	the sun
Death of Firstborn	Exodus 11:1–12:36	Ra, ***Pharaoh	the sun

*Chart adapted from A. Hill and J. Walton, *A Survey of the Old Testament* (Grand Rapids: Zondervan, 2009), 115.
**Scholars are divided about which Egyptian deity correlates with a given plague.
***Death of the firstborn is a direct attack against Pharaoh himself, who is the "firstborn" of Ra.

By Brian Peterson

obvious claims of the biblical account. Moreover, the ten plagues must be understood as a direct attack against the pharaoh and Egypt's gods.

The tenth plague serves as the impetus for the institution of the Passover feast—a feast that has been observed longer than any other human feast. With the end of the tenth plague, Pharaoh allows the Israelites to leave, but not before Israel despoils Egypt—in a sense, payment for many years of forced labor (12:36; cf. Gen 12:16).

The Journey to Sinai: Exodus 12:37–18:27

God leads the people by a pillar of fire by night and a pillar of cloud by day (13:21-22). However, Israel soon faces the obstacle of the Red/Reed Sea (ch. 14). The exodus is the defining moment in Israel's history, and the Red Sea crossing is the defining miracle—an event that Paul characterized as a type of baptism (1 Cor 10:2). With the Egyptian army closing in on the Israelites on one side and the Red Sea on the other, Moses calls for his people to "stand still, and see the salvation of the Lord" (14:13 KJV), whereupon he raises his staff toward the Red Sea, which then divides, making a path of "dry ground" upon which Israel escapes to freedom. The horsemen and chariots of Egypt pursue, only to be destroyed when the divided waters crash in upon them (14:28). The Israelites celebrate with a song (ch. 15), led by Moses's sister, Miriam—a song that some have viewed as Scripture's first psalm. As Israel marches to Sinai, God miraculously provides quail (16:13), manna (16:14), water (17:1-7), and protection (17:8-16)—clear examples of God's role as covenant provider and protector.

Statue of Thutmoses III from the Luxor Museum. Depending on the date of the exodus, Thutmoses III has been proposed as the pharaoh of the exodus era. Photo courtesy of Michael Luddeni.

At Sinai: Exodus 19–40

Once at Sinai, God manifests in a theophany (God appearance) of blazing fire on top of Sinai and gives his law to the people in the form of the Ten Commandments (20:3-17) and subsidiary legislation (21:1–23:33). Once the elders and people agree to the covenant and solemnize it through a ritual of sacrifice (24:7-8), they become accountable to God. For this reason, disobedience to the covenant from this point on brings swift justice and retribution. God also lays out the precise plan for the tabernacle, its vessels, and the priests' garments (chs. 25–31). In the ANE it was common to have temples crafted after a heavenly prototype or plan and disseminated to kings by the gods (cf. Exod 26:30; Ezek 43:10-11; 1 Chron 28:11-19; and the *Dream of Gudea* in *COS* 2.155:417–33).[8]

Sadly, in the midst of this watershed moment for Israel, the nation falls into grievous sin by breaking the first two of the Ten Commandments by fashioning the gold calf (chs. 32–34). Because Moses delays in coming down from Sinai (he was there for 40 days and nights), the people begin to grumble, prompting Aaron to sculpt a god that would "go before them" (32:1, 23 KJV). At that moment God alerts Moses to the sin of Israel and Moses descends Sinai (32:7). With great anger Moses breaks the tablets that God had written with his own hand, no doubt signifying the breaking of the covenant. Moses in turn grinds the gold calf into dust, mixes it with water, and forces the perpetrators to drink the mixture (32:19-20). Next, Moses commands those who stand with him to go throughout the camp and kill anyone associated with the idolatry—3,000 people die (32:26-35). Here we see a clear picture of the gravity of keeping the covenant and the repercussions for those who break it. They had gone through a blood ceremony in agreeing to the covenant, now their blood was required (24:8). After Moses's intercession for Israel (33:12-17), God relents of his plans to abandon them, and he renews the covenant (ch. 34).

Chapters 35–40 follow a similar pattern as that of chapters 25–31. Here the people implement the exact construction of God's dwelling, or tabernacle, its vessels, and the priests' garments "just as the LORD had commanded Moses." This phrase appears 14 times in the last two chapters alone, thus showing that the people had learned their lesson and now were following Moses's words to the letter.

Before leaving the book of Exodus, one final comment needs to be made concerning the covenant ceremony on Sinai, the copies of the Ten Commandments, and the ark of the covenant. The Ten Commandments on the two stone tablets were no doubt exact copies—each tablet bearing all Ten Commandments. In the ANE, when two individuals or nations entered into a covenant, each was given a copy of the treaty stipulations. Those individuals would in turn take the treaty to their own temples and store them there, signifying that their gods would oversee the treaty, its stipulations, and its curses/blessings. When Israel entered into covenant with God, God was both the second party of the covenant *and* the God of Israel. As such, Israel placed both copies within the ark of the covenant, in their tabernacle where God could oversee both his and their faithfulness to the stipulations of the covenant (25:16; 40:20; cf. Num 17:10; 1 Kgs 8:9; Heb 9:4; Exod 16:33-34).

Finally, while the Indiana Jones movie *Raiders of the Lost Ark* has cemented in our collective minds Hollywood's perspective of the power of the ark, in reality the ark was merely the footstool of God (that is not to say that one could touch it—cf. 1 Sam 6:19; 2 Sam 6:7). In ANE thinking, the gods were carried along and protected by cherubim (cf. Ezek 1). In the case of the ark in Exodus, the cherubim statuettes on top of the ark symbolically served this function. They were a buffer between the holy (i.e., God) and the

---

8. For more on temple building protocols, see Brian Peterson, "Ezekiel's Rhetoric: ANE Building Protocol and Shame and Honor as the Keys in Identifying the Builder of the Eschatological Temple," *Journal of the Evangelical Theological Society* 56, no. 4 (2013): 707–31.

profane (i.e., the earthly). When the ark was carried by the priests, the cherubim symbolically carried God's presence as well.

Debated Issues (aka Great Paper Topics)

1) Who was the pharaoh who did not know Joseph?

2) When did God reveal his name—in the period of the patriarchs (Gen 4:26) or the time of Moses?

3) Why did God attempt to kill Moses in Exodus 4?

4) What are the theological and ethical issues of the hardening of Pharaoh's heart?

5) Should the plagues be explained naturally or miraculously or both?

The Message of the Book

In light of Gen 12:1-3, the message of Exodus is that God keeps promises. Looking at Exodus itself, the message is that God is a covenantal God who hears the cries of the people, redeems, provides, protects, and forgives those who belong to God.

Closing the Loop

The book of Exodus tells the most pivotal and crucial story of the Old Testament. Unlike the Genesis narrative, which swiftly covers many generations, Exodus slows down and zooms in on only one. Indeed, one grand episode, one single plotline, and the dramatic mission of one human leader, Moses, are featured. No story is recalled more often and attracts more subsequent attention in Scripture than the exodus story—an outcome that the story itself instigates and anticipates by setting forth the ceremonial observance of Passover as a part of the story. Clearly, this story, more than any other, is defining for the people of Israel and for the God of Israel—something quite appropriate for a book with a Hebrew title that means "Names."

For Israel, the exodus from Egyptian bondage, what later Scriptures call the "iron furnace" (Deut 4:20; 1 Kgs 8:51; cf. Jer 11:4), forges Israel's existence and identity as a nation. From this point on, Israel will know itself and be known as the people whom God brought "out of Egypt with a strong hand and an outstretched arm" (cf. Exod 6:6; Deut 26:8; Jer 32:21). What God first brought about in *the creation of God's people* in Genesis, is here established for all time through *the liberation of God's people* in Exodus. In fact, this latter event points back to the former, as God's dividing of the waters of the Red Sea in Exodus 14 (to make what has often been described as Israel's "birth canal") recalls God's dividing of the waters of creation in Genesis 1. Thus, this signature event for Israel, by reflecting the very script of creation, is shown to bear significance for the whole world. Accordingly, Israel's exodus story has inspired liberation movements the world over from ancient times to the present day, including the movement to end slavery in the United States. It is arguable that no other story, ancient or modern, has had as much social and political impact on the history of humankind as this narrative. By way of Exodus, Israel bears witness to the world that the God who sits high over all creation looks low—low enough to take notice of slaves languishing under the load of their oppressors. And what's more, this Most High God is moved by the outcry of these slaves to come down in order to raise them up to be "a kingdom of priests" and "a holy nation" (Exod 19:6) mediating God's name to all the world.

The significance of God's name is clearly of primary concern in Exodus. The book is about not only *the liberation of Israel* but also *the revelation of God's name.* Indeed, the crux of Exodus turns on how these two matters are inextricably intertwined. The most prominent refrain in Exodus, declared by God's own voice as the purpose for most every major divine action in the book, is "that you (or they) may know that I am YHWH!" (cf. Exod 6:7; 7:5, 17; 8:10, 22; 9:14; 10:2; 14:4, 18; 16:12; 29:46). And this most important name, "YHWH," first becomes the special focus of attention when the mission of Moses is introduced in Exodus 3. Here, when God sends Moses to go lead the Israelites out of Egypt, Moses asks God as to how he should identify this divine one who is sending him. God's answer, which comes forth from the burning bush, is *revealing* and *concealing* all at the same time—a point that has been abundantly evidenced throughout the ages by the fact that interpreters disagree on how to interpret it, theologians disagree on how to explain it, and even translators disagree on how to translate it: "I am who I am" or "I will be as I will be" or "I cause to be as I cause to be." Could it be that the elusiveness of this name is part of the point? In response to Moses's request for God to reveal the divine name, God offers a "handle" that no one is entirely able to handle, any more than one can handle the flame of the burning bush out of which this name of God is spoken. All this would appear to convey that God wants to be known, but he wants to be known only on his own terms, not ours. Thus, God's name could be likened to an incomplete sentence that we must wait for God and God alone to unfold—as if God were saying, "*I am . . .*" The ensuing story of Exodus, you could say, provides the initial unfolding of this self-identifying sentence, and by the time we reach the high point of the story, God is ready to speak out of the fire once again and continue the sentence with the words, "*I am* [*YHWH*] your God who brought you out of Egypt, out of the house of slavery" (Exod 20:2). Here the revelation of God's self comes to light through the liberation of God's people. God's identity is brought forth as Israel is brought forth—brought forth from slavery unto the establishment of their own identity as the people *of YHWH.*

Thus, from this revelation of *who God is* flows the revelation of *who Israel is,* but then still more, namely, the revelation of *what Israel is supposed to do.* The sentence, "*I am* [*YHWH*] your God who brought you out of Egypt, out of the house of slavery," is the statement by which God introduces the Ten Commandments (Exod 20:2-17). By its occurrence here, this gracious, first-person declaration of YHWH highlights two important things: (1) Israel's law is grounded in grace and flows from grace just as surely as Mount Sinai follows the Red Sea; and (2) Israel's ethic is all about responding to a divine person and not just to human principles. In other words, the law is a direct outflow of the graciousness of YHWH and unfolds an ethic whereby Israel is called in the presence of God to reflect the same graciousness, compassion, and justice of God's own person, God's very being and doing.

This revelation of God's presence, encountered by Moses before the fiery bush of Sinai and then by Israel before the fiery mountaintop of Sinai, is clearly something that is not supposed to be left behind. The call to build YHWH a tabernacle, which dominates the last major section of Exodus (chs. 25–40), makes a place for the fire of God to keep on burning at the very center of Israel's existence. Thus, even as YHWH's saving power is the *fountainhead* of Israel's life, YHWH's burning presence is the continuing *focal point* of Israel's life. As the feast of Passover commemorates the former, the feast of Pentecost comes to commemorate the latter, and especially so after these two feasts are taken up and filled with new meaning in the New Testament—when Jesus transposes the Passover in his Last Supper with his disciples and when the Holy Spirit transforms the Day of Pentecost in Acts 2 by coming as a rushing, mighty wind with cloven tongues of fire sitting upon 120 believers gathered in an upper room in Jerusalem.

Too many times God's people, both individually and corporately, have found ways to co-opt, to domesticate, to quench, or to extinguish the burning revelation and the wondrous liberation that the story of Exodus sets forth. Yet the God of Exodus, of Passover and Pentecost, in mighty graciousness has found ways at various places down through time, such as the upper room in Acts 2 or the meeting house on Azusa Street in 1906, to reignite among the people of God a fresh outbreak of holy fire so that we may know the Holy One, who, once again, says, "*I am who I am.*"

LEVITICUS

"You shall be holy; for I the Lᴏʀᴅ your God am holy."
　　—Leviticus 19:2 (RSV)

When I think about the book of Leviticus,

the oft-circulated e-mail attachment entitled "Why Can't I Own a Canadian?" comes to mind. This may be due to the fact that I am both Canadian by birth and an OT professor. The letter, supposedly sent to a well-known radio personality, is an attempt to discredit any moral relativity of the OT law for today. In it, the author sarcastically cites a number of Levitical laws and asks how one is to implement, in a modern context, the practice of whole burnt offerings (1:9), owning slaves (hence the title "Why Can't I Own a Canadian," 25:44), eating shellfish (11:10), cutting the edges of one's hair (19:27), mixing crops (19:19), and touching the skin of a dead pig (11:6-8). As I will discuss below in more detail, what makes the letter so problematic is the author's failure to comprehend the differences between legislation germane to the old covenant and that which is still applicable under the new covenant as reiterated in the NT (e.g., Lev 18:22; 20:13//Rom 1:26-27; 1 Cor 6:9; 1 Tim 1:10, etc.). What's more, the author does not realize that what makes the book of Leviticus applicable today (cf. 2 Tim 3:16) is the principles set in place by God, not necessarily a particular law. As a professor, I often get students in class proposing arguments similar to those in that letter. It's always a good icebreaker for a discussion on the importance of the book of Leviticus for the Christian today.

Quick Facts

Title: *Leviticus* comes from the Septuagint title and connotes "pertaining to the Levites." In Hebrew the title is *Wayyiqra*, which means, "and he called."

Date: Based on source-critical theory, the majority of the book (labeled as "P" in Wellhausen's JEDP theory; see "Introduction to the Pentateuch") has been dated to the postexilic period (ca. 500 BCE). However, some argue that portions of the book, such as the putative Holiness Code (chs. 17–26, also labeled "H"), was a separate law code that was written before the exile (ca. 600 BCE or earlier) and later edited into the "Priestly source." Traditional dating places it in the period of Moses (ca. 1446–1406 BCE).

Authorship: As with Genesis and Exodus, the authorship of Leviticus is unknown, although traditionally, like the rest of the Pentateuch, Leviticus has been attributed to Moses (cf. 4:1; 5:14; 6:1, et al.). Source-critical theorists propose that priests from as early at the seventh century BCE and/or later formulated the laws.

Audience: Regardless of when one chooses to date Leviticus, there can be little doubt that the audience was Israelite. The book has been authoritative for the Jewish people in every age (even today). Obviously, the portions dealing with ritual sacrifices (e.g., chs. 1–7, 16) have undergone changes in application since the temple destructions of 586 BCE and 70 CE.

Genre: Leviticus predominantly contains laws connected to ritual and sacrifice, and can be subdivided into categories such as sacrificial rules, rules regulating ritual cleanliness and uncleanness, a curse list, and regulations dealing with vows. Chapters 8–10 fall under the category of narrative.

Purpose: Directly connected to the theme of Leviticus is the purpose of the book: to teach a holy people how to live and exhibit holiness to the Lord in the presence of God.

Structure

Any number of structural outlines could be offered for Leviticus. The easiest way to view the book is as follows:

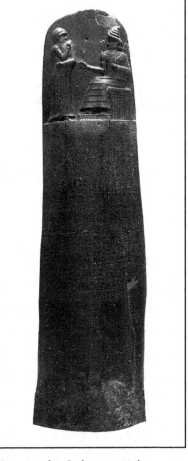

Hammurabi Stele ca. 18th century BCE. On the upper portion of the stele, Hammurabi is depicted receiving the law directly from the sun god Shamash. Photo courtesy of Michael Luddeni.

- rules for sacrifices 1–7

- ordination of the priests and the death of Nadab and Abihu 8–10

- regulations of cleanliness and uncleanness for the people and priests 11–15

- transitional chapter on the Day of Reconciliation 16; the Holiness Code for personal holiness 17–22

- miscellaneous laws 23–27: laws regarding feasts (23); care for the sanctuary (24); rules for the sabbatical years (25); blessings and curses (26); laws on vows (27)

Summary

Leviticus picks up where Exodus leaves off. By the end of Exodus, the tabernacle, its articles and utensils, and the priests' garments are completed and ready to be used. Leviticus shows how those things are to be implemented in the daily life of the nation. The book also answers the question of how Israel is to survive the truly awesome prospect of a holy God taking up residence in an earthly tabernacle situated in the midst of the Israelite camp.

Laws of Sacrifice: Leviticus 1–7; 16

The first seven chapters of Leviticus sound strange to a modern reader. At first glance, the sacrificing of animals, washing certain parts of the animal's body, the placing of blood on or around an altar, the waving of a piece of raw meat in the air by a priest, and so on, do not resonate with a Christian audience. Nevertheless, for the original audience these sacrifices made perfect sense, and when the basic principles behind the sacrifices are understood, even a modern Christian reader should find affinity with what God was asking the people through the sacrificial system. These offerings were performed when Israel gathered for their three required feasts: Passover (spring); Pentecost (summer); and Tabernacles/Booths (fall; see ch. 23).

The first offering listed in Leviticus 1 is the whole burnt offering. This offering was to be without blemish (either a bull, a male sheep or goat, or a turtledove or pigeon), and it was to be killed by the devotee and offered in totality to God. The principle here was that no person approached a holy God without a blood "covering." Indeed, the whole burnt offering was a substitute for the individual. Today, most Christians believe that Jesus's death on the cross fulfilled the sacrificial system (see the book of Hebrews). As such, his sacrifice takes the place of this first offering, as all people may now come before a holy God. The second offering is the grain offering mixed with frankincense (i.e., incense; Lev 2). This offering was purely an act of worship and is much costlier than most realize. For the wilderness generation, grain and/or flour would not have been easily attainable (no doubt purchased from caravan traders). This offering was given in part to God and in part to the priests. Today this would be similar to a Christian giving a special offering to the church (and by extension to the pastor) as an act of worship and devotion to God.

The third offering was a peace offering, or well-being sacrifice (Lev 3), which could be practiced in three ways: as a thanksgiving offering (general thankfulness for God's provision); as a votive offering (for the fulfillment of a vow); and as a freewill offering (merely to acknowledge God is good). This offering was a way for the devotee to show his or her gratitude to God for some blessing or simply for God granting forgiveness through the whole burnt offering. In a practical sense, this offering also allowed the devotee to extend hospitality to those less fortunate who did not have meat in their diet. The only things sacrificed on the altar were the fat portions, kidneys, and liver. The remainder of the animal was for a shared "barbecue" before the Lord with the priests, friends, and neighbors (cf. Deut 12:17-18; 16:10-12). Today, this kind of practice is paralleled in acts of Christian kindness to others (cf. Matt 25:34-40).

Feasts and Sacrifices of the OT					
Feast	**Purpose**	**Reference**	**Sacrifice**	**Purpose**	**Reference**
Passover*	Commemoration of the Israelite deliverance during the tenth plague in Egypt	Exod 12:1-14; Lev 23:5; Num 9:1-14; 28:16; Deut 16:1-3a, 4b-7	Whole burnt offering	Offering for general sinfulness	Lev 1:3-17 6:8-13
Unleavened Bread*	Commemoration of leaving Egypt in haste; participants eat unleavened bread	Exod 12:15-20; 13:3-10, 23:15; 34:18; Lev 23:6-8; Num 28:17-25; Deut 16:3b, 4a, 8	Sin / purification offering	Offering to atone for a specific sin (unintentional)	Lev 4:15, 13 6:24-30
First fruits	To thank God for the bounty of the land during barley harvest	Lev 23:9-14	Guilt / reparations offering	Offering when making reparations to God or neighbor	Lev 5:14–6:7 7:1-10
Pentecost / Weeks*	To show Israel's gratefulness for the bounty of the wheat harvest	Exod 23:16a; 34:22a; Lev 23:15-21; Num 28:26-31; Deut 16:9-12	Grain offering	Good-will offering to God (priests benefit)	Lev 2:1-16 6:14-23; 7:10
Trumpets	An assembly before the Lord to receive his favor marked by trumpet blasts	Lev 23:23-25; Num 29:1-6	Peace/praise / free-will offerings	A sacrifice to God for his blessings (communal sacrificial meal)	Lev 3:1-17 7:11-21, 28-36; 22:18-24; Num 15:3; Deut 12:6-18; 16:10-12
Day of Atonement	A day of sacrifice for the covering of the nation's collective sin	Lev 16; 23:26-32; Num 29:7-11	Vow offerings	Offered when a vow was fulfilled	Lev 22:21
Tabernacles / Booths*	A feast to commemorate the sojourn in the wilderness	Exod 23:16b; 34:22b; Lev 23:33-36a, 39-43; Num 29:12-34; Deut 16:13-15; Zech 14:16-19			
Sacred Assembly	A day to celebrate the end of the cycle of feasts	Lev 23:36b; Num 29:35-38	*Required attendance for all the males of Israel (Deut 16:16) Note: Passover and the Feast of Unleavened Bread coincided with one another. Chart adapted from Bush, Hubbard, and Lasor, *Old Testament Survey: The Message, Form, and Background of the Old Testament*, 83, 92-93.		
Purim	A feast to commemorate the salvation of the Jews during Esther's era	Est 9:18-32			
Sabbath	Rest on the seventh day each week	Exod 20:8-11; 31:12-17; Lev 23:3; Deut 5:12-15			
Sabbatical year	Fields lay fallow one year in seven	Exod 23:10-11; Lev 25:1-7			
Jubilee	In the fiftieth year all debts canceled and land returned to owners	Lev 25:8-55; 27:17-24; Num 36:4			

By Brian Peterson

Chapters 4–7 deal with the guilt/sin/purification offering and general housekeeping details for the priests when offering sacrifices. The purification offering (Lev 4–5) was the offering that truly showed the inward repentance and the work of God in the devotee. If a devotee had, say, inadvertently cheated someone, he or she could offer a sacrifice and pay back what he or she had cheated the neighbor (plus 20 percent more; cf. 5:16). Other uses of this offering were to cover general uncleanness if a devotee became defiled in some way (touching a corpse or an unclean animal, etc.; cf. Lev 14:12-14) or through sin (e.g., Lev 19:20-22). Guilt offerings were also offered daily by the priest on behalf of the nation (Lev 7:1-7; 10:16-20). While certain aspects of this type of sacrifice are indeed foreign to us today (issues of unclean foods; cf. Acts 10), the principle of allowing the Spirit to work in one's life is certainly not. The truly repentant believer will allow the Spirit to convict of sin and in turn make right those things that are wrong—even to the point of making restitution with a neighbor (cf. Matt 5:23-24; Luke 19:18).

Finally, the Day of Reconciliation sacrifice (also known as Yom Kippur or the Day of Atonement; Lev 16) was a general covering for the nation (16:16, 32). There were always those within the nation who did not sacrifice for their sin as they were required to do, thus bringing defilement upon the nation (cf. Deut 21). As such, this yearly sacrifice "cleaned the slate," so to speak, and made the nation right before God. While this sacrifice did not absolve individuals of their willful sin—they still were responsible before God—it did absolve the nation as a covenant community. As elaborated in the book of Hebrews, the sacrificial death of Jesus has done away with the need for these sacrifices. As with any sin, repentance is still required, the difference is that Jesus's blood has covered it all. The author of Hebrews highlights this, asserting the superior nature of Jesus's sacrifice vis-à-vis the Levitical law (Heb 10:10-12).

Nadab and Abihu: Leviticus 8–10

The narrative portion of Leviticus centers on the ordination of the priests for service in the tabernacle. Central to this account are the strange events surrounding the deaths of Nadab and Abihu. The Bible says God killed them for offering "strange" (KJV), or "unauthorized," fire before him (10:1). This account can be understood only in light of the context of chapter 10 on the one hand, and through an appreciation of "inceptive moments" in God's salvation history on the other. As for the former, 10:8-10 makes it clear that priests are not to drink alcohol when working in the tabernacle. One can assume that due to drunkenness, Nadab and Abihu did not follow procedures in lighting their incense burners and performing their duties in the tabernacle. Indeed, they may have walked directly into the tabernacle's most sacred chamber, the holy of holies (Lev 16:1-2)! As for the latter, throughout salvation history inceptive moments were solemn events, the violation of which brought swift judgment. For example, the inception of creation brought swift judgment on Adam and Eve when they broke God's law (Gen 3). This is again true for the post-Flood generation at Babel (Gen 11); the death of the ten spies (Num 14:37); the execution of Achan and his family in the conquest generation (Josh 7); the judgment on Saul as Israel's first king (1 Sam 13; 15); Uzzah when the ark, or God's chest, was brought into Jerusalem (2 Sam 6); and Ananias and Sapphira in Acts 5.

Purity Laws, the Holiness Code, Feasts, and Miscellaneous Laws: Leviticus 11–27

The last three-fifths of Leviticus explain how Israel is to live in the presence of a holy God. As such, most of the finer details of these laws are not directly applicable to Christians today (cf. Acts 10; 15). Nevertheless, application of deeper principles of faithfulness are important for the believer. As will be addressed in the next section, there are portions of the Levitical law that have to be considered by Christians today, even if particular punishments do not apply, because of their echoes in the NT. For example, the laws pertaining to sexual ethics for the Israelites in Leviticus 18 and 20 are reaffirmed in the NT, including restrictions against incest, adultery, and homosexuality (cf. Matt 5:27-28; Mark 10:11-12; Luke 16:18; Rom 1:18-32; 1 Cor 5; 6:9-11; 1 Tim 1:9-11, etc.). Finally, the Holiness Code forms the heart of the last half of Leviticus (chs. 17–26) and offers a detailed look at what it means to live a holy life before a holy God. How we apply these laws today is vital to our discussion on the role the OT plays in the life of the believer.

Application of the Law Today

As noted in the introduction to this chapter, how one applies the Levitical law—or any of the OT law, for that matter—is a topic that dominates many discussions. Five basic factors are crucial when applying the law to contemporary contexts. First, one needs to determine whether the particular legislation is reiterated in the NT as part of the requirements for Christian living. Second, for laws that are not directly applicable, one needs to consider why they were given and what is the basic principle that lies behind the legislation. Remember that many of the laws of Leviticus served to keep the nation of Israel holy before God; the Christian believer and the Christian community are likewise called to live a holy life (Titus 1:8; 1 Pet 1:15-16; 2:5, 9; 2 Pet 3:11). An example of an applicable principle might be seen in the law prohibiting mixing materials in clothing (Lev 19:19). This law aimed to distinguish the Israelites from the surrounding nations by the very way they dressed. The principle for believers is that even our clothes (i.e., the way we dress) should bring honor to God and reflect God's holiness. If we dress immodestly, then we are not following the principle of the law (1 Pet 3:3-5). Third, what is the required punishment? If the law requires the death penalty, then it's probably viewed as being very serious to God, affecting the community as a whole. If it carries a lesser penalty, chances are it involves issues of personal holiness and needs to be handled on a personal level between God and the believer. Fourth, the reader must ask, does the legislation have a redemptive trajectory in which OT legislation is being transcended by a NT ethic? This is particularly the case for the difficult legislation dealing with slavery and patriarchy. By the NT period, the seeds had been sown for the dissolution of both of these institutions (cf. Judg 4–5; 2 Kgs 22:14; Rom 16; 1 Cor 7:3-4; 12:13; Gal 3:28; Col 4:1; 1 Tim 6:2; 2 Pet 2:18-19; Phlm). Fifth, discerning God's ethical will for our lives must be done in the context of the faith community. We have been given more than an inscripturated word to be deciphered by each believer individualistically. The very presence of God has been promised to us, comes to us, and calls to us corporately (cf. Lev 1:1) as the people of God. This, then, is the context in which we will together be able to discern God's word, hear God's voice, and heed God's will for our lives.

Debated Issues (aka Great Paper Topics)

1) What was the sin of Nadab and Abihu in Lev 10:1-5?

2) In a modern context, how is one to deal with the laws related to slavery?

3) Is the legislation against same-sex acts in Lev 18:22 and 20:13 applicable today?

The Message of the Book

God's people in any generation are to live holy and pure lives before a holy God. Holiness is not an option—it is a requirement of God's people.

Closing the Loop

Leviticus, the book of the Pentateuch that might seem most distant from us, is closely joined to Exodus. It even begins with the conjunction *and* in the first phrase, "And the Lord called" (KJV), which constitutes, in the Hebrew, the original title of the book, *Wayyiqra*. This phrase and the words that follow make it clear that Leviticus is a book that is not just for the priestly Levites, as our name for it might suggest. It continues YHWH's call from Sinai to Moses and all the people of Israel. And as it extends the Sinai revelation of Exodus, it adds a most important, even crucial, dimension and emphasis to it, summarized in its most famous sentence, "You must be holy, because I, the Lord your God, am holy" (19:2; cf. 11:44-45; 20:26). Beyond this repeated declaration, various forms of the word *holy* (*qadosh*) occur more than 100 times in Leviticus, far more than in any other book of the Bible, making this Scripture's prime revelation on this important theological theme and ethical concern.

Leviticus's focus on *the holiness of God's being* provides a crucial complement to Exodus's focus on the *justice of God's doings*. As Exodus elaborates the most defining *divine action* ("I am [YHWH] who brought you out of Egypt"—20:2), Leviticus accentuates the most defining *divine attribute* ("I . . . am holy"—Lev 19:2). Justice and holiness are both essential to God's character and identity, but whereas God's justice brings YHWH near to the people, as shown in Exodus, God's holiness sets this God apart. Indeed, the very concept of "holy" and "holiness" is rooted in the notion of being "set apart." God's holiness, more than anything else, is what sets God apart from us and makes God "other" than us. It is essentially God's "otherness," God's very *Godness*.

The reason this is such a crucial matter is that we as human beings are ever prone to fashion gods in our own image or, as the people of God, to refashion the God of Scripture into our own likeness—a mere super-sized reflection and projection of our own selfish aspirations, vested interests, and egos. This bent toward idolatry, whether by making other gods or by making light of God's otherness, is the very first thing YHWH condemns in the commandments that make God's top ten list: "You shall have no other gods before Me; You shall not make for yourself a carved image—any likeness of anything that is in heaven above, or that is in the earth beneath. . . . You shall not take the name of the Lord your God in vain" (Exod 20:3-4, 7 NKJV).

If we think of the book of Exodus here driving down the stake of condemnation against any affront to God's supreme otherness, we can think of Leviticus as erecting Scripture's full-blown barricade against it. Everything in the book of Leviticus—the laws for sacrifice (Lev 1–7), the laws on priestly ordination and the account of Nadab and Abihu (Lev 8–10), the purity laws (Lev 11–15), the Day of Reconciliation (Lev 16), the Holiness Code (Lev 17–26), and laws on vows and other matters (Lev 27)—serves to *provide access* to the presence of this God who has come to tabernacle in the very midst of the people, while at the same time *preserving the necessary and proper distance* from this God whose holy presence can never be domesticated and must never be regarded or treated as a light or common thing. To offer an analogy, God's presence in the midst of his people is something like a critical mass of enriched uranium, radiating a zone of awesome, invisible, mysterious, and dangerous power. To paraphrase the famous line of C. S. Lewis, this God is good, but he is not safe. And anything less than this unsafe God of Leviticus is not the God of Scripture, but a mere image and idol of our own making. The God of Exodus justice is also the God of Leviticus holiness, and we cannot know the one apart from the other, in all of God's holy "otherliness." This is what's at stake in all the laws, rituals, and taboos of Leviticus that are so strange, ancient, and foreign to us. From an ancient context, they pose for us the ultimate cross-cultural experience and thereby the ultimate challenge to our relentless ethnocentric and egocentric bent.

We, as the people of God, desperately need this ancient revelation in our current times. We live in a world, and even more and more in a church world, that approaches every ethical issue through the lens of contemporary mores and cultural codes as something to be completely subsumed under considerations of human justice and civil rights without consideration of divine holiness and sacred rites. We are quickly losing any place in our worldview for the concept of "the holy" and the "awe," indeed "the fear of God," that it evokes. Where everything is awesome, nothing is awesome, and then the term itself becomes trivialized and we forget what *awesome* once described. Consequently, we have come to a time marked by ethical impasses—such as homophobia and what could be described as homophobia-phobia squaring off against each other—but *Theophobia*, "the fear of God," is nowhere to be found on the landscape of our ethical debate. And by losing sight of what is truly awesome, it is a world that, as famed sociologist Max Weber realized many years ago, has lost its enchantment.[9]

Nevertheless, right in the very midst of the disenchanted worldview of modernity, there has emerged a countermovement that, over the last century, has spread across the entire globe. It is a movement that has borne fresh witness to God's *Holy* Spirit, the Spirit of God's *holiness*, coming down and becoming manifest in the lives of individuals and communities, and doing so in ways that restore among its adherents what some have described as "the re-enchantment of the world."[10]

---

9. Max Weber, *The Protestant Ethic and the Spirit of Capitalism* (London: Routledge), 24.

10. Morris Berman, *The Reenchantment of the World* (Ithica, NY: Cornell University Press, 1981).

NUMBERS

"In the wilderness . . ."
    —Numbers 1:1 (KJV)

When I think about the book of Numbers,

I recall a recent family outing to a park known as Rock City. This site, near my home in Tennessee, is a favorite of my daughter Maddie. While the site has breathtaking views and is great for stimulating the imagination of children, I often find myself bored, having seen the gnomes for the umpteenth time. Nevertheless, during one of my last visits, I was pleasantly surprised to find a section of the tour that I had somehow missed during previous visits. This short side trail had a number of plaques that recorded the progression of the population of the United States over the past century. Of course, the American census, which occurs every ten years, records much more than the number of people in America—it collects information about changes in the population as it relates to demographics, poverty, migration, and so on. Among other things, such information enables the government to know where and how best to plan for future spending. In a way, the two censuses in the book of Numbers serve a similar function (chs. 1 and 26). Instead of being ten years apart, like American censuses, the Numbers censuses were 40 years apart. The first was taken for the purpose of assigning military leaders before Israel entered the land. Sadly, immediate possession of the land had to wait. Israel's rebellion against God brought about God's judgment of 40 years of wilderness wandering. The second census, just before entering Canaan, was taken of the following generation of Israel to ensure the land was evenly divided on the basis of tribal population. However, there is much more lurking behind the numbers of the censuses; they also reveal God's judgment on particular tribes, such as Simeon due to the sin of idolatry (note the diminished population from 1:23 [59,300] to 26:14 [22,200]).

Quick Facts

Title: *Numbers* comes from the Septuagint title, *arithmoi*, from which we get "arithmetic." The title reflects both the censuses and the numerous lists in the book. In Hebrew the title is *B^emidbar* ("in the wilderness").

41

Date and Authorship: Numbers is set within the period of the wilderness wandering and covers approximately 40 years. If the book is attributed to Moses, then the date would be either in the 15th century (ca. 1446–1406 BCE) or the 13th century (ca. 1290–1250 BCE), depending on the early and late-date perspectives of the exodus. Source-critical theorists place it much later in the exilic period, or even later, seeing it as a combination of the Yahwist, Elohist, and Priestly sources. Even if Moses wrote the majority of the book (cf. 33:2) some of the material still appears to be from a later hand (e.g., 12:3; 15:32-36).

Audience: The audience is Israelite. The message fits well within the wilderness period and, as Torah, has instructional importance for the Jewish people in any era.

Genre: Aside from the overall classification as Torah, Numbers incorporates several genres, such as: census lists (1; 4 [extended from chap. 1]; 26); marching orders (2); genealogies (3); prayers (6:24-26); legislation (5; 6; 8; 9; 15; 18; 19; 27:1-11; 28–30; 35–36); lists (7; 13:3-15; 32:33-42; 34); a succession narrative (27:12-23); travelogues (20:1–22:1; 33); prophecy (24:5-9, 16-24); spy reports (13:26-33); and war reports (31).

Purpose: The book of Numbers serves as a history of the roughly 40 years from the time Israel left Sinai until they reached the plains of Moab. It also functions as a repository for specific legislation germane to a sedentary life (e.g., Num 36) and as a warning against rebellion.

Structure

Apart from the numerous theme-related ways of viewing the structure of the book, two structural outlines work well for Numbers. The first is based on the two censuses and the respective sections they introduce, whereby chapters 1–25 deal mainly with the first generation and chapters 26–36 deal with the second generation (of course, the two generations share some chronological overlap). The second is based on geography: from Sinai to Kadesh (1–19); from Kadesh to the plains of Moab (20–21); at the plains of Moab (22–36).

Summary

The book of Numbers records the shaping of Israel into a nation. This period is much like army boot camp for Israel—God brings order to their once-chaotic lives in every area: religiously, socially, cultically, and even militarily when they march and encamp. God takes a ragtag group of slaves and shapes them into a mobilized military organization and nation. As they prepare to leave Sinai, they have their own covenanted God in their midst, they have the tabernacle, they have God's Law, and they have direction in life—on to Canaan! Unfortunately, rebellion against God becomes the hallmark of this period in Israel's history.

Preparations to Leave Sinai: Numbers 1:1–10:11

The book of Numbers picks up after the giving of the Levitical law (i.e., the book of Leviticus) as the people prepare to move from Sinai to Canaan. One year, one month, and 20 days had transpired from the time Israel had left Egypt until they left Sinai (10:11). Chapters 1–10 record the process of preparations. For example, chapter 1 records the census that was needed to prepare for war (military leaders were assigned to the numbered groups); chapter 2 gives the specifics on how the camp is to be ordered and prepared to march; chapters 3–4 number the tribe of Levi and record the assignments given to the three sons of Levi: Gershon, Merari, and Kohath. These three men and their families are to take care of and transport the tabernacle and all that pertained to it: the Gershonites are to care for the tabernacle proper (3:25-26), the Kohathites are to carry God's chest (the ark) and the other utensils of the tabernacle (3:31); and the Merarites are to take care of the outer structure of the court of the tabernacle, God's movable dwelling (3:36-37). Finally, Num 5:1–10:9 presents miscellaneous legislation and preparations for departure (i.e., laws pertaining to the unfaithful wife—5; nazirites—6; offerings of the leadership for the tabernacle—7; consecration of the Levites—8; celebration of the first Passover since leaving Egypt—9:1-15; and orders for camp movement—9:16–10:10).

From Sinai to Kadesh: Numbers 10:11–19:22

This portion of Numbers is marked by rebellion at every level: the people rebel as they ask for meat and water (ch. 11); Miriam and Aaron rebel against Moses (ch. 12); ten of the spies give a negative, or "evil" (KJV), report (ch. 13); upon hearing the evil report, the people rebel again (ch. 14); and then Korah, Dathan, and Abiram challenge the leadership of Moses and Aaron (chs. 16–17). In each case, God passes judgment upon those who rebel. They either die immediately (11:33—the people; 14:37—the ten spies; 16:32—Korah, Dathan, and Abiram and families) or they are forbidden to enter the promised land (14:29-35—the people; 20:1—Miriam dies; 20:12, 24; 27:14—Moses and Aaron).

Three of these accounts stand out as noteworthy in this block: the people's request for meat (ch. 11); the story of the 12 spies (chs. 13–14); and the events of Korah, Dathan, and Abiram (ch. 16). The first account is eerily similar to Exodus 16. Source-critical scholars have long suggested that this is the same story told from two different perspectives and placed in two different narratives. However, not only are the accounts told differently, but God's reaction in each case is radically different. In the first account (Exod 16:1-30), God gave Israel the meat they asked for and nothing happened to the people. In the second account (Num 11:4-33), God gives the people quail for meat and then strikes down a number of people with a plague because of their request. What changed? In one sense, the answer lies in the geographical progression of the narrative. The first event took place before Israel arrived at Sinai in the wilderness of Sin between Elim and Sinai. The second event happened between Sinai and Kadesh on the way to Canaan. The key change involved the events at Sinai—the covenant changed everything! Once Israel entered into the blood covenant at Sinai, God required more of them. Here in Numbers 11, God is holding them to account for their evil actions because they are in fact now a covenanted people.

The second account dealing with the 12 spies entering the land is a sad but noteworthy episode (chs. 13–14). After spending 40 days in the land of Canaan, the spies return and give an evil report to the people, causing them to want to return to Egypt. Of course, Caleb and Joshua want to go immediately and take the land, but the voices of the other ten spies win the day. To convince the people that the land is full of fearful warriors, the other ten spies conjure up the old bogymen from the pre-Flood era—the Nephilim! Further, they say "we were like grasshoppers in their eyes" (13:33, paraphrased; how the spies know what the Canaanites were thinking is not at all apparent). Their fear tactics work. The people become scared and murmur against God, Moses, and Aaron, seeking to return to Egypt (14:2-4). Recall that the miracle of the Red Sea was the moment when Israel closed the proverbial door on returning to Egypt. So, what they are doing here is a direct affront to God in light of all that God had done for them. What's more, the people hide behind their children, suggesting that God had brought them to the land of Canaan to give their *children* as prey to the giants of the land. God's anger is kindled, and God decrees that the people will spend 40 years in the wilderness, one year for every day the spies were in the land. Once again the covenant has changed everything. The people respond to God's decree again with rebellion, declaring that they had sinned and are now ready to enter the land. A stern warning from Moses is not enough to deter a number of the people who then try to enter the land—the results are disastrous, as Amalek hands Israel their first defeat (14:40-45). This is the beginning of a long, thirty-eight-and-a-half-year trek through the wilderness. The irony is that the people's children, whom they had, in a sense, hidden behind, would be the ones God would bring into the land (14:31).

The last episode to be noted here is the rebellion of Korah and his cohorts (ch. 16). When Korah, Dathan, Abiram, and 250 of the elders of the people stand against Moses and Aaron, Moses places a challenge before them. They are all to come and offer incense to the Lord along with Aaron. God would choose who would stand before him; Aaron and Moses or Korah and his lot. Moses then announces a means of proof before the people: if God has sent him, then the earth would open up and swallow the rebels alive; if God had not sent him, then they would die natural deaths (16:29-30). Immediately the earth opens up, and Korah and all that he owns are swallowed alive into the "pit" (KJV; pit = *Sheol*, 16:32-33). Next, fire comes out from the Lord and devours the 250 elders who had sided with Korah (16:35). As if this were not enough, the next day the people once again murmur against Moses for killing their friends (16:41)! At this moment God sends a plague throughout the camp and begins to kill the rebels. Quick intercession on the part of Aaron and Moses stop the plague, but not before 14,700 people had died (16:49).

Apart from the theme of rebellion running through these three passages, three things stand out as important:

1) Covenant had changed everything. Now God required obedience from his people. Of course, this is no less a requirement for us today when we become Christians—God requires more from us.

2) This period was an inceptive moment in Israel's history. The covenant had just been given, and now, to prove the gravity of what had happened at Sinai, God reacted decisively to get the people's attention.

44

3) Finally, it is vital to recognize the power of intercessory prayer. No fewer than four times in these three accounts, Moses and Aaron fell on their faces before God, asking him to spare the people (14:5-20; 16:4, 22, 45; cf. 20:6). This is why Moses is often viewed as the great intercessor—an example worthy of emulation even today.

Kadesh to the Plains of Moab: Numbers 20–21

Having arrived at Kadesh, Moses and Aaron are once again faced with the rebellious acts of the people; this time they desire water, not once, but twice (20:1-13; 21:4-9). In the first instance, God tells Moses to speak to the rock in order to attain water for the people. Moses instead strikes the rock, thus drawing the ire of God and causing Moses and Aaron to be forbidden from entering Canaan. God's harsh response reveals the divine reaction to humanity's efforts to take God's place. Moses and Aaron had taken credit for bringing water out of the rock when they said, "Must *we* bring water out of this rock" (20:10 HCSB, emphasis added). In that moment Moses and Aaron had stolen the glory of God. The message is clear: God shares the divine glory with no one!

The second account of rebellion in chapter 21 comes about after Edom refuses to give Israel safe passage through their land (20:14-21), thus forcing Israel to travel through the barren wilderness (21:4). Being deprived of water, once again the people rebel. God responds by sending a plague of fiery serpents among the people. Through Moses's intercession (21:7) the hand of the Lord relents and the people are saved. The same key themes again appear here: rebellion, covenantal accountability before God, and intercession.

Chapter 21 draws to a close with the Israelites finally reaching the plains of Moab, but not before they are confronted by Sihon and Og, kings of the Amorites (21:21-35). The defeat of these two foes not only serves as a precursor to the conquest of the land, but also opens up territory outside of the promised land that will eventually be settled by the tribes of Reuben, Gad, and half the tribe of Manasseh (32:33).

At the Plains of Moab: Numbers 22–36

The account of Balaam in chapters 22–24 is perhaps one of the most perplexing events in Numbers. Once the Israelites arrive on the plains of Moab, the king of Moab, Balak, becomes fearful that they will take over his land as they had done with Sihon and Og. Balak thus sends for the well-known seer, Balaam, to come and curse Israel. After one failed attempt by Balak's envoys (22:5-14), Balaam finally agrees to come, but not before he and his donkey have an encounter with the angel of the Lord, who is sent to kill Balaam. At this juncture in the account, God opens the mouth of Balaam's donkey, and his donkey begins to speak with Balaam (22:28-30). Whether one realizes it or not, this strange event is actually the key to answering the question as to whether Balaam was a prophet of God. The author wants the reader to realize that if God can use a donkey to deliver his word, God can certainly use a pagan prophet. This is exactly what happens when Balaam arrives in Moab. After three failed attempts to curse Israel (23:1, 14, 27), and after seven words from the Lord concerning Israel and her enemies (23:7-10, 18-24; 24:3-9, 15-19, 20,

21-22, 23-24), Balak sends Balaam away in frustration. However, this is not the end of the story. One must read on to chapters 25 and 31 to realize that Balaam does not actually go home; he stays in the area and attempts to bring a curse upon Israel another way—through luring Israel into idolatry.

Realizing that he could not curse Israel directly, Balaam encourages the Midianites (close neighbors of Moab) to send their women among the tribes of Israel (Simeon in particular) to entice them to worship Baal of Peor (31:16). Balaam knows that the God of Israel will punish Israel, thus fulfilling Balaam's original attempt to curse Israel directly. And this is exactly what happens—24,000 Israelites die of plague (25:9). Note that a comparison of the two census numbers shows that the tribe of Simeon (25:14) was most affected by this sin (cf. 1:23—59,300//26:14—22,200). On the other hand, chapter 31 tells of God's retribution on Midian and Balaam for their attempt to lead Israel astray. A war of extermination is launched, during which Balaam is killed (31:8). Interestingly, when the captains of Israel tally the number of casualties under their commands, they realize that they have not lost a single man (31:48-49)! What appears to be a minor detail in the account actually serves as an example of the kind of protection that God will give to Israel during the conquest if they obey.[11]

The last portion of Numbers reads more like a laundry list than a narrative. These chapters record those things that Moses needed to take care of before he died. These include making Joshua his new replacement (27:15-23); the institution of the daily, Sabbath, and New Moon sacrifices (28:1-15); a rehearsal of the three feasts that all Israelite males were required to attend—Passover, Pentecost/Weeks, and Tabernacles/Booths (28:16–29:40); laws on women taking vows (ch. 30); and a travelogue of Israel's journey from Egypt to the land of Canaan (ch. 33). Finally, the hallmark of this block of material is the distribution of inheritance and land allotments for each tribe on both sides of the Jordan (chs. 32, 34–35). Along with the cities granted to the Levites, six "cities of refuge"—three on each side of the Jordan—are established as safe havens for individuals who commit manslaughter (35:6 RSV). Of further importance is the question of what to do if a father has only daughters; could they inherit property? On this issue God sides with the daughters of Zelophehad (Mahlah, Tirzah, Hoglah, Milcah, and Noah), in response to their special appeal for equitable treatment, and grants them an inheritance, provided they marry within their tribe. Interestingly, the two passages that present this concern for the women in Israel form an *inclusio* (a literary frame) around the closing portion of Numbers (27:1-14; 36:1-13).

After 40 years of waiting and wandering, Israel is now ready to enter Canaan. However, one thing needs to happen—Moses needs to deliver his final words of encouragement and warning to the people. The book of Deuteronomy serves this purpose.

---

11. Before leaving the Balaam account, one further point of clarification is in order. Some scholars insist that the 1967 discovery of the Deir Alla inscription (ca. 9th–8th century BCE) in the country of Jordan creates a major problem for the reliability of the biblical account of Balaam. This later text tells of Balaam, the son of Beor (cf. Num 22:5), who is a seer/prophet for the gods. The problem is not so much that this Balaam is a prophet for false gods, but rather that the text is much later than the time of Moses (15th/13th century BCE). Scholars assume that the biblical text relies on this later text, thus proving the late date of the biblical account and its apparent reliance on this localized myth of Balaam. However, this argument is extremely speculative. Is it not possible that the legend of Balaam continued in the region for centuries? Indeed, source-critical scholars suggest the same for much of the material of the Pentateuch.

Debated Issues (aka Great Paper Topics)

1) What was the sin of Moses and Aaron in 20:1-12?

2) What about the accuracy of the extremely large numbers found in the book of Numbers?

3) Was Balaam a prophet of God (22:18)?

The Message of the Book

God honors obedience but punishes disobedience in his people.

Closing the Loop

The story of the people of God that unfolds in the book of Numbers is not a flattering story for the Israelites. Numbers shows the dreadful consequences of what happens when God's holy presence and will, so strongly emphasized in Leviticus, are violated by the nation as a whole. An old generation perishes in the wilderness and a new generation struggles to move beyond it. Thus, Numbers, at its core, presents a tragic chapter in Israel's story—a tragedy aptly reflected in the meaning of the Hebrew name for the book, "In the Wilderness."

This is not the kind of story that nations and peoples, even the people of God, are quick to tell on themselves. Yet it is the kind of story that journeying through this world with God will inevitably generate, because God is holy and we fall short. And so, the Apostle Paul, writing to the Corinthian church in the New Testament, makes reference to the story of Numbers and indicates that it should serve as a sobering model for God's people. In his words:

> Brothers and sisters, I want you to be sure of the fact that our ancestors were all under the cloud and they all went through the sea . . . all ate the same spiritual food and all drank the same spiritual drink . . . However, God was unhappy with most of them, and they were struck down in the wilderness . . . These things happened to them *as an example and were written down as a warning for us to whom the end of time has come* (1 Cor 10:1, 3-5, 11; emphasis added).

In this light, several characteristics of the kind of story Numbers tells are especially relevant for us: First of all, it is *a story in which God is the central character*. The entire Pentateuch exemplifies this, but Numbers shows it in a particularly pointed way. Even as Numbers emphasizes God's tabernacle presence at *the center of Israel's camp*, the book shows the urgency of recognizing God at *the center of Israel's story*. Israel's tragic move to take God's place at the center results in being consigned to the periphery, the margin, indeed, to wander and even perish "in the wilderness." As a number of God's people down through the ages have recognized, history is ultimately "God's-story," and if God is missing from the center of the story of our lives—whether our individual lives or our corporate lives as a congregation, a denomination, a nation, or a generation—we, like the ancient Israelites, will lose our way. The global Spirit movement of the last century has done much to restore God to the center of the stories of many lives.

Secondly, the book of Numbers tells *a self-critical story*. It is remarkable, when you stop and think about it, that the ancient Israelites did not whitewash their national story, like we see being done so pervasively today, whether by nations or congregations or denominations or even individuals such as ourselves who are constantly polishing our online profiles and touching up our status updates. In Numbers we open *God's Face Book* "page" and face the only one who can enable us to get our story straight. Doing so will undoubtedly humble us and glorify God alone. Pentecostalism has widely emphasized the importance of us telling our story or "giving our testimony." But Numbers would serve to remind all of God's people that this testimony that we are talking about, for God's sake, is not just any story we would tell, but it is *the story we tell when God gets us told*!

Finally, Numbers tells *a story that sees our life with God as a journey*. Numbers goes a long way in making *journey* a central metaphor for biblical faith—a journey with ups (cf. Num 1–10) and downs (cf. Num 11–25) and in-betweens (cf. Num 26–36). Journey is not a static concept that views our spiritual life only in terms of a state of existence or a position we hold with respect to God, but it is a dynamic concept that sees our spiritual life in terms of an unfolding movement. This accords with Pentecostalism's emphasis on *life in the Spirit*, for Spirit is wind, and wind is not wind without movement. It is this movement of the Spirit in the book of Acts that had something to do with why the earliest Christians were called followers of "the Way" (Acts 24:14; cf. 9:2). They realized that the outpouring of God's Spirit upon them was propelling them forward on a journey through time and space (indeed, "to the uttermost part of the earth"—Acts 1:8 KJV). The movement of the Spirit in the last century, in a similar way, has recovered this dynamic among God's people on every continent—a stunning development that calls to mind the expressed wish of Moses in Num 11:29, "Would that all the LORD's people were prophets, that the LORD would put His Spirit upon them!" (NASB).

DEUTERONOMY

These are the words that Moses spoke . . .
    —Deuteronomy 1:1

When I think about the book of Deuteronomy,

the closing scene in the Tolkien trilogy, *The Lord of the Rings: The Return of the King*, comes to mind. This is due not specifically to the content of Deuteronomy but to how both the book and the movie end. Spoiler alert: at the end of the movie, unbeknownst to Frodo's friends, especially his best friend, Sam, the hobbit Frodo makes the decision to leave the beloved Shire in order to travel to the celestial land of the Elves with Gandalf. When Gandalf turns to Frodo and says, "It is time, Frodo," Sam and the others are caught off guard. A tearful Sam struggles with what Frodo's departure means. They had been through so much together over the course of their short lives: travels to new lands, hardships and privations, battles, climbing Mount Doom under the searching eye of Sauron, intrigues and rebellions within their midst, and more. The salvation of the Shire had been their goal, and now that task was complete. For Frodo, his job was done. A solemn Frodo hands a book to Sam—a record of their adventures—and says, "The last pages are for you, Sam."[12] I am almost certain that Moses's good-bye to Joshua was no less heartfelt. They had been through so much together in their mission of bringing salvation to the Israelites and preparing them to enter the promised land. Indeed, their list of adventures sounds very similar to that of Frodo and Sam: they had traveled to and through new lands (e.g., Sinai, Midian, Kadesh, Edom, Moab); suffered hardships and privations (lack of bread, water, and meat in the wilderness); endured intrigues and rebellions (from Korah, the people, Aaron and Miriam); fought battles (with Arad, Sihon, and Og); and faced the awesome dread of Mount Sinai together. And now Joshua was faced with the reality that Moses was leaving for good—leaving this earthly life to be with YHWH. One can even imagine Moses handing Joshua his copy of the Torah—at least the portion he was responsible for writing down (Deut 31:9, 19-26)—and saying, "The last pages are for you, Joshua." Without doubt, the occasion of Moses's final farewell gives Deuteronomy a dramatic force and gravity that command our special attention.

---

12. *The Lord of the Rings: The Return of the King*, directed by Peter Jackson, film, New Line Cinema, 2003.

Quick Facts

Title: The title derives from the Septuagint translators—a term meaning "second [*deuteron*] law [*nomos*]" and thus reflects the recognition that Deuteronomy presents for the second time a version of the covenant law revealed first at Sinai in the book of Exodus. The original Hebrew title, coined from the book's first words, *Elleh ha-devarim*, means "These are the words."

Date and Authorship: Deuteronomy begins with the claim that "these are the words that Moses spoke to all Israel" (1:1a) "in the fortieth year" of their wilderness sojourn after leaving Egypt (1:3), right before their crossing of the Jordan River to possess the promised land (see Josh 1). Deuteronomy ends with the account of Moses's death (chap. 34), thus making Deuteronomy the last words of Moses to the new generation of the children of Israel, after the old generation had perished in the wilderness (cf. Numbers). As such, Deuteronomy is presented as the Bible's primary instance and example of the transition and the transmission of the faith from one generation to the next, showing how the old covenant word is to be brought forward to the new generation and to the new context—a model not just for the new generation that stood before Moses but for *every* subsequent new generation that would arise in the future of God's people (cf. Deut 29:14-15, which expands the sense of "*all* Israel" in 1:1).

Accordingly, there are two subsequent times in the Old Testament itself when later generations are shown to have found in the words of Deuteronomy the key resource for renewing their covenant faith. We see this in the story of 2 Kings 22–23 in the seventh century BCE when King Josiah's officials found in the Jerusalem temple the book of Torah (a scroll that appears to have contained a version of Deuteronomy; 2 Kgs 22:8), and this discovery had the effect of spurring a national revival that Josiah had been leading. And later still, in Nehemiah 8, after the Hebrew people returned from the Babylonian captivity in the sixth century BCE, we see Ezra the scribe assembling all the people and leading them in a covenant renewal by reading to them the book of Torah (Neh 8:1), which, here again, registers the import and impact of Deuteronomy for still another new generation.

A prominent theory of modern scholarship has claimed that the book of Deuteronomy was not merely *discovered* in King Josiah's time but was instead *composed* during this time by someone or some group who fictiously ascribed these words to Moses to give the book an ancient authority that it otherwise would not have had. Thus, this theory disputes Deuteronomy's opening claim that "these are the words that Moses spoke" and attributes the book instead to a so-called Deuteronomistic author or school in the seventh century BCE. While this view has found widespread support among modern OT scholars, these same scholars have not been able to agree on the specific social circle or tradition that the Deuteronomistic author(s) represented. The possibilities proposed include priestly, judicial, prophetic, and wisdom circles. The fact that Deuteronomy contains elements associated with each of these circles has been seen by some scholars as support for the alternative possibility that the book comes from a time before these tradition circles branched apart, even from the time when all of these elements were originally united in the figure of Moses.

Advocates of the seventh century dating of Deuteronomy have reinforced their view by claiming archaeological support from the excavated Assyrian treaties from this later time period that feature curse formulas that have striking parallels to the covenant curses of Deuteronomy 28. On the other hand, supporters of the Mosaic dating of Deuteronomy have found archaeological support for their view in the Mosaic-era suzerain-vassal treaties of the Hittite empire that are structured in a pattern that appears in the broad structure of the book of Deuteronomy but does not appear in the later treaties of the Assyrian Empire.

During the years that this debate has been going on, both sides have moderated their arguments. Those who support Mosaic authorship have shown more willingness to concede that Deuteronomy does not claim that Moses wrote every word of the book, but rather only certain portions of it (see Deut 31:9, 24-25, 30). They readily admit the later hand of a narrator in the book's introduction and its conclusion, which includes Moses's death narrative, and many have even shown increased openness to the possibility of later editorial hands in the shaping of the final form of the book. On the other hand, many who support later Deuteronomistic authorship have increasingly conceded the strong likelihood that Deuteronomy contains at least some materials and traditions that are much older than the time of Josiah in the seventh century BCE. So what finally is the difference between an earlier authorship of the book with later editing and a later authorship of the book using earlier materials? Perhaps it comes down to how much room one is inclined to make and how much respect one is inclined to have for Deuteronomy's opening claim, "These are the words Moses spoke to all Israel . . . just as the LORD had commanded him to speak to them" (Deut 1:1, 3 NRSV).

Audience: As indicated earlier, the audience to whom Deuteronomy is addressed is the new generation (or generation*s*) of the people of Israel who succeed Moses and the exodus generation.

Genre: Deuteronomy features a variety of literary genres at the level of its specific passages and sections. These include: historical review (chs. 1–3); legal material (chs. 4–26); lists of curses and blessings (chs. 27–28, 30, 33); a covenant renewal liturgy (ch. 29); a succession narrative (ch. 31); a song (ch. 32); and a death notice (ch. 34). Scholars have put forward differing opinions as to the general, overarching genre of Deuteronomy that holds all of these together. The various proposals include: legal commentary, priestly preaching (sermons), wisdom instruction, catechetical teaching, covenant-renewal ceremony, and political treaty (see above) or constitution. While each of these genre identifications has some merit, the book of Deuteronomy quite literally (and not just from a Pentecostal perspective!) presents a *camp meeting*—a solemn, set-apart gathering where the entire faith community comes together (indeed "all Israel . . . in the wilderness"—1:1 NRSV), for the purpose of hearing a word from God.

Purpose: God's word through Moses in Deuteronomy is all about *renewing the covenant faith of the new generation of God's people* by focusing on three things: (1) the *testimony of the past* that has led up to their current location and situation in their journey of faith (chs. 1-4); (2) *God's word for the present* that details what they need to see, to know, and to do in order to take the next steps forward (chs. 5-28); (3) and *God's promises, provisions, and projections for the future* to secure the success and the succession (from generation to generation) of the people of God in the land of promise (chs. 29–34).

Structure

The preceding purpose statement, with its three parts, points to an overall shape to the book of Deuteronomy that moves essentially from past to present to future—a temporal sequence that can be detected as well in the previously noted treaty structure that undoubtedly played some role in Deuteronomy's overall shaping. Yet, as OT scholar Dennis Olson has so aptly shown, Deuteronomy has its own explicit device for marking the major structural segments of the book, namely, a series of parallel headings (superscriptions) that introduce the six major sections of the book: "These are the words . . ." (1:1); "This is the Torah . . ." (4:44 CJB); "This is the commandment . . ." (6:1 NASB); "These are the statutes and ordinances . . ." (12:1 NRSV); "These are the words of the covenant . . ." (29:1); and "This is the blessing . . ." (33:1).[13]

Summary

"These are the words": Deuteronomy 1:1–4:43

These words, which introduce the entire book as well as the first section, are identified first of all as "*words that Moses spoke to all Israel*" (1:1) "*just as the LORD had commanded him to speak to them*" (1:3 NRSV) as he "*undertook to expound this law*" (1:5 NRSV). What then follows in the rest of this opening section is a swift recap of the story told in the previous chapters of the Torah, from the middle of Exodus to the end of Numbers—the story of the Israelites' journey from Mount Sinai (= Horeb) to their current location on the plains of Moab, just outside the promised land. Deuteronomy here recalls and retells this story in a way that highlights two things: (1) Israel's disobedience and the resulting divine judgment, which had caused a generation to languish and perish in the wilderness (1:26–2:15); and (2) God's gracious covenant faithfulness, which had enabled the new generation to survive and even begin at last to taste the firstfruits of the promised land through God-given victories over the kingdoms of Og and Sihon in the lands east of the Jordan River (2:16–3:29). This retracing of the steps of Israel's journey serves to take the new generation of Israel back, as it were, through an act of humbling remembrance, so they can begin anew to hear God's Torah word coming to them from Sinai (4:1-43).

"This is the Torah" (CJB): Deuteronomy 4:44–5:33

As Moses takes this new generation of Israelites back to God's Sinai revelation, he sees this holy word from Horeb *coming forward* to them, becoming a present word to God's people "*right now.*" As Moses expresses it near the beginning of this section: "The LORD our God made a covenant with us at Mount Horeb. The LORD didn't make this covenant with our ancestors but with us—all of us who are here and alive right now" (5:2-3). Moses then proceeds to re-present the Ten Commandments, the Decalogue, recorded previously in Exodus 20. He not only repeats this central nucleus of Torah law

---

13. Dennis T. Olson, *Deuteronomy and the Death of Moses: A Theological Reading* (Eugene, OR: Wipf & Stock, 2005), 14–17.

(5:6-21), but he also surrounds this core text of Israel's covenant with emphatic reminders of the fire of God out of which these ten words were first spoken and the fear of God that this evoked (5:4-5; 22-33; cf. 4:9-36). What's more, in the midst of this memory, Moses recalls how God himself exclaimed, "Oh, that they had such a heart as this always, to fear me and to keep all my commandments" (5:29 ESV). Moses concludes this section by pointing to the intended outcome of all this: "You shall walk in all the ways which the LORD your God has commanded you, that you may live and that it may be well with you, and that you may prolong your days in the land which you shall possess" (5:33 NASB). This brief but pointed section of Deuteronomy thus serves to show how life for God's people will keep coming from nothing other than obediently keeping the word of God in the light of the fire of God, *from which the word keeps coming.*

"This is the commandment" (NASB): Deuteronomy 6:1–11:32

This section of Deuteronomy moves forward from the previous section's focus on the Ten Commandments by drawing down to a pin-point focus on one, single commandment, announced in the heading of 6:1 and then presented in 6:4-5: "Hear, O Israel: The LORD our God, the LORD is one! You shall love the LORD your God with all your heart, with all your soul, and with all your strength" (NKJV). This most famous and familiar Scripture text for the Hebrew people, recited daily by Jewish children for centuries, is known as the *Shema*, which is the Hebrew term for "hear"—a term that actually combines the nuances of both "listen" and "obey," like our English word *heed.*

The momentous theological claim of this text, in radical counterpoint to the surrounding polytheistic world of that time, is that "YHWH is one." Yet scholars ponder the various possible connotations of this statement, recognizing it could point to YHWH's uniqueness (there is only *one* God), YHWH's supremacy (he is number *one*), YHWH's integrity (of *one* pure essence), or YHWH's exclusiveness in relation to Israel (the *one* and only God of Israel). That these multiple connotations are all alive within the *Shema* only adds to its singular significance.

Yet one thing is for sure: YHWH *is the one* who commands his people to have *just one ultimate allegiance*—one unique, supreme, singular, exclusive devotion to YHWH—for the command to love YHWH with all one's heart, soul, and strength could mean nothing less than this. Clearly, this holistic devotion to one God makes a person whole, indeed one whole person, and then makes one whole family (as children are taught "when you are sitting around your house and when you are out and about, when you are lying down and when you are getting up" and when God's word is on "your house's doorframes"—6:7, 9), and then one whole city (when God's word is signed on "your gates"—6:9 NKJV), and finally one whole people (when "the LORD your God has brought you into the land . . . full of large and wonderful towns that you didn't build"—6:10).

The rest of this entire section of chapters 6–11 serves as an extended commentary on the *Shema* and begins to unpack the many implications of this first and greatest commandment—the commandment that, as Jesus eventually confirms (Matt 22:36-37), encompasses all the others.

"These are the statutes and ordinances" (NRSV): Deuteronomy 12:1–28:68

After the honing of the Ten Commandments (in ch. 5) down to just one (in chs. 6–11), chapters 12–28 fan out and unfold the many specific stipulations that God is requiring of his people in relation to the particulars of their given context. The plurality of the heading signals this multiplicity, and the words that immediately follow point to this contextual specificity: "These are the statutes and ordinances which you shall be careful to do *in the land which the* LORD, *the God of your fathers, has given you*" (12:1 RSV). This entire legal section is replete with such references to the time when God's people come into the land (e.g., 12:10, 20, 29; 15:7; 17:2, 14; 19:1,14; 20:1,13, 16; 21:1, 10; 25:19; 26:1; 27:2). This section thus emphasizes the need for ethics to address timely contextual specifics as well as timeless universal norms (as in the Ten Commandments and the *Shema*). In other words, it stresses the dynamic unfolding of God's ethical will as well as the law set in stone. And in line with the thrust of the entire book, this demonstrates how God's word aims to address each and every new generation in ways specifically and dynamically related to the respective context of each one.

Along with their multiplicity and contextual specificity, the laws in this section of Deuteronomy show great variety. We see laws that relate to all social levels (from personal issues to family matters to national and international affairs) and to all arenas of human activity (from worship to work to social welfare, to warfare to government to judicial practice to marriage to sexual behavior to commerce to construction to apparel to animal husbandry to hygiene to eating to farming to festivity). Some measure of organization is imposed on this variety by the grouping of laws into a number of obvious subcollections (e.g., 15:19–16:17—laws on feasts; 16:18–18:22—laws on leadership; 19:1–22:8—laws related to killing), but orderly arrangement is not always apparent. Some scholars argue for an overarching order that reflects the topical sequence of the Ten Commandments, starting with laws about worship (chs. 12–13—reflecting the Decalogue's first three commands), then moving to matters of sacred times and observances (14:22–16:17—reflecting the Sabbath command), then laws on leadership (16:18–18:22—reflecting the command to honor parents), and then laws relating to the treatment of other human beings (chs. 19–25—as in the remaining commands of the Decalogue).

There is much in these laws that is very strange and foreign to us, and this is so because, at many points, they reflect the conventions, concepts, and customs of a culture that is both ancient and Middle Eastern. This makes any easy, direct application to our culture quite impossible and any relevance for our context very elusive. Yet on the positive side, our encounter with these laws is like a cross-cultural experience, and there is no more potent way to be critically challenged and enlightened about our own ethical mind-set than to be exposed to that of others. We see new things about ourselves when we encounter "the other." It can even serve to open us to the "otherness" of God, the ultimate cross-cultural being.

While these detailed laws of Deuteronomy reflect ancient Near Eastern culture at many points, they are, in some other significant respects, remarkably *counter*cultural. This has essentially to do with the way Israel's ethics flow directly from Israel's Exodus faith. The memory of God's compassion, justice, and liberation for the enslaved Israelites instigates and inspires an ethical orientation and expectation for the people of Israel to act similarly on behalf of the oppressed and the vulnerable of society (e.g., 24:17-22), especially the oft-mentioned trio of the widow, the orphan, and the alien (10:18; 14:29; 16:11, 14; 26:12-13; 27:19). Quite revolutionary for their ANE context, these kinds of laws in Deuteronomy read like an ancient precedent for the Bill of Rights.

This section of Deuteronomy culminates with a series of observances that are commanded of the people of Israel when they first enter the promised land. First, there is a thanksgiving observance at the end of their first harvest (26:1-11), followed by a special ceremony in their third year in the land, when they must pay a tithe (tenth) of their produce to the poor (26:12-15), and then a grand, outdoor, oath-taking ceremony on two mountains, Ebal and Gerizim, which overlook the city of Shechem (chs. 27–28). Here half the tribes of Israel are to stand on one peak and half on the other and solemnly record and responsively proclaim the consequences of either obeying or disobeying the covenant laws: the blessings and the curses.

"These are the words of the covenant": Deuteronomy 29:1–32:52

The full sentence introduced by this heading reads: "These are the words of the covenant the LORD commanded Moses to make with the Israelites in the land of Moab in addition to the covenant he had made with them at Horeb" (29:1). Whereas chapters 1–28 emphasized how the *past* Horeb covenant was *presently* being brought forward to the Israelites in Moab (cf. 5:2), this section of Deuteronomy emphasizes the need for the *present* generation to make a new covenant commitment in Moab that will extend into the *future* (so 29:14-15: "I'm not making this covenant . . . with you alone but also . . . with those who aren't here with us right now"; cf. 29:22–30:14).

Thus, chapters 29–32 present the words that lead this new generation of God's people in a new covenant-making observance, *a covenant renewal*. These words are presented in three parts: First, chapters 29–30 lay out *a liturgy*, which has the solemn and formal feel of something like a wedding ceremony, especially when it culminates with the declaration: "I call heaven and earth as my witnesses against you right now: I have set life and death, blessing and curse before you. Now choose life—so that you and your descendants will live" (30:19).

Second, chapter 31 presents a series of divinely ordered *provisions for leadership transition*. These include: Moses bringing Joshua forward and commending him as the new leader (vv. 7-8); Moses writing down the Torah and ensuring its ongoing preservation and propagation as scripture (vv. 9-13, 24-26); and Moses teaching Israel *a song* (KJV), or poem, which, together with the witness of the Scripture (v. 26), would serve as a witness against Israel's tendency to forget and forsake the covenant (vv. 19-21). Yet, in addition to *leadership, scripture, and a song*, chapter 31 highlights one more provision that will be crucial to Israel's future beyond Moses, and this is *God's own presence* in the midst of his people. This is promised both to all Israel (v. 6) and to Joshua (v. 8), and then Moses and Joshua are called into "the meeting tent" where God's very presence appears for the very first time in Deuteronomy. God's presence is made manifest by a thick cloud and a prophetic revelation about the future that God speaks to Moses and Joshua (vv. 14-23). Thus, God shows in the present a manifest presence that is promised for the future.

Third, chapter 32 presents the lyrics of the song that Moses was earlier commanded to teach the people of Israel (31:19; often called "The Song of Moses," it is a song that YHWH gives him). The prophetic revelation about Israel's future, given in the previous chapter, looked forward only to Israel's future covenant failure and punishment (31:16-21); however, these song lyrics project a story that moves through and then beyond this failure, all the way to the promise of God's restoration of his people on the other side of their devastation (32:36-43).

"This is the blessing": Deuteronomy 33:1–34:12

Just as covenantal blessings overtake the curses in the song of chapter 32, they do so as well in chapter 33 when Moses carries out one of the last acts expected of a departing patriarch—he blesses the children of Israel. He pronounces a special word of favor and future prosperity to each individual tribe. This brings Moses to the final chapter (ch. 34), where he climbs his last mountain (Mount Nebo), looks across the Jordan River, and surveys the promised land (34:1-4). Then Moses dies, and God himself conducts the burial, in a place known only to God (34:5-6). The final paragraph offers something of a blessing upon Moses in the form a tribute eulogizing his life and legacy. The tribute declares that "never since has there arisen a prophet in Israel like Moses, whom the LORD knew face to face" (34:10 NRSV)—a statement celebrating Moses's past but perhaps intending, like the book of Deuteronomy itself, to sow a seed of expectation as to the prophetic possibilities of the future (cf. Deut 18:18).

The Message of the Book

God through Moses issues a fervent call to every (new) generation to hear and heed (*Shema*) the word—indeed these words, this Torah, the (Great) Commandment, the statutes and ordinances, the words of the covenant, the blessing—in order to be renewed as God's covenant people and move forward into God's promised future.

A panoramic view looking west toward the promised land from atop Mount Nebo. Photo courtesy Michael Luddeni.

Debated Issues (aka Great Paper Topics)

1) What are the scholarly arguments concerning the late versus the early date of Deuteronomy?

2) What arguments are presented for the different views on the genre of Deuteronomy?

3) How do the detailed laws of Deuteronomy relate to their ANE cultural context?

4) How does Deuteronomy serve as a model of contextual theology and ethics?

Closing the Loop

Deuteronomy is a book of great gravity, not only by being the last book of the Pentateuch but also by being the last words of Moses. If you knew you were down to your last words—especially your last words to your children—wouldn't you want them to count? Wouldn't you want them to last?

Deuteronomy is all about the passing of the torch from one generation to the next. And for Moses there is no question that this torch was all about the revelation that was first ignited in him when he stood before the burning bush and then for those in his entire generation when they stood before the burning mountain of God and heard God's voice coming "from the midst of the fire" (5:22). So, in this final message, "these are the words that Moses spoke" to ignite the fire of the word of God in the coming generation, indeed in *all* the generations to come.

Deuteronomy, then, gives sustained focus—more than any other book of Scripture—to the words that carry and convey the revelation of God. It gives us what could be considered a virtual *theological primer on the word*. Indeed, the parallel headings that begin each new section of the book, as noted earlier, identify a rich array of words that are used to make manifest God's holy word:

- "These are the words" (1:1);

- "This is the Torah" (4:44 CJB);

- "This is the commandment" (6:1 NASB);

- "These are the statutes and ordinances" (12:1 NRSV);

- "These are the words of the covenant" (29:1); and

- "This is the blessing . . ." (33:1).

These words that Deuteronomy uplifts and commends to all God's people for all generations are not just words written on a page to be read. Granted, Deuteronomy strongly emphasizes the importance of Scripture, God's written word, and the solemn necessity of reading it (31:10-11), yet it presents the word of God as something that involves much more than this—something that conveys a living Voice, which comes *through our past, into our present, and unto our future*.

The early chapters of Deuteronomy (chs. 1–4), as we saw, highlight how God speaks *through our past*: Moses recounts Israel's past journey with God from Sinai to Moab and brings home the point, "Don't forget the things [or "words," *devarim*, in the Hebrew] your eyes saw . . . so they never leave your mind as long as you live. Teach them to your children and your grandchildren. *Remember . . .*" (4:9b-10a). The Pentecostal emphasis on recounting our experiences with God, on telling our "God stories," our testimonies, finds explicit biblical grounding here.

The middle chapters of Deuteronomy (chs. 5–28) emphasize not merely the reading of God's written word but the heeding of God's spoken word that speaks *into our present*. The golden text of the entire Torah, the *Shema*, as we saw, boils it all down to one word—and that word is not "*Read*, O Israel" but rather "*Heed*, O Israel" (6:3). And Deuteronomy 5, as we saw, gives its own emphasis to the point: "Hear, O Israel, the statutes and ordinances that I am addressing to you today . . . The LORD our God made a covenant with us at Horeb. Not with our ancestors did the LORD make this covenant, but with us, who are all of us here alive today" (5:1-3 NRSV). This verse bears powerful witness to something that has been important in Pentecostalism's understanding of the living dynamic of God's word, namely, how a word of God first spoken in the past can leap forward into the present to become a "now" word to "*all of us here alive today.*"

The final chapters of Deuteronomy (chs. 29–34) reach forward from the present *unto the future*, even unto the people of God who are yet to be born, as Moses indicates in 29:14-15 (NRSV): "I am making this covenant . . . not only with you who stand here with us today . . . but also with those who are not here with us today." God's presence, which attends his word, makes all the difference. Even as it can make his past word leap forward into our present (5:2), it can make his present word spill forward unto the future (29:14-15). What's more, it can cause God's word to overcome the boundaries of space as well as time. As Moses says of God's word in 30:12-14:

> It isn't up in heaven somewhere so that you have to ask, "Who will go up for us to heaven and get it for us that we can hear it and do it?" Nor is it across the ocean somewhere so that you have to ask, "Who will cross the ocean for us and get it for us that we can hear it and do it?" Not at all! The word is very close to you. It's in your mouth and in your heart, waiting for you to do it.

This dynamic view of God's word coming to us in and through God's living presence, which is so pronounced here in Deuteronomy, is surely one of the main thrusts of Pentecostal faith and spirituality—one that moves in one accord with the words declared by Peter on the Day of Pentecost in Acts 2:39, "For the promise is unto you, and to your children, and to all that are afar off, even as many as the LORD our God shall call" (KJV).

INTRODUCTION TO THE HISTORICAL BOOKS

The 12 books from Joshua through Esther comprise the Historical Books in our English Bibles. These same 12 books were originally arranged differently in the Hebrew canon, with Joshua, Judges, Samuel, and Kings forming the four-book collection called "Former Prophets," and Ruth, Chronicles, Ezra–Nehemiah, and Esther distributed among the Writings. The Historical Books are labeled as such because they cover material directly related to the history of Israel from the time of Joshua (Late Bronze Age ca. 1406 or 1220 BCE, depending on one's dating of the exodus/conquest) until the postexilic period of Nehemiah (Late Iron Age ca. 445 BCE). While other OT books, such as the Torah and the Latter Prophets, contain historical narrative, the Historical Books are predominantly comprised by this genre.

Noth's Deuteronomistic History

In 1943 a German scholar named Martin Noth wrote a book in which he proposed a theory that attempted to answer the question of why and when the Former Prophets were compiled. He argued that early in the exilic period (ca. 550 BCE) an unknown author(s), whom he called the Deuteronomist (abbreviated as Dtr), compiled and/or wrote the books of Joshua, Judges, Samuel, and Kings in order to explain why the nation of Israel had gone into exile. He called this block the Deuteronomistic History (abbreviated as DtrH). The Deuteronomist was so named because Deuteronomy was seen to serve as the author's introduction for these four books. Noth's theory was rooted in the belief that the book of Deuteronomy did not come from the time of Moses but rather from the time of King Josiah in the seventh century BCE. In fact, Noth saw the story of 2 Kings 22 about the discovery of "the book of the law" (v. 8 KJV) in the temple during Josiah's time (621 BC) as a story written in order to fabricate a Mosaic origin for Deuteronomy. Deuteronomy thus became the dominant theological influence on the Deuteronomist as he compiled his perspective of Israel's history, a history marked by the nation's disobedience to the teachings of Deuteronomy. Since the time of Noth, numerous revisions of his theory have been proposed that focus on the date (i.e., strands as early as David, Hezekiah, and Josiah) and the number of contributors to the DtrH (e.g., a priestly family from Anathoth; Dtr 1 and 2 who wrote in Josiah's day and during the exile respectively; DtrP—for a prophetic strand; DtrN—for a nomistic/legal strand etc.).

Despite different views on such aspects, Noth's theory of the Deuteronomistic History has been widely followed in OT scholarship. However, this is merely one theory of how the OT historical books began to

THE ARCHAEOLOGICAL AGES AND OLD TESTAMENT HISTORY

© Bryant G. Wood 2016

Period	Date, BCE	Significant Events	Biblical Periods
Early Bronze I[1]	ca. 3100–2900		
Early Bronze II	ca. 2900–2600		
Early Bronze III	ca. 2600–2300		Period of the Patriarchs
Early Bronze IV	ca. 2300–1900		
Destruction of Sodom & Gomorrah in 2067 during the EB IV period			
Middle Bronze I (IIA)[1]	ca. 1900–1750		
Middle Bronze II (IIB)	ca. 1750–1650	Second Intermediate (Hyksos)	
Middle Bronze III (IIC)[2]	ca. 1650–1485	Period 1668–1560[3]	Egyptian Sojourn, 1876–1446
Subjugation of Canaan by Thutmose III in his 22nd year, ca. 1485			
Late Bronze IA[4]	ca. 1485–1445	**Exodus Spring 1446**	
Late Bronze IB	ca. 1445–1400	Wilderness Wanderings 1446–1406	Conquest 1406–1400
Late Bronze II (IIA)	ca. 1400–1305	Campaign of Seti I, ca. 1305	
Late Bronze III (IIB)[5]	ca. 1305–1173		Period of the Judges, ca. 1400–1051
Philistine invasion in the 8th year of Ramses III, ca. 1173			
Iron IA[6]	ca. 1173–1140/30		
Iron IB	ca. 1140/30–980	Saul 1051–1009, David 1009–969, Solomon 971–	United Monarchy,
Iron IIA[7]	ca. 980–841	Solomon –932, Campaign of Shishak ca. 925	1051–932
Jehu coup 841			
Iron IIB	ca. 841–701	Fall of Samaria 723, Campaign of Sennacherib 701	Divided Monarchy,
Iron IIC	ca. 701–587		932–587
Fall of Jerusalem to the Babylonians June/July 587			
Babylonian Period	587–539		Exile
Persian Period	539–332		Return

1. Dates for the Early and Middle Bronze Ages are those of Douglas Petrovich (https://www.academia.edu/4167872/Archaeological_Ages_in_the_Levant).
2. The end of the Middle Bronze Age is correlated with the campaign of Thutmose III in ca. 1485 (*Qashish* [2003], 327).
3. Egyptian dates are those of Douglas Petrovich in *Gleanings from the World's Oldest Alphabet: Hebrew as the Proto-Consonantal Script* (2016).
4. For general agreement for LB IA, see *Yoqne'am* III (2005), 243, and for general agreement for late MB and LB, see *Tel Beth-Shean* II (2007), 12.
5. The end of Late Bronze Age is correlated with the invasion of the Philistines in ca. 1173.
6. Iron Age I dates are those of Amihai Mazar in *The Ancient Pottery of Israel and Its Neighbors from the Iron Age through the Hellenistic Period* 1, ed. S. Gitin (2015), 7.
7. Iron Age II dates are based on Amihai Mazar, "The Debate over the Chronology of the Iron Age in the Southern Levant: Its History, the Current Situation and a Suggested Resolution," in *The Bible and Radiocarbon Dating—Archaeology, Text and Science*, eds. T. E. Levy and T. Higham (2005), 14.

By Bryant Wood

emerge—one that is similar, by the way, to Gerhard von Rad's well-known theory of how the first books of Scripture first emerged not as a Pentateuch but as a six-book Hexateuch that included Joshua—a book that von Rad saw as providing needed closure to the promise of the land that is introduced in Gen 12:1-3. Both Noth and von Rad looked for literary closure at the conclusions of these first two divisions of the Hebrew canon, no doubt in line with modernity's closed worldview. Yet there is perhaps more to be said for the Hebrew canon's preference for open endings, such as can be seen at the end of the Pentateuch (Deut 34) and in the last paragraph of the Former Prophets (2 Kgs 25:27-30)—open endings that accord with a Hebrew worldview broken open by the ever-present prospect of the in-breaking of God.

Ancient History versus Modern History Writing

When studying the Historical Books, one must also bear in mind the clear distinctions between ancient and modern history writing. To begin, even though many modern history writers attempt to give an unbiased presentation of history, agendas are nonetheless present. Thus, someone living in Alabama writing about the US Civil War might be more apt to present it as a struggle for state's rights against Northern aggression. Conversely, someone living in New York writing about the same struggle may argue that the war was more about the preservation of the Union and emancipation. Of course, the ancient biblical history writers often had theological agendas that drove their writing. In the case of the Former Prophets, the word of the prophet was central to the nation and a king's success or failures. As such, many of the narratives have the word of a prophet as a central feature (e.g., Josh 1; Judg 6; 1 Sam 8, 15; 2 Sam 7, 12; 1 Kgs 11–14; 2 Kgs 1–4, etc.).

Also, unlike modern history writers, biblical history writers were not as focused on chronology when writing. Two key examples appear in Judges 17–21 and 2 Sam 21:1-14 (note also the book of Jeremiah). In the former case, the narratives of chapters 17–21 appear to be from a period much earlier than the time of Samson, recorded in chapters 13–16. In this case, the author's agenda was to show what happens when Israel does not have a king (cf. Judg 17:6; 18:1; 19:1; 21:25). In the latter case, the material in 2 Sam 21:1-14 appears to fit best before or in close proximity with the period noted in 2 Samuel 9 (see chapter on 2 Samuel for the possible reasons for the chronological changes). Addressing questions about how and why history is written falls into the category of historiography. That is, historiography examines the *way* history is written: it examines the sources, and why authors wrote the way they did.

One feature of history writing common throughout the ancient Near East but noticeably lacking in OT historical narrative is the authors' obvious decision to avoid saying anything negative about the nation and/or king from whence the history originated. This is one of the reasons one should not expect to find events such as the exodus of Israel in ancient Egyptian records. Another example from ancient Egypt involves how they recorded battle reports. We have archaeological records that attest the victory of Ramses II against the Hittites at the Battle of Kadesh, circa 1275 BCE. However, Hittite sources intimate that their king, Muwatalli, won as well! This sort of discrepancy is a common feature of the ancient histories. In many cases, the kings took their historians with them into battles so that a "proper" rendition of the events of battles reached those at home. After all, the kings ruled at the behest of the gods, and if a king lost too many battles, the people might want to replace the king.

While the global reach of the Internet is quickly changing people's ability to falsify their history, even today in some Middle Eastern contexts, defeats are often downplayed for the purpose of "saving face" and/ or keeping the real truth hidden from the homeland. For example, during the First Gulf War in the early 1990s, Iraqi propaganda minister Muhammad Saeed al-Sahhaf, also known as "Bagdad Bob," regularly reported to the Iraqi people that Iraq was winning the war, even though the multinational coalition led by the United States was beating at the doors of Bagdad. Conversely, in biblical history writing, the "good, the bad, and the ugly" were regularly recorded. This was in keeping with a history recorded for the purpose of teaching theological truths. Therefore, even though David may be seen as the king to emulate, the text also records his failures (2 Sam 11–20). Throughout the history of Israel, the biblical authors were selective in their reporting of negative facts about the nation and people. Where the author(s) of Samuel tended to show David with his flaws, the later Chronicler ignored these negative aspects almost entirely.

Selectivity also relates to how the biblical authors reported world events. Israel's authors rarely mentioned events going on in the world beyond their borders. For this reason, events such as the battles of Qarqar (853 BCE), Kadesh (1275 BCE), Carchemish (605 BCE), Marathon (490 BCE), or the major exploits of the Neo-Assyrian, Neo-Babylonian, and Persian empires are not recorded in the biblical account. However, whenever world empires clashed with Israel or Judah, the Bible often included the event. Thus, Sennacherib's invasion of Judah during the reign of Hezekiah in 701 BCE (cf. 2 Kgs 18–20) or Nebuchadnezzar's capture of Jerusalem in 586 BCE (cf. 2 Kgs 24–25) appear in the Bible because of the direct contact of the ancient empires with the people of the Bible.

Finally, there is also much conflict between modern historians and the Bible because of the inclusion of the supernatural in biblical history. Many modern thinkers refuse to accept these events as "history." For example, Joshua's longest day (Josh 10) has been variously interpreted from both a supernatural and a more naturalistic perspective.

Archaeology and History

Another important issue to keep in mind when reading biblical history is the strong influence of archaeology on the interpretation of the history contained in the Historical Books. Secular archaeologists tend to put more faith in their *interpretation* of archaeological "facts" than in the authority of the Bible. Here one must be very careful in assessing claims of archaeologists on both sides of the debate. It is true that the field of archaeology has opened our understanding to the world of the ancients; yet caution must be taken when putting too much weight on the conclusions of an archaeologist when there is a clear disagreement with claims of the biblical text. As noted above, the art of history writing in the ancient world was not the same as the more scientific methods today; however, there can be little question that the authors of the Historical Books desired their readers to understand what they were writing as real history, not mere mythology.[14]

At the same time, archaeology has also been used to help vindicate the Bible. Over the past 200 years or more, various scholars have claimed that the Bible included material that was not factual. For example, some claimed that the Hittites were a fabrication of the biblical historians, that Belshazzar in Daniel 5 never existed, and that David was a petty chieftain and not the ruler of a large kingdom. Yet, archaeology has proven that the Bible is in fact correct in all of these cases.

Israel and the World Empires

Before concluding this chapter, it is important to note that the Historical Books record Israel's interaction with no fewer than four world empires. Israel's history did not transpire in a vacuum. The people of Israel consistently interacted with Egypt from their earliest history recorded in Genesis. Egypt dominated the Near East until its defeat by the Neo-Assyrian Empire. Pharaohs mentioned in the OT include: Shishak (1 Kgs 11:40; 14:25, etc.), So (2 Kgs 17:4), Tirhakah (2 Kgs 19:9; Isa 37:9), Neco (2 Kgs 23:29-35), and Hophra/Apries (Jer 44:30). With the rise of the Neo-Assyrian Empire, and particularly Tiglath-pileser III (745–727 BCE), the power of Egypt largely recedes from biblical history. Assyrian rulers appearing in the OT include: Tiglath-pileser III (2 Kgs 15:29; 16:7, 10); Shalmaneser V (726–722 BCE; cf. 2 Kgs 17:3; 18:9), Sargon II (721–705 BCE; cf. Isa 20:1); Sennacherib (704–681 BCE; cf. 2 Kgs 18:13; 19:16, etc.), and Esarhaddon (680–669 BCE; cf. 2 Kgs 19:37; Ezra 4:2; Isa 37:38). The Assyrian Empire met its demise at the hands of the Babylonian ruler Nabopolassar (626–605 BCE) and his son, Nebuchadnezzar II, in three key battles; the fall of Nineveh in 612 BCE, the Battle of Haran in 609 BCE, and the Battle of Carchemish in 605 BCE. Neo-Babylonian rulers appearing in the OT include: Nebuchadnezzar (605–562 BCE; cf. 2 Kgs 24:1, 10, 11, etc.), Awil-merodach, or Evil-merodach (562–560 BCE; cf. 2 Kgs 25:27; Jer 52:31), and Belshazzar (ca. 550–539 BCE), who co-ruled with his father, Nabonidus (Dan 5). Finally, Persia defeated Babylon in 539 BCE and ruled the Near East until the rise of Alexander the Great in 333 BCE. Persian kings appearing in the OT include: Cyrus the Great (559–530 BCE; cf. 2 Chron 36:22-23;

---

14. Over the past century or more, a growing skepticism concerning the historicity of the Historical Books has pervaded scholarly circles. Three of the key assertions based on archaeology that have driven this skepticism are: (1) Kathleen Kenyon's conclusion that Jericho was not destroyed in 1406 but rather in the mid-16th century BCE; (2) the assertion that the proposed site of Ai (et-Tell) was not occupied during the suggested conquest periods; and (3) the discovery of numerous 13th-century settlements in the highlands that reflect Canaanite culture. While space will not allow for a thoroughgoing discussion on these topics, suffice it to say that Kenyon's 16th-century date for the destruction of Jericho and the traditional site of Ai have been called into question and rejected by a number of archaeologists (see the chapter on Joshua). Second, the rise of settlements in the highlands after the 13th century is in keeping with the settlement patterns of Israel during the judges' period. They moved from seminomadic pastoralists during the late 15th and early 14th centuries BCE to sedentary life in the 13th century and later. Furthermore, most of the cities they inhabited during the sedentary phase of their settlement tended to be Canaanite cities that they had captured (cf. Deut 6:10; Josh 24:13). When the Sea Peoples (i.e., the Philistines) drove the Canaanites to the highlands throughout the 13th and 12th centuries, the Canaanites built cities in the highlands, in some cases beside Israelite settlements. As a result, Israel adopted much of the Canaanite culture (cf. Josh 17:12-18; Judg 1:19-36; 3:1-7). This settlement pattern is in keeping with the raucous period of the judges and Joshua's challenge to Israel to completely dispossess the Canaanites (Josh 18:3). Slowly, from the period of Joshua until the united monarchy, Israel conquered most of the Canaanite regions.

Ezra 1:1; Isa 44:28; 45:1; etc.); Darius I (522–486 BCE; cf. Ezra 4:5, 24; Neh 12:22; Hag 1:1; etc.); Ahasuerus/Xerxes I (485–465 BCE; cf. Ezra 4:6; Esther 1:1, 2 etc.), and Artaxerxes I (464–424 BCE; cf. Ezra 8:1; Neh 2:1; 5:14; etc.).

It is quite remarkable upon reflection to realize that, while Israel would have seemed small when all of these ancient empires held sway across the ANE world, it is the history of Israel that in the end has had the largest impact by far on the subsequent history of the world. It should be enough to make even a skeptic wonder where the real power that moves history is to be found. It should also be enough to encourage us now to dig a little deeper into the OT Historical Books.

JOSHUA

"Arise, go over this Jordan . . . to the land which I am giving . . ."
    —*Joshua 1:2 (NKJV)*

When I think about the book of Joshua,

I cannot help but ponder the key ethical issue that is inevitably raised with the conquest, namely, genocide. Against traditional interpreters that would accept the conquest of Joshua as a just and holy war, others see it in terms of unjustifiable genocide. For a culture that has witnessed and/or read about the atrocities of the Holocaust, the Rwandan genocide, and the Balkan wars of the 1990s, the events of the book of Joshua appear problematic, to say the least. Yet, can we draw a one-to-one parallel between the biblical account of the conquest and these modern acts of violence and injustice? While a number of scholars have addressed this topic from both sides of the debate, Paul Copan, in his books *Is God a Moral Monster?*[15] and his more recent work with Matthew Flannagan, *Did God Really Command Genocide? Coming to Terms with the Justice of God,*[16] presents a number of considerations that lessen, even if not eliminate, the ethical difficulty of this part of Israel's story.

These considerations begin with the term *genocide,* which is defined as the deliberate extermination of a large group of people from a particular ethnic or religious class/nation. At first glance what the Israelites under Joshua did to the Canaanites appears to meet this definition. After all, didn't Israel leave a land of oppression only to become the oppressors of Canaan? Building on Copan's line of argument, several key factors indicate that what's going on in Joshua may not fit modern definitions of genocide. First, the language dealing with the complete extermination of the Canaanites could be understood as hyperbole (note the formulaic language of 10:28, 35, 37, 39, 40; 11:11-12; 18:1); many Canaanites actually remained and lived with the Israelites (13:1-7; 17:12-18; 16:10; cf. Judg 1:19, 21, 27-36; 3:1-6). Second, the Canaanites were given a chance to leave peacefully—Israel did not pursue them into other areas. In fact, Israel's wars against the southern and northern Canaanite coalitions appear to be defensive (Josh 11:19). Third, God actually drove out many before Israel arrived (Josh 23:5; 24:12). Fourth, according to the biblical witness,

---

15. Paul Copan, *Is God a Moral Monster? Making Sense of the Old Testament God* (Grand Rapids: Baker, 2011).

16. Paul Copan and Matthew Flannagan, *Did God Really Command Genocide? Coming to Terms with the Justice of God* (Grand Rapids: Baker, 2014).

God extended grace to some Canaanites, who later became part of Israel through acceptance of YHWH or through shrewdness (Rahab and her family and the Gibeonites). Fifth, the command to annihilate everything that breathed (Deut 7:1-6; 20:15-17) should be understood within the context of war and conquest as opposed to genocide—most of those who died would have been combatants, not women and children. Sixth, only Jericho was totally devoted to YHWH as the "first fruits" of the conquest. Seventh, much of the problem for modern readers is failing to recognize the covenantal nature of the OT and the unique relationship Israel had with God—God used the people to execute divine justice. Leviticus 18 lists several of the sins that caused God to expel the Canaanites from the land (Lev 18:3, 28): incest, adultery, bestiality, child sacrifice, and same-sex practices. As part of God's long-suffering, he allowed the inhabitants of Canaan to remain in the land for more than 400 years while God kept his own people in harsh conditions in Egypt (Gen 15:13-16). When the sin of the Canaanites had reached its peak, it was then that God allowed judgment to fall. Yet, when Israel began to fall into these same sins, God cast them out of the land and brought the horrors of war against them as well. Eighth, this was a once-in-a-lifetime event within salvation history as the Israelites claimed the land that God had promised to their forefathers (e.g., Gen 13:14-15).

After all this is said, there still remains an ethical difficulty with God's command to annihilate the Canaanites that continues to confront us. Yet perhaps it's only right that we should continue to be confronted by these kinds of biblical texts. Perhaps it's part of their purpose to make us struggle with the ethics of war, which are never easy, or at least never should be. Their special difficulty here in this chapter of Israel's history is due in part to the inevitable issues raised by total war. They are due also in part to the particular challenge of evaluating the conventions of an ancient ethos by those of a contemporary one. Yet most of all there is the special yet ever present difficulty of trying to come to terms with the vexing gap between our ways and the ways of God in these extreme matters of life and death.

On this point, the words of Francis Chan ring true when he warns, "When we begin an argument with the words 'Well, I wouldn't believe in a God who would'—who would what? Do something you wouldn't do? Or think in a way that is different from the way you think? Do you ever even consider the possibility that maybe the creator's sense of justice is actually more developed than yours . . . and that maybe his love and his mercy are perfect and that you could be the one that is flawed?"[17] Indeed, all we need to do is consider the "genocide" western nations in particular are committing against the unborn—should we really be pointing the finger at God for commanding Joshua to enact God's justice?

Quick Facts

Title: The title comes from the main character of the book. Joshua means "YHWH is salvation."

Date and Authorship: As with most OT books, date and authorship are closely connected. If Joshua wrote portions of the book, then the date would be sometime in the early 14th or late 13th century BCE.

---

17. See "Erasing Hell by Francis Chan," YouTube video, 9:41, posted on May 19, 2011, by David C. Cook, https://www.youtube.com/watch?v=qnrJVTSYLr8.

Some have noted that portions of the conquest read like an eyewitness account, perhaps reflecting details indicative of the historical time period of Joshua. A couple of examples can suffice to support this point. First, Josh 6:20 tells how the Israelites went "up into the city" of Jericho (KJV). Archaeologists have found that the mud-brick walls of the city actually fell down over the lower revetment wall making a ramp up into the city. Second, Josh 5:10-11 records that the conquest of Jericho took place in the spring of the year because Israel had just celebrated Passover. Excavations at Jericho unearthed storage jars full of scorched grain showing that the spring harvest had just taken place.

If the Deuteronomist is the author (see "Introduction to the Historical Books"), then the date of the book would fall closer to the sixth century BC or after. Of course, this would not preclude earlier material from being incorporated in the book. In this vein, I have argued elsewhere that Abiathar may have been instrumental in editing and/or compiling preexisting material for this book.[18] In keeping with this Davidic-era dating for compilation and/or the editing of Joshua, it seems, at least according to 16:10 that the book was compiled before the period of Solomon, when Gezer was finally conquered (cf. 1 Kgs 9:16).[19]

Audience: The audience is clearly the Israelite people. The argument for a sixth-century BCE date or later would entail seeing the book being composed to give hope to an exilic audience longing to return to the land. The case for the early dating of Joshua would see the book providing the conquest generation with a record of YHWH's great acts on behalf of Israel.

Genre: While the overarching genre of the book is history, the genres used for individual passages include: a commissioning notice (1:1-9); an account of battle preparations (1:10–3:17); battle reports (6:1–7:5; 8:1-29; 10:1–11:23); legal proceedings (7:6-26); lists (12:1–21:45); an exhortation (23:1-16); and covenant and ritual ceremonies (4:1–5:15; 8:30-35; 24:1-28).

Purpose: As the first book of the Historical Books in our English Bibles, Joshua serves as a history of the conquest period, while teaching about the dangers of disobedience (e.g., Achan's sin—ch. 7) and of not asking God for direction in important decisions (e.g., the Gibeonites' covenant through deception—ch. 9). As the first book of the Former Prophets in the Hebrew canon, Joshua not only records Israel's early conquest history, but it also serves to introduce God's work through Israel's leaders in the prophetic sphere (e.g., 3:13; 10:12-14; 23:12-16; 24:19-20).

Structure

The book of Joshua can be outlined as follows: God's commissioning of Joshua (1:1-9); preparations for the conquest (1:10–5:15); conquest of Canaan (6:1–12:24); division of the land (13:1–22:34); Joshua's commissioning of Israel (23:1-16); epilogue: covenant renewal (24:1-28) and death notices (24:29-33).

---

18. See Brian Peterson, *The Authorship of the Deuteronomistic History* (Minneapolis: Fortress Press, 2014). Specific texts that reflect possible editorial notions include: Josh 1:1; Judg 1:1; 1 Sam 1:1; the updating of place names 15:9-11; the possible editorial use of the phrase "unto this day" (KJV) in Josh 4:9; 5:9; 6:25; 7:26; 8:28-29, etc.; and perhaps the duplicate account of Caleb and Othniel. Also see 15:14-19 and Judg 1:12-15.

19. Brian Peterson, "The Authorship of Samuel: 70 Years after Noth," *Bibliotheca Sacra* 172, no. 688 (2015): 416–32.

Summary

God's Commissioning of Joshua: 1:1-9

God's words in the opening nine verses confirm to Joshua that God is with him just as he had been with Moses. God reaffirms his promise of the land and warns Joshua to remember to keep the Torah as revealed through Moses.

Preparations for the Conquest: Joshua 1:10–5:15

Preparations to invade the land of Canaan included practical things, such as: arranging food provisions (1:10-11); mustering the Transjordan tribes to join the conquest (1:12-18); doing proper reconnaissance of the land (2:1-24); crossing the Jordan (3:1–4:24); and undergoing ritual preparation of circumcision and observing Passover (5:1-12). One of the most memorable portions of these chapters is the two spies' encounter with Rahab, a prostitute in the city of Jericho. Here the reader is alerted to the reality that the people of Canaan are already defeated psychologically (2:9-11). Furthermore, Rahab serves as a fitting picture of God's grace to those who would submit to Israel and its God. Yet, ethically, one is also faced with the dilemma of Rahab's lying to her own people to save the two spies (cf. Heb 11:31; Jas 2:25). This is a typical example of what happens when two ethical principles come into conflict: lying versus the preservation of life. In a way, this is the ancient equivalent of hiding Jews from Nazis. Rahab chose to preserve the lives of the two Israelite spies at the expense of being honest with the king's soldiers.

In chapters 3–5 the author also presents key accounts that parallel events in the life of Moses to show the reader that Joshua is the new Moses (Josh 4:14)—the Spirit that was once upon Moses now rests on Joshua. In chapters 3–4, these parallels include: the parting of the Jordan, similar to the parting of the Red/Reed Sea (Josh 3:13-17; 4:23//Exod 14:20-22); and the setting up of memorial stones to commemorate a key event (Josh 4:1-9//Exod 24:4). In chapter 5, the circumcision scene of 5:1-9 (cf. Exod 4:24-26) and the cryptic meeting between Joshua and the angel of the Lord (5:13-15//Exod 3:2-5) harks back to similar events in the life of Moses in Exodus 3–4. As the representatives of YHWH, the Israelites, just like Moses earlier, had to align themselves with the Abrahamic covenant through circumcision. The house of Moses and now Israel had to be in order before they could serve as God's instruments of judgment on the respective nations of Egypt and Canaan.

Conquest Theories

Before discussing the content of the conquest chapters, it is important to present the dominant scholarly theories associated with the conquest. The four main theories are: (1) the biblical model, which entails the rapid initial takeover of major strongholds followed by a slower, more gradual overtaking of holdouts, as presented in Joshua and Judges respectively; (2) the peaceful infiltration theory; (3) the peasant-revolt theory; and (4) the Canaanite migration theory.

The *biblical model*, as introduced in Joshua, reports a rapid takeover of the land of Canaan in approximately six to seven years (cf. Josh 14:7-10). This was accomplished by a three-pronged attack on Canaan. A central campaign, which divided Canaan in half, took out Jericho and the strategic border city of Ai and its ally Bethel. Next, Joshua launched the defensive campaign against the southern coalition, which was led by Adoni-zedek, king of Jerusalem. Once it was subdued, Joshua then marched north to defeat the northern coalition, which was led by Jabin, king of Hazor.

The biblical model, as it is further unfolded in Judges, depicts a much slower process of overtaking the remaining Canaanites after Joshua's initial onslaught—a process taking several generations to accomplish. As Israel moved into the land, they gained strength and formed alliances with each other, thus enabling them to take over cities one at a time (cf. Judg 1). Some scholars have theorized that the entire conquest happened this way, rejecting the biblical claims of the rapid takeover by Joshua. This is the view of the *"peaceful infiltration theory"* of Albrecht Alt and Martin Noth. Alt proposed that Israel joined with other discontented Canaanites and some of the local nomads and began to infiltrate into Canaan. As the coalition participants grew over an extended period of time, they then began to overthrow the city-states one at a time.

The *peasant-revolt theory*—proposed by George Mendenhall and very similar to the Marxist-based "agrarian social revolution" theory of Norman Gottwald—argues that the Israelites did not conquer the land from without but rather were part of the local Canaanite peasantry who were under the control of feudal-like city-states in the lowlands of Canaan. The Canaanite overlords, influenced by Egyptian hegemony, levied heavy taxation and oppressive policies that led to the revolt of the "peasant" class. These Canaanites moved to the highland region and built cities. Only later did these "peasants" identify themselves as Israelites, after a group of escaped slaves from Egypt, whose god was YHWH, entered the region.

The *Canaanite migration theory*, rooted heavily in archaeology, is the dominant scholarly theory today. Variations of the theory have been proposed by various scholars, such as Israel Finkelstein and William G. Dever, who both argue that the Israelites were in fact predominantly Canaanites. Some suggest that the Canaanites were living in the lowlands next to the Mediterranean before the invasion of the Sea Peoples (i.e., the Philistines) in the 13th to 12th centuries BCE. When the Sea Peoples invaded, the Canaanites migrated to the central highlands and established new, defensible cities. Other variations of this theory hold that the migration came from the Transjordan. Whichever version of this theory one holds, most proponents agree that in time, these Canaanites adopted a desert god named YHWH and took on the designation of "Israel."

All of these theories claim some degree of grounding in either archaeology and/or biblical data. Yet, one is left wondering why, if Israel was once Canaanite, is the Bible so anti-Canaanite? It is true that archaeology has revealed Canaanite/Israelite culture as dominant in the highlands during the transition between the Late Bronze Age and the Early Iron Age (ca. 1200 BCE), yet this would in no way conflict with the biblical account of Israelite occupation of Canaanite cities (Deut 6:10-11; Josh 24:13). Indeed, the unfolding biblical picture is that, for the first 200 years or more of Israel's existence in the land, the Israelites adopted many of the Canaanite cultural practices, and this is explicitly emphasized as the reason for their undoing during the period of Judges. Finally, most of these theories give more weight to archaeological evidence than the biblical witness as a valid source for Israel's history, something more conservative readers of Scripture see as an unjustifiable methodological bias.

As for the biblical model, while scholars have pitted the accounts of Joshua and Judges against each other, they can be seen as complementing each other. Joshua's rapid conquest essentially took out the Canaanite leadership and subdued the heavy resistance in the strategic areas of the land. God points out at the end of Joshua's life that there was much land yet to conquer (13:1-6). The book of Judges presents a picture of Israel unwilling to complete what God had commanded. As such, God allowed many of the nations to stay in the land as a test for Israel in consequence of their disobedience (Judg 3:1-5).

Conquest of Canaan: Joshua 6:1–12:24

According to Joshua 6, the Israelites' conquest of Jericho was accomplished after they circled Jericho once a day for six days and then seven times on the seventh day. At the word of Joshua, the entire army shouted, the walls fell down, and the city was plundered for YHWH and burned. The only survivors from the city were Rahab and her immediate family members. The main problem with this account, according to some archaeologists, is whether or not Jericho was actually inhabited at this time. Kathleen Kenyon, who excavated the city in the 1950s, concluded that the city was destroyed at the transition of the Middle and Late Bronze Age (ca. 1550 BCE), thus arguing that the biblical account is in error. However, Bryant Wood, who is a specialist in Late Bronze Age Canaanite pottery, refutes this conclusion, positing a date of 1406 BCE for the destruction.[20] To this day, the dating of the destruction of Jericho remains a vigorously debated issue.

Chapters 7 and 8 present an account of the conquest of Ai, which is located in the central highlands about 15 miles west of Jericho. Israel's first attempt to conquer this small border fortress fails due to the sin of Achan, who had stolen gold and garments from Jericho against the command of YHWH (7:1). Once Achan's sin is revealed and punished, Joshua returns to Ai a second time and defeats both Ai and its ally, Bethel (8:17). Two issues in these two chapters are worth noting. First, the story of Achan's plight poses a striking contrast to the Rahab account. In the Rahab story, we see a female foreigner who accepts the will of YHWH and saves herself and family, and in the other, we see an Israelite male (from Judah, no less) who rejects God's commands and is executed with his family.

As with the Jericho account, the second issue concerning Ai involves controversy over the historicity of the account. Since famed 20th-century archaeologist William F. Albright concluded that Et-tell was biblical Ai, scholars have propagated his position. Because "Ai" can mean "the ruin," Albright and other archaeologists identified it with the largest ruin in the approximate location of where Ai was thought to

---

20. Bryant Wood, "Did the Israelites Conquer Jericho? A New Look at the Archaeological Evidence," *Biblical Archaeology Review* 16, no. 2 (1990): 44–58.

Artist's reconstruction of the city of Ai (by Tom Miller). Courtesy of ABR.

have been, namely, Et-tell. The problem once again is that the occupation levels at Et-tell do not match the biblical account. Et-tell was unoccupied from the Early Bronze Era until the Iron Age I.[21]

Chapter 9 presents the story of the Gibeonites, a Canaanite group who deceives the people of Israel. Having heard that Jericho and Ai had fallen, the leaders of Gibeon and its cities send envoys to Joshua to sue for peace. The envoys, having disguised themselves by wearing worn-out clothing and travel accessories and carrying dried-out bread, tell Joshua that they are from a distant land (9:4-5). Without consultation from YHWH (9:14), Joshua and the elders of Israel make an irrevocable covenant with the Gibeonites (9:15; cf. 2 Sam 21:1-14). Once Joshua realizes that the Gibeonites are Canaanites, he puts them to forced labor in service of the nation and the tabernacle (9:21-23, 27).

Chapter 10 records the fallout of the Gibeonites siding with Israel. The southern city-states form a coalition to go and attack the Gibeonites. As the suzerain of the Gibeonites, Israel is responsible to defend its vassal. It is within this context that Joshua makes a forced march and attacks the southern coalition (10:9). During the battle, Joshua prays to God to extend the daylight hours so he can defeat the five kings of the south. Along with the extended day, God also sends hailstones from heaven and kills more of the enemy

---

21. This has been cited as proof that the biblical chronology is in error. However, the Associates for Biblical Research, under the leadership of Bryant Wood and Scott Stripling, have proposed an alternate site for Ai at Khirbet el-Maqatir about one kilometer (0.6 miles) west of Et-tell, and their work has unearthed a number of significant findings that support details from the biblical story of Ai, including the topographical considerations, ceramic typology (refired Late Bronze Age pottery), the size of the city (smaller than Gibeon—Josh 10:2), and the orientation of the city (gates facing north Josh 8:11)—enough to convince many that Albright identified the Ai of Abraham's day but not the Ai of Joshua's day (Wood 2008). The recent discovery of an Egyptian scarab (Amenhotep II; ca. 1450–1425 BCE), just inside the city gates, adds to the amassed evidence.

than the Israelites did (10:11). The remainder of chapter 10 and most of chapter 11 are written in very formulaic language showing the systematic conquest of the southern and northern regions of Canaan (10:28-43; 11:1-23).

Division of the Land: Joshua 13:1–22:34

Land allotment lists comprise most of the second half of the book. Once the land is subdued, Joshua casts lots and assigns each of the tribes their respective inheritance (18:6-10). With the exception of the two and a half tribes from the Transjordan (13:1-33), each tribe receives a portion of the land (13:1–19:51). The Levites receive their portion from within each tribe's allotment, perhaps serving as a metaphorical representation that God is within the midst of Israel (21:1-45).

Amenhotep II (ca. 1450–1425 BCE) scarab found in 2013 at the proposed site of Ai (Khirbet el-Maqatir). Photo courtesy of Michael Luddeni and ABR.

Joshua's Commissioning of Israel: Joshua 23:1-16

Similar to YHWH's commissioning of Joshua in chapter 1, Joshua commissions Israel to complete the conquest (23:1-5), follow YHWH's law (23:6-7), trust in him alone (23:8-11), and abstain from adopting the ways of Canaan (23:12-16).

Epilogue: Covenant Renewal (24:1-28) and Death Notices (24:29-33)

Following the basic covenant formulary of Deuteronomy and the Covenant Code of Exodus 20–23, chapter 24 records the covenant renewal ceremony at Shechem. The format includes: the preamble, 24:2a; historical prologue, 24:2b-13; stipulations, 24:14-15, 23; blessings, 24:16-18, 20c; curses, 24:19-20b; witnesses, 24:21-22, 24, 27; and the document clause, 24:25-26. The book of Joshua closes abruptly with the death notice of Joshua (24:29-30), the burial of Joseph's bones (24:32), and the death of Eleazar (24:33). Of particular importance is the notice concerning Joseph's bones, which harks back to Genesis (Gen 50:24-26). With the conquest of the promised land, all the promises of God to Abraham are fulfilled, at least in part.

Debated Issues (aka Great Paper Topics)

1) Where did Joshua set up the stones of memorial noted in chapter 4: in the midst of the Jordan (v. 9) or at Gilgal (v. 20)?

2) What are the scholarly opinions concerning the location of Ai?

3) Why did Joshua order the destruction of Achan's family in addition to Achan (Josh 7:24-25)?

4) What are the scholarly explanations of Joshua's longest day?

The Message of the Book

God is a promise-keeping God, who protects his people and gives them rest in the land.

Closing the Loop

There are some striking parallels between the roles of the book of Joshua in the OT and Acts in the NT—the biblical book that has been so theologically significant for Pentecostalism. As Acts follows the foundational canonical story of the Gospels, so Joshua follows the foundational story of the Torah (the Pentateuch). In each case, these books extend the primary story to the following generation of leadership, after the primary leader (Moses and Jesus, respectively) passes from the scene. Both Joshua and Acts are biblical books that tell a triumphant story of progressive territorial expansion. For Joshua it is a military conquest that progressively extends to encompass the entire land of Canaan, according to the promise of YHWH (1:2-6). For Acts it is a spiritual conquest that progressively extends from Jerusalem, to Judea to Samaria to "the end of the earth," according to the promise of Jesus (Acts 1:8). In both cases these campaigns are wonderful—indeed full of wonder—for they are generated and propelled forward by signs and wonders (Josh 3:5; Acts 2:43).

Yet these triumphant conquests in both cases are also shown to have a downside. When God's people are being swept along in a season of successive victories, it becomes easy to be triumphalist, equating God's cause with our cause and collapsing the divine agenda and interests into our human agenda and interests. This comes out not only in blatant attempts by individuals to exploit and capitalize on God's victories for his people, as with Achan in Joshua 7 and Ananias and Sapphira in Acts 5, but also in more pervasive and subtle ways for God's people as a whole. Any time "our group," as a collective body, gets into conquest mode, we can quickly get caught up in seeing God on our side until it becomes easy to see everything in terms of only two sides: "us versus them."

However, in both the conquest in Joshua and the conquest of Acts we find stories that challenge this two-sided way of seeing things, for God is not always found fighting for "us" against "them," but at times he is seen moving for "them" against "us" (cf. the Gibeonites in Josh 9 and the Gentiles, including a Roman military officer, in Acts 10). God even makes this point explicitly and emphatically in both Joshua and Acts as God's people in each case stand at the starting point of their conquests. In Acts 10 God gives Peter a prophetic vision to carry the gospel to the Gentiles and says to him, "Never consider unclean what God has made pure" (v. 15). And in Joshua 5, on the eve of Israel's first battle in the promised land, Joshua, all alone, suddenly finds himself facing a mighty swordsman, whose startling presence prompts Joshua to say, "Are you on our side or that of our enemies?" But this divine messenger declares, "Neither! I'm the commander of the Lord's heavenly force" (5:13-14). He then speaks to Joshua, in an echo of YHWH's words to Moses, "Take your sandals off your feet because the place where you are standing is holy" (v. 15).

These divine declarations in both Joshua and Acts should give us pause in relation to the stands we take for the causes and movements we take up. For *holy* land is not *our* land, and *holy* war is ultimately not *our* fight. It is vital to remember this anytime we get into a fight or a debate—even a debate over holy war in the book of Joshua! We might be surprised, as Joshua surely was, to hear that God's side in the battle is not so easily or completely identified with "our side." And this most certainly is a truth that extends to the movement of the Holy Spirit, whether in the book of Acts or in our day. A movement of *Holy* Wind is not a movement we can claim as *our own*. It is bigger, wider, deeper, and infinitely purer and more wondrous than the Pentecostal movement. Yet regardless of the movement or group to which we belong, whenever the Wind of God begins to propel us forward in conquest, this lesson coming to us from Joshua through Acts is most crucial. It's no doubt time for us to check out where we stand with God, for it just might be that we are standing on holy ground.

JUDGES

In those days . . . everyone did what was right in his own eyes.
  —Judges 21:25 (NASB)

When I think about the book of Judges,

I see parallels between ancient Israel of the Judges' era and 21st-century America. As we saw at the close of the previous chapter on Joshua, the Israelites had established their new life in a new land by reaffirming their faith and trust in God; yet within one generation, the cracks in the spiritual foundation of the nation began to show. The sad downward cycle of sin and servitude is the hallmark of Judges, even though the 300 or so years of this period are marked by moments of renewal. By the end of the book, the sad refrain "each person did what they thought to be right" (Judg 17:6; 21:25) becomes the punctuation of the book, pointing to the moral depravity of the period—in many cases directly related to a plummet in spiritual and sexual ethics (cf. Judg 17–21).

Of course, one doesn't have to think too long before the obvious parallels between Israel and contemporary America (and many other enlightened nations) become apparent. America is a nation that was founded upon Judeo-Christian principles and trust in God. It has had a history punctuated by moments of God's inbreaking through awakenings of faith, including the First Great Awakening of the 18th century, with George Whitefield and Jonathan Edwards; the Second Great Awakening of the late 18th to early 19th century, with the Wesley brothers and Charles Finney; the Azusa Street revival beginning in 1906 with William Seymour, or the charismatic renewal and Vineyard movements of the 1960s, led by Dennis Bennett and John Wimber, respectively. Yet, despite these powerful times of renewal, America and many other cultures, just like Israel, are at serious risk for decline, which happens in any nation or culture that becomes increasingly mired in debased sexual practices and a faulty spiritual ethic. Indeed, today the phrase "Every person did what was right in his or her own eyes" can be said of many Western nations. It should be our hope and prayer that in the midst of the moral and spiritual chaos, God will see fit to send another "Samuel" to help bring clarity—for as "the word of the LORD was rare in those days and there was no vision breaking through" (1 Sam 3:1, author's translation), we are facing the same dilemma: the need for a word from God through his prophets.

75

Quick Facts

Title: The title comes from the main characters of the book—the judges. Both the Hebrew title, *Shophetim*, and the LXX title, *Kritai*, mean "judges."

Date: The date of Judges is much debated. On the one hand, Judg 1:21 records that the Benjamites could not drive out the Jebusites; so they were still living among them "to this day" (NASB). It was only after the period of David, in about 1000 BCE, that Jerusalem was conquered and seized from the Jebusites. On the other hand, some scholars see Judg 18:30 as pointing to a post-722 BCE date, insofar as this text makes a reference to "the captivity of the land" (NASB), which sounds like a reference to the Assyrian conquest of the northern kingdom of Israel in 722 BCE. However, this "captivity of the land" could be referring to a phase of the Philistine wars before David's reign (cf. 18:31; Ps 78:60; Jer 7:12-14; 1 Sam 4–5). If one opts for the theory that the so-called Deuteronomist (Dtr) was the author, then Judges would date to the late seventh or early sixth century BCE. Fortunately, many questions related to the date of the book of Judges can be resolved by turning to the issues of authorship and purpose.

Authorship: The general scholarly consensus is that the Dtr wrote the book of Judges. Of course, this does not preclude the possibility of earlier material being edited into the whole. To be sure, ascribing the authorship to the Dtr would accord well with the theory that 18:30 refers to the Assyrian captivity of 722 BCE. However, another possibility appears more fitting, one that would see the Dtr as no more than an editor of the material. A number of scholars now conclude that the character parallels between Saul and the judges, along with several of the narrative portions of Judges (e.g., chs. 1; 9; 19–21), present an anti-Saul/pro-Davidic perspective. This slant is clearest in chapters 19–21, where the author puts Saul in a bad light by highlighting the rebellion of Benjamin (Saul's tribe), the sin of Gibeah (Saul's hometown), and the unfaithfulness of the men of Jabesh-gilead (the ancestors of Saul). Because any serious pro-Saul support for the throne was all but stamped out by the middle of David's reign, the most fitting date for Judges would fall in the early reign of David. In light of this, it is arguable that Abiathar, David's priest (cf. 1 Sam 22–23; 30:7), could easily have written the book in support of his friend David during the roughly seven-year civil war between Saul's son Ishbosheth and David (2 Sam 2–4).[22]

Audience: The book is clearly addressed to the people of Israel. If Judges reflects support for David's claim to the throne, as suggested above, then it may have been especially aimed at the tribes allied with Ishbosheth (2 Sam 2:5-7; 3:17).

Genre: Judges is predominantly historical narrative, although a few other genres are featured in several passages: Deborah's song (5:1-30), the Midianite's dream report (7:13-15), Jotham's fable (9:7-15), and Samson's riddle (14:13, 18). The genre of battle report also appears frequently in the book (1:1-13, 22-26; 3:27-30; 4:14-24; 7:16-25; 9:35-57; 12:4-6; 15:14-19; 20:14-48).

---

22. For more on this theory, see Brian Peterson, "Could Abiathar, the Priest, Be the Author of Judges?" *Bibliotheca Sacra* 170, no. 680 (October–December 2013): 432–52. See also Brian Peterson, *The Authors of the Deuteronomistic History: Locating a Tradition in Ancient Israel* (Minneapolis: Fortress Press, 2014).

Purpose: As noted earlier, Judges may have served as a narrative aiming to support and promote Davidic rule. It also served the greater purpose of recording the history of the transitional period between the conquest and the monarchy. Theologically, it served to highlight the Canaanization of the Israelites (cf. 3:6; 6:25-32; 11:39; 17:1-13; 19:13-30; 20:11-48; 21:9-23) and the reality that despite Israel's unfaithfulness, YHWH remained faithful to the covenant.

Structure

Judges is one of the least debated books of Scripture when it comes to the structure of the final form. Its three-part structure unfolds as follows: an introduction that previews the cyclic pattern of Israel's life that will follow (1:1–3:6, see esp. 2:11-19); a series of stories of individual judges, with each following the same recurring cycle of *sin, servitude, supplication, salvation,* and *security* (3:7–16:31); and a conclusion or appendix to the book that further highlights the need for a king in Israel (17:1–21:25).

Summary

Introduction: Judges 1:1–3:6

As with Josh 1:1, Judg 1:1a shows clear evidence of the editorial activity of the Historical Books (note also Josh 15:15-19; Judg 1:11-15). This is the first time since leaving Egypt that Israel did not have a clearly designated leader. Instead God says here that Judah (the tribe) will lead the nation. This declaration at the beginning of the book is echoed near the end of the book in 20:18, forming a framing device (inclusion or *inclusio*) that serves the book's pro-David agenda, since Judah is the tribe from which David will come. In this regard, almost all of chapter 1 depicts Judah as the tribe to emulate in the conquest of Canaan in contrast to the glaring failure of the tribe of Benjamin, from which Saul will come (cf. 1:8, 21). There is also the issue of what many have seen as a second introduction to the book in 2:6-10—a passage that returns to the topic of the last days of Joshua and his death, which was previously covered in 1:1. Thus chapter 1 may have been added purposely to emphasize Judah as the ideal kingly tribe.

The cycle, which structures the body of the book, is first introduced in 2:11-19: *sin*—the Israelites did things that the Lord saw as evil (2:11-13; cf. 3:7, 12; 4:1; 6:1; 10:6; 13:1); *servitude*—God delivered Israel into the hands of its enemies (2:14-15b); *supplication* and *salvation*—the distress of Israel caused God to send a deliverer (2:15c-18); *security*—Israel served God in safety until the judge died, only thereafter to return to its old ways, thus starting the cycle all over again (2:19). Finally, 3:1-6 records that God allowed many nations to remain in Canaan as a means of testing his people. Sadly, Israel intermarried with the nations, once again drawing the ire of God (3:6).

The Cycle of the Judges' Period: 3:7–16:31

Following the pro-Judah/David perspective, the first judge to be highlighted is Othniel—a Judahite judge—who serves as the paradigmatic judge for Israel (3:7-11). With the Spirit of God upon him (3:10), he delivers Israel from Cushan-rishathaim of Mesopotamia. Not surprisingly, Othniel is one of the few judges to have a positive influence on Israel.

Ehud, a Benjamite, succeeds Othniel. Ehud's unique ability to use his left hand (3:15) is the means for achieving deliverance for Israel from Eglon, king of Moab. The brief account is full of intrigue as the left-handed Ehud conceals a two-edged sword under his cloak on his right thigh (most soldiers were right-handed and wore their swords on their left side). Once inside of the king's palace at Jericho (or Palm City, 3:13), Ehud pretends that he has a message for the king. When Ehud is alone with Eglon, he draws out his sword and thrusts it into Eglon's belly. Eglon is so overweight that his belly fat closes around the sword, forcing Ehud to leave the sword there (3:22). Ehud then locks the doors to the upper chamber, where he and Eglon had been meeting, and he escapes and rallies all Israel against Moab to bring about a great deliverance (3:27-30).

After an 80-year reprieve, Israel again returns to their evil ways and God puts them into the hand of Jabin, king of Canaan, who reigned in Hazor (4:2). This time God sends an unlikely deliverer, Deborah, a woman who is both a judge and prophetess—the only judge before Samuel with this dual identity. For a patriarchal audience this would have been surprising for sure. Nevertheless, God uses Deborah and her general, Barak, to deliver Israel by bringing a great victory in the Jezreel Valley (the future site of Armageddon; cf. Rev 16:16). Yet, Deborah is not the only heroine in the story. Jael, a descendant of Moses's father-in-law (4:11), is the person who actually kills Jabin's general, Sisera, by driving a tent peg through his head while he slept in her tent (4:21). Judges 5, perhaps one of the most archaic pieces of literature in the Bible, presents another version of the same episode in the form of a song. Here one hears the added detail that YHWH fought on behalf of Israel by using a great rainstorm that made the Jezreel Valley and the region around the Kishon stream a miry bog, causing the chariots of Sisera to become immobilized. The account of Deborah accentuates God's readiness to send his Spirit upon women and men to bring about God's plans and purposes (cf. Gal 3:28).

Other than the story of Samson (chs. 13–16), the account of Gideon (chs. 6–8) is the most well-known story in Judges. God recruits Gideon, a man who is the youngest or least in his family (6:15), to deliver Israel from the Midianites. Gideon's response is to ask God for a sign, not once, but twice. Gideon places a wool fleece on the ground overnight and asks God to keep the ground dry from the dew but to make the fleece wet (6:37-38). When God answers this request, Gideon asks for a second sign on the following night, that the fleece would be dry and the ground wet (6:39-40). God answers this request as well. This act of Gideon has become known in Christian circles as "putting a fleece before God." It is still practiced by many believers even today, even though the "fleece" is usually metaphorical. The rest of the story of Gideon is the focus of many Sunday school lessons. Gideon goes to fight the Midianites, but God tells

The Judges of Israel ca. 1367–1050 BC

Judge	Tribe	Length of Judgeship/ Years of Rest**	Oppressor	Length of Oppression	Reference
Othniel	Judah	40 years 1367–1327	Cushan-Rishathaim of Mesopotamia	8 years (3:8) 1375–1367**	3:7-11
Ehud	Benjamin	80 years 1309–1229	Eglon of Moab	18 years (3:14) 1327–1309	3:12-30
Shamgar*	Dan?	1230–?	Philistines	?	3:31
Deborah and Barak	Ephraim	40 years 1230–1190	Jabin and his general Sisera of Canaan	20 years (4:3) 1250–1230	4:1–5:31
Gideon	Manasseh	40 years 1183–1143	Midian	7 years (6:1) 1190–1183	6:1–8:35
Abimelech†	Manasseh	1143–1140	3-year civil war	NA	9:1-57
Tola*	Issachar	23 years 1140–1117	NA	NA	10:1-2
Jair*	Manasseh	22 years 1117–1095	NA	NA	10:3-5
Jephthah	Manasseh	6 years 1100–1096	Ammon and Philistines	18 years (10:8) 1118–1100	10:6–12:7
Ibzan*	Judah	7 years 1100–1093	NA	NA	12:8-10
Elon*	Zebulun	10 Years 1093–1083	NA	NA	12:11-12
Abdon*	Ephraim	8 years 1083–1075	NA	NA	12:13-15
Samson	Dan	20 years 1130–1110	Philistines	40 years (13:1) 1150–1110††	13:1–16:31
Eli	Levi	40 years 1144–1104‡	Philistines	?	1 Sam 1:1–3:18
Samuel and Sons; Joel* and Abijah*	Levi/ Ephraim?	54 years 1104–1050	Philistines	NA (see 1 Sam 7:13-14)	1 Sam 3:19–25:1

*Denotes a minor judge

†A usurper

**Most dates are approximate and in many cases may have overlapped with other judges

‡The Battle of Aphek is variously dated from 1104 to 1050 BC. Here I follow Merrill's date of 1104 (*Kingdom of Priests*, 195).

††The Philistines started their oppression from the west, which first affected the tribes of Dan and Judah ca. 1150 BCE or before (Judg 13–16). By 1104 they had penetrated north into the region of Ephraim at Aphek (1 Sam 4–7). Samuel defeated the Philistines and gave Israel rest during his days (1 Sam 7). By the period of Saul (1050–1010 BCE), the Philistines destroyed Shiloh (ca. 1050/40 BCE) and controlled farther north into the tribal territory of Manasseh (e.g., Beth-shean). It was not until their defeat by David ca. 1000 BCE that they became less of a threat (2 Sam 8:1)

By Brian Peterson

him he has too many men. After letting those who are fearful return home (7:3), and after putting them through a test involving how they drink water, God narrows the army to just 300 men (7:4-7). God does this to show Israel that he does not need a vast army to deliver his people. With the army whittled to just 300 men, Gideon divides them into three companies and goes into battle under the cover of night. With pitchers, torches, trumpets, and a great amount of psychological warfare (7:13-22), God brings victory to Israel. Sadly, after this great victory Gideon causes Israel to sin by making a "priestly vest" or ephod (i.e., an instrument of divination) out of the spoils of war, an object that became a spiritual stumbling block for the nation (8:27). On a personal level one lesson from the life of Gideon is clear: when God gives victory in a particular area of your life, do not allow the "fruits" of that victory to be the focus of your worship and take the place of the worship of God.

At the end of the Gideon account, the book of Judges takes a marked turn toward a downward spiral, which ends in all-out civil war in chapters 19–21. Serving as a transitional chapter, Judges 9, which tells the story of a man named Abimelech who tried to make himself king over Israel, is often interpreted as promoting a negative perspective on kingship and therefore posing a problem for those who see Judges as a pro-David writing. However, the account of Abimelech's treachery against his 70 brothers (9:1-5, 16-20) and Israel's failed attempt to make him king (9:6, 22-57) only highlight the fact that condemnation is being leveled at only a certain *type* of kingship: that which is not sanctioned by God. Jotham's fable about the trees having little success in finding a qualified candidate to rule over them (9:7-15; cf. 1 Sam 8) thus serves as a prophetic exhortation to wait for God to appoint Israel's leaders in God's own time.

As part of Israel's continuing downward slide, Jephthah's sad tale paints an all-too-clear picture of what happens when a nation turns from God. For the first time in the book, God refuses to deliver the nation from their enemies but instead tells Israel to cry out to their false gods (10:13-14). Therefore, much like the men of Shechem in the Abimelech fiasco, the men of Gilead beg their illegitimate half brother Jephthah to save them from the Ammonites (11:4-11). After a series of failed negotiations with the Ammonites (11:12-28), Jephthah and Israel are forced to go to war. In a moment of insecurity, Jephthah makes a rash vow before God by saying that he would sacrifice whatever met him coming out from his house when he returned in peace (11:30-31). To Jephthah's dismay, his daughter meets him upon his return (11:34-35). Some argue that Jephthah's vow to sacrifice whatever (or whomever) met him coming out of his house on his return from battle is merely a continuation of the theme of the "Canaanization" of Israel, by raising the specter of child sacrifice. While this may be true, there may be another way to read this account. First, the houses of Iron Age Israel generally had two floors: the bottom floor, where the best animals were kept, and a second floor where the people lived. When Jephthah made his vow, he may have been expecting a prized animal would be wandering out of the house to "meet" him, not a person per se. Second, some argue that Jephthah did not actually sacrifice his daughter but rather offered her in perpetual service in the tabernacle. This may be the reason his daughter mentions her virginity and her childlessness in lamenting her plight (11:37-39). This finds further support in the story of Samuel and Hannah where Hannah vows to give her child to the Lord (1 Sam 1:11) and where we also see women serving at the tabernacle (1

Sam 2:22). Whichever way one reads the text, it does appear that Israel is quickly sliding into the state of anarchy, as indicated in the intertribal war recorded in 12:1-6.

The account of Samson in chapters 13–16 brings the cycle of the judges to a close. Most people know the account of Samson the "strongman." Samson's miraculous birth to his barren mother (13:2-3) is supposed to be the beginning of deliverance for Israel from the oppression of the Philistines. Instead it reads like a Greek tragedy. Born under a special, so-called nazirite vow (13:5), Samson is not to drink wine or "strong drink" (KJV), cut his hair, or eat or touch any unclean thing, including touching dead people and animal corpses (cf. Num 6). It is both

An artist's reconstruction of the typical Iron Age Israelite four-roomed house. Courtesy of the Madaba Plains Project excavations at Tall al-`Umayri, Jordan. Artist: Rhonda Root ©2001.

explicit and implicit that Samson broke all of these rules at some point in his life (cf. 14:8–10, 19; 15:8, 15-16; 16:19). Moreover, Samson falls in love with all the wrong women. First he pursues marriage to a Philistine woman from Timnah (14:1-2), a decision that ends with his enemies murdering his wife and Samson burning their wheat fields in revenge (15:1-5). Then he visits a prostitute in the Philistine town of Gaza, an excursion that ends with him being trapped inside until he rips up the city gates and carries them more than 35 miles to Hebron (16:1-3). Finally, he falls in love with Delilah, a Philistine woman bent on finding out the secret of his strength for monetary gain (16:4-19). For Samson, the third time is not "a charm." His course of disobedience, which finally leads to the cutting of his hair in violation of his nazirite vow, causes the Spirit of the Lord to depart from him. After blinding Samson, the Philistines make sport of him by giving him the job of an ox (16:21-25). Samson's life ends tragically in a Philistine arena when he pulls the building down upon himself, killing 3,000 Philistines (16:26-30). The message of Samson's life is clear: the believer who chooses to ignore the commands/law of God will end up "blindly" stumbling to a tragic end and spiritual death.

The Appendix: Judges 17:1–21:25

The final five chapters of Judges are out of chronological order with what comes before, presumably for rhetorical reasons, to show how the lack of God-ordained leadership (i.e., a king; cf. 17:6; 18:1;

19:1; 21:25) causes anarchy to abound. Theft (17:2; 18:18, 27), idolatry (17:3-5; 18:30), and self-centeredness propel the downward spiral of these closing chapters (18:15-31; cf. 19:15; 20:13), which in this case leads to sexual depravity on par with Sodom and Gomorrah (19:22-25; cf. Gen 19:1-11)—even Levites are not safe (20:4-5). The sin of the Benjamites triggers a civil war that almost brings about the annihilation of their tribe (20:35-48; 21:4, 17). In the midst of the chaos of these closing chapters, violence (18:25, 27-28; 21:10-12), sexual deviance (19:22-25), callousness (19:27-29), civil war (20:14-48), rash vows (21:1, 5, 7), and sanctioned kidnapping and rape (21:12, 20-23; cf. 19:25) are the defining marks of the era. Indeed, the narrative highlights this state of affairs quite well by ending with the somber refrain "each person did what they thought to be right" (12:25).

Debated Issues (aka Great Paper Topics)

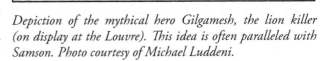

Depiction of the mythical hero Gilgamesh, the lion killer (on display at the Louvre). This idea is often paralleled with Samson. Photo courtesy of Michael Luddeni.

1) How do people reconcile the apparent contradiction between Josh 15:63 and Judg 1:8?

2) What can explain the two death notices for Joshua in Judg 1:1 and 2:8-9?

3) Did Jephthah actually sacrifice his daughter (Judg 11)?

4) What is the merit of the theory that the Samson account is based on the Greek myth of Hercules?

5) Does Judg 18:30 support a late or early date for the book of Judges?

The Message of the Book

Never allow the attractions of the world to draw you away from your commitment/covenant to God.

Closing the Loop

Judges, true to this book's name, focuses on stories of a specific group of leaders, who played the most prominent leadership role in Israel between the death of Joshua and the rise of Israelite kingship. These judges executed justice more as military deliverers than as adjudicators of legal matters. Yet perhaps the most striking characteristic of their leadership is its charismatic nature. In other words, they did not come to their leadership position by heredity, that is, by being born into a certain family or dynastic line (as in the case of priests or kings); these judges were "raised up" by YHWH (2:16, 18; 3:9, 15) and empowered by having the Lord's spirit come upon them (3:10; 6:34; 11:29; 13:25; 14:6, 19; 15:14).

These leaders and their charismatic gifts and callings can be affirmed and celebrated for the crucial role they played in helping God's people survive in a very dark period of Israel's history. And indeed, we see some of this affirmation registered in the roll call of the faithful in Hebrews 11, which uplifts "Gideon, Barak, Samson, [and] Jephthah" alongside "David, Samuel, and the prophets" (Heb 11:32).

However, the book of Judges, as we saw, also reflects a more critical perspective on this entire period of charismatic leadership—and it does so by showing us not only the flaws of individual leaders but also a failure that extended to the entire people of Israel during this sad time, where "*each* person did what they thought to be right" (emphasis added). This culminating message of Judges thus poses a strong and searching word to any community of faith, whether ancient or contemporary, that depends heavily on charismatic leaders, gifts, and revival moments to the neglect of sustained faithfulness to God's covenant and calling. It is a word that is meant to turn us from the cycles of sin that can soon turn into downward spirals that lead directly to our demise.

RUTH

"Wherever you go, I will go . . . Your people will be my people, and your God my God."
—Ruth 1:16

When I think about the book of Ruth,

I am taken back to my Bible college days. Two of my good friends, Katie and Brandon, got married in our third year and moved into an apartment on campus. Katie was one of those young women who could fit in with the guys while we watched sports and just "hang out"; yet she could also dress up and wow any crowded room.

One day a mutual male acquaintance of ours approached Brandon and in a half-jesting manner said to him, "If anything happens to you, Brandon, I want to be Katie's kinsman redeemer!" Now every time I teach Ruth, I cannot help but think of this humorous line. In an ancient Near Eastern context, Ruth, as a widowed woman, was definitely in need of a "kinsman redeemer." Boaz was just that man, who changed what otherwise could have been a bleak existence for Ruth and her widowed mother-in-law, Naomi. If ever there was a picture of the love of God for the outsider, the book of Ruth is it.

Quick Facts

Title: The title comes from the name of the main character in the book, the only book of the Bible to be named after a Gentile woman. The title is the same in the LXX and Hebrew.

Date and Authorship: While the setting for Ruth is in "the days when the judges ruled" (1:1a), the date and authorship of the book are unknown. Jewish tradition assigns authorship to the prophet Samuel. However, 1:1 and 4:7 seem to imply some distance between the events and the time of writing. Because the genealogy in chapter 4 ends with David, some place the date of the book close to his reign (4:22). Others propose that it was written in the postexilic period as a means of challenging the teaching of Ezra and Nehemiah opposing marriage to foreign women (Ezra 10; Neh 13:23-29).

Audience and Purpose: If the book was written as a means of legitimating the kingship of David despite his Moabite descent (cf. Deut 23:3), then the first audience would have been those Israelites who may have been embroiled in challenges to David's right to the throne. If the book is postexilic, then it may have served to teach the returning exiles that God was welcoming even Gentiles into the community of faith (cf. Isa 19:19-25; 56:1-8). As part of the five *Megilloth* ("scrolls"), it is read at the Feast of Pentecost.

Genre: Narrative dominates the book with the exception of the genealogy in 4:18-22. In today's terms, "romance story" may be a better designation, for indeed, metaphorically speaking, Ruth is a flower garden in the cesspool of the judges' period.

Structure

There is no absolute consensus on the structural divisions of this small book. However, the four chapters of Ruth may offer the best way to divide it. As a good romance, the five parts can be designated as the curse: the loss of husbands (1:1-22); the solution: Boaz, a kinsman redeemer (2:1-23); the proposal: Ruth proposes marriage (3:1-18); the resolution: obtaining a husband and a child (4:1-17); the blessing: a genealogy (4:18-22).

Summary

The Curse: Ruth 1:1-22

The book of Ruth opens with little fanfare by giving the setting as the period of the judges, by pointing out the fact that there was a famine in Bethlehem (Hebrew for "house of bread"; note the irony), and by noting that Elimelech, his wife (Naomi), and their two sons went to live in Moab to escape the famine. Within the terse narrative the reader is told that Naomi lost her husband and two sons—what certainly would have been seen in that ancient context as a curse. She decides to return to Judah with her two daughters-in-law, Orpah and Ruth, in tow. In the ancient world when a married man died without an heir, his brother was expected to marry his widow and raise up a son to carry on his brother's name (4:5-10; cf. Gen 38:8-10). This was known as levirate marriage. With this practice in view, in 1:8-14, Naomi notes that she could not physically produce another male child to be a husband for Orpah or Ruth. Naomi encourages her daughters-in-law to return to the houses of their fathers in hopes that these men could provide for them or perhaps help them each get another husband. Orpah returns but Ruth stays with Naomi and utters the well-known pledge, "Wherever you go, I will go; and wherever you stay, I will stay. Your people will be my people, and your God will be my God" (1:16). Once back in Bethlehem, Naomi tells her old friends to call her Mara ("bitter"—1:20), because God had dealt harshly with her. The scene is set; who will deliver Naomi and Ruth from their curse?

The Solution: Ruth 2:1-23

Chapter 2 offers the solution to all of the woes of Naomi and Ruth. Ruth finds a place to glean grain (a source of food is found—2:14, 17); she finds favor with Boaz and is told to stay with his gleaners and maids (friendships are forged—2:8-9); and Boaz offers her protection (security is gained—2:9, 15). More important is how the chapter starts and finishes—we learn that Boaz is a *wealthy* "relative" of Elimelech and can "redeem" the family of Naomi by marrying Ruth through a levirate-like marriage (2:1, 20 KJV)! Interestingly, the word for blessing (*barak*) is found three times in this chapter (2:4, 19, 20), a perfect answer to the curses of chapter 1.

The Proposal: Ruth 3:1-18

Ruth works with Boaz for five months during the barley and wheat harvests (March–July). Naomi, realizing it is now her responsibility to secure Ruth's future (3:1), devises a plan to convince Boaz to marry Ruth. Ruth is to put on her best "outfit" and her best perfume and go down to the threshing floor where Boaz is working and lure him to marry her by "sleeping" with him (3:2-5). Scholars are divided on what Naomi is actually proposing. Is Naomi telling Ruth to have relations with Boaz when she tells Ruth to "uncover [Boaz's] feet" (sometimes used in the ancient world as a euphemism for the male genitalia, 3:4)? After all, Naomi tells her to wait until Boaz finishes "eating and *drinking*" (implying intoxication?) before she lies down with him (3:4, emphasis added). Whatever Naomi may have been implying in her instructions, Ruth carries them out by acting as a righteous woman, going no further than *literally* uncovering Boaz's feet (3:7). When he awakens and looks down where she is lying, Ruth proposes marriage by saying "spread your covering ["wing" in the NKJV; Heb *kanaph*) over your maid" (3:9 NASB; cf. Ezek 16:8). Ruth is asking Boaz to fulfill the blessing that he had uttered over her the first day they met when Boaz said, "May you receive a rich reward from the LORD, the God of Israel, under whose wings [*kanaph*] you've come to seek refuge" (2:12). Boaz's response is immediate. Yes! He will marry her provided that the relative closer in line does not want to assume this role (3:12-13). In an effort to protect Ruth's reputation, and as a means of showing his righteous character, Boaz tells Ruth to stay until morning but to leave before the sun comes up so no one will know she had stayed the night (3:14). Once home, Naomi knows that Boaz will complete the formalities before the day is done (3:18).

The Resolution: Ruth 4:1-17

The setting of chapter 4 at the city gate is important from an ancient Near Eastern perspective. Much like a modern courthouse, the city gate was where formal business transactions took place and legal cases were settled. It was here that the elders of the city congregated literally to "sit" in the chambers of the gate. Boaz goes through the formalities of acquiring the property of Elimelech, which had passed to Mahlon, Ruth's deceased husband. Although the nearer relative presents himself and expresses interest in redeeming the land of Elimelech, he apparently does not have the financial means to support Ruth (perhaps as a second wife), so he declines (4:6). In the presence of the witnesses/elders of the city, Boaz makes it public that he will marry Ruth (4:10-11). The elders' response is to offer blessings by recalling a similar levirate-like union of Judah and Tamar in Genesis 38. With the legal proceedings complete, the author jumps ahead to the day that Ruth delivers her first son, whom the local women name Obed, the child who will eventually turn out to be the grandfather of David!

The Blessing: Ruth 4:18-22

The oft-cited genealogical "addition" to the book of Ruth serves as a perfect conclusion to the book. Whereas Naomi and Ruth had experienced the curse of no children and lost husbands, now they are blessed with a lineage—one that begins with Perez (the son of the levirate union of Judah and Tamar) and ends with the greatest of Israel's kings, David!

Debated Issues (aka Great Paper Topics)

1) What actions on the threshing room floor were prescribed by Naomi and then carried out in the encounter between Ruth and Boaz in chapter 3?

2) Why did the nearest kinsman redeemer refuse to marry Ruth (4:6)?

3) What are the scholarly arguments concerning the date for the genealogy of 4:18-22?

The Message of the Book

Even though we may not always see it, God's plan for all people, even a perceived "outsider," is one of redemption, love, and blessing.

Closing the Loop

As previously seen, the period of the judges, in which the book of Ruth is set, was a dark time of great covenant unfaithfulness interrupted periodically by the interventions of charismatic leaders and their Spirit-empowered exploits. The book of Ruth, on the other hand, tells a story that completely contrasts Judges in this respect. It features no charismatic leaders or miraculous events or supernatural revelations or divine manifestations whatsoever—the first book in our Christian Bible to exhibit a complete absence of all these things—but it presents one of the most remarkable examples of covenant faithfulness in all of Scripture. What makes this all the more remarkable is that this beautiful example of faithfulness features a person who is both a foreigner (a Moabite), living as a resident alien in an ethnically tense Israelite world, and a woman who, alongside another vulnerable woman, is struggling to survive in a very male-dominated world.

When the Hebrews placed the book of Ruth in Scripture as one of the five books of the *Megilloth* ("scrolls"), which they used respectively for the five major holidays that came to mark their annual calendar, they made Ruth the primary Scripture reading for the Feast of Weeks (Heb *Shavuoth*) or Pentecost, as it came to be known. Thus, Ruth can be seen as an ancient biblical witness to the covenant faithfulness of God that, even without featuring any charismatic phenomena, nevertheless anticipates the Day of Pentecost in Acts 2 and even the present-day Pentecostal movement. It does so particularly in its Pentecost emphasis on God's gracious and empowering outreach to women as well as men (indeed to "sons *and daughters*"—Acts 2:17, emphasis added; cf. Joel 2:28) and to people "from every nation under heaven" (Acts 2:5), indeed, "to everyone who calls on the name of the Lord" (Acts 2:21).

1 SAMUEL

The LORD! He brings death, gives life, takes down to the grave, and raises up!
    —1 Samuel 2:6

When I think about the book of 1 Samuel,

I am reminded of my visit to ancient Shiloh a couple of years ago. While there I had the opportunity to visit the newly opened visitor center with museum and theater. This complex was made possible by a generous donation from a wealthy US couple who had visited the site a few years before. The woman's name was Hana, and yes, she was childless, as Samuel's mother, Hannah, had been. While there she prayed a prayer similar to the one that Hannah had prayed over 3,000 years earlier—"God, please give me a child." When she returned to the United States, she soon found that she was pregnant. As a show of her and her husband's appreciation to God for giving them a child, they donated the money to erect the building, so all who would visit the site could learn about the biblical account related in 1 Samuel 1. As I sat there and watched the presentation, I was moved to tears at the nearness of God and his ability to answer prayer. For that 21st-century couple, God's word had come alive, and in that moment they experienced the reality that God is indeed still the Lord who gives life, lifts up those in need, and rules the far corners of the earth (cf. 1 Sam 1:6-10).

Quick Facts

Title: The title comes from the main character in the book and is the same in the LXX and Hebrew. Samuel's name means "name of God" or "asked of God" (cf. 1 Sam 1:20).

Date and Authorship: Jewish tradition attributes the book to the prophet Samuel. As such, the date would be sometime in the 11th century BCE (ca. 1100–1010 BCE). The problem with this theory is that by 1 Sam 25:1, Samuel is dead. A number of other authors have been proposed for portions of both 1 and 2 Samuel: Nathan, Gad, David, Ahimaaz, Hushai, Abiathar, and the Dtr (cf. 1 Chron 29:29; 2 Chron 9:29). The dominant scholarly theory is that Dtr wrote it in the sixth century BCE.

Audience and Purpose: The audience is Israelite. First Samuel serves as a record of the early history of the united monarchy. Scholars have noted that large portions of 1 Samuel may have served as a pro-Davidic argument to show that David did not steal the throne from Saul, but rather was given the kingdom by divine fiat. From this perspective, the purpose and date would be closely intertwined. Therefore, the book may have been written for an audience that included those who were challenging David's right to the throne in the late 11th century BCE.

Genre: Historical narrative is the overarching genre. Other genres featured in the book include: prayers (2:1-10), prophecy (2:27-36; 3:11-14; 8:11-18; 9:16, 20; 10:2-8; 13:14; 15:1-3, 28), and a vision (28:15-19).

Structure

First Samuel is driven by a focus on several key characters and follows a basic pattern of ebbing and flowing from one dominant figure to the next. Each of the three people who fade into the background and die before the book concludes (Eli—4:18; Samuel—25:1; and Saul—31:6), leaving David to emerge as God's chosen leader. Thematically, 1 Samuel may be divided as follows: Samuel's birth and childhood (1–3); the ark narratives and Philistine assault (4–7); Israel's request for a king (8); Saul's rise and fall (9–15); David's successes (16–19); David's fleeing from Saul (20–27); the contrasting ways Saul and David face the threat of death (28–31).

Summary

Samuel's Birth and Childhood: 1 Samuel 1–3

In this first section the author sets up a parallel between two dysfunctional families: Elkanah's and Eli's. Here the focus is on either God's blessing or cursing of offspring. For the barren Hannah, Elkanah's wife, God honors her prayer and gives her the child (i.e., Samuel) she had prayed for while at Shiloh where the tabernacle was located during the judges' period (1:3-19). Hannah vows to give Samuel to God in service at the tabernacle (1:11), and when God answers her prayer, her response is one of prayer and praise (2:1-10). On the other hand, God speaks to Eli through an unnamed prophet and tells him that he will lose his two sons in one day (2:34) because of their blatant disregard for God and his laws (2:27-36; cf. 2:12-17, 22-25).

Chapter 3 begins with the sad report that the word of the Lord was rare in those days and visions were infrequent (3:1). It is amid this spiritual void that the young Samuel first hears the voice of God and receives a prophetic word for Eli and his house (3:2-9), thus confirming the word spoken by the unnamed prophet (cf. 2:27-36; 3:10-14). The repeated prophetic word confirmed to Eli that God would bring about his judgment. Throughout the OT, the duplicating of dreams, visions, or prophecies was

God's way of confirming his word (e.g., Gen 28:12-15; 31:10-13; 37:5-10; 41:1-7; 13:14; 15:28; 1 Kgs 3:5-14; 9:2-9; Dan 2; 7).

The Ark Narratives and Philistine Assault: 1 Samuel 4–7

This portion of the book sets up the situation that will pit the kingship of YHWH against Israel's desire for an earthly king. First Samuel 1–7 shows a continuation of the leadership pattern of the judges. Eli (4:18), Samuel (7:15), and his two sons, Joel and Abijah (8:1-2), are the last judges to rule. Thus, when Israel is confronted in battle, there is no human king to lead them. In chapter 4 after the Philistines defeat Israel, the Israelite people decide to reach for their "genie in the bottle" (i.e., the ark of the covenant, or the Lord's chest) to help them win. In the battle that follows, the Philistines not only defeat Israel again, inflicting on them 30,000 casualties, but what's more, the ark is taken, the sons of Eli are killed, and Eli himself dies from a fall when he hears the battle report (4:10-18). Without doubt, this is a tragic day, but in the midst of the sorrow, YHWH is trying to teach Israel a lesson. Israel does not need an earthly king to lead them into battle; YHWH can fight his own battles without their help. This is precisely the picture that unfolds in chapter 5. In the span of seven months, YHWH defeats Dagon, the god of the Philistines (5:2-7) and smites three of their five major cities (Ashdod, Gath, and Ekron) with plagues, as he had done to Egypt (cf. 4:8; 6:6). The Philistine response is to send the ark back to Israel (6:1-16). The return of the ark ignites a revival in Israel during which Samuel leads the people in a period of repentance (7:3-6) and military victories over the Philistines (7:7-14). The revival is short-lived, and the people soon forget what YHWH and Samuel had done for them.

Israel's Request for a King: 1 Samuel 8

Despite God's deliverance, Israel still asks for a king. While some of this is attributable to the corrupt leadership of Samuel's sons, Israel also desires to be like the other nations, particularly in order to have someone who will lead them in battle (8:20). God's response is to give the people what they want, for they had not rejected Samuel; they had rejected God (8:7; cf. 10:19; 12:12)! Before agreeing to the people's demands, Samuel warns Israel of how a king will treat them. Centralized governmental control will mean a loss of their freedom and wealth (8:11-18)!

Saul's Rise and Fall: 1 Samuel 9–15

Israel's new king, Saul, is introduced in chapter 9 (9:21; cf. Judg 6:15) and anointed in chapter 10 as king over Israel at Mizpah. Saul is a handsome man who is head and shoulders above every man in Israel (9:2; 10:23)—the ideal man to lead an army. Almost immediately, Saul is faced with the Ammonite war in which he has great success. This military victory solidifies the kingship in Saul's hands, causing Samuel to renew Israel's pledge to Saul as king (11:14-15). Nevertheless, in Samuel's final soliloquy he reminds the Israelites about their wickedness in rejecting God as their king (12:17).

Scholars have long struggled with the perceived vacillating perspectives in chapters 8–12 as to whether Samuel is for or against kingship. Most scholars see this as evidence that the biblical materials in this section were composed by multiple authors presenting divergent views. However, this need not be the case when one understands how this transition from judgeship to monarchy must have affected Samuel (cf. 12:1-11). It seems just as logical to conclude that what the reader is witnessing in the text is the anguish of an aging Samuel, who has been rejected by his people (8:6-7) and yet entrusted by God with a mandate to reveal God's plan for a new king (8:9; 9:15-16; 12:13). Added to this mix is Samuel's prophetic foresight, which enabled him to foresee the eventual costs of this experiment (8:11-18; 12:15, 25).

Chapters 13–15 serve as the turning point in Saul's kingship. Chapter 13 reveals Saul's lack of respect for the prophetic/priestly office when he usurps Samuel's job by offering the sacrifice before battle. As a result, Samuel declares that the kingdom will be taken from Saul (13:14). Moreover, chapter 14 juxtaposes the character flaws of Saul (e.g., his rashness 14:24, 39-44) with the battle prowess and wisdom of his son Jonathan (14:1-14, 29-30). Surprisingly, it is Jonathan who points out the folly of his father in making his rash vow (14:29). Finally, chapter 15 shows Saul's unwillingness to follow God's commands in the war with Amalek. Once again Samuel prophesies that Saul will lose the kingship (15:23). Instead his "neighbor" will receive the kingdom (15:28 NKJV; note that geographically, Judah, David's tribe, is adjacent to Benjamin, Saul's tribe).

Before leaving this section, one further point is worth noting concerning Samuel's seemingly conflicting actions with Saul in 15:25-31. Because of God's rejection of Saul, Samuel refuses to return with Saul to offer sacrifices (v. 26). However, once Saul falls on his face and grabs Samuel's robe, Samuel relents and returns. What changed Samuel's mind (v. 31)? The answer is found in the actions of Saul when he grabbed the edge (or "hem" HCSB; Heb *kanaph*) of Samuel's garment (v. 27). In an ancient context, humbling one's self and seizing the hem of someone's garment obligated that other person to act. That is why Samuel quickly responds that God is not one to change his mind (15:29). Saul may have forced Samuel's hand by invoking the ancient custom, but it did not change the fact that God had spoken! This action also helps explain the later actions and remorse of David when he cuts Saul's *kanaph* in the cave and when, in the NT story, the hemorrhaging woman seizes Jesus's garment (1 Sam 24:4-5; Matt 9:20-21; Luke 8:43-48).

David's Successes: 1 Samuel 16–19

After God rejects Saul, Samuel anoints David to be the next king (16:1-13). Showing no awareness that David had been anointed, Saul secures his services as a harpist to calm his tormented soul (16:15-23). After taking up this role, David soon gains legal access to the throne through his marriage to Saul's daughter, Michal (18:20-28). Even though there may be some chronological questions on the relationship between chapters 16 and 17 (i.e., when did Saul meet David? cf. 16:16-23; 17:55-58),[23] the author sets out to show in the encounter between David and Goliath and in the following chapters that David is the better choice

---

23. See Robert Polzin, *Samuel and the Deuteronomist: A Literary Study of the Deuteronomistic History II: 1 Samuel* (San Francisco: Harper & Row), 171–76.

for king. While Saul fears Goliath, David goes and fights the giant in the power of the Lord (cf. 17:11, 32, 37, 45-47). One must remember that Saul is the "giant" of Israel (9:2; 10:23); who better to face Goliath? When Saul sees David's bravery and abilities, he takes him as a soldier for his army (18:2; cf. 8:11). With God's Spirit resting upon David, he excels wherever Saul places him (18:5, 14; 19:8). Soon the women are singing songs about David: "Saul has killed his thousands, but David . . . his tens of thousands" (18:7). These words make Saul all the more paranoid. He now realizes the identity of the "neighbor" Samuel said would take away his throne (18:8-9, 15, 29; cf. 15:28). From this point forward, Saul seeks how he can kill David, either directly (18:10-11; 19:1, 10-17) or indirectly, through military actions (18:17, 25).

David's Fleeing from Saul: 1 Samuel 20–27

Chapter 20 records a final test that Jonathan and David devise to determine whether Saul intends to kill David (20:5-7). When the test proves that Saul's intent is to kill David at his first opportunity (20:27-33), David is forced to run for his life from Saul. From this point until the end of 1 Samuel, David becomes a fugitive in his own land. After receiving a few provisions from Ahimelech, the priest at Nob (21:1-9), David tries unsuccessfully to hide in the land of the Philistines (21:10-15). David is then forced to hide in the hills of Judah, where he slowly gathers a small army of dissenters around him (22:1-2). When the paranoid Saul finds out that an unwitting Ahimelech aided David's escape, he orders the slaughter of the entire city of Nob (22:9-19). The sole survivor, Abiathar, runs to David and becomes his priest (22:20-23).

Even while David runs from Saul, he performs the duty of a true king by delivering the city of Keilah from the hands of the Philistines (23:1-13). Yet, Saul is not deterred in his desire to capture David. He pursues him relentlessly throughout the region of Judah (23:14-29). On two separate occasions during this time, David has the opportunity to kill Saul: once while Saul is relieving himself in a cave near En-gedi (ch. 24), and once when Saul's men fall asleep while they are supposed to be guarding the king (ch. 26). David's primary reason for refusing to kill Saul when he has these opportunities is because Saul is God's anointed king (24:10; 26:9-11, 23). And David surely did not want to set a precedent that may come back to haunt him (cf. 2 Sam 1:1-15; 4:1-12)! The account of David's retaliatory pledge to destroy every male in the household of a man named Nabal, who had refused to return his goodwill (ch. 25), makes it clear that David is not above avenging himself. Despite Saul's change of mind after David spares him, David calculates that it is just a matter of time before Saul will resume his attempt to capture him. Therefore, for a second time David flees to Achish, the Philistine king of Gath (27:1-7).[24]

---

24. Scholars have often noted the so-called doublets in this portion of 1 Samuel (i.e., chs. 21// 27; and 24//26) as evidence of variant traditions regarding the same accounts. However, there is another way of understanding these alleged "duplications." First, chapters 21 and 27 happened years apart (although we cannot be certain, there could have been up to ten years between the events). Second, the first time Achish met David, David was alone and had little to offer him from a political standpoint. The second time David flees to Achish, David has a well-trained army that served as an excellent addition to Achish's forces. Indeed, 28:1-2 reveals that David became the very bodyguard of Achish! Moreover, Achish had planned on David and his men being a part of his campaign against Saul (29:1-7). And once Saul was dead, Achish had intended to make David a vassal king in Israel (27:12). As for the second doublet of chapters, 24 and 26, these two accounts again appear to have been separated by several years. The only real parallels between them are David's response not to kill Saul and Saul's remorse. A careful reading of the two texts shows that there are at least seven major differences in the two accounts: (1)

The Contrasting Ways Saul and David Face the Threat of Death: 1 Samuel 28–31

The final section of 1 Samuel serves to highlight the differences of the two anointed kings when each is faced with the possibility of death. When the Philistines attack Israel, Saul is in distress and fears for his life (28:5). As a result, he consults a witch (28:7-21) because God is silent (28:6). When David is confronted with the Amalekite attack and is in distress (30:6) he consults his priest and God answers (30:7-8). David is rewarded by victory in the battle, thereby saving his entire family and the families of his men (30:16-24). Conversely, Saul loses the battle, his sons, and his life (31:1-6). Finally, David brings spoil to all of his supporters (30:26-31), while Saul's supporters lose their homes and cities (31:7). It is clear by the end of 1 Samuel who God's choice is for king—David!

First Samuel ends on a bittersweet note; Saul is dead and David is victorious. However, the Philistines have gained the upper hand, and David's best friend, Jonathan, is dead. One would think that David's path to the throne over all Israel is assured. However, this is not the case. One more obstacle stands in his way—Saul's son Ishbosheth.

Debated Issues (aka Great Paper Topics)

1) Based on Gen 49:10, Num 24:17, Deut 17:14-20, and 1 Sam 2:10, was it right for Israel to ask for a king?

2) How do scholars explain the apparent pro-monarchic and anti-monarchic portions of 1 Samuel?

3) How can one reconcile the ethical dilemma of God telling Samuel to tell a half-truth (16:1-3)?

4) Does 1 Sam 16:14 and the surrounding passage support the idea that God sends "evil spirits" upon people?

5) Did Samuel actually come back from the dead in 28:11-19?

The Message of the Book

Two equally important messages can be gleaned from 1 Samuel, both dealing with the process and timing of God's will being realized in our lives. We see this (1) in Israel's untimely desire and impatient push to get a king like the nations, and (2) in David's long and trying wait between his anointing as a young person and the fulfillment of his calling to become king at the age of 30 (2 Sam 5:4).

---

the region: En-gedi versus Hachilah; (2) the setting: a cave versus an open field; (3) the time of day: day versus night; (4) who initiated contact: Saul coming to David versus David coming to Saul; (5) the circumstances of the encounter: accidental versus intentional; (6) what David took from Saul: part of Saul's garment versus Saul's spear and water; and (7) who was to blame for the lapse in security for Saul: Saul himself versus Saul's general, Abner. Therefore, this portion of 1 Samuel can be read as presenting one coherent account of similar episodes rather than as presenting different versions of the same episodes.

Closing the Loop

After the dark days of Judges, 1 Samuel tells the story of a period that features the rise of new leadership in Israel. It highlights the rise of the monarchy, to be sure, but this book, together with 2 Samuel, with which it was originally united, addresses the issue of leadership in a way that extends far beyond just the rise of kingship in Israel. And the song of Hannah in 1 Samuel 2 reveals and expresses this in powerful, poetic form. This song is a *manifesto on leadership* that puts the prime focus on the rule of YHWH—how YHWH rules to "the far corners of the earth" (2:10), how he both brings down (especially the high and mighty; vv. 3, 6-7) and raises up (especially the poor and lowly; vv. 5-8), and how he is, above all others, "the God who knows" and "weighs every act" (vv. 2-3). A significant implication here is that God's rule does not take up all the action. God's agency makes room for human agency and initiative. And the overlapping stories of Samuel, Saul, and David that unfold from here, bear out this truth along with all the other claims made in this magnificent song that celebrates how YHWH rules.

Thus from the outset, one can see the delicate interplay between human leadership and divine leadership that gives the Samuel narrative its dramatic tension, dynamism, and power. God raises up Samuel to judge and prophesy in Israel in response to a barren mother's cry and pledge that if YHWH would give her a child, she would give her child back to YHWH (1:11). The child God gives Hannah is named Samuel, whose name means "asked of God." Later the elders of Israel ask Samuel (as opposed to God) for a king in order to be "like all the other nations" (8:4-5, 19-20), and God, against his own better wishes, grants them Saul, whose name, rather tellingly, means "asked for." So, the people of Israel get what they "asked for." In the beginning it is the kingship of Saul, and in the end (2 Kgs 25) it will be the kingdom of Babylon—from beginning to end, just like they "asked for," indeed just "like all the other nations!"

Yet God does not just leave his people to the tragic consequences of their own willful choices. In tenacious commitment to this chosen people, God works to redeem Israel's choice for kingship. One way God does this is by bringing down Saul and by choosing and raising up David. And God does all of this, here again, in ways that make room for human choices and their consequences, whether for good or for evil.

This gives us a prime biblical example of how God leads and develops leadership among covenant people. And it gives us a prime example as well of how God's Spirit plays a crucial role in this process, for 1 Samuel makes mention of God's Spirit more than any biblical book before it (see 10:6, 10; 11:6; 16:13, 14, 15, 16, 23; 18:10; 19:9, 20, 23). Indeed, the book's pivotal moment is defined when God's Spirit departs from Saul and comes upon David (16:13-14). Yet the full story reveals that the role of God's Spirit, powerful and decisive though it may be, does not overpower the place of human choice or the role of human decision. Indeed, this is a most instructive lesson for people of the Spirit, whether in ancient times or in the present day.

2 SAMUEL

"I took you from the sheepfold, from following the sheep, to be ruler over My people, over Israel."
   —2 Samuel 7:8 (NKJV)

When I think about the book of 2 Samuel,

the importance of godly family lineage/"succession" comes to mind. This is directly related to the last half of 2 Samuel, which focuses on the question of who will succeed David (chs. 9–20; 1 Kgs 1–2). David obviously showed shortcomings in passing on to his children his godly habits and love for God. As we will see, this lapse caused chaos in the kingdom. For me personally, I have extremely positive memories about all my mother and my grandparents did for me in their desire to make possible a godly "succession." As a third-generation Pentecostal Christian, I am truly appreciative of the example they set for me and my siblings. My grandfather experienced "Pentecost" when he was a teen living in Detroit, Michigan, in the early 1920s. He and his brother returned to my region of rural New Brunswick, Canada, and began to spread the message of Christ and the power of his Spirit. I can vividly recall my grandfather sitting at the head of the family table, praying over the meal we were about to share, with hands raised in the air, giving thanks for his ten children and their children and their children. And then there were the numerous times I would watch my grandfather and my mother praying at the altar, asking God for a renewed touch of his Spirit, or the times I would see my mother standing at the kitchen sink with soapsuds up to her elbows, praying to God and asking for his blessing on her family of eight. These are the memories of "succession" I recall when I think of my loved ones who have gone on to their eternal reward. My family did not have much in the way of monetary wealth, but we were "millionaires" when it came to the blessings and heritage that God gave us. Now, as a father myself, I realize that since my grandparents and my parents are now with God, it is my responsibility to facilitate this succession to my children. As I read the book of 2 Samuel, the importance and weight of this responsibility become palpable for me. My prayer daily is that I would not falter in this sacred trust; for David, despite his many great achievements, surely missed the mark in this regard and paid a very high price for it.

Quick Facts

Title, Authorship, and Date: The only thing to add to the previous chapter's discussion of these matters is that 2 Samuel covers a time span from about 1010 to 970 BCE.

Audience and Purpose: As noted previously, scholars have posited that good portions of 1 Samuel up to 2 Samuel 5:10 served as a tractate to convince those of David's era that David did not steal the throne from Saul. In a similar way, others argue that 2 Samuel 9–20 functions as a "succession narrative" to validate Solomon's right to the throne, thus placing the original audience in Solomon's period. If Dtr wrote this book, as many now believe, then it was written to show why the kingdom started on its downward spiral toward exile. In the latter case, the audience would be exilic or postexilic. While the theory of Dtr authorship dominates the current scholarly discussion, in reality no complete consensus has been reached on authorship, date, or purpose. What we can be assured of is that the text first of all functioned as a history of the united monarchy. What's more, there is no reason not to place the writing of most of the book at a time during, or shortly after, David's reign.

Genre: Although the book's overall genre is historical narrative, it incorporates a number of other genres, including a eulogy (1:17-27), battle reports (2:17-32; 5:17-25; 8:1-14; 10:1-19; 12:26-31; 18:6-17; 20:15-22), laments (3:33-34), a covenant declaration (7:5-17), prayers (7:18-29), lists (5:14-16; 8:16-18; 20:23-26; 23:8-39), prophecies (12:10-14; 24:12-13), and songs (22:2-51).

Structure

Second Samuel has five clearly defined sections: civil war with the house of Saul (1:1–5:3); David's consolidation of his throne (5:4–10:19); David's fall from grace (11–12); the fourfold judgment on David (13–20); appendix: preparations for the next king (21–24).

Summary

Civil War with the House of Saul: 2 Samuel 1:1–5:3

Second Samuel begins with an Amalekite man admitting before David that he had just fled from a battlefield where he had killed Saul and plundered his body (1:2-10). Little did this man realize that an Amalekite would be the last person from whom David would want to get this bad news, especially only three days after David's own battle against the Amalekite marauders (cf. 2 Sam 1:2; 1 Sam 30). David responds by executing the Amalekite for touching God's anointed king. In further response to the tragic news, David sings a eulogy for Saul and Jonathan (1:17-27). From this song you would never know that Saul had hunted David for years; David is truly disheartened.

As king of Judah, David chooses a new capital at Hebron (2:1) and makes overtures for peace with Saul's old allies at Jabesh-gilead (2:5-9). When this fails, a seven-and-a-half-year civil war breaks out between Ishbosheth, Saul's remaining son, and David. Although the opening battle goes in David's favor (2:30-31), the death of Asahel, Joab's brother, at the hands of Abner during the battle (2:19-23) sets up a rivalry between Joab and Abner that ends with Joab's murder of Abner (3:27) and Joab receiving the death penalty (1 Kgs 2:28-34). As the civil war drags on and David gains the ascendency (3:1), Abner, Ishbosheth's general and the real muscle behind the ongoing struggle (3:6), decides to align himself with David (3:7-13). Joab takes the opportunity to avenge his brother's death by murdering Abner in cold blood. Chapter 4 records the last act of treachery against the politically weakened Ishbosheth. Two of his own men murder him and bring his head to David (4:2-8). David's response is the same as it was for the Amalekite in chapter 1; he has them executed (4:9-12)! Soon the elders of Israel come to Hebron and swear allegiance to David. The civil war is over; David is finally king over all Israel (5:1-3).

David's Consolidation of His Throne: 2 Samuel 5:4–10:19

With the nation united, David makes a brilliant political move. He captures Jerusalem from the Jebusites and makes it his capital (5:6-9). This is a political move that is similar to the one made by the founding fathers of the United States in 1790. When Washington DC was made the national capital, it was "neutral" land in that it did not belong to any one state, and in a similar way Jerusalem had been a Canaanite city on the *border* between Judah and Benjamin. By making Jerusalem the capital, Israel now has a capital city that bridges the two tribal regions from which Israel's first two kings hailed. After a double defeat of the Philistines (5:17-25), David consolidates his government in Jerusalem and lays the foundation for the centralization of worship by bringing the ark, or God's chest, into Jerusalem (ch. 6). This action includes two tragic details: the death of a man named Uzzah when he reached out to steady the ark during its transport, and the cursing of David's wife, Michal, after she mocks David for his celebratory dancing over the occasion (6:7, 23). These details are no doubt intended to teach a lesson based on an earlier theme: do not touch the ark of God (1 Sam 6:19) and do not "touch" God's anointed king (cf. 1 Sam 24:10; 26:9-11, 23; 2 Sam 1:14).

Chapter 7 records how God establishes an everlasting covenant with David and his descendants after him. This Davidic covenant is widely regarded as the fourth major covenant of the Old Testament, after the Noahic, Abrahamic, and Mosaic covenants. In response to David's proposal to bless God by building God a "house," God declines the offer and instead promises to build a "house" for David (7:11, 16 KJV). The Davidic covenant in many ways resembles the Abrahamic covenant. God promises to make a name for David (7:9//Gen 12:2), he promises to give him and Israel a place/land (7:10//Gen 12:1), and he promises him descendants (7:12//Gen 12:2), through whom will come eternal blessing (7:16//Gen 12:2-3)—a promise fully realized in the coming of Jesus. Much like Hannah's response in 1 Samuel 2, David's reaction is to offer a prayer of thanksgiving (7:18-29).

Finally, chapters 8–10 show how military conquest and general acts of kindness enable David to establish his throne. David defeats the Philistines, Moab, Zobah, Aram, Ammon, Amalek, and Edom (chapter 8 is not in chronological order with the chapters surrounding it). Moreover, chapters 9 and 10 must be read together. Chapter 9 shows what the proper response should be when David, God's anointed, shows kindness to someone. In this case, Mephibosheth, Jonathan's son, is blessed when he accepts the mercy and kindness shown to him (9:6-13). Conversely, the Ammonite king, Hanun, rejects David's overtures and in turn is crushed militarily because

In the center of the picture you can see the stone ramparts excavated at Jericho. Above the rampart stood a mud-brick wall. Photo by Brian Peterson.

of his insolence (10:1-14). This could bring to mind Ps 2:12a: "Kiss [i.e., pay homage to] the son lest he become angry and you perish in the way when his wrath is kindled even a little" (author's translation).

David's Fall from Grace: 2 Samuel 11–12

Chapter 11 is one of the saddest chapters in the OT. Instead of going to war with his men (11:1), David stays in Jerusalem and commits adultery with the wife of one of his soldiers (11:2-4). Some have argued that Bathsheba knew exactly what *she* was doing when she bathed under the rooftop view of the king's palace; after all, the text notes that she was going through the ritual purification after her menstrual cycle had ended, perhaps indicating her awareness that she was fertile (11:4-5)! Did she have an eye for power and the throne (cf. 1 Kgs 1)? Others argue that David knew exactly who Bathsheba was and what *he* was doing; that this was nothing more than lust, carried out with coercive force (for who could refuse the king?). After all, Bathsheba is married to Uriah, one of David's mighty men (23:39). Bathsheba's father, Eliam, is also one of David's choice men (23:34) and Bathsheba's grandfather, Eliam's father, is none other than David's most trusted counselor, Ahithophel (16:23). By yielding to his passions, David sets in motion events that will cause his family to fall apart.

Yet, in the midst of this sad account, several things stand out as particularly troublesome. It is not enough that David sleeps with Uriah's wife; after she becomes pregnant he then tries to cover it up by trying to get Uriah, while he is home on furlough, to sleep with her too (11:8-13). Uriah may have known the truth. In any case, he refuses to sleep with his wife and thereby frustrates David's cover-up plan. Even a drunk Gentile (Hittite)—Uriah—is more righteous than a sober Israelite David (11:11-13)! David's final solution is to send word to his general, Joab, to put Uriah in the most dangerous part of the battle so that he will die. To cap off this diabolical plan, David actually has Uriah carry the letter, his own death warrant, back to Joab (11:14). After Uriah perishes in battle, David takes Bathsheba as a wife (11:27). David assumes that all is covered up!

Chapter 12 shows otherwise when God tells Nathan the prophet to confront David. Wisely, Nathan does not accuse David directly, since David just might react by having him killed, too. Therefore, Nathan chooses to tell a story about a poor man whose only lamb was taken and killed by a wealthy neighbor (12:1-4). Why did Nathan tell this story? Perhaps it took David back to a more innocent time in his life when, as a boy, he faithfully tended his father's sheep. David's response to Nathan's account is one of anger at the man who had wronged the poor man—he will pay fourfold for his wickedness, declares David (12:6)! In pronouncing judgment on the wealthy man, David passes judgment on himself. Nathan then pronounces a prophetic word that includes the judgment that the sword will never depart from David's house (12:10). Indeed, this is the price David would pay. Furthermore, the fourfold judgment pronounced against David comes to fruition when death comes to four members of his own house, the first of which is the son conceived in the illicit act with Bathsheba (12:14, 18).

The Fourfold Judgment on David: 2 Samuel 13–20

The next eight chapters, along with 1 Kings 1–2, are directly connected to the events of chapter 12. Chapter 13 records a story of the incestuous rape that David's oldest son, Amnon, plans and perpetrates against his half sister Tamar (13:1-4). After Amnon carries out this heinous plot (13:5-14), Tamar's full brother, Absalom, plots a way to murder Amnon for raping Tamar (13:20-33). Surprisingly, David does nothing to hold either of his sons accountable. In view of the similarities between their sins and his own sin with Bathsheba and Uriah, David may have felt hard-pressed to "judge" them. In any case, Nathan's prophecy is coming to pass. A second son of David is now dead as the sword descends upon his house! Chapter 14 relates the roundabout way that Joab got David to bring Absalom back to Jerusalem from Geshur, where he had fled after killing Amnon (14:1-20). Without realizing it, both Joab (14:28-33) and David (15:1-6) invite trouble upon themselves by this act.

Chapters 15–18 show the extent to which Absalom acts to rid himself of his father—he devises a coup. Absalom forces David and all of his loyal men to flee from Jerusalem to the Transjordan, but not before David leaves several spies to help thwart the coup: Abiathar and Zadok the priests, their two sons, Jonathan and Ahimaaz, and Hushai, one of David's counselors (15:14-37). In David's moment of despair, old enemies come out to curse him (i.e., Shimei, 16:5-13) while others take advantage of his distressed state (i.e., Ziba, 16:1-4; cf. 19:24-30). Meanwhile, back in Jerusalem, much like what one would find in a good spy novel, David's planted spies go into action. Hushai undermines the counsel of Ahithophel, leading to Ahithophel's suicide (17:1-14), and Jonathan and Ahimaaz serve as couriers for the spy network (17:17-21; Ahithophel no doubt sided with Absalom on account of David's sins with his granddaughter, Bathsheba). The work of the spies buys David enough time to make it to the fortified city of Mahanaim in the Transjordan and to plan a counter attack (17:24-29).

The battle between David and Absalom does not go in Absalom's favor. In the midst of the battle, Absalom's head (perhaps his long hair; cf. 14:26) gets caught in a branch when he is riding under a tree limb; he is left dangling in the air (18:9). When it is told to Joab, he rushes to the spot and kills Absalom, something David had told his men not to do (18:5, 12). With the death of Absalom, the coup is over. Sadly, this fulfills the third part of the fourfold judgment on David. He has now lost three sons! David does not take the death of Absalom easily (18:33). His mourning for his son is so severe that David's army returns without fanfare to the city (19:3). However, Joab's quick and forceful advice snaps David out of his public mourning, and moves him to go greet his army (19:8) and pay proper respects. With the coup over, a quarrel ensues between Judah and the other tribes of Israel over who should reinstate the king (19:41-43). Even Shimei, who had cursed David on the day of his retreat from Jerusalem, sees which way the political winds are blowing and comes to show his allegiance to David (19:16-23). As Judah rallies around David's kingship, the other Israelites, under the leadership of Sheba of Benjamin, rebel. A short-lived civil war breaks out that ends with the death of Sheba (20:13-22). David's throne is again established over all of Israel.

Appendix: Preparations for the Next King, 2 Samuel 21–24

The appendix of 2 Samuel appears to lack thematic and chronological ties with what comes before and after it (cf. 21:1-14; 9:1). However, the purpose of this block of material is evident when viewed as a precursor to David's last days and death recorded in 1 Kings 1–2. What appear to be haphazard accounts cobbled together at the end of this book actually serve a rhetorical function. These chapters show that a new king is needed now that David is old (21:15-17), and that everything is prepared for the successor.[25] For example:

1) David removes the curse of famine on Israel that carries over from Saul's misdeeds and, in the process, any possible contenders for the throne from Saul's family (21:1-14);

2) the Philistine giants in the land are dead (21:15-22);

3) David sings a final song of praise to his God and speaks his last words (22:1–23:7; cf. Deut 32–33; Josh 23–24; 1 Sam 12);

4) David is leaving a faithful bodyguard for the next king (23:8-39; cf. 1 Kgs 1:8-10);

5) God's anger against Israel is appeased (24:1-16); and

6) the site for the temple is chosen and purchased (24:17-25).

Even with these preparations, there still is one more part of the fourfold judgment yet to fall on David and his house. Indeed, this may explain why some manuscript traditions (e.g., LXX[L] and Josephus's *Antiquities*, book 8) actually continue 2 Samuel until the death of David in 1 Kgs 2:12.

---

25. See further, Brian Peterson, "The Gibeonite Revenge of 2 Sam 21:1–14: Another Example of David's Darker Side or a Picture of a Shrewd Monarch?" *Journal for the Evangelical Study of the Old Testament* 1, no. 2 (2012): 201–222.

Debated Issues (aka Great Paper Topics)

1) Why does David seem to get a pass for offering sacrifices whereas Saul lost the throne for doing it (cf. 1 Sam 13:9-14; 2 Sam 6:13, 17-18)?

2) How does one explain the apparent brutality of David against the Ammonites noted in 12:31?

3) What may have caused the Lord to get angry with Israel in 24:1?

4) Who caused David to number the people? Was it God (2 Sam 24:1) or Satan (1 Chron 21:1)?

The Message of the Book

Do not take the blessings of God as a license to sin; for whatever a person sows, that is what he or she will also reap (cf. Gal 6:7). David had been blessed with much, yet he allowed his lusts to undermine those blessings. In the end he reaped what he had sown.

Closing the Loop

David is Israel's ideal king. God's everlasting covenant with David and his descendants in 2 Samuel 7 establishes this. The enduring remembrance of this covenant throughout the rest of Scripture expands this, opening up the grand hope for the coming of a supreme ruler in David's line, the ultimate "anointed one" or Messiah. In light of this, it is quite remarkable how the narrative of 2 Samuel presents David not just in all his glory but also in all of his flawed reality. No other nation in the ancient world has a narrative like this for one of its favoured kings—none that treats an "ideal" ruler with such critical realism.

Scholars have long struggled to explain what could account for Israel's producing and preserving such a story. A leading explanation is that this must have resulted from some intellectual development in ancient Israel, a time of enlightenment (such as the so-called Solomonic Enlightenment), in which a more naive, religious view of reality gave way to a more sophisticated, rational, and critically realistic view of political and social reality.

Not to take anything away from the advancement of Israel's intellectual level, one might find a far greater determining factor for Israel's realistic portrayal of David at the theological level. YHWH is the ultimate king over Israel and over every other kingdom of this world, and this means that the human king in Israel, unlike what happened in the kingdoms that surrounded ancient Israel, could never be elevated to divine status. Israel's kingship, in this respect, was definitely *not* "like all the other nations" (1 Sam 8:5, 20). This being the case, Israel's king, even King David, was subject to, accountable to, and answerable to the rule of YHWH and the ultimate critical standard of his holiness. Indeed, Hannah's song voices this critical truth near the beginning of 1 Samuel: "No one is holy like [YHWH]—no, no one except you! There is no rock like our God!" (1 Sam 2:2). And David comes close to echoing this very same verse in his own song near the end of 2 Samuel: "Now really, who is divine except [YHWH]? And who is a rock except our God?" (2 Sam 22:32).

What this would suggest is that the story of David is presented in a critical light because David himself came to see his own life in a critical light. In this light, David says in his last words, "The Lord's spirit" speaks through me; his word is on my tongue. Israel's God has spoken, Israel's rock said to me: 'Whoever rules rightly over people, whoever rules in the fear of God, is like the light of sunrise on a morning with no clouds" (2 Sam 23:2-4a). These words are spoken by a king who had confessed at times that he had not ruled rightly, had not ruled in the fear of God, and had consequently seen dark days and heavy clouds descend upon his house and his nation. Yet even more significantly, these last words of David identify the Spirit of the Lord as the source of this *critical analysis*. Indeed, the revelation of the Spirit—what could be called *a hermeneutic of the Spirit*—is the real source behind the humbling of David and also the hope for the future *son of David, the Messiah*, who at last will be totally and utterly "like the light of sunrise on a morning with no clouds."

1 KINGS

"You will never fail to have a successor sitting on Israel's throne as long as your descendants carefully walk before me."
—1 Kings 8:25

When I think about the book of 1 Kings,

I am drawn to the account of the prophet Elijah. After a mountaintop experience of seeing (literally) the fire of God fall and a revival ensue, Elijah entered the most depressing period of his life—a true valley experience. Jezebel, King Ahab's wife, threatened his very life (19:1-3). Elijah's response was to run for his life to the mountain of Horeb/Sinai (19:4-8). This spiritual roller coaster of sorts exhibits a pattern that is experienced by many great men and women of God. A number of my pastor friends have told me that it is often after delivering a great sermon or experiencing a period of great spiritual awakening and revival that they have a lonely valley experience where the enemy often attacks. It is during these "valley" experiences that they must hold on to the promises of God and the truthfulness of his word. Nevertheless, it is at those moments that people can truly meet God and be sustained by his Spirit. Even though many believers try to live their spiritual lives by jumping from one spiritual "mountaintop" to the next, I have learned, like a lot of my pastor friends, that the valley experiences are just as important, if not more so, to my spiritual growth. For it is in those valley experiences of death, disease, rejection, and adversity that I have met with God and been sustained. It certainly draws you closer to God in a way that can bring more depth to that next mountaintop experience. Of course, this is exactly what happened to Elijah. After running for his life and experiencing a period of depression and self-pity (19:4), Elijah's next (literal) mountaintop experience at Horeb was marked by intimate communication with God himself (19:9-18). Finally, when we encounter those valleys—and we certainly will—and when we feel all alone, we can know for sure that we are not alone. In fact, we might just learn that there are even as many as 7,000 "whose knees haven't bowed down to Baal and whose mouths haven't kissed him" (19:18)!

Quick Facts

Title: The title comes from the main topic in the book. The Hebrew title is *Melachim* ("Kings").

Date and Authorship: First and 2 Kings were originally one book but were divided when the Hebrew text was translated into Greek (ca. third century BCE or later). While 1 and 2 Kings span more than 400 years (ca. 970–560 BCE), 1 Kings covers a period from roughly 970 to 850 BCE. The date for the authorship of the material in the book is debated. Jewish tradition attributes the authorship (both 1 and 2 Kings) to Jeremiah, which seems possible in light of the way 2 Kings ends (chs. 24–25) in close similarity to the book of Jeremiah (40–41; 52:1-27). This does not mean that there could not have been older material in Kings. Jeremiah could easily have compiled earlier material and merged it together. Another prominent theory is that the Dtr compiled much of Kings in the late seventh or early sixth century BCE, with final notations added circa 560–550 BCE (cf. 2 Kgs 25:27-30).

Audience and Purpose: Audience and purpose are closely connected. If the book of Kings was first written in the seventh–sixth centuries BCE in order to show how and why the nation went into exile, then the audience would be from the same time period or later. However, if there were several versions of the book produced in sequence during the divided monarchy (i.e., in Hezekiah's era and/or during Josiah's reforms) then the audience would have been from several eras. The purpose would not only be for history's sake alone, but perhaps for particular polemical reasons at a given time (e.g., countering Jeroboam; countering Ahab).

Genre: Historical narrative is the overall genre of the book with several other genres incorporated at various points: dreams/visions (3:5-15; 9:1-9; 22:19-22); prayers (8:23-54; 17:20); lists (4:1-19); prophecies (9:4-8; 13:1-3; 14:7-16; 17:1, 14; 20:13-14, 28, 42; 21:19-26; 22:17, 23, 25); building reports (6:1–7:51); miracle reports (17:16, 21-22; 18:38; 19:9); and an account of a theophany (19:9-18).

Structure

First Kings can be divided as follows: the struggle for the throne (1–2); Solomon's rise and fall (3–11); the kingdom divided (12–16); the Elijah–Elisha cycle begins (17–22).

Summary

The Struggle for the Throne: 1 Kings 1–2

First Kings picks up where 2 Samuel left off; only now David is advanced in years. Because David has not declared his successor, his eldest surviving son, Adonijah, claims the throne with the support of Joab and Abiathar (1:5-7, 9-10). However, another group supports Solomon: Nathan, Zadok, Benaiah and the mighty men of David (i.e., his bodyguard; cf. 1:8, 11-27). While Adonijah celebrates his self-appointment, Nathan and Bathsheba approach David and tell him the news. David immediately chooses Solomon as his successor. Within hours Solomon is declared the next king of Israel (1:38-40); Adonijah can do nothing but fall on the mercy of his half brother (1:50-53). With Solomon on the throne, David quickly passes from the scene, but not before giving final instructions to Solomon, namely, to keep the law (2:3-4), execute Joab for his crimes (2:5-6), treat Barzillai well (2:7), and punish Shimei (2:8-9).

Shortly thereafter, Adonijah tests Solomon's earlier show of mercy by asking for David's nurse, Abishag, as a wife (2:13-25). In this roundabout way Adonijah still has his sights on the throne (cf. 2 Sam 16:20-22). Solomon's response is swift—Adonijah is executed. In a way, God shows mercy to David because he does not see his fourth son die. Nevertheless, the fourfold judgment pronounced against David is hereby fulfilled (cf. 2 Sam 12:6). Solomon also takes this opportunity to squelch any further attempts on the throne by exiling Abiathar the priest (who had sided with Adonijah; 2:26-27), and by executing Joab for his crimes (2:28-34). Solomon also places Shimei under "house arrest" with the threat of death if any terms are broken (2:36-38)—Shimei breaks his word and is executed (2:39-46). By the end of chapter 2, Solomon has paved the way for what should have been a very successful reign.

Solomon's Rise and Fall: 1 Kings 3–11

Scholars are divided on how to assess Solomon's reign. With the exception of chapter 11, is it meant to be read positively or negatively? It seems as though the entire narrative is meant to critique Solomon's reign, sometimes in a positive manner (3:3; 4:25), at other times negatively (9:11; 11:1-10). For example, the first comments about Solomon's reign are that he entered into a covenant with Egypt by marrying the pharaoh's daughter—not a great way to start. Moreover, the motif of foreign wives serves as a thematic frame, or *inclusio*, to Solomon's reign (cf. 3:1//11:1-10). On the other hand, the first dream Solomon receives from the Lord informs the reader whence Solomon's wisdom and wealth derive (3:4-15). This accounts for the story of Solomon's wise judgment in deciding the case of two prostitutes (3:16-28)—God had fulfilled his word by giving Solomon unsurpassed wisdom (cf. 4:29-34). Similarly, chapter 4 serves to show God's blessings of wealth. Yet in the midst of chapter 4 we see the makings for dissention in the nation; Solomon divides the nation into twelve sectors with an official over each; however, the region of Jerusalem and good portions of central Judah are missing (4:1-19 note the mention only of Socoh and Hepher, v. 10). Was this area exempt from taxes?

Chapters 5–8 focus entirely on Solomon's construction projects and the dedication of the temple. Hiram, the king of Phoenicia, aids Solomon in these enterprises by providing skilled labor and materials. In exchange Solomon gives him food (ch. 5). First Kings 6:1 sets the exact date for the beginning of the construction of the temple, namely, 480 years after Israel had departed Egypt. Taken at face value, this would place the Exodus circa 1446 BCE. The chapter continues by giving design instructions for the temple (see also 7:14-51). In 6:38 and 7:1, some see a possible negative assessment of Solomon's priorities; he spent 13 years building his own house but only 7 years building God's house. Nevertheless, the author shows great interest in the temple, the dedication ceremonies, and Solomon's extended prayer (8:23-53)—perhaps evidence of a Priestly author, such as Jeremiah.

Chapters 9–11 present Solomon's declining years. In 9:1-9, Solomon receives from God his second dream, in which God warns him about idolatry—the very thing that will be Solomon's undoing. Furthermore, 9:10-14 shows evidence of a negative assessment of Solomon's reign by noting that the king used northern cities in the Galilee region (many of them priestly) as partial payment to Hiram for all of his building services, something Israel was forbidden to do (Lev 25:23). Chapter 10 may seem more positive toward Solomon until one recognizes the excess of Solomon's building projects (10:16-20; cf. 12:4). The multiplying of gold and horses (10:21-29) is a direct contradiction of Moses's commands in Deut 17:14-20. This chapter is thus a critique of Solomon's policies and his actions, the harshest of which is reserved for chapter 11 and his multiplying of wives (11:1-3; cf. Deut 17:17). These many women lead Solomon into flagrant idolatry (11:4-8). As a result, God promises to split the kingdom (11:13) and raise up adversaries to plague Solomon (11:14-28). It is Jeroboam who will cause the most grief. Through the word of the prophet Ahijah, Jeroboam is told that he will one day rule the ten northern tribes—a reality that takes place in the days of Solomon's son, Rehoboam (11:29-40).

Archaeological remains of the Gezer gate complex from the period of Solomon. Photo courtesy of Christine Curley.

The Kingdom Divided: 1 Kings 12–16

In keeping with the Hebrew categorization of these materials in the canonical collection called "Former Prophets," this section is dominated by a prophecy-fulfillment pattern. Rehoboam's rejection of the wise counsel of his elders in favor of that of his friends causes the kingdom to split, thus fulfilling the earlier prophecy of Ahijah (11:29-40//12:15; see also 12:22-24). The ten northern tribes break away and choose Jeroboam I as king, and this has immediate negative consequences: he institutes the worship of golden calves in Bethel and Dan; he appoints non-Levitical priests; and he changes established feast days (12:26-33). Ironically, when Jeroboam sets up the calves, he uses the same language that Aaron used in Exodus 32: "Behold your gods, O Israel, that brought you up from the land of Egypt" (12:28 NASB; cf. Exod 32:4). The handwriting was on the wall for the northern kingdom of Israel.

Repercussions follow in chapter 13, again through the prophetic word. There is another prophecy-fulfillment in 13:3//13:5, which features the sudden collapse and destruction of Jeroboam's altar at Bethel. This sequence, however, is encompassed by a greater prophecy-fulfillment sequence, featuring the prediction here of the coming of Josiah to cleanse Israel of its cult places—something that does not happen for another 300 years (13:2//2 Kgs 23:14-18). The strange account here of the interaction between two unnamed prophets from Judah and Samaria, when first read, might seem out of place; however the entire incident, in addition to featuring a prophecy that will reach forward to a fulfillment three centuries in the future (2 Kgs 23:17-18), shows how God is working on both sides of the divide between Israel's northern and southern kingdoms, raising up but also judging the shortcomings of prophetic messengers from each respective side, and thus indicating that God is not ignoring or abandoning either side of this division, for it is a division that will not last forever (as signaled earlier in Ahijah's prophecy in 11:39).

Chapter 14 is transitional, featuring an account concerning the illness of Jeroboam's son. Because of Jeroboam's incessant idolatry, three prophecies are given, which are either fulfilled within the immediate chapter or soon thereafter. These include Jeroboam's loss of his dynasty and rule (14:9-11, 14//15:27-30), the death of his son (14:12-13//14:17-18), and God's promise to exile Israel beyond the Euphrates (14:15-16//2 Kgs 17). Unfortunately, Judah has the same chinks in its spiritual armor (14:21-31; 15:3); the message is clear: Judah will also be exiled in due time!

Literarily, chapters 14–16 move away from a narrative-driven format to one that is more like a formal report. For example, kings are now measured against the righteous rule of David or the wicked behavior of Jeroboam (i.e., X did evil/right in the sight of the Lord like Jeroboam/David (evil: 15:26, 34; 16:7, 19; 22:52; right: 1 Kgs 15:11; cf. 2 Kgs 15:34; 16:2, 25-26, 30; 18:3; 22:2). Similarly, the phrase: "now the rest of the acts of [X] . . . are they not written in the book of the chronicles of the kings of Judah?" (or "Israel") (NKJV) appears throughout the remainder of 1 and 2 Kings (14:29; 15:7, 23, 31; 16:14; 22:39; 2 Kgs 10:34; 12:19, etc.). These formulae, along with a number of others, may be evidence of a change in authorship. Nevertheless, what remains constant is the prophecy-fulfillment motif (16:1-4, 7//16:11-13; 16:34//Josh 6:26). Adding to the formulaic presentation is the downward spiral of the northern kings. In this vein, chapters 15 and 16 are marked by the chaos of war between Israel and Judah (15:6, 16, 32) and conspiracies and dynasty changes. The conspiracy of King Omri leads to the wicked rule of his son Ahab, which dominates the remainder of 1 Kings.

One can see a striking parallel between Omri's dynasty in the north and David's dynasty in the south. First, both kings establish a new capital (Jerusalem//Samaria). David accomplishes this legitimately by conquest, but Omri goes against the law of God and purchases Samaria (cf. Lev 25:23). Second, each of these kings has a son who establishes organized worship of his deity (Solomon builds a temple for YHWH//Ahab institutes Baal worship). Finally, the grandson of each of these kings presides over a major loss (for Rehoboam, the division of the united monarchy//for Ahaziah, the fall of the dynasty itself). Because of the wicked practices of Omri's dynasty, especially Ahab, the prophet Elijah is raised up to prophesy.

The Elijah–Elisha Cycle Begins: 1 Kings 17–22

The abrupt introduction of Elijah has caused many scholars to see the Elijah–Elisha narrative as an originally separate and independent story complex. This theory does have merit in that the text shifts focus primarily to the northern kingdom and Elijah's attack on the wicked reign of Ahab and the influence of his wife, Jezebel (a Baal worshiper from Phoenicia). In this regard, the narrative begins with a direct challenge to the Canaanite storm god, Baal. Elijah declares that it will not rain for three years (17:1). Even though ravens miraculously feed him, Elijah himself soon feels the effects of his own prophetic word when the brook he is living beside dries up (17:2-7). At the word of the Lord, Elijah moves to the very heartland of Baal worship, Zarephath in Phoenicia, and begins performing miracles: a miracle causing a poor widow's tiny supply of oil and flour to continue replenishing itself (17:10-16), and then the raising of her son after he suddenly dies (17:17-23). Interestingly, this foreign woman is the first person to acknowledge that Elijah is a prophet of God (v. 24).

Chapter 18 presents one of the best-known episodes in the OT: Elijah's contest with the prophets of Baal on Mount Carmel. Already by verse 17 the two sides are drawn when Elijah meets Obadiah, Ahab's God-fearing servant, and Ahab himself. Obadiah calls Elijah his "master" (v. 7) and Ahab calls Elijah the "troubler of Israel" (v. 17 NKJV). Ahab accepts Elijah's challenge to call all the prophets of Baal to Carmel. The simple challenge is this: the deity who, in response to a sacrifice, "answers with fire" is the true God (v. 24). For Baal worshippers this makes sense. Baal is supposed to control the thunder and the lightning! In the account that ensues, Baal's prophets fail to get a response from their god even though they

Ancient water system at Beersheba. Cities survived long sieges because of the inhabitants' ability to build elaborate underground water systems to protect their water supply. Photo by Brian Peterson.

pray, shout, and cut themselves (vv. 26-29). After watching this for most of the day, Elijah takes his turn, but what he asks is strange indeed. He wants water poured over his sacrifice three times (vv. 33-35)! Then after a simple prayer, fire falls from heaven, consuming the sacrifice, the stones of the altar, the dust, and the water in the trench around the altar (v. 38). The people's response is immediate; "YHWH is God!" Elijah's command for the people to kill the false prophets is in strict adherence to the law (Deut 13:1-5). After this, Elijah prays for rain. When it begins to rain, the Spirit comes upon him and he outruns Ahab's chariot to Jezreel (vv. 46-48).

As noted in the introduction above, chapter 19 shows Elijah's spiritual valley due to Jezebel's response of issuing a threat on his life (19:2). An important lesson that Elijah learns from this low point in his life is that he is not alone in his devotion to God (19:18). When he comes to Horeb, the mountain of God, he has an encounter with God (a theophany) that dramatically shows that YHWH is not like Baal. God is not to be narrowly identified with natural phenomena such as wind, earthquake, and fire—this is the thinking of the Canaanites. Instead, YHWH is a God of relationship who comes and speaks directly and personally (19:13). Furthermore, the God of Israel does not just rule over a geographical region (cf. 20:23, 28), but instead rules the entire earth and sets up and takes down leaders as he sees fit. This is why God tells Elijah to anoint Jehu as the next ruler of Israel *and* Hazael as the new king of the neighboring nation of Aram (19:16). Elijah also is directed to anoint Elisha as his successor (19:16). From this point forward, Elijah will mentor Elisha (19:19-21)—an important practice for any man or woman of God.

As seen throughout the second half of 1 Kings, the prophecy//fulfillment motif continues (20:35//20:36; 21:21-24//22:37-38; 22:17//22:36). Chapters 20–22 also relate how and why Ahab meets his demise. Within this section several prophets are featured: the prophet Micaiah (22:8-23) and an unnamed prophet (20:13-14, 22, 28), as well as Elijah again (ch. 21). This reinforces the point that Elijah is not alone in his ministry (cf. 19:18); there will be others to deliver God's word when he departs (2 Kgs 2). In this regard, the Micaiah narrative features a confrontation between this prophet and Ahab's prophets that harks back to Elijah's Mount Carmel experience (22:7-28), while the battle scenes following Micaiah's confrontation (ch. 20) reinforce the Carmel declaration of YHWH's supremacy and sovereignty. YHWH is not a localized deity confined to mountains or valleys (20:23-28; cf. 19:15; 2 Kgs 5:17), he rules over the nations. Indeed, God's victories for Israel, despite Ahab and Jezebel's wickedness, are to show Aram and Israel that YHWH is Lord (20:13, 28).

Sandwiched between the two battle accounts we find the seemingly out-of-place narrative about an Israelite named Naboth and his vineyard. This account relates how and why Ahab will die. King Ahab acts on his desire to obtain Naboth's vineyard—an action that harks back to his father, Omri, and his initiative to purchase Samaria (cf. 16:24; 21:2). Ahab thinks that he can purchase or trade for whatever land he wants, in disregard for the Torah's provisions for tribal allocation and covenant inheritance (Lev 25:23). When faced with Naboth's refusal, Ahab allows Jezebel to order the death of an innocent man (and no doubt his family). This is the final act that brings forth judgment on Ahab's house, and Elijah is there to deliver the bad news (21:17-26). In chapter 22, Elijah's prophecy is fulfilled; Ahab dies.

Debated Issues (aka Great Paper Topics)

1) How does one account for David's apparent flip-flop on the matter of how to respond to the offense of Shimei (2 Sam 19:23; 1 Kgs 2:8-9)?

2) How do scholars interpret the reference to Josiah in 13:2?

3) What is the meaning of the widow's words to Elijah in 17:18?

4) How should we understand God sending "a lying spirit" upon people in 22:19-23?

The Message of the Book

Two messages stand out in 1 Kings. First, God's word is sure. God's promises or prophecies will come to pass in God's own timing. Second, God honors those who honor him. Those who put God first will endure; those who reject God will not!

Closing the Loop

While this book is entitled "Kings," it was placed into the canon of Scriptures in a collection of "historical books" that the Hebrews entitled "Former Prophets." Thus, these two titles—one for the book and one for the book collection—point to the two streams of leadership in Israel—kings and prophets—that can be seen clashing and generating much of the drama and dynamic that we see in 1 Kings.

After David dies, something seems to die with him, namely a certain posture of royal respect for YHWH's prophetic messengers.[26] While Solomon's kingdom gets off to a great start with a prophetic dream and revelation that he would be blessed with wisdom to rule Israel, the rapid rise of the wealth and splendor of his kingdom soon seems to produce what appropriately could be called "a non-*prophet* organization." Solomon's wisdom was widely celebrated, but the absence of the voice of the prophet was surely one of the noteworthy marks of his reign.

What followed in Solomon's wake was a kingdom that broke in two under the strain of his legacy of oppressive taxation of his people (ch. 12) and idol worship, imported along with his many wives from other nations (ch. 11). And then came a whole string of kings, in both the southern and northern kingdoms, who to a large extent followed the precedent that Solomon had set. This in turn further fulfilled Israel's earlier wish for a kingship "like all the other nations." These were kings who showed little of the respect that David showed for the prophets, not merely ignoring them but more and more even openly opposing them, as we have seen.

The height of this royal opposition in the northern kingdom comes near the end of 1 Kings with King Ahab and his foreign wife, Jezebel, versus the prophet Elijah. Yet what is so very striking when one comes to this culminating part of 1 Kings is that, whereas the literature of the book before this is dominated by *royal reports* on the actions, initiatives, and projects of the kings, here the *stories of prophets*, beginning with Elijah, take over the spotlight of the narrative.[27] These stories follow the prophets to out-of-the-way places, far from the royal palace, where prophetic wonder rather than royal wisdom carries the day—all this to suggest that when human kingdoms go their own way, this is where and this is how God might be most at work in the world. In this light, the literature of 1 Kings can point us to and prod us into becoming the prophetic heirs of these stories, answering the call to stand up and to speak up against the presumptuous pretentions of the royal power centers that still hold sway in our world today.

---

26. Walter Brueggemann, *2 Kings*, Knox Preaching Guides (Atlanta: John Knox Press, 1982), 1–3.
27. Walter Brueggemann, *Hope within History* (Atlanta: John Knox Press, 1987), 55–56.

2 KINGS

"Where is the LORD God of Elijah?"
    —2 Kings 2:14 (KJV)

When I think about the book of 2 Kings,

I am awed by the power of the Holy Spirit at work in the inspiration process preparing readers for the coming of Jesus. One of the clearest examples of this occurs in the life of Elisha (whose name means "God saves"). More than 800 years before Jesus (whose name means "YHWH saves") came to the earth, Elisha performed a series of miracles (cf. 2 Kgs 4–6; 13), which are mirrored by many of Jesus's miracles. Elisha raised a woman's only son at Shunem (4:32-37), as did Jesus at Nain, only a few miles from that same OT site (Luke 7:11-15). Elisha fed 100 men with twenty loaves of barley bread and cobs of corn (4:42-44), and Jesus fed thousands with a few fish and loaves (Mark 6:44; 8:19-20). Elisha healed Naaman the leper (2 Kgs 5), and Jesus healed ten lepers (Luke 17:12-19; cf. Luke 4:27). Elisha caused an ax head to float on water (6:1-7), and Jesus walked on the water (Matt 14:25-27). Elisha knew what men were planning/ thinking (6:8-12) as did Jesus (Luke 6:8; John 1:48). Finally, after Elisha died, mere contact with his bones caused a dead man to come back to life (13:21), and when Jesus died, graves were opened and people were resurrected (Matt 27:50-53). Even Elisha's forerunner, Elijah, finds NT connections to Jesus's forerunner, John the Baptist, who was even recognized as an "Elijah" come back to life (Matt 17:12-13; Luke 1:17; cf. Mal 4:5). What I find especially fascinating is the way Jesus goes above and beyond the works of Elisha as God's only begotten Son. Seeing parallels like these stirs my appreciation for God's Word and my awareness of God's Spirit moving from the OT to the NT, from then to now.

Quick Facts

The previous chapter on 1 Kings covers matters of **title**, **authorship**, **date**, **audience**, and **purpose** that apply as well to 2 Kings. However, 2 Kings spans the years 850–561 BCE.

Genre: Historical narrative dominates the text, with a number of other genres incorporated: prophecy (1:3-6; 3:16-19; 4:16; 5:27; 6:32; 7:1-2; 8:10-12; 9:6-10; 13:15-19; 19:6-7, 20-34; 20:1-6, 16-18;

22:15-20); miracles (1:10, 12; 2:14, 19-22; 4:1-7, 32-36, 38-41, 42-44; 5:10-14; 6:1-7, 18; 13:20-21; 20:7-11); coronation ceremony (11:4-12); and a parable (14:9).

Structure

Second Kings focuses on several leading characters, especially the godly examples of Elijah, Elisha, Hezekiah, and Josiah. The lives of these leaders stand in stark contrast to the parade of ungodly kings in both Judah and the northern kingdom of Israel, among whom Manasseh is the most notorious example. Thus, the book's structure can be viewed in terms of the following sections: the rest of the Elijah–Elisha stories (1–13); Israel's slide into Assyrian exile (14–17); Hezekiah's reign (18–20); Manasseh's evil reign (21); Josiah's reforms (22–23); Judah's slide into Babylonian exile (24–25).

Summary

The Rest of the Elijah–Elisha Stories: 2 Kings 1–13

Once again, in line with the title "Former Prophets," used for the book collection in which this book was first grouped, the prophecy-fulfillment motif continues to be prominent (cf. 1:3-6//1:17; 3:16-19//3:20-25; 4:16//4:17; 5:27a//5:27b; 6:32//6:33; 7:1//7:16-20; 19:6-7, 20-34//19:35-37; 22:15-20//23:29-30; 25:1-11). This is displayed in Elijah's prophecies against the house of Ahab (2 Kgs 1:1-8, 16-18). Within the first chapter we also find the troubling account of Elijah calling fire down from heaven to consume 100 men (1:9-15). Thus, the narrative shows the ministry of Elijah coming to an ending that is much like its beginning, namely, on a mountain with fire falling from heaven—the first time to consume a sacrifice, the last time to consume the belligerent soldiers of Ahaziah. The message of these two events could not be clearer: YHWH is God and Elijah is his prophet—both demanded respect! With this word from the Lord, the ministry of Elijah ends as abruptly as it began when he is taken up to heaven in a whirlwind (2:11); but not before Elisha asks for a double portion of Elijah's spirit (2:9 KJV). While any number of interpretations could be given to this request, one possibility is that the "double portion" could point to the doubled number of prophecies and miracles wrought by Elisha as compared to Elijah. Indeed, Elisha's parting of the Jordan with Elijah's mantle—a miracle that replayed Elijah's wondrous feat that itself recalled Moses's—showed those who were watching that the same power of God that rested upon Elijah now rested upon Elisha (2:13-15). Finally, the troubling account of Elisha's cursing of the "children" (KJV; no doubt a gang of teenagers, 2:23-24; cf. Lev 26:22) needs to be understood in light of Elijah's calling fire down upon the soldiers. Elisha, like Elijah, is now the prophet of God and is to be respected as such: to disrespect the prophet is to disrespect God.

As a part of God's continuing judgment on Israel, Mesha, the king of Moab, rebels against Israel after the death of Ahab's son, Ahaziah. The discovery of the Mesha Stele in 1868 in modern Jordan serves

The Double Portion of Elisha Compared to Elijah's Prophecies and Miracles

Elijah's Prophecies		Elisha's Prophecies	
Prophecy	Text	Prophecy	Text
1. 3-year drought	1 Kgs 17:1	1. Victory over Moab	2 Kgs 3:14-19
2. Coming storm and end of drought	1 Kgs 18:44	2. Birth of a son to the Shunammite	2 Kgs 4:16
3. Ahab's demise for stealing Naboth's vineyard	1 Kgs 21:17-24	3. The Syrian army's plans revealed	2 Kgs 6:8-23
4. Ahaziah's death	2 Kgs 1:6	4. Meeting the king	2 Kgs 6:13
		5. Abundance of food but death to the royal officer	2 Kgs 7:1-20
		6. 7-year famine	2 Kgs 8:1-3
		7. Ben-hadad's death	2 Kgs 8:7-15
Totals: Elijah 4/ Elisha 8		8. Jehoash's defeat of the Syrians	2 Kgs 13:14-19

Elijah's Miracles		Elisha's Miracles	
Miracle	Text	Miracle	Text
1. Fed by ravens	1 Kgs 17:2-6	1. Parting of the Jordan	2 Kgs 2:14
2. Flour and oil multiplied	1 Kgs 17:6	2. Two bears tear youths	2 Kgs 2:23-25
3. Resurrection of the woman's boy	1 Kgs 17:17-24	3. Waters healed	2 Kgs 2:19-22
4. Calls down fire from God on Mt. Carmel	1 Kgs 18:16-40	4. Oil multiplied	2 Kgs 4:1-7
5. Outruns Ahab's chariot	1 Kgs 18:46	5. Resurrection of the Shunammite's boy	2 Kgs 4:33-35
6. Two times he calls down fire upon 50 soldiers	2 Kgs 1:10-12	6. Purified Stew	2 Kgs 4:38-41
7. Parting of the Jordan	2 Kgs 2:8	7. Feeding of the 100	2 Kgs 4:42-44
		8. Naaman healed	2 Kgs 5:1-19
		9. Gehazi cursed with leprosy	2 Kgs 5:26-27
		10. Axe head floats	2 Kgs 6:5-7
		11. Servant sees angels	2 Kgs 6:17
		12. Syrian soldiers are blinded	2 Kgs 6:18-19
		13. Syrian soldiers receive their sight	2 Kgs 6:20
Totals: Elijah 7/ Elisha 14		14. Elisha, post-mortem, raises a dead man	2 Kgs 13:20-21

By Brian Peterson

as archaeological support for this biblical account. The latter portion of the biblical account records yet another disturbing event, the king of Moab's sacrifice of his eldest son. Sadly, many of the peoples surrounding Israel believed that sacrificing one's eldest son was a way of getting a god's attention; a trump card of sorts. Some have argued that the biblical text appears to indicate that this pagan ritual worked, producing the desired supernatural effect. However, there are two other ways of understanding 3:27. Either the spectacle of human sacrifice was so horrifying that it caused Israel to stop fighting or the sight inflamed the Moabites to fight with new vigor.

Chapters 4–6 (see introduction above) present stories of Elisha performing miracles similar to those of Elijah, and twice as many (see chart). Within this block some may question why Naaman the leper asks for two of his mules to be loaded with earth after Elisha heals him (5:17). This request makes sense in light of the ancients' belief that the gods were localized (cf. 1 Kgs 20:23). In essence, Naaman is asking to take a "piece" of Israel back to Aram so he can worship on YHWH's "land." Chapter 5 also serves as a comparison between Elisha's unfaithful servant, Gehazi, getting cursed with leprosy, and the repentant Gentile leader Naaman, getting healed of leprosy (cf. Rahab and Achan in Josh 2–7). Elisha's servant Gehazi is by no means the type of man who would succeed Elisha in the way Elisha had replaced Elijah. Among "the sons of the prophets" that Elisha mentored (6:1 KJV), no primary successor emerges in the narrative. Jonah (14:25; ca. 769 BCE) and Amos (ca. 755 BCE) would be the next named prophets of Israel.

Chapter 6 addresses further the spiritual blindness of Elisha's "servant" (whether this is Gehazi is not clear) when the Arameans surround the city where Elisha is staying (6:8-18). Elisha's prayer to open the spiritual eyes of his servant so that he can see the heavenly armies could be seen as indicating the spiritual state of even those closest to the prophet. Indeed, chapters 7–8 continue to relate the spiritual blindness of the kings of Israel and their blatant rejection of Elisha and YHWH. This is exemplified when the king of Israel (not named here, but likely Ahab's son Joram) threatens Elisha's life because of the famine and siege overtaking Samaria (6:24–7:20).

Even though there are those in Israel and Aram who recognize Elisha as the true prophet of God (8:1-15), the effects of Ahab's wickedness spread into Judah when Jehoshaphat's son, Jehoram, marries Ahab's daughter, Athaliah (8:16-29). By the end of chapter 8, the scene is set for the great purge of the evil of Ahab's dynasty by Jehu, the Israelite king's hard-driving charioteer and general. Jehu would rise to lead the next dynasty of Israel.

Jehu's purge of Ahab's line is rapid, bloody, and thorough. After Elisha's servant anoints him king (9:1-14), Jehu goes on a rampage, killing King Joram; his nephew Ahaziah, king of Judah; and Ahab's wicked wife, Jezebel (9:15-37). This fulfilled the prophecy of Elijah against the house of Ahab, pronounced when Ahab killed Naboth and his sons (cf. 9:36-37; 1 Kgs 21). Jehu proceeds not only to have the 70 sons of Ahab executed (10:1-10) but also to kill all those remaining of Ahab's family, together with the king's close friends and priests (10:17). Finally, Jehu devises a plan to entrap all the worshippers of Baal and execute them as well (10:18-28). Jehu obviously sees and attributes all of this to his zeal for the Lord in his fulfillment of Elijah's prophecy (10:16), but one can find two things in the biblical text that raise serious questions about how fully Jehu's agenda is representing God's agenda: (1) His failure to remove the calves at Dan and Bethel prompts God to send Aram to inflict heavy losses on Israel (10:29-36), and this belies a telling lack in his godly zeal; (2) Years later the prophet Hosea looks back on the bloodletting of Jehu and sees it as an atrocity for which the "house of Jehu" is still being punished (Hos 1:4).

Unfortunately, remnants of Ahab's line still remained in Judah in the person of Athaliah, Ahab's daughter. No sooner had Jehu killed Athaliah's son, Ahaziah, than Athaliah in turn kills all the royal offspring so she can rule over Judah (11:1). Her rule lasts six years before the priest Jehoiada sets the sole survivor of Athaliah's massacre, Joash, on the throne. He then orders Athaliah to be executed. With this act, the purge of Ahab's house is complete.

In chapters 12 and 13 the author closes out the Elijah–Elisha materials by presenting accounts of kings from both Judah and Israel; the reign of Joash in Judah in chapter 12 and the reigns of two of Jehu's descendants in chapter 13. The material here can be confusing due to the similarity of kings' names, the lack of strict chronological order, and the rapid pace of the narrative. For example, in chapter 13 alone, the narrative swiftly presents the reigns of the son (Jehoahaz) and grandson (Jehoash) of Jehu as well as the final prophecy and postmortem miracle of Elisha (13:14-21). In the latter case, some scholars insist that the author invented the account of Elisha's postmortem miracle in order to make the number of Elisha's miracles exactly double that of Elijah's. However, as noted earlier, for Christian interpreters this miracle comes to serve the larger canonical function of adding to the parallels between the miracle stories of Elisha and those of Jesus.

Israel's Slide into Assyrian Exile: 2 Kings 14–17

The rapidity of the narrative continues in these chapters, producing the rhetorical effect of showing the accelerated slide of the northern kingdom into exile. Although Jonah is the only prophet mentioned in this section of 2 Kings (14:25), the historical period covered in these chapters parallels a number of writing prophets, including Amos, Hosea, Micah, and Isaiah. Typical of this raucous period are wars (14:7, 8-14; 15:29), intrigue and conspiracies (14:19; 15:10, 14-15, 25, 30; 17:4; cf. 21:23), and idolatry and child sacrifice (14:4; 15:4, 35; 16:3-4; 17:9-17, 35). As a result of these ungodly activities, God sends foreign invaders against both Israel and Judah. One of the major powers at this time is the Neo-Assyrian Empire to the northeast of Israel. Under the expansionist policies of Tiglath-pileser III (745–727 BCE), Assyria begins to press their conquests into the northern reaches of Israel. At this time, Tiglath-pileser captures Samaria and subjugates the northern kingdom (15:29; 16:7-10). In the midst of this chaos, Ahaz, the king of Judah, makes his nation a vassal to Assyria by paying Tiglath-pileser to fight against Ahaz's enemies, the Syro-Ephraimite coalition of Aram and Israel (16:7-10). As a result of relying on foreign powers as opposed to God, Judah will struggle under the yoke of Assyria until the period of Josiah (ca. 640–609 BCE). These are the actions of Ahaz that are condemned by the prophet Isaiah and punctuated by his famous "Christmas prophecy," which begins in Isaiah 7:14 (KJV), "Behold, a virgin shall conceive . . . and shall call his name

Immanuel." Israel's failure to adhere to the stipulations of the Assyrian rulers brings swift retribution. After a three-year siege (17:5), Shalmaneser V (726–722 BCE), Tiglath-pileser's son, comes and destroys Samaria and sends the northern kingdom into exile (ca. 722 BCE; cf. 17:6). As was Assyrian policy, Shalmaneser deports the people of the northern kingdom and then relocates other defeated nations into the region of Israel (17:23-41). The final section of chapter 17 gives a running list of the reasons why God exiled the northern kingdom. The central reason for the exile is rooted in Israel's failure to listen to YHWH's prophets (17:13, 23) and to keep God's commands (17:15, 19, 34-40). Tucked into this explanation is an implied warning for Judah not to follow in the path of Israel (17:13-19). Sadly, Judah's leaders did not pay heed. From this point on in 2 Kings, with the northern kingdom of Israel having been exiled, Judah becomes the sole focus.

Hezekiah's Reign: 2 Kings 18–20

These chapters, which present the reign of Hezekiah, are repeated almost verbatim in Isaiah 36–39. Hezekiah (715–686 BCE) and Josiah after him (640–609 BCE) are the last two reforming kings in Judah before its exile in 586 BCE. After the death of Sargon II, king of Assyria (721–705 BCE), Hezekiah rebels against Assyria. The new Assyrian king, Sennacherib (705–681 BCE), comes to put down Hezekiah's rebellion in 701 BCE. After Sennacherib conquers 46 of Judah's cities and villages, Hezekiah acknowledges his error in rebelling (18:14-16). However, when Sennacherib's field commander, Rabshakeh (KJV), mocks YHWH's ability to defend Jerusalem (18:17-35; 19:4, 10-13, 16) the prophet Isaiah prophesies of Sennacherib's defeat and downfall (19:6-7, 20-34). That night the angel of the Lord comes and kills 185,000 Assyrian soldiers, forcing Sennacherib to return to Assyria. There Sennacherib is killed in a conspiracy (19:35-37). What is interesting in relation to this account is the fact that the annals of Sennacherib, unearthed by modern archaeologists, actually record the siege of Jerusalem but not its capture. And even though Sennacherib's death is 20 years later, the author of Kings notes the fulfillment of Isaiah's prophecy within the same chapter to show that the word of God's prophet always comes to fruition.

Chapter 20 recounts the story of Hezekiah being struck by a terminal illness. As a sign that Hezekiah will arise from his deathbed and be given 15 more years, Hezekiah asks Isaiah to request a sign from God, which God grants, specifically causing the shadow on the sundial to move backwards several steps. Soon after these events, envoys from Babylon come to visit Hezekiah. Hezekiah responds most hospitably by showing them all the treasures of Judah. This brings about Isaiah's harsh prophecy that Babylon will one day come and plunder Jerusalem and make eunuchs of Hezekiah's children, but not in Hezekiah's own days (20:14-19). Scholars have noted the lack of chronological ordering of chapter 20 with what comes before it. Here, as in Isaiah 39, the author appears to be placing the visit of the envoys last in the sequence as a literary device to set up for the material that follows this chapter, highlighting who will be coming to conquer Judah.

Manasseh's Evil Reign: 2 Kings 21

The wicked reign of Manasseh is perhaps a sad commentary on the fathering abilities of Hezekiah. Manasseh reverses all the spiritual reforms of his father (21:2-9). According to Jewish tradition, Manasseh was responsible for Isaiah's death (cf. 21:16; Heb 11:37). Even though the Chronicler notes that Manasseh repents of his sin in the end (2 Chron 33:11-13), the author of Kings does not include this fact. The author wants to show the sin of Manasseh as the final straw that causes God's judgment to fall on Judah (21:10-15; 23:26-27; 24:3-4).

Josiah's Reforms: 2 Kings 22–23

After the brief reign of Manasseh's wicked son Amon (21:18-23), Josiah, Manasseh's grandson, comes to the throne of Judah at age eight (22:1). Josiah is known for being the last great reforming king of Judah. At age 18 he orders the renovation of the temple (22:3-9), at which time the Instruction scroll, or book of the law, is found (22:8). Most scholars today insist that this is the book of Deuteronomy (see chapter on Deuteronomy). From this moment forward, Josiah enters into a covenant with YHWH, carries out extensive reforms that include the removal of idols and cult sites that have caused Judah to sin, and celebrates Passover (23:2-25). Due to the weakness of the Assyrian Empire at this time, Josiah even ventures into the former northern kingdom and destroys the cult sites at Bethel and Samaria (23:15). At this point the prophecy of the unnamed prophet from Judah comes to pass (cf. 1 Kgs 13:1-2; 2 Kgs 23:16-18). Sadly, Josiah's reforms cannot undo all the wickedness perpetrated by his grandfather Manasseh (23:26-27). In 609,

A scarab from one of the Psamtik pharaohs of the 26th dynasty in Egypt. Pharaoh Neco, who killed Josiah (2 Kgs 23:29), was from this period. The scarab was found at Khirbet el-Maqatir, the proposed site of Ai. Photo courtesy of Michael Luddeni and ABR.

Josiah is killed in battle while trying to stop the Egyptian pharaoh Neco from going to help Assyria against Babylon at the battle of Harran. With Josiah's death, the last hope for reforms in Judah comes to an end.

Judah's Slide into Babylonian Exile: 2 Kings 24–25

Judah's rapid return to its old ways is evidence that the people did not embrace Josiah's reforms with their whole heart. From 609–586 BCE four kings rule in rapid succession: Josiah's sons Jehoahaz (23:31-33) and Jehoiakim (23:34–24:6), his grandson Jehoiachin (24:8-16), and finally a third son, Zedekiah (24:17–25:4). The author's refrain for each is that they "did evil in the sight of the Lord" (KJV), especially

Jehoiakim and Zedekiah (23:32, 37; 24:9, 19). This is the era when the prophets Jeremiah, Ezekiel, Zephaniah, Habakkuk, and perhaps Obadiah minister. Through these prophets, God gives the nation plenty of warning about the coming destruction of the city and temple.

With the defeat of Assyria by Babylon at the battle of Carchemish in 605 BCE, Assyria passes from the world scene never to return. This paves the way for the dominance of the Neo-Babylonian Empire under the rule of Nabopolassar (626–605 BCE) followed by his son Nebuchadnezzar II (605–562 BCE). This is why Babylon, and not Assyria, is responsible for taking Judah into exile in three stages: 605/4—Daniel and the choicest of Judah's elite go into exile; 597—Jehoiachin, the royal family, and many others, including Ezekiel, go into exile; and 587/6—Jerusalem is destroyed and looted along with the temple (25:8-17), and the rest of the people go into exile to Babylon with the exception of some of the poorest who are left to take care of the land; cf. 25:12. As a result of Zedekiah's rebellion against Babylon, Nebuchadnezzar executes Zedekiah's sons and then puts out his eyes (25:5-7). This is the last thing Zedekiah will ever see. The book of Kings ends with a glimmer of hope when Nebuchadnezzar's son Awil-merodach (KJV: Evilmerodach), releases Jehoiachin from prison, allowing him to eat at the Babylonian king's table (25:27-30). It is this notation that is often used to date the book of Kings to the period after 562 BCE, the date when Evilmerodach came to the throne of Babylon.

Debated Issues (aka Great Paper Topics)

1) What are the scholarly views on Elisha's "double portion" (2:9 KJV)?

2) How many times did Sennacherib attack Jerusalem (chs. 18–20)?

3) In view of Josiah's sudden and surprising death in battle, was the prophetess Huldah wrong when she prophesied that Josiah would die in peace (22:15-20)?

The Message of the Book

Second Kings, together with 1 Kings, shows that God's prophetic word presides over human kings and kingdoms, bringing judgment against sin, yet leaving a door open in the end for hope beyond the judgment (as with Jehoiachin's prison door in the exile).

Closing the Loop

The originally unified book of 1–2 Kings begins with the demise of King David (1 Kings 1–2) and ends with the demise of the Davidic kingdom (2 Kings 25). It thus tells a tragic story—a *story of kings* that, from beginning to end, fulfills the *words of prophets*. And so fittingly, the Hebrews used it to conclude the collection of books they called "Former Prophets."

The Kings of Israel and Judah*

DAVID 1011-971
Solomon 971-931

BC	ISRAEL		JUDAH		co-regency	Prophets	Ancient Near East
1000							
	JEROBOAM I	930-910	Rehoboam	931-913			Shishak, 945-924
	Nadab	910-909	Abijah/Abijam	913-910			
			Asa	910-869			Ben-Hadad I, 900-860
900	BAASHA	909-886					
	Elah	886-885					
	Zimri	885 (7 days)					
	Tibni	885-880					
	OMRI	885-874					Ashurnasirpal II, 853
	Ahab	874-853	Jehoshapat	872-848		Elijah 860-850	Ben-Hadad II, 860-841
						Elisha 850-798	
850	Ahaziah	853-852	J(eh)oram	853-841		Obadiah 845?	
	J(eh)oram	852-841	Ahaziah	841		Joel 840?	Shalmaneser III, 841
							Hazael, 841-806
	JEHU	841-814	Athaliah	841-835			Tel Dan & Mesha Stela
	Jehoahaz	814-798	J(eh)oash	835-796			Adad-Nirari III, 806
800	J(eh)oash	798-782	Amaziah	796-787		Jonah 770	
	Jeroboam II	793-753	Uzziah/Azariah	791/739		Amos 762	
						Earthquake c. 760	
	Zechariah	752 (6 month)				Hosea 755-730	
750	Shallum	752 (1 month)			co-regency:		
	MENAHEM	752-742	Jotham	750-731	751-736		Tiglath-pileser, 744-727
	Pekiah	742-740					
	Pekah	752/740-732	Ahaz	735-715	743-728	Isaiah 740-686?	Shalmaneser V, 726-722
	Hoshea	732-722	Hezekiah	715-686	728-696	Micah 735-690	Sargon II, 722-705
722	Assyrian Conquest/Exile						Sennacherib, 705-681
			Manasseh	696-642			Ashurbanipal, 669-627
			Amon	642-640		Nahum 640	
			Josiah	640-609		Zephaniah 635	Neco, 610-595
			Jehoahaz	609 (3 mo)			
			Jehoiakim	609-598		Habakkuk 608	Nebuchadnezzar, 605-562
			Jehoiachin	598/7 (3 mo)		Jeremiah 627-580	
			Zedekiah	597-586		Daniel 605-530	
586			Babylonian Conquest/Exile			Ezekiel 593-570	
							Evil-Merodach, 562-560
							Nabonidus, 556-539
538			Return & Restoration				Cyrus, 539-530
						Zechariah 520	
						Haggai 520	
						Malachi 425	

CAPITALS indicate new dynasty

*Adapted from E. Thiele, *The Mysterious Numbers of the Hebrew Kings*, Kregel: 1983. Appendix B

Courtesy of W. Schlegel, Satellite Bible Atlas.

Prophets loom large in this overarching drama of 1–2 Kings in still another way, which has to do with the sheer amount of material devoted to the lives and deeds of prophets. Indeed, the central section of this writing—no less than a full third of the Kings material—features a dramatic shift away from accounts focusing on kings to stories focusing on prophets, primarily Elijah and Elisha (1 Kings 17–2 Kings 13). And at the very center of this central section stands a story of special prophetic significance, featuring the passing of the mantle of prophetic leadership from Elijah to Elisha (2 Kings 2).

This story has been especially important in the history of Pentecostalism.[28] Its reference to a "double portion of spirit," along with wondrous manifestations involving fire, wind, and transport into the heavens, all yield some rather obvious parallels to the outpouring of the Holy Spirit in Acts 2. Yet this story has an important role in its own context in the book of Kings that should not be missed. It offers a powerful example of *successful spiritual succession* that stands right in the midst of a long string of royal successions that end in tragic failure.

Elijah's enduring legacy was centered in passing on a spiritual inheritance that the kings of Israel after David, for the most part, failed to pass on. Elijah's role in this is so significant that it is recognized both at the very end of the OT (in terms of the promise that Elijah would come again to turn the hearts of elders and children toward one another; Mal 4:5-6) and at the very beginning of Luke's Gospel in the NT (in terms of the promise that John the Baptist would be raised up in the spirit of Elijah to reactivate this intergenerational work of turning hearts; Luke 1:17).

All of this should help us to see that the prophetic Spirit, both then and now, is not only about revealing something new but also about repairing the broken connection between the old and the new. Indeed, this is the inheritance, the "promise . . . for you [and] your children," that comes with "the gift of the Holy Spirit" (Acts 2:38-39).

---

28. See Walter Bruggemann, "Elisha as the Original Pentecost Guy: Ten Theses," *Journal for Preachers* 32.4 (Pentecost 2009): 41–47.

1 AND 2 CHRONICLES

"If my people who belong to me will humbly pray, seek my face, and turn from their wicked ways, then I will hear from heaven, forgive their sin, and heal their land."
    —*2 Chronicles 7:14*

When I think about the book of Chronicles,

I cannot help but reflect on how many Christians often speak about, or even long for, the "good old days" of a bygone era. I am acutely aware of this, as I have personally witnessed rapid spiritual digression in America in my short lifetime. I can recall waiting as a youth at the altar for God's touch upon my life and being changed by the power of God's Spirit. Yet today the "altar services" of many Pentecostal churches are the exception rather than the rule. In many ways the "good old days" were a time of spiritual and national blessing, notwithstanding a number of national sins during those days that cannot be denied. The author of Chronicles (the Chronicler, so-called) appears to have had a similar outlook as he wrote his version of the history of Israel. It seems he looked back wistfully at the "good old days" of David and Solomon. Having lived through, or at least known about, the period of the Babylonian Exile, the Chronicler looks back to a better time when Israel experienced God's blessing. As a means of magnifying this bygone era, the Chronicler purposely removed many of the negative aspects of the reigns of David and Solomon. Israel had paid for their sin by means of a 70-year exile; now was not the time to reminisce about the negative aspects of Israel's past, it was the time to recollect the many blessings that they had once experienced. Undoubtedly the Chronicler thought that, if his audience would listen, they could once again experience those same blessings.

Quick Facts

Title: The authors of the LXX used the title *Paraleipomenon* ("The things set aside/omitted") whereas the Hebrew title is *Divrei hayyamim* ("the events of the days"). The title in English Bibles comes from the influence of the title given to this book first by Jerome and then by Martin Luther.

Date: Chronicles is postexilic even though the author used much older sources. The exact period of authorship is uncertain. Based on internal evidence (e.g., 1 Chron 3:17-24; 29:7; 2 Chron 16:9; 36:22-23), the dating could range from the late sixth century (ca. 538 BCE) to the late fifth century (ca. 420 BCE) or even later. Most scholars settle on a date in the early Persian period (ca. 500–400 BCE). Chronicles' content indicates the likelihood that it was written in Jerusalem.

Authorship: Jewish tradition (*Baba Bathra* 15a) assigns the authorship of Chronicles to the priest and scribe Ezra. This makes sense in light of the way Chronicles ends and Ezra begins with the same statement (cf. 2 Chron 36:22-23; Ezra 1:1-3). Some scholars think that multiple unknown authors wrote it over a period of time. In this vein, some see factors weighing against Ezra's authorship in such things as the placement of Ezra–Nehemiah before Chronicles, ideological outlooks that differ slightly between the two bodies of literature, and certain linguistic differences between them. Even though the authorship of Chronicles bears resemblance to that of Ezra (e.g., in its priestly focus), we cannot be certain about authorship.

Audience and Purpose: The audience was postexilic and Jewish. The purpose of the book was to relate a theologized history of Israel whereby the Davidic kingship was the archetype for all Israel to follow. It was in essence a book of encouragement in the midst of postexilic hardships.

Genre: Although Chronicles is written as historical narrative, other genres predominate. This is most evident in the nine chapters of genealogy that begin 1 Chronicles. Other genres incorporated in Chronicles include: psalms (1 Chron 16:8-36); laments (2 Chron 35:25); lists (e.g., 1 Chron 11:26-12:36; 15:4-24; 23-27; 2 Chron 17:14-18); and prayers (e.g., 1 Chron 29:10-19).

Structure

Chronicles originally was one book but was later divided into two. It can be divided as follows: 1 Chronicles: genealogies (1–9); the death of Saul and the reign of David (10–29); 2 Chronicles: Solomon's reign (1–9); the reigns of the kings of Judah (10–36).

Summary

The book of Chronicles repeats many parts of the books of Samuel and Kings. First Chronicles covers material from 1 Samuel 31–1 Kings 2, and 2 Chronicles presents much of the content of 1 Kings 3–2 Kings 25. Because of this, in what follows we will discuss the major areas of divergence between the Chronicler's History and the Deuteronomistic History (DtrH). The most obvious departure from DtrH is the addition of the extended genealogies in 1 Chronicles 1–9. If you want to write a best seller, this is not the way to begin your book; yet the Chronicler opens his book by tracing Israel's lineage back to Adam. This has rhetorical importance. The Chronicler connects the Jews of the postexilic community to their past. It had been all too easy for the dislocated people to lose their connectedness to their ancestors and their heritage. These genealogies remedy that problem.

The Chronicler's next major departure from the DtrH is that he skips over the lives of Eli, Samuel, and the early years of David and Saul (1 Sam 1–30). Instead he jumps immediately to the death scene of Saul (cf. 1 Chron 10; 1 Sam 31). There are probably at least two main reasons for this major gap in the Chronicler's History. First, the Chronicler's purpose is to highlight the godly rule of David and the positive aspects of Solomon's reign. Second, the Chronicler apparently does not want to present David in an unfavorable light. By eliminating the early days of David and his time as a fugitive from Saul, the author begins the reign of David on a positive note (however, see 1 Chron 12:1). This conclusion is reinforced by the fact that the Chronicler does

Jewish men being impaled on poles by Assyrian soldiers at the battle of Lachish (ca. 701 BCE), Judah's second largest city. Photo courtesy of Michael Luddeni.

not address the seven-year civil war between Saul's son Ishbosheth and David (cf. 2 Sam 2–4). Instead he skips over that span of time and moves directly to all Israel coming to David at Hebron and declaring him to be the next ruler of Israel after Saul's death (1 Chron 11:1-3).

At certain spots the Chronicler's chronological ordering is also different from the DtrH. In chapters 11–12 the Chronicler presents a list of the mighty men of David that actually appears at the end of 2 Samuel in chapter 23. This serves to show that, even before David's reign, men joined themselves to him because of YHWH's blessing upon David (11:10; 12:18, 22). Nevertheless, sections such as 1 Chronicles 13–19 follow closely the same ordering and basic content of 2 Samuel 5–11. Two of the key changes occur in how the Chronicler reports Nathan's prophetic word concerning the Davidic covenant (cf. 1 Chron 17; 2 Sam 7). First, the Chronicler diverges from 2 Samuel 7 in that he gives the reason for David's inability to build the temple—he shed too much blood in war (1 Chron 22:8). Second, unlike the DtrH, the Chronicler names Solomon as the son who will build the temple (cf. 1 Chron 22:9; 2 Sam 7:12). This is in keeping with the Chronicler's positive stance toward both David and Solomon.

First Chronicles 20 presents the next major difference between the Chronicler and the DtrH. Here verses 1-8 repeat content from several 2 Samuel passages (2 Sam 11:1; 12:30-31; 21:18-22). However, these verses exclude any mention of David's sin with Bathsheba (2 Sam 11:2-27) along with the repercussions of that sin (2 Sam 12–20), and the Gibeonite account as well as the near death of David at the hands of a Philistine giant (2 Sam 21:1-17). These accounts are passed over in a way that once again presents David in a more favorable light.

The next departure of the Chronicler from the DtrH is the content of chapters 23–29, which is unique to the Chronicler. These chapters, which conclude 1 Chronicles, record the preparations that David made for the smooth transition of Solomon to the throne. David's preparations included gathering materials for the construction of the temple and putting in place the administrative apparatus of the temple, which is highlighted by the extended lists of Levites, priests, temple workers, and officials (chs. 23–29). The scene of Solomon's coronation also diverges from that of 1 Kings. Unlike 1 Kings 1, where David is aged and appears unaware of the struggle for the throne between Adonijah and Solomon, the Chronicler presents a smooth transition to Solomon's reign, with David appearing much more in control of the situation (1 Chron 28–29). Unlike 1 Kings 1, all the officials of Israel, the army, and even the king's sons are shown supporting Solomon (1 Chron 29:21-25).

Second Chronicles follows a more narrative style without the predominant use of lists and genealogies as seen in 1 Chronicles. Second Chronicles begins by omitting any mention of the power struggle for the throne recorded in 1 Kings 1:1–3:3. By starting Solomon's reign with his encounter with the Lord at Gibeon (cf. 2 Chron 1:3; 1 Kgs 3:4), the Chronicler also excludes mention of Solomon's alliance with the Egyptian pharaoh and his marriage to the pharaoh's daughter. In line with this, the Chronicler also does not mention the downfall of Solomon due to his many wives, as noted in 1 Kings 11. Perhaps indicative of the Chronicler's priestly interests is his increased focus on the construction and dedication of the temple (2 Chron 2–7). Solomon's reign ends on a positive note, leaving responsibility for the downfall of the Davidic line to Rehoboam and those who follow him (2 Chron 8–9).

The first appearance of a prophet in 2 Chronicles is during Rehoboam's reign (12:5). The motif of prophecy-fulfillment that dominates 1 and 2 Kings is all but absent in Chronicles. Of course, Nathan's prophecy to David concerning the Davidic covenant is given prime placement in 1 Chronicles 17, but the rest of the appearances of the prophets have a more supportive role in the Chronicles narrative. These include the mention of Samuel (1 Chron 11:3); Shemaiah (2 Chron 11:2-4); Azariah (2 Chron 15:1-7); Micaiah (2 Chron 18:6-27); Jahaziel (2 Chron 20:14-17); unnamed prophets (2 Chron 24:19; 25:7-9, 15-16); Zechariah (2 Chron 24:20); Obed (2 Chron 28:9-11); Isaiah (2 Chron 32:20); and Jeremiah (2 Chron 36:12). Of interest is the complete absence of the prophetic activities of Elijah and Elisha with the exception of Elijah's letter to Jehoram (2 Chron 21:12). This movement away from emphasis on the prophetic voice might be due to the actual fulfillment of many of the prophecies recorded in 1 and 2 Kings by the time the Chronicler begins to compose his work; and here again, why rehearse all of the past failures of Judah as foretold by the prophets? Another possible reason for the Chronicler's omission of the Elijah–Elisha stories is the fact that the prophetic ministries of Elijah and Elisha were primarily focused on the northern kingdom, not Judah. The Chronicler mentions the northern kingdom and its kings only when Judah has direct interaction with them (e.g., Ahab in 2 Chron 18). This is the case with the account of the division of Israel under Rehoboam and his interaction with Jeroboam I, the first king of the northern kingdom of Israel.[29]

---

29. 2 Chron 10:2, 3, 12, 15; 11:4, 14; 12:15; 13:1-20.

Another peculiarity of the Chronicler is his increased emphasis on the godly reforming kings of Judah. Having already noted the central focus on David and Solomon from 1 Chronicles 11–2 Chronicles 9, in what remains of 2 Chronicles, no fewer than 13 chapters are devoted to the godly reigns of Asa (14–16), Jehoshaphat (17–20), Hezekiah (29–32), and Josiah (34–35). Remarkably, even the wickedest king of Judah, Manasseh, is shown repenting—something completely absent in 2 Kings. Finally, the Chronicler repeats a number of motifs that perhaps betray his priestly background. He makes a point of showing that godly kings sought God's help in battle and that God fought for his people;[30] along with highlighting the actual preparation and construction of the temple by *both* David and Solomon, the Chronicler emphasizes the role of the temple in the lives of the kings and people of Judah;[31] he repeatedly notes the importance of the book/Law of Moses/YHWH to Judah;[32] five times he records covenants made between godly kings and the Lord;[33] throughout his book the work and role of the priests and Levites are prominently presented;[34] and lastly, he notes that judgment came upon the people for forsaking or disobeying God.[35] This is particularly poignant in light of how the Chronicler ends his work. He concludes by noting the reasons why Judah had gone into exile: they were unfaithful to the covenant; they defiled the temple (2 Chron 36:14); they forsook the word of the prophets (36:15-16); and they failed to give the land its Sabbath rest (36:21). Because of these sins Judah went into exile at the hands of the Babylonian king, Nebuchadnezzar in 586 BCE. Yet, similar to the way that 2 Kings ends with a glimmer of hope, shown in the release of King Jehoiachin from prison (2 Kgs 25:27-30), the Chronicler also gives a final ray of hope by noting the decree of the Persian king, Cyrus (2 Chron 36:22-23) in 538 BCE. This decree allowed for the Jewish people to return to their homeland.

Debated Issues (aka Great Paper Topics)

1) How do scholars account for the differences between 2 Sam 24:13 and 1 Chron 21:12, and 2 Sam 24:25 and 1 Chron 21:24?

2) What are the key differences in the portrayals of King David in the books of Samuel and in the Chronicles corpus, and what might account for these differences?

---

30. 1 Chron 5:20; 10:14; 2 Chron 13:14-15; 14:11; 18:4, 31; 20:3; 26:7; 32:8.

31. 2 Chron 20:9; 23:3-10; 24:4-27; 26:19-21; 29:3-35; 30:1-15; 31:10-21; 33:4-15; 34:8-17, 30; 35:2-8; 36:7-19.

32. 1 Chron 16:40; 22:12; 2 Chron 6:16; 12:1; 14:4; 17:9; 23:18; 25:4; 30:16; 31:3-4; 33:8; 34:14-19; 35:12, 26.

33. 1 Chron 11:3; 2 Chron 13:5; 15:12; 29:10; 34:31.

34. 1 Chron 9:2; 13:2; 15:11, 14; 23:2; 24:6; 28:13, 21; 2 Chron 7:6; 8:14-15; 11:13-14; 13:9-10; 17:8; 19:8; 23:4-6; 24:5; 29:4, 16, 26, 34; 30:15-16, 21, 25; 31:2, 4, 9, 17, 19; 34:30; 35:8-18.

35. 2 Chron 7:22; 12:1-5; 21:10; 24:20, 24; 26:16-21; 28:6, 19; 29:6; 32:26; 34:25.

The Message of the Book

The great heritage of the Jewish people, especially in the covenant traditions of temple worship established through David and Solomon, provides important foundations for rebuilding life in their homeland after almost two generations of exile.

Closing the Loop

The book of Chronicles retells the story of Israel from the perspective of and for the benefit of the postexilic Jewish community. It is much like what Moses did for the pre-conquest generation in the book of Deuteronomy, but with the Chronicler now looking back, obviously, over a much longer span of time. As such, Chronicles reinforces the long-established biblical understanding that God's covenant is designed to be renewed, reclaimed, and sometimes even re-presented with fresh articulation for new contexts and new generations of God's people.

The new context that Chronicles is so very concerned to address involves the crisis of postexilic survival. In order to survive, the Jewish people must restore and re-establish their foundations—not only the foundations of their physical infrastructure in terms of their capital city with its walls, its buildings, and especially the temple, but also the foundations and infrastructure of their faith, which had been beaten down by 70 years of captivity.

Thus Chronicles appreciates the new context and the new expression of the covenant faith that is needed, yet it also realizes how vital it is to connect the new with the old—a conviction graphically signified and represented by the long genealogical lists. What the people of Israel do in this new day must be based on and rooted in the old ways that were established by the founders of their faith, especially David, for David is the one, above all others, who laid the foundations of Israelite worship and temple practice. And there are no foundations in the postexilic situation that are more crucial than these when it comes to Israel's effort to survive.

As a relatively *new* movement in the history of Christianity and one that has championed re*new*al, Pentecostalism has had a special attraction toward and flair for the "new." And nowhere has this been more evident than in the area of worship practice. Pentecostal worship has emphasized free expression and has pushed away from formal liturgy, even to the point of seeing it as an encroachment upon the freedom of the Spirit. Yet ironically, while celebrating its freedom from form, Pentecostal worship in many ways has fallen into its own established forms and routine patterns. This could well serve as a reminder that the issue here is not whether or not we will have worship forms but rather whether or not Pentecostal forms of worship will be *in*formed by our theological heritage and historic roots, which reach deeply into the ages past. It is at this very point that Chronicles can offer us fresh light from the past upon this vital work of renewal.

EZRA—NEHEMIAH

Then Nehemiah the governor, Ezra the priest and scribe, and the Levites who taught the people said to all of the people, "This day is holy to the LORD your God."
—*Nehemiah 8:9*

When I think about the books of Ezra and Nehemiah,

I am prompted to draw a connection between their teaching forbidding the marrying of foreigners (Ezra 9–10; Neh 13:23-31) and my own experience as a Canadian marrying an American. Although Ezra and Nehemiah were specifically forbidding the union of God-fearing Israelites with foreigners (that is, those who do not worship the same God as Israel)—a similar perspective taught by Paul in 2 Cor 6:14a, "Do not be unequally yoked together with unbelievers" (NKJV)—I am still moved with compassion for all those women and children who were forced to return to their own lands with no real prospects for the future without a husband/father. As a parent, I cannot imagine what it would be like if a law were passed out-lawing Canadian–American marriages. The pain that I would experience of not being able to be with my children and my wife would be excruciating. I can assume that the pain felt by the families in the day of Ezra and Nehemiah was no doubt much more agonizing. For me, I know that being married to a believer makes all the difference. The Israelites, however, had broken God's law by their actions, and the innocent suffered the consequences. The lesson is no less applicable today. When we as believers choose to date or marry unbelievers, all too often the innocent, and even ourselves, suffer the effects. In any era, it is best to obey the voice of the Lord in these matters and avoid suffering the painful consequences.

Quick Facts

Title: These two books, which were originally one, have titles that come from the two key figures of the books. This is the case in modern Bibles, both Christian and Jewish. The LXX uses the title Esdras, the Greek translation for Ezra.

Date: As with many books, pinpointing the date of Ezra–Nehemiah is not easy. We know that Ezra ministered during the reign of Artaxerxes I/Longimanus (464–424 BCE). According to Ezra 7:8 and Neh

1:1, Ezra and Nehemiah came to Jerusalem circa 458 and 445 BCE, respectively; Nehemiah returned to Babylon circa 433 BCE (Neh 13:6). However, the genealogy of Neh 12:22, dated to the reign of Darius II (ca. 423–403 BCE), would make the date for the final form sometime during Darius II's reign.

Authorship: Jewish tradition assigns these books to Ezra (*Baba Bathra* 15a), which fits the first-person discourse that appears in the book (e.g., 7:28–9:15). If this is the case, it is likely that Ezra used Nehemiah's memoirs (i.e., 1–6; 7:1-5; 11:1-2; 12:27-43; 13:4-31; cf. 2 Macc 2:15) for the book of Nehemiah.

Audience and Purpose: The audience is the postexilic Jewish returnees from Persia and Babylon. Along with the historical aim of the books, the purpose is to instruct the returnees on the proper lifestyle and separateness as the people of God in the midst of hostile neighbors, and on the importance of rebuilding the city of Jerusalem.

Genre: These books are written as historical narrative; however other genres are incorporated: genealogies (Ezra 7:1-5; 8:1-14); lists (Ezra 2:1-67; 10:18-44; Neh 3:1-32; 7:7-73; 10:1-27; 11:4-36; 12:1-22); letters/decrees (Ezra 4:9-22; 5:7-17; 6:6-12; 7:12-26; Neh 6:6-7); a memorandum (Ezra 6:2-5); and prayers/confessions (Ezra 9:6-15; Neh 1:5-11; 9:5-38).

Structure

Ezra and Nehemiah can each be further subdivided as follows: a brief history of the rebuilding of the temple (Ezra 1–6); Ezra teaches the law (7–10) // Nehemiah rebuilds the walls of Jerusalem (Neh 1–7); the spiritual status of the returnees (8–13).

Summary

A Brief History of the Rebuilding of the Temple: Ezra 1–6

Because they are ordered thematically as opposed to chronologically, chapters 1–6 are somewhat difficult to follow. In these chapters the author goes back to the first return in 538/7 BCE and gives a history of the rebuilding of the temple. Chapter 4 is the most confusing in that the author moves from the period of Cyrus to the beginning of Darius I's reign (ca. 539–522 BCE) in 4:1-5, then jumps ahead to Ahasuerus/ Xerxes I (485–465 BCE) in 4:6, and ahead again to Artaxerxes I (464–424 BCE) in 4:7-23, only to return back to the second year of Darius I (ca. 520 BCE) in 4:24. Verses 6-23 thus seem to be added by the author to show a history of opposition by the enemies of the Jews. After chapter 5 describes the prophetic influence of Haggai and Zechariah in effecting the completion of the temple in 516 BCE (6:15), chapter 6 shows the sovereign hand of God in thwarting the enemies of Israel. Those who were opposed to the rebuilding of the temple had to pay for the costs of rebuilding it at the decree of Darius I (6:8-13)!

Ezra Teaches the Law: Ezra 7–10

Having been given a mandate by Artaxerxes I to return to Jerusalem and teach the law (7:11-26), Ezra sets out with 1,754 men plus their families (8:1-20) with many gifts from the king and his officials (8:25-27). However, once they arrive, Ezra is faced with the widespread practice of foreign marriages among the Jewish people, a violation of the law (Deut 7:3). Ezra confronts the people about this issue (9:1-4) and prays to God for forgiveness (9:5-15). As a result, the people repent and willingly, under oath, divorce their foreign wives (10:1-44).

Nehemiah Rebuilds the Walls of Jerusalem: Nehemiah 1–7

Whereas Ezra focuses on the spiritual state of Jerusalem, Nehemiah is devoted to rebuilding the city. In 445 BCE, Nehemiah, working as a cupbearer for Artaxerxes I in Susa, Persia, hears about the desolated state of the city of Jerusalem. He prays to God for its people and that he will find favor in the king's sight to return and rebuild the city (1:5-11). The king grants him permission and Nehemiah goes to Jerusalem as governor of Judah for 12 years (cf. 2:1-8; 5:14; 13:6). No doubt sensing a loss of political power with Nehemiah's arrival, the local non-Jewish leaders led by Sanballat, Tobias, and Geshem immediately oppose him (2:10, 18-20; 4:1-12; 6:1-14, 17-19). Under the cover of darkness, Nehemiah surveys the ruined city and rallies the Jews to rebuild the walls by working in family units (2:12-16; 3:1-32). Even though Sanballat and his cronies try desperately to thwart the rebuilding of Jerusalem, even threatening armed attack, Nehemiah's response is resolute. He arms his workers and sets guards to keep watch for any attack (4:13-23). When the wealthy nobles begin to enslave their own people and charge interest on loans, Nehemiah confronts them and puts them under oath to stop (5:1-14). Despite this setback and the threats by the locals, they complete the city walls in 52 days (6:15).

The Spiritual Status of the Returnees: Nehemiah 8–13

In chapter 8 we are reintroduced to Nehemiah's contemporary, Ezra. Here Ezra reads the law to the people in a formal gathering and celebrates the Festival of Booths (8:1-18). Scholars have noted the chronological issues with Ezra teaching the law over 13 years *after* he arrived in 458 BCE. One solution is to suggest that chapter 8 is out of chronological order (i.e., it should be after Ezra 10 or between Ezra 8 and 9). It is also possible that Ezra chose this occasion to re-present the law. Whatever view one takes, the reading of the law in any case leads to national repentance and a written confession (9:1-38), which is signed by the people (10:1-27). Under oath, the people agree not to intermarry with the locals (10:30), not to buy or sell on the Sabbath (10:31), and to support the temple and priests by taxes and tithes (10:32-39).

After the city walls are rebuilt, there are still only a few people actually living there. As a remedy, the leaders move into the city and the people cast lots so that one in ten will relocate there (11:1-36). Next, in conjunction with great festivities, Nehemiah dedicates the walls of Jerusalem (12:27-45). At the end of 12 years (ca. 445–433 BCE), Nehemiah returns to Susa. After an unspecified time, he returns to Jerusalem and finds that the people had not only allowed foreigners to live in the very temple precincts (13:4-8), but they had also broken their oaths, which they earlier had agreed to in writing. They had not paid their tithes to the priests (13:10-11), they had worked and conducted commerce on the Sabbath (13:15-21), and they had intermarried with the locals (13:23-24). As a result, Nehemiah reinstitutes the former lawful state of affairs (13:11-12, 19-22, 30-31), resorting to forced compliance at several points (13:19, 21, 25, 28).

Excavated portions of Nehemiah's wall. Photo courtesy of Michael Luddeni.

Debated Issues (aka Great Paper Topics)

1) How do scholars account for the discrepancies between the lists of Ezra 2:1-70 and Neh 7:6-69?

2) How do scholars handle the issue of Ezra teaching the law 13 years *after* arriving (Neh 8)?

The Message of the Book

Two messages resonate within these two books. First, despite opposition to the plan of God, God will have the final say. Second, God is the God of the "perpetual second chance." Indeed, the returnees came to realize that God forgives the truly repentant.

Closing the Loop

The originally united books of Ezra and Nehemiah continue and complete Chronicles to form the composite set of books that has become widely known as the "Chronicler's History." The Ezra–Nehemiah materials are addressing the same postexilic survival concerns of Chronicles and supporting its same general vision of national reconstruction and covenant renewal. The Ezra–Nehemiah narrative moves this vision forward, not only in a chronological way, but also in a theological way. It does this by supplementing Chronicles' previously noted theological emphasis on the Davidic covenant tradition with renewed stress on the Mosaic covenant tradition, as specifically shown in Ezra's bringing all the people of God together, just as Moses did, so they could hear the reading and teaching of the Instruction scroll, or book of the Torah (Neh 8).

What this shows is how important it is for God's people to be solidly grounded in the full scope of God's covenant heritage, from the old covenant to the new, and to be keenly attentive to both the authenticity of its worship and the authority of the word. God's people are sometimes prone to become divided by embracing one of these to the neglect of the other, with one tradition exalting their form of worship and another championing their faith in the word. Yet the God of all people is at work to bring these covenant foundation stones together as surely as he brought together a priestly teacher of the word named Ezra (who was much like Moses) and an administrative restorer named Nehemiah (who was much like David). And surely the Holy Spirit is still at work across all divisions in our world today, to separate a holy people from the world in order to bring all things and all people together in the light of the coming kingdom of God.

ESTHER

"Yet who knows whether you have come to the kingdom for such a time as this?"
    —*Esther 4:14 (NKJV)*

When I think about the book of Esther,

I am encouraged by the fact that even though we cannot see God working in our lives in the midst of painful experiences and oppression, God is very much active in and through those circumstances. Sometimes I wonder if Paul had the book of Esther in mind when he penned the words, "We know that God works all things together for good for the ones who love God, for those who are called according to his purpose" (Rom 8:28). While we do not find a direct reference to God in Esther, his fingerprints are all over this story, reflecting his work through the lives of Esther and Mordecai to bring about his purposes.

Quick Facts

Title: The title comes from the main character in the book. It is the same in the LXX. In Hebrew it is Hadassah. *Esther* means "star" or "myrtle tree."

Date: The book is set in the reign of Ahasuerus/Xerxes I (485–465 BCE; cf. 1:1), however, the reference to the period after the death of this Persian king in 10:2 would indicate a date after 465 BCE. Scholars have suggested composition dates from the mid-fifth century to the mid-second century BCE. Others note that the lack of Greek influence would suggest a date before 333 BCE. Thus, a date shortly after the events of the book (ca. 450–400 BCE) seems most appropriate.

Authorship: Jewish tradition assigns this book to the Great Synagogue (*Baba Bathra* 15a). Scholars have proposed a number of authors: Mordecai, Ezra, or Nehemiah. The fact of the matter is that we cannot be sure. At best we can agree with the consensus that it was written by a Jew.

Audience and Purpose: The original audience was undoubtedly Jews, who, for whatever reason, did not return to Judah after the exile ended. Some have suggested that Esther was written to validate the new feast of Purim. As part of the five *Megilloth* ("scrolls"), the book is read annually at the feast of Purim—the Jewish festival that is established at the end of the book of Esther to celebrate the Jewish victory therein recounted. Practices associated with this feast have been used to explain the absence of the divine name in the book. According to Jewish tradition, people were expected to get so intoxicated during the feast that they could not tell the difference between the names of Haman and Mordecai—a condition that could lead someone to slander the name of the Almighty.

However, finding the sole purpose of the book in the desire to explain the origin of Purim does not seem credible due to the fact that the feast receives only secondary attention in the book (cf. 3:7; 9:24, 28-32). The purpose of the writing is perhaps best seen as revealing the providential work of God to protect and care for his people wherever they may be located.

Genre: Historical narrative is the genre of the entire book.

Structure

Esther divides into three scenes: Esther's promotion to Queen (1–2); the feud of Haman and Mordecai and the resulting crisis for the Jews (3–8); Jewish victory and the celebration of Purim (9–10).

Summary

Esther's Promotion to Queen: Esther 1–2

In scene 1, Ahasuerus, the king of Persia, celebrates a great feast for more than 180 days, during which time he asks queen Vashti to don her crown and appear before the drunken crowd. She refuses (1:12). Some believe that he was asking her to appear wearing *only* her crown. At the advice of his friends, the king decides to remove Vashti from power. This scene sets the stage for the beauty contest that brings Esther to the throne (2:17). However, her cousin and guardian, Mordecai, who is an important man in the capital city of Susa/Shushan (2:5, 21), will not allow Esther to tell anyone that she is a Jew.

The Feud of Haman and Mordecai and the Resulting Crisis for the Jews: Esther 3–8

Scene 2 covers chapters 3–8, which detail the feud that develops between Haman and Mordecai. This feud actually has roots that go all the way back to 1 Samuel 15, when Mordecai's ancestor Saul tried to destroy all of Haman's people, the Amalekites (cf. Esth 2:5; 3:1). Because Mordecai refuses to bow before Haman, Haman seeks the king's permission to destroy all the Jews (3:6-15). The king grants the permission without realizing that his wife, Esther, falls within the scope of the execution order. The response of Mordecai and the other Jews is to put on sackcloth (a mourning garment) and fast for deliverance. Mordecai then asks Esther to approach the king to try and save her people. Even though going before the king without being summoned could cost Esther her life, she agrees to do so (4:8-16).

After three days of fasting, Esther approaches the king and is received with favor. She requests that Ahasuerus and Haman attend a banquet that day. Once at the banquet, the king asks Esther to disclose her petition. She asks again that he and Haman attend a second banquet the next day, at which time she would reveal her request. Haman is delighted, because he sees it as a sign of his prestige in the kingdom (5:9, 11-12). Nevertheless, Mordecai's refusal to pay him homage enrages him (5:9, 13). Haman's wife and friends suggest that Haman erect a gallows on which to hang Mordecai (5:14).[36] Meanwhile, during the night, the king is unable to sleep and begins reading the records of the court. He comes across an entry noting that Mordecai had thwarted an attempt on the king's life (cf. 6:2-3; 2:21-23). When Haman arrives the next morning, the king asks him how he should honor someone who deserved it. Haman, thinking that the king is referring to him, says that the man should be robed in the king's robe, placed upon the king's horse, and paraded through the square by one of the king's nobles. Much to Haman's chagrin, the king orders *him* to do this for Mordecai. After fulfilling the king's request, Haman goes home enraged. Interestingly, at this point Haman's wife and friends tell him to stop going after Mordecai. Their reason is, because Mordecai is a Jew, Haman would not be able to succeed in his plot (6:13).

During the banquet the next day, Esther reveals to the king that Haman's plan targets her as well as her people to be annihilated (7:3-6). The king leaves the room enraged, but when he returns, he finds Haman lying on Esther's couch, begging for mercy. The king, assuming that Haman is assaulting the queen, orders Haman to be hanged on the gallows Haman had prepared for Mordecai (7:7-10).[37] As just retribution and in an ironic twist, the king gives Esther all of Haman's possessions. The queen in turn installs her cousin Mordecai over Haman's house. Because the laws of the Medes and the Persians are unalterable, Haman's decree to kill the Jews must go forward; however, to offset the decree, the king authorizes Mordecai to send a second letter to all the provinces of the empire stating that the Jews could defend themselves against their enemies, a decree that is greeted with festivities (8:1-17).

Jewish Victory and the Celebration of Purim: Esther 9–10

Scene 3 records the results of the Jewish defense of their lives. On the assigned day the Jews attack their enemies, killing whoever had intended to do them harm. But the Jews do not take any of the plunder, in order to show those of the empire that they are not attacking their enemies for financial gain, but only for the right to exist (cf. 9:10, 15-16; 8:11). As a means of celebrating this victory, the feast of Purim is instituted (9:26-32). Mordecai's promotion to second in the kingdom is noted in the epilogue (10:3).

Debated Issues (aka Great Paper Topics)

1) Do scholars view the book of Esther as history or fiction?

2) What is the history of the feast of Purim?

---

36. The CEB renders this "a pointed pole."

37. In the CEB we read that Haman was "impaled . . . on the very pole that he had set up for Mordecai."

3) How do scholars respond to the fact that Esther is the only book in the Hebrew Scriptures unattested so far among the Dead Sea Scrolls discovered at Qumran?

The Message of the Book

God will not tolerate anti-Jewish hostilities. Haman would have been well served to take to heart the words of Prov 26:27, "Those who dig a pit will fall in it; those who roll a stone will have it turn back on them."

Closing the Loop

The book of Esther has characteristics that have tended to make it less important to the Christian tradition than to the Jewish tradition. These include its focus on the crisis of a threatened Jewish genocide and its culminating attention to the establishment of the Jewish festival of Purim, which has no place in Christian practice and very little place even in Christian awareness. What's more, the book has additional features that have no doubt further muted its interest for the Pentecostal and charismatic streams of Christianity. These include, as in the case of the book of Ruth, the complete lack of any miracles, prophetic experiences, or supernatural revelations. Yet even more than that, there is the oft-mentioned absence in the book of any reference whatsoever to God. These features of the book of Esther tend to make it of marginal interest to traditions that are enthusiastically focused on the manifest presence of God.

Yet perhaps this very set of characteristics is what could and should make the book of Esther especially valuable to these more charismatically oriented tradition streams. Esther well represents those times that invariably come for every community and individual of faith, even charismatic ones, where God's wonders, God's work, God's presence, and even God's name appear nowhere in sight. These are the times of exile when God's people suffer the life-threatening forces of alienation—the absence of home, the presence of marginalization and even persecution, and perhaps worst of all for people of faith, the silence of God. It is precisely in such times that Mordecai's famous words resonate with the most force, "Yet who knows whether you have come to the kingdom for such a time as this?" (4:14 NKJV). It is in "such a time as this" that *the gift of discernment* is most needed, most tested, and most proven. Indeed, it is proven to be a most vital gift of the Spirit.

INTRODUCTION TO THE POETIC BOOKS

The grouping of books traditionally designated as Poetic Books in our Bible are Job, Psalms, Proverbs, Ecclesiastes, and Song of Songs. In the original Hebrew canonical arrangement of the *Tanak*, these five books were distributed among the Writings (*Ketuvim*). Psalms came first in the Writings, followed by Proverbs and then Job, but the Song of Songs and Ecclesiastes were placed in the five-scroll collection called the *Megilloth* (i.e., Song of Songs, Ruth, Lamentations, Ecclesiastes, and Esther). These five books were grouped together to form a series that corresponded to the five major holidays that were practiced in postexilic Judaism (more on that as we come to each of these books). It is not obvious why the Hebrews placed Psalms, Proverbs, and Job at the beginning of the Writings (though it might suggest the prominence of their usage), and it is not clear why the Greek canon (LXX) changed the sequence of this threesome by putting Job before Psalms.

In any case, the canonical grouping called Poetic Books in our Protestant Bible, as inherited from the LXX, highlights the common poetic nature of these writings. They are not the only books of the OT to feature poetry, for so does Lamentations and most of the oracles of the Major and Minor Prophets. Yet the Poetic Books certainly appear to be the writings of Scripture where poetic artistry is most prominently on display.

Ancient Hebrew poetry, in its features and techniques, has much in common with poetry the world over (meter, symbolism, imagery, metaphor, simile, alliteration, etc.) and even more with particular poetic conventions and styles of the surrounding ANE cultures. Hebrew poetry's most prominent feature by far is *parallelism*. Bishop Robert Lowth (1710–1787) drew attention to this long ago. *Parallelism* is the term used to designate consecutive poetic lines (phrases or statements) that parallel one another in some way. A parallelism typically consists of two lines (a bicolon) but can extend to more than two. One could think of a parallelism as a "thought rhyme," which, unlike sound rhyme, has the advantageous quality of being translatable into any language. Scholars have often designated three main types of parallelism: *synonymous* (where the poetic lines express similar thoughts), *antithetic* (where the lines express contrasting thoughts), and *synthetic* (where the subsequent line branches in a new direction). An example of each of these types of parallelism can be found in Proverbs 15:9-11:

Antithetic Parallelism:
The LORD detests the path of the wicked,
> but loves those who pursue righteousness.

Synonymous Parallelism:
Discipline is severe for those who abandon the way;
    those who hate correction will die.

Synthetic Parallelism:
The grave and the underworld lie open before the Lord;
    how much more the hearts of human beings!

Yet this threefold scheme can in no way fully categorize the various and manifold ways that the poetic lines of Hebrew parallelism play off of one another.

Another literary device used often in Hebrew poetry is *chiasm*. The term *chiasm* comes from the Greek letter *chi*, which looks like the letter *X*. Like the shape of this letter, it is a symmetrical pattern, where the structure of the first half of a literary unit is paralleled in inverse order in the second half (i.e., a pattern of A-B-B-A). Psalm 70:5b (ESV) provides a good example of how a chiasm is used to structure a single parallelism:

A   Hasten to me, O God!
  B   You are my help
  B   and [you are] my deliverer;
A   O Lord, do not delay.

Psalm 70 also provides an example of how a chiasm is used to structure an entire psalm:

A   Verse 1: Prayer for God to hurry and help
  B   Verses 2-3: Curse on those "who seek my life"
  B   Verse 4: Blessing on those "who seek you [God]"
A   Verse 5: Prayer for God to hurry and help

A chiasm can involve more than four parts (e.g., A-B-C-D-D-C-B-A), and it can sometimes highlight one central element standing alone at the center (e.g., A-B-C-B-A). What's more, chiastic structures appear often in the patterning of OT prose narrative writings as well as OT poetic writings.

The *acrostic* is another literary device featured prominently in OT poetry. An acrostic is an alphabetic composition where the consecutive lines or sets of lines (stanzas) begin with the consecutive letters of the Hebrew alphabet. Psalm 119 is the most well-known example. Other examples include: Psalms 9–10, 25, 34, 37, 111, 112, 145; Prov 31:10-31 (the poem on the competent wife); and chapters 1–4 of Lamentations.

When we turn our attention to the subject matter of the OT Poetic Books, we find three major categories: *wisdom literature* (Job, Proverbs, and Ecclesiastes), *worship writings* (Psalms), and *love poetry* (Song of Songs, which sometimes is also placed in the wisdom category). Since the upcoming chapters on Psalms and Song of Songs will give adequate opportunity to introduce the latter two categories, our focus here will be on wisdom literature.

All human cultures, from ancient times until today, have their deposits of wisdom that come to expression in wisdom literature—whether it be an inscription on a tomb from antiquity or the latest trending tweet. Thus, ancient Israel's wisdom literature is a part of a universal literary discourse that is not unique to Israel but common to peoples of all times and places. In fact, the wisdom tradition has often been understood in terms of "common sense." In the Hebrew tradition, one could say that the wisdom literature teaches people how to share life in common, indeed in community with each other.

Wisdom literature is distinguished by a certain *set of emphases* that come to expression in a particular *set of literary forms*. The characteristic emphases include the following: (1) accent on human observation and investigation rather than divine revelation; (2) focus on creation or nature rather than the events of history; (3) attention to order or recurring patterns of life rather than novel or unique events; (4) emphasis on universal truth rather than particularities; and (5) stress on individual experience and responsibility rather than corporate life. Every one of these emphases can at times be found outside the orbit of wisdom, but when we see them all aligning together in a unified constellation, then we are definitely in the domain of the wisdom tradition.

As regards wisdom's distinguishing literary forms, the most prominent of these by far is the *proverb* or *aphorism*. Also identified by such terms as *maxim* or *wise saying*, it is the wisdom form that is found most universally—from ancient Chinese proverbs to the latest bumper sticker. One popular definition of a proverb (itself proverbial!) is "a short sentence based on long experience" (Miguel de Cervantes). Another memorable definition calls the proverb "the wisdom of many and the wit of one" (Lord John Russell). A more formal definition would be: a pithy, poetic statement that reflects the order of the world and human experience by capturing an instance of it in a memorable turn of phrase. A proverb, if it is to work, must "ring true" at once, without having to be explained. Obviously, the book of Proverbs features an extensive collection of wisdom literature cast in this literary form. Such lists of proverbs have also been found in the archaeological remains of other ANE nations, especially Egypt.

The wisdom *dialogue* or *debate* is another important wisdom literary form. The book of Job is, of course, the prime biblical example. This form is particularly suited to exploring the major philosophical questions of the meaning of human life, divine justice, innocent suffering, and the like. Israel's ANE neighbors also utilized this form, especially in Mesopotamia. Scholars often characterize such texts as "speculative wisdom" in contrast to the "practical wisdom" that tends to dominate in proverb collections.

The *numerical saying* represents another common ANE wisdom form. It consists in identifying a prescribed number of items that fall in a specified category, using a numerical pattern of "x, x+1," as illustrated in Prov 30:18-19:

Three things are too wonderful for me,
four that I can't figure out:
the way of an eagle in the sky,
the way of a snake on the rock,
the way of a ship out on the open sea,
and the way of a man with a young woman.

Several examples of this form are featured in Proverbs 30 (see also Prov 6:16-19). The form invites pondering the parallels and connections between things universally observed in human experience.

The *onomasticon* is another common form used in ANE wisdom literature. It consists in the mere listing of things found in nature that belong to a given category, such as a listing of plants or animals. Some believe that 1 Kgs 4:33 indicates Solomon's use of this wisdom form and that God's speech in Job 38–41 may have been patterned after an onomasticon.

One last wisdom form worth noting is the *autobiographical saying*. Here a sage, speaking in first person, describes some personal experience that is put forward as a representative observation about the way things are in universal human experience. This form, which can be as brief as a single verse (e.g., Eccl 10:7), can also be developed as an extended monologue, such as what appears in the book of Ecclesiastes, particularly in the first two chapters. Like the dialogue, this extended monologue form of the autobiographical saying lends itself to probing the deep questions of human existence, such as we see in Ecclesiastes and in a number of Mesopotamian wisdom texts.

In the same way that David is the leading figure of Israel's worship writings, Solomon is the leading figure of the OT wisdom literature, as shown in the way his name and voice have marked the books of Proverbs and Ecclesiastes (as well as Song of Songs). The story of Solomon in 1 Kings (cf. chs. 3, 4, and 10) provides the background for this king's surpassing gift of wisdom. Yet the failures that mark the end of Solomon's story (cf. 1 Kgs 11) could no doubt be seen to register a warning that, although human wisdom is affirmed as a good gift that ultimately comes from God, it is not by itself the ultimate source of life. Wisdom has its limits. This truth is also powerfully registered in how both Ecclesiastes and Job, each in its own way, point up the limits of human wisdom.

The Poetic Books are significant in the way they give powerful affirmation to poetry as a medium of revelation. The way they appropriate and celebrate the poetic art is a testimony to the innate human need and drive to reach for poetry when trying to give expression to the deepest and most searching and elusive matters of the soul, such as the search for meaning in the face of suffering (Job) and mortality (Ecclesiastes); or the worship of God amid the full range of human experience (Psalms); or the ways and wonders of human erotic love (Song of Songs). And if we indeed are poetic beings in our very nature, it is because we bear the image of a God of poetry and song—a God who is both a singer (Zeph 3:17) and a songwriter (Deut 31:19 KJV). Accordingly, we are called not only to know and to do God's word but also to delight in it.[38]

No doubt one of Pentecostalism's greatest contributions to Christendom has been the freedom, exuberance, and passion of its poetic art as expressed through music.[39] In this light, we will now take a closer look at each of the Poetic Books. So, as we turn our eyes to the content, let's open our ears and our hearts to the music.

---

38. Ps 1:2 KJV; see Lee Roy Martin, "Delighting in the Torah: The Affective Dimension of Psalm 1," *Old Testament Essays* 23, no. 3 (2010): 707–27.

39. Harvey Cox, *Fire from Heaven: The Rise of Pentecostal Spirituality and the Reshaping of Religion in the Twenty-First Century* (Reading, MA: Addison-Wesley, 1995), 139–57.

JOB

My ears had heard about you, but now my eyes have seen you.
—Job 42:5

When I think about the book of Job,

I am reminded of the unexpected deaths of my mother, father, and best friend, Sandie. I was in my third year of college when my father passed away at 70 due to a stroke. I was finishing my PhD when my friend Sandie died at 37 from ovarian cancer. My mom passed away from cancer at 80 when I was in the middle of my third year of full-time teaching. These deaths of people close to me were difficult times in my life. I did not understand why my father had to die the same year he retired. After working for almost 60 years, and after becoming a Christian at age 60, my dad and mom would have had at least ten to 15 good years to enjoy retirement. My friend Sandie had her entire life ahead of her, and felt called to minister to children in the inner city. My mom had been healthy her entire life and had dedicated herself to her family of eight, her husband, and the church, yet she died a slow death. Some may immediately say, "Why?" Why would a good God allow what appears to be such unfairness? In moments like these, many Christians take refuge in the book of Job. Indeed, Job does address what a believer's response should be when bad things happen to "good" people. Two verses from the book of Job have helped me through these dark valleys. First, one night while I was praying during my first year of Bible school, I read Job 13:15a, which says, "Though he slay me, yet will I trust in him" (KJV). In that moment this verse came alive to me, and I dedicated myself to that reality; regardless of what came my way, I would trust in God. Little did I know exactly how that would unfold. The second verse, 42:5, is Job's response to seeing the theophany of God: "My ears had heard about you, but now my eyes have seen you." Job's reply is a poignant reminder that his book is not so much about suffering but rather relationship. Before Job's trials he had "heard" about God and served him based on that limited knowledge; however, when he had a personal encounter with God (i.e., he "saw" God), his perspective changed. Much like many believers' experience, we serve God because of what we have heard, perhaps from our parents or grandparents. But it is only when we have an experience with God for our-selves—that is, we "see" God—that we will truly appreciate God's working in our lives whether good or bad. Indeed, that type of relationship will cause one to say, "Though you slay me, yet will I trust in you!"

Quick Facts

Title: The title comes from the main character in the book. It is the same in both the Hebrew and the LXX. Job means "hated"/"oppressed."

Date: The book of Job has both a date for the setting and for its writing. While the book seems to be set within the ancestral era (ca. 2000–1500 BCE), the date for its writing is much debated. Jewish tradition views it as one of the oldest books in the Bible, dating it as early as the 15th century BCE. Others suggest that the book should be assigned to the Solomonic era because of its wisdom themes. Still others propose an exilic date based on similar literature from Babylon, such as the *Righteous Sufferer*, often labeled the "Babylonian Job." What is certain is that the discovery of the Targum of Job (11QtgJob) at Qumran precludes a date after the second century BCE.

Authorship: Jewish tradition assigns this book to Moses (*Baba Bathra* 14b), as did some of the church fathers (Origen, Jerome, et al.). Today few follow this attribution, choosing rather to assign it to an unknown author(s) in the exilic or postexilic period. For a long time scholars also challenged the book's unity, arguing that some of the poetic sections were written first (chs. 3–27; 29–31) with chapters 28 and 32–41 being added by another author(s), and the prologue and epilogue being added later still by the final author. This theory has been challenged based on the logical need for the prologue to introduce the main reason for Job's suffering as well as the main characters. Also, the epilogue serves to bring the entire book to a resolution.

Audience and Purpose: If one follows the Jewish tradition, then Moses would be seen as writing the book of Job sometime during his sojourn in Midian (ca. 1486–1446 BCE), possibly receiving his information about Job (probably a non-Israelite) from Elihu, while living in this region, which is close to Uz (cf. Job 1:1). The book could have served as an encouragement to the Israelites living under Egyptian bondage: trust God in the midst of your suffering; he will deliver you in the end. Those who posit an exilic date suggest that it served as a parable of Israel's suffering in exile. This latter theory does not really fit the facts of Israel's exile. Israel was in exile because of the sin they had committed; Job was innocent in his suffering. Moreover, if Uz is in the region of Edom, an Edomite hero such as Job would be unlikely to appeal to Israel during this time, given Edom's ill treatment of Israel leading up to the exile (see the book of Obadiah). As a theodicy, the book may have served simply to show humanity's limitation in knowing the ways of the Divine.

Genre: Job contains a mixture of prose and poetry. The narrative prologue (chs. 1–2) and epilogue (42:7-17) form a literary frame, or *inclusio*, for the book. The body of the book unfolds like proceedings in a courtroom setting; Job's friends put him on trial, whereas Job puts God on trial (chs. 4–27). We also find a lament (ch. 3), dialogues (4–27), a wisdom poem (ch. 28), monologues (chs. 29–37), and a theophany (38:1–42:8).

Structure

In many ways, the structure of Job follows the genre forms in the previous section. The book can be divided into seven parts: prologue (1–2); Job's lament (3); the dialogue of Job and his three friends (4–27); a wisdom interlude (28); the monologues of Job, Elihu, and God (29–41); Job's response (42:1-6); and the epilogue (42:7-17).

Summary

Prologue: Job 1–2

The book opens by introducing the reader to Job. He is from the land of Uz (1:1), the exact location of which no one knows for certain. Some suggest it is in ancient Syria (cf. Gen 10:23; 22:21) while most point to northwest Arabia in the region of Edom (cf. Lam 4:21). The ancestral period is indicated by the following factors: Job's wealth is measured in livestock; like the patriarchs, Job offers sacrifices (1:3-5; cf. Gen 12:7-8; 13:18; 26:25; 31:54; 33:20; 46:1); and Job lives to be 140 years old (42:16; cf. Gen 25:7; 35:28). Similar to Noah, Job is introduced as a man of absolute integrity (cf. 1:1, 8; 2:3; Gen 6:9). Verse 6 pivots from an introduction of Job to the conversation between God and Satan. The appearance of Satan ("adversary") with "the sons of God" (KJV; cf. 38:7 KJV; Gen 6:4 KJV) places the meeting in heaven (1:6-12). Some argue that God is capricious toward Job when he allows Satan to attack him, even though Satan is prohibited from touching Job's physical body. What seems to be most important here is that God trusts Job's integrity and character (2:3). Satan brings calamity from the four points of the compass by alternating between human invaders and natural calamities: from the south the Sabeans attack; from the west, the normal direction of thunderstorms, fire falls; Chaldean raiders swoop down from the north; and a sirocco storm wind from the desert to the east completes the devastation of Job's wealth and family (1:13-19).

Thwarted in his attempt to cause Job to curse God, Satan again comes before God. In almost a taunting fashion, God again asks Satan to "consider" his servant Job, who is blameless and upright (2:3 RSV). Satan's response is to ask God to allow him to afflict Job's body. Clearly, Satan is betting that Job worships God because of the blessings God has given him, including good health. God grants

The Nabatean remains at Petra, the ancient homeland of the Edomites. Job is believed to have been connected to the line of Esau/Edom. Photo courtesy of Steve Rudd.

Satan permission to afflict Job's body but not to kill him. At this point Job's wife is introduced. She tells Job to curse God and die. Job's response is to upbraid her for speaking as a foolish person (2:10). A key mark of a wise person in the wisdom tradition was prudent speaking; did one's speech show wisdom? On this score, the narrative points out that Job does not blame God or sin with his lips (1:22; 2:10). The prologue ends by introducing the three "comforters" of Job: Eliphaz, Bildad, and Zophar (2:11). These three along with Job are featured in the dialogues of chapters 4–27. As they approach Job, they are shocked by his physical state. As was typical of mourning in the ancient world, they tear their garments and throw dust on their heads. Out of respect for Job, they do not speak for seven days (2:11-13).

Before leaving this portion of the discussion, it is important to note that the question of the historicity of Job is often raised. It is generally reasoned that the heavenly discussions between God and Satan would be unknowable, and that surely one person could never experience such calamity. To be sure, the book of Job is written in a highly stylized fashion. However, this does not preclude the possibility that Job did in fact exist or that he could have experienced such great loss. Both the prophet Ezekiel and James acknowledge the existence of a man named Job (Ezek 14:14, 20; Jas 5:11). As for the heavenly conversation between Satan and God, the prophet Micaiah had a vision of the divine council conversing about the fate of Ahab (1 Kgs 22:19-23), as did Zechariah concerning Joshua the high priest (Zech 3:1-10). Finally, would any of us deny that people in our own time have experienced Job-like sufferings? In this light, there appears no reason to deny the possibility that the book of Job is based on actual historical events.

Job's Lament: Job 3

In what appears to be a stark contrast to Job's response to suffering in chapters 1 and 2, Job's lament in chapter 3 has caused some scholars to posit another author at work. Yet others have read this lament as showing the development of Job's response and the surfacing of his human side. In the midst of his pain and sorrow, Job wishes he had never been born (cf. 10:18-19). Again, as is typical of the wise man, Job does not curse God, nor does he curse his parents for his birth (cf. Lev 20:9; Prov 20:20). Instead he curses the *day* of his birth. Interestingly, the godly prophet Jeremiah also cursed the day of his birth in the midst of his affliction (Jer 20:14-18).

The Dialogue of Job and His Three Friends: Job 4–27

There are three dialogic sequences in these chapters that follow a similar pattern (chs. 4–14; 15–21; 22–27). Eliphaz (chs. 4–5; 15; 22), Bildad (chs. 8; 18; 25), and Zophar (chs. 11; 21) all speak in turn, followed each time by Job's responses (chs. 6–7; 9–10; 12–14; 16–17; 19; 21; 23; 26–27). Several scholars argue that the brevity of the third sequence of dialogues for Bildad and the absence of a third speech from Zophar show that material has been lost from the text. As such, scholars have suggested a number of emendations or rearrangements of the text. However, it is possible, as some have argued, that the third dialogue sequence has been shortened for rhetorical import, specifically to show the dialogue breaking down due to the tension and frustration of the participants.

The basic content of the speech rounds exhibits an increasing level of hostility between Job and his "comforters" as Eliphaz, Bildad, and Zophar attempt to pinpoint the cause of Job's suffering. Indeed, the first dialogue sequence is more friendly than the second (cf. 4:1-9; 8:1-7; 11:1-6; 15:1-6; 16:1-5, 20; 17:2, 10; 18:1-4; 19:1-6, 28-29; 20:1-5; 21:1-3, 34), and the third is more abrasive than the first two (cf. 22:1-11; 25:1-6; 26:1-4; 27:12). Characteristic of the increased harshness of his friends' accusations, Bildad even suggests that Job's children died because of sin (8:4). Job's friends embraced the ancient Near Eastern belief in divine justice and retribution, the idea that someone would invariably reap punishment for doing evil and blessing for doing good (e.g., 4:7-9; 8:20; 11:20; 15:20; 18:1-21; 20:6-29; 21:28; 22:8; 27:13-23; cf. Prov 13:21). This is the dogma that appears to be in the minds of Jesus's disciples when they asked about the man born blind in John 9. In this case, Jesus set the record straight by pointing out that neither the man nor his parents had sinned but rather this was all part of the greater plan of God to heal the blind man. Similarly, in Job the reader has already been made aware that Job's suffering is for a purpose having nothing to do with retributive punishment. Of course, Job and his three friends are not privy to this information.

Job's friends encourage Job to repent of his sins (5:8-16; 8:5-7; 11:13-19; 22:1-30), noting that he should be happy that God is reproving him before he gets too far off course (5:17; 8:19-22). Job's response is defiant, because he knows he is innocent (6:10, 22-24, 29-30; 9:20-21; 10:7; 16:17; 23:11-12; 27:1-6). Moreover, Job knows that his friends' perspective about the evil person being punished is the normal expectation according to wisdom thinking (9:2; 12:3, 9; 13:2, 13). However, his situation does not fall under the normal category, he insists, because he is innocent. He also asks his friends to stop adding to his pain by their unfair words (13:4-5), but rather to pity him (19:21-22). Also of importance is the fact that, unlike his three friends, Job consistently directs most of his complaints toward God (7:11-21; 10:2-22; 13:20-28; 14:13-22; 16:6-17).

Throughout the dialogue cycles a number of themes serve as unifying features. These include: the sovereignty of God (e.g., 12:13-25); court language (9:32; 16:21; 23:4-7); the notations on death and *Sheol*, the Hebrew term for the underworld and/or grave (see 7:9, 21; 10:21-22; 14:7-12; 17:13-16); the brevity of life (7:7-10; 9:25-26; 10:20; 14:1-2; 16:22); and how the wicked seem to prosper (21:7-26; 24:1-25). Also, cosmological (22:14; 26:11-12; 38:4-11) and creation motifs (9:5-10; 26:5-14; 28:23-27; 36:27-30; 37:1-13; 38–39) serve to link the dialogues with the monologue section.

Wisdom Interlude: Job 28

Chapter 28 presents a poem about wisdom that serves the dual function of ending the dialogues between Job and his three friends and transitioning to the three monologues that follow. Here Job points out how wisdom is precious and hard to attain. Job uses the analogy of mining for precious stones and metals in the bowels of the earth (28:1-11) to show that, even though this is difficult, they are nonetheless attainable by people. However, none of this wealth can purchase wisdom (28:12-19). Only God can give true wisdom, which begins with the fear of the Lord (28:28)—a point similarly sounded in the introduction of Proverbs (1:7).

The Monologues of Job, Elihu, and God: Job 29–41

The first monologue in chapters 29–31 is from Job, who begins by reminiscing about the way things were before his affliction. He had God's blessing (29:2-3, 6), his children were close to him (29:5), he sought justice in the city gate (29:7-20), and his counsel was heeded by those who heard him (29:21-25). He in turn takes these recollections and juxtaposes them to his present state of humiliation. The young and those who were previously restrained by his justice now mock him (30:1-15), his body is racked with sickness (30:16-23, 30), and his call for justice in no longer heard (30:25). Despite the pain, however, Job maintains his integrity in the face of the opposition. Against his friends' accusations, he claims that he has not looked lustfully on any virgin or another man's wife (31:1, 9-12); he has treated his servants justly (31:13-15); he has cared for the poor, widow, and orphan (31:16-23; cf. Exod 22:22; Deut 10:18; 27:19; Isa 1:17; Jer 7:6; 22:3; Zech 7:10); he has not trusted in his riches (31:24-28); he has not prayed for the destruction of his enemies (31:29-30); and he has cared for the foreigner (31:31-32). With this oath of innocence, Job ends his defense.

In chapters 32–37, a new character appears for the first time. Apparently during the entire dialogue sequence, a younger man by the name of Elihu sat listening to the interactions (32:11-12; 33:8). Following ANE protocols, Elihu had waited for his elders to finish speaking (32:4), but at this juncture he can wait no longer (32:18-20). He is angered by the comments of Job and his three friends (32:2-3, 5). Elihu begins by challenging Job (33:5, 31-33), and then he defends God's right either to speak or to remain silent in the midst of a person's troubled life (34:10-29). Elihu even declares that Job had indeed sinned, because of his attitude of rebellion toward God (34:34–35:16). Elihu continues by affirming that God is just and God will vindicate in his good time (36:5-16), for there is none like the sovereign God (36:22-26; 37:1-13, 21-24). Finally, Elihu challenges Job to answer his questions concerning the cosmological wonders of God's creation (37:14-20).

These questions could be viewed as a segue into the monologue of God in chapters 38–41. God appears in a theophany in the midst of a whirlwind and begins by asking Job 70 questions concerning creation and the functioning of the earth and cosmos (38:4-38). God next narrows his questions to the animal kingdom, perhaps in a move to lighten up on Job by asking "easier" questions (38:39–39:30). In a brief interlude, Job acknowledges his insignificance in the face of the Almighty (40:3-5). God then upbraids Job for attempting to "annul" the judgment of God so that he may be justified before the Almighty (40:8 NASB). Next, God narrows his focus even further by asking Job about two great creatures of the earth, the identities of which are not altogether clear to modern scholars: Behemoth (the hippopotamus?) and Leviathan (the whale?) (40:15–41:34). God asks Job if he can tame the former or catch the latter with a hook (40:24; 41:1).

Job's Response: Job 42:1-6

Job gives the only response that one can give when confronted by the Almighty—awe and repentance (42:6). Job's "knowledge" is nothing before God. Indeed, as we noted in the introduction, Job thought he knew God, but now that he has seen God, his relationship and knowledge of God have been transformed.

Here many of the loose ends of the foregoing dialogues and prologue are tied together. First, God chastises Job's three friends for not speaking correctly with respect to God as compared to Job (42:7). God directs them to offer a sacrifice and have Job pray for them (42:8-9). God then restores Job's wealth and gives him twice as much livestock as he had before (42:10-12). Job is also given seven more children and enough wealth to give an inheritance even to his daughters (42:15). Finally, the reader is told that Job lived to be 140 years old.

Several questions still linger as the reader comes to the end of Job. First, was Elihu correct in his assessment of Job and God? Second, if Job's response to God, in contrast to his three friends' response to God, was "correct" (42:7), why did God challenge Job so severely in his monologue? And three, why did God fail to answer any of Job's questions? These questions and perhaps more serve to prompt and to provoke us to struggle (not unlike Job!) over the message of the book (see below).

Debated Issues (aka Great Paper Topics)

1) Based on Satan's attack of Job in chapter 1, can we attribute certain calamities in our lives to the work of Satan?

2) How do scholars interpret 19:25-27?

3) What are some alternate understandings of "Leviathan" in 41:1?

4) What do scholars feel is the reason for God not passing judgment on Elihu (42:7)?

The Message of the Book

Because we live in a fallen world, suffering is a universal part of the human experience. When suffering comes, it is important to acknowledge that God's sovereign plan is greater than we can ever know or fathom. The message of Job finally appears to have less to do with answering the question "why do we suffer?" than posing the question "how will we suffer?" Surely we are most blessed to have Job as an example.

Closing the Loop

Job has become a timeless example of innocent suffering. His friends were inclined to turn his experience of suffering into a theological discussion and debate. Much modern interpretation of Job has approached the book in this same way—as a theological exposition on the problem of suffering. What tends to get overlooked in all this, both by Job's ancient friends and his modern interpreters, is that Job's primary concern is not to theologize but *to pray*, in other words, not just to talk *about God* but to talk *to God*. Again and again throughout the debate section, Job, unlike his friends, keeps pushing past the dialogue with them to speak directly to God (see instances in chs. 7, 9, 10, 13, 14, 16, and 17). Job even vigorously implores God for a direct audience with him (10:2; 13:22; cf. 30:20-23) and culminates his monologue with an urgent expression of this wish (31:35-40).

Job is keen on *speaking directly to God* in still another way. Throughout the book he dares to speak to God with bold, contentious, and confrontational directness, even going so far as to express his wish to put God on trial (cf. 9:3; 13:3, 18-24; 23:2-7). Job's friends rebuke him for this way of speaking (e.g., 8:2-3; 15:12-13). However, in the final judgment expressed by God at the end of the book, Job's way of speaking is declared "right," while their way is condemned as "not . . . right" (42:7-8 KJV). What's more, this final statement of God appears to be drawing particular attention to how Job had spoken, so God says, "*to* me" rather than just "*about* me," for the Hebrew preposition used here (*el*), while having "about" as a possible secondary meaning, has "to" as its primary meaning, as every first-year Hebrew student learns. Although most modern translations of this verse assume the secondary meaning of the preposition (The Lexham English Bible is an exception), could it be that, like Job's friends, they are too prone, here again, to see the main issue of Job as talking "about" God rather than talking "to" God?

Yet throughout the book, Job talks to God. He talks to God directly by going over the heads of his friends, and he talks to God directly also in the sense of being boldly confrontational. In the end God confronts Job, but at least God thinks enough of Job's words to pay him a visit, and a lengthy visit at that. What's more, God finally commends Job to his friends for speaking "right" (KJV)—and in light of the simple, primary meaning of the Hebrew preposition, we can see God affirming Job more specifically for "speaking right *to me*." This shifts the focus from theology to prayer. No wonder God immediately follows this affirmation of Job with the demand that Job's friends go directly to Job so he can pray for them (42:8), for the issue, here again, is primarily and finally about prayer.

Thus, Job not only offers a timeless example of innocent suffering; Job provides one of Scripture's greatest examples of prevailing prayer—what has long been known in Pentecostal circles as "praying through." This is prayer that entails struggling—indeed, wrestling with God—as Jacob did when he wrestled all night and gained his new name, Israel—a name that literally means "he wrestles/prevails with God" (Gen 32:24-31). This is not just polite, polished prayer, but it is raw, risky, and gutsy, so much so that it can be provocative and, as in Job's case, even offensive to the theological platitudes and protocols of others. Yet Job stands as a lasting testament to God's willingness to host, to engage, and finally to affirm this kind of prayer—prayer that might very well leave one walking away with a limp, as Jacob did, but nevertheless knowing, honest before God, like Job (42:1-6), the unspeakable blessing of "praying through."

PSALMS

Let everything that has breath praise the LORD! Praise the LORD!
  —Psalm 150:6 (ESV)

When I think about the book of Psalms,

the 1998 movie *Saving Private Ryan*, starring Tom Hanks, comes to mind. This might seem strange, given the fact that the Psalms are about prayers and songs to God, whereas the movie is about events connected to the World War II D-Day invasion and its aftermath. Few readers of the Psalms realize that some of the psalms were actually written for a context of war (e.g., Ps 144). In the movie, one character in particular, Private Daniel Jackson (played by Barry Pepper—a fellow Canadian, I might add) is marked by his frequent practice of quoting the Bible. However, these are not just random quotations, but rather, he quotes the Psalms in the midst of intense battle scenes. On three such occasions, Jackson quotes from Psalms 22, 25, and 144. Jackson's quotations are actually his prayers to God for help. In essence, that is what many of the Psalms are; they are prayers to God from a variety of people and from a variety of circumstances in life. When we read the Psalms, it is as though we are standing behind the author and looking over his or her shoulder and reading or listening to the psalmist's prayer to God in a moment of grief, inner turmoil, praise, thanksgiving, and so forth. This is no doubt why the Psalms are so timeless. While we may not use the exact same words as the ancient authors used, we certainly have the same emotional spectrum that is displayed in the Psalms. As demonstrated by Private Jackson's character, this is why many people in times of distress or anguish turn to the Psalms and allow them to speak to God for them. For indeed the Psalms not only "speak to us"; they also "speak for us."

Quick Facts

Title: The English title comes from the LXX title *Psalmoi/Psalter*, a term of music (i.e., songs or hymns). In Hebrew the title is *Tehillim*, meaning "praises."

Date: There are two issues in play when dating the Psalms: the date for the writing of individual psalms and the date of their final compilation as a book. When dealing with the former, dates for individual psalms range from the period of Moses (cf. Ps 90) to the postexilic period (cf. Ps 126). As regards the compiling of individual psalms into a book, this is likely to have started in the period beginning with the reign of David in the 11th to 10th centuries BCE. Because the book of Psalms is a collection of individual psalms that grew over a long time, the book likely looked different at various junctures in Israel's history. Support for this is indicated by the different Psalms collections found in the LXX and at Qumran (e.g., 11QPs^a). The LXX adds a psalm (viz., 151, which the authors of the LXX note is "outside of the number" of the 150) and reorders several others (the LXX joins Pss 9 and 10 and 114 and 115, while splitting Pss 116 and 147). At Qumran additional psalms are attested (e.g., two psalms that appear to be Hebrew counterparts to the two halves of LXX Ps 151). The final form of the book of Psalms that has come down to us is divided into five sections, or "books." Most scholars agree that Books 1–3 of the Psalms were the first to form, and that Books 4 and 5 remained in flux well into the late Intertestamental Period. The final form of Psalms found in English Bibles today was probably fixed at some point between the first century BCE and the first century CE.

Authorship: Jewish tradition assigns the Psalms to David, but sees David incorporating the work of many others, including Adam, Melchizedek, Abraham, Moses, Heman, Yeduthun, Asaph, and the three sons of Korah (*Baba Bathra* 14b–15a). Whenever the NT authors quote the Psalms, they connect them to David (Matt 22:41-45; Mark 12:35-37; Luke 20:42; Acts 1:16; 2:25; 4:25; 13:34-35; Rom 4:6-8; 11:9-10; Heb 4:7). This probably flowed from the assumption that David wrote most of them, although not necessarily all of them. The Hebrew Bible attributes as many as 73 psalms (cf. 2 Sam 23:1-2; Amos 6:5) to David, and the LXX assigns an additional ten to him (e.g., Pss 91–99). The psalm headings in the Hebrew Bible as well as in our English Bibles indicate a number of people contributing psalms to what is now the final form of our Psalter. These people include Moses (90), Solomon (72; 127), Heman (88), the Korahites or sons of Korah (42–49; 85; 87), Asaph (50; 73–83; cf. 2 Chron 29:30), and Ethan (89). When the psalm heading or superscription names David (e.g., Pss 3:1; 4:1; 5:1; etc.; cf. Hab 3:1) this is not necessarily an indication of authorship, for the Hebrew preposition *l^e* in the phrase "of [*l^e*] David" can also mean: "to," "for," "dedicated to," or "concerning." Even though there is evidence for the antiquity of the superscriptions, as opposed to their being added at a much later date, with such ambiguity in the meaning of the preposition, it is hard to be certain as to the authorship of individual psalms.

Audience and Purpose: The audience in view in the book of Psalms is the Israelite people, spanning a wide range of time periods. The book's original purpose was to serve as a hymnbook of praise and worship for Israel, particularly for worshipping at the temple.

Genre: Psalms is the Bible's most extensive example of poetry. Among the variety of its literary forms, one finds prayers (e.g., 4; 17; 51; 55; 61), laments (e.g., 58; 69), songs (e.g., 8; 30; 45; 46; 48; 65–68), prophecies (messianic promises, e.g., 22; 110), and wisdom sayings (e.g., 1; 34; 37; 119; 127; 128; 133). The form-critical study of the Psalms by OT scholar Hermann Gunkel in the 1920s has helped scholars understand the specific genres or literary forms found in the Psalter. He identified a number of psalm

Classification of the Psalms		
Class	**Basic Characteristics**	**A Few Examples**
Hymns	Songs of praise and thanksgiving	8, 29, 33, 89, 138, 146–150
Penitential	Express sorrow for sin	51
Wisdom	General observations of life	1, 14, 27, 49, 112, 119, 127, 133
Royal	Focus on David as God's chosen king	2, 45, 72, 101, 110
Messianic	Describe the person and ministry of the Messiah	2, 16, 22
Imprecatory (Curse)	Call for judgment on the Psalmist's enemy	35, 58, 69, 109, 137
Laments (Communal and Individual)	Lamentation of one's condition	Individual: 3–5, 7, 9–10, 13–14, 17, 25–26 etc. Communal: 12, 44, 58, 60, 74, 90, 94, 123, 137 etc.

By Brian Peterson

types—a typology that has been added to and/or modified throughout the years by scholars who have taken up Gunkel's approach. Some of the major psalm types are: communal and individual laments (including imprecatory or curse psalms), royal and messianic psalms, communal and individual psalms of thanksgiving and praise, "ascent" or pilgrimage songs, psalms of Zion, and wisdom psalms.

Structure

The book of Psalms, as previously noted, has been divided into five "books": 1–41; 42–72; 73–89; 90–106; 107–150. Most scholars believe this fivefold division of the Psalms was done to correlate scheduled (lectionary) readings from Psalms with readings from the five books of Torah. Each of the first four "books" of the Psalms ends with a doxology, that is, a concluding statement of praise (41:13; 72:20; 89:52; 106:48). Psalms 146–150 (and especially Ps 150) are often seen as a doxology for the entire book, what some have viewed as a virtual "Hallelujah Chorus." Also of interest is the fact that the editors of Books 1, 4, and 5 prefer using the divine name YHWH, (Yahweh), usually translated "Lord," whereas many of the Psalms in Book 2 use Elohim/God. Book 3 shows a mixture in this regard. Some psalms are repeated in two different books. The best example of this is Psalms 14 and 53. The former, appearing in Book 1, uses the divine name YHWH, whereas the latter, appearing in Book 2, uses Elohim/God. Other instances of repeated psalms include: Ps 40:14-18 = Ps 70; Ps 31:2-4a = 71:1-3; and Ps 108, which combines Pss 57:8-12 and 60:7-14.

151

Summary

Given the sheer number of the psalms, this summary will not attempt to address each psalm individually. This discussion will instead focus on a few of the prominent topics related to the ordering and unique features of the Psalms and certain psalm types.

Psalms 1 and 2 as an Introduction

Wisdom psalms and messianic or enthronement psalms play an important role in the Psalter. The first two psalms in the Psalter actually fall into these categories. Psalm 1, a wisdom psalm, serves as the introduction to Book 1 (chs. 1–41) of the Psalms and perhaps should even be seen as an introduction to the entire Psalter. The message contained in Psalm 1 is that the wise person meditates on the law (or teaching) of God and does not associate with scoffers and sinners. Indeed, the righteous will prosper (1:3) but the wicked will perish (1:4-5). In essence the "door" to the Psalms is to be entered through meditating on the law of God. Some also see Psalm 2 as serving as a second half to that doorway for "entering into" reading the Psalms. Psalm 2 is an enthronement psalm that can be interpreted with messianic expectations. Verse 7 promotes this idea when God says, "You are my Son; today I have begotten you" (ESV; cf. Acts 13:33; Heb 1:5; 5:5; Luke 9:35). Following this, a choice is given—a choice either to accept the Lord's anointed King or to reject him and face the consequences (Ps 2:12; cf. Acts 4:25-27). Interestingly, and in line with some ancient Psalms manuscripts, it is possible that Psalms 1 and 2 may originally have been one psalm, framed by the *inclusio* phrase, "how blessed . . ." found in Pss 1:1 and 2:12 (NASB, both). Thus, an introductory blessing is held forth for those who practice true wisdom and offer true praise by studying God's law and honoring God's King.

The Unity of the Psalms

Gerald Wilson, in his book, *The Editing of the Hebrew Psalter*, has developed a holistic approach to the Psalter whereby he argues that Books 1–3 focus on the kingship and covenant of David. Solomon's words in Psalm 72 at the end of Book 2 serve as an appropriate means to highlight the rule of Solomon, the promised offspring foretold in the Davidic covenant (cf. 2 Sam 7:12-16). When this covenant was broken and the historical Davidic kingship came to an end with the exile in 586 BCE, the compilers of the Psalter, according to Wilson, used Books 4–5 to address this dilemma. Moses's words at the beginning of Book 4 in Psalm 90 point back to a time before Israel's monarchy when YHWH was the sole king and leader of Israel (90:1). The theme of punishment within Psalm 90 can be seen to point forward to the hardships of the exile (90:7-9). In the context of exile, YHWH once again became Israel's true King and refuge who would lead and protect the nation. In accord with this context, many of the psalms in the final two books appear to have been written during the exilic and postexilic periods. What's more, the pilgrimage songs, or psalms of ascent (Pss 120–134) in Book 5 were appropriate songs to sing as the returnees came from

Babylon and ascended the slopes to Jerusalem and climbed on up to the temple mount. Finally, we come to the concluding cluster of Hallelujah Psalms (Pss 146–150)—each of which begins and ends with "Praise the Lord!"—thus placing culminating focus on YHWH, the only king worthy of all praise.

One scholar has suggested that the Psalter as a whole represents something like a "literary sanctuary."[40] It is to be entered only by the righteous who delight in God's law (so Ps 1) and who then can meet and bow down to God and his Messiah (so Ps 2). Then all of the following psalms comprise the songs and prayers, the laments and praises that lead up to the final crescendo of praise in Psalms 146–150, before exiting the sanctuary.

Historical Context of the Psalms

Many of the psalms appear to have been rooted in actual historical circumstances that birthed the psalmist's cries of anguish, forgiveness, and praise. A number of events in David's story can easily be correlated with the content of particular psalms, and indeed some of the psalm superscriptions that have come down to us have made these historical connections. A prime example is the prayer for forgiveness in Psalm 51, which has a superscription that attributes this prayer to David after his sin with Bathsheba (2 Sam 11). Other examples include Psalm 3//2 Sam 15–18; Psalms 34 and 56//1 Samuel 21:10-15; Psalm 52//1 Sam 22:9-19; Psalm 54//1 Sam 23:19-29; Psalm 57//1 Sam 24:1-22; Psalm 59//1 Samuel 19; Psalm 60//2 Samuel 8; Psalm 63//1 Samuel 22; Psalm 142//1 Sam 22:1. A few psalms "of David" have superscriptions that refer to events in David's life that do not appear in the biblical narratives of David (e.g., Pss 7; 30). In other cases there are psalms from the Psalter that actually reappear in slightly altered forms in the historical books of the Bible (e.g., Ps 18//2 Sam 22). This shows us that the psalms were not written in a vacuum; they were birthed out of human experience.

Messianic Psalms and Prophecy

The messianic Psalms, as they are often called, can be read in the context of prophecy, as indeed they are by NT writers who note ways in which Jesus's life met the expectations of the Messiah as projected in these psalms. While there is no scholarly consensus on the exact list of psalms that belong to this category, the most obvious examples include Psalm 22 with its correspondences to the crucifixion of Jesus (cf. 69:21), and Psalm 110 with its reference to the priest after the order of Melchizedek (Ps 110:4), which the writer of Hebrews sees as referring to Christ (cf. Heb 5–7). There are several other psalm references that NT writers see as pointing to events in Jesus's life: Jesus's zeal for the temple (Ps 69:9//John 2:17); his resurrection (Ps 16:10//Acts 13:35); Jesus's betrayal (Ps 41:9//Luke 22:47-48); Jesus being falsely accused (Ps 35:11//Mark 14:57-58); Jesus praying for his enemies (Ps 109:4//Luke 23:34); and Jesus's rejection (Ps 118:22-23//Matt 21:42; Mark 12:10-11; etc.).

---

40. Tremper Longman III, *Introducing the Old Testament* (Grand Rapids: Zondervan, 2012), 92–93.

The Psalms and Music

As noted earlier, the Psalms are a combination of different genre forms, one of which is hymns/songs. This is evidenced by the appearance of details in the Psalms themselves and in the superscriptions relating to how a psalm is to be sung or musically performed. The ancient musicians used instruments such as the lyre (e.g., Pss 33:2; 43:4; 71:22), flutes/pipes (Pss 5; 150:4), *shofars* (47:5), timbrels (81:2 KJV), trumpets (98:6), and cymbals (150:5) when singing these psalms before God. Some psalms also followed certain tunes or rhythms (see the headings of Pss 7; 22; 45; 53; 56; 60). The singing and reciting of the Psalms promoted and advanced the spiritual life not only of the ancient Israelites but also of the Jewish community and the church throughout history.

Psalm 119 as Poetry

Every person who has ever attempted to read through the Bible has certainly had the "joy" of reading the longest chapter in the Bible. No one psalm displays the characteristics of Hebrew poetry more than Psalm 119, a wisdom psalm. Even though other psalms display poetic devices, Psalm 119 by its very length allows for a wide range of examples. In this regard, what makes Psalm 119 so long is that it employs a poetic device known as an acrostic, where the lines of text begin with letters that follow the sequence of the Hebrew alphabet. While other psalms employ this same device (e.g., Pss 25; 34; 145), only Psalm 119 has stanzas of eight verses assigned to each letter! Most modern English translations actually note these stanzas (e.g., CEB, NASB). Psalm 119 is also important for its focus on studying the law and allowing it to guide one's path (119:105). Interestingly, Psalm 1, another wisdom psalm, and Psalm 119 begin with the same refrain, "How blessed . . ." (NASB), showing the blessings that flow from learning and following the law. Indeed, wise individuals hide God's Law in their hearts so that they do not sin against him (119:11). So vital is the law of God for one's life that the psalm repeats "thy word" 35 times, the "law" of God 25 times, the "statutes" and "testimonies" of God 22 times each, the "precepts" and "commandments" of God 21 times each, and the "judgments" of God 18 times (KJV all).

The Psalms and ANE Motifs

Another feature of the Psalms is the parallels between select psalms and ANE themes/motifs. Frank Moore Cross, in his book *Canaanite Myth and Hebrew Epic*, addresses this issue at length, especially for the divine warrior motif in Psalms 24 and 132.[41] An even more pronounced parallel is that of Psalm 29 and the Canaanite *Baal Myth*. However, these psalms, rather than imitating or borrowing Baal references, may have been intentionally taking them over to serve the polemical purpose of refuting the lordship of Baal.

---

41. Frank Moore Cross, *Canaanite Myth and Hebrew Epic* (Cambridge, MA: Harvard Press, 1973), 91–111.

Psalms of Lament

This category of psalms is one of the largest in the Psalter, comprising close to half of all the material in the book. It is a broad category of prayer that includes both individual and corporate expressions of negativity—negativity over the full gamut of life's painful and threatening experiences, from the personal to the national level. They give vent to a heavy array of passions, including anger, grief, desperation, despair, guilt, shame, disappointment, and especially complaint. The complaint is often directed against my "enemies" or "adversaries" (e.g., Pss 69; 137), but sometimes against God (e.g., Pss 22; 44; 88).

The sheer volume of laments in the Psalms reveals what an important place they hold in biblical worship. However, the laments have often been ignored or marginalized in the worship of Christian churches, which like to keep to what is upbeat and positive and not linger for long on the negative. Yet the Psalms of lament are shown to have a close and inseparable relationship to praise. This is seen in the way most laments, after pouring out the sorrows of the soul, break through at the end to positive affirmations of faith and expressions of praise (e.g., Pss 13; 22). While this positive turn does not happen in every case (e.g., Pss 88; 137), it has often been noticed that in the book of Psalms as a whole, laments are more prominent near the beginning of the book and praises more prominent near the end. This might be a further indication that in the book of Psalms, lament is a primary pathway to the heights of praise.

Imprecatory Psalms

No one genre in the Psalter creates more problems for the believer than the imprecatory psalms, which are a subcategory of lament psalms. The term *imprecatory* comes from the noun *imprecation*, which means "curse." Many times in these psalms we see the psalmists praying curses upon their enemies. The problem that is immediately evident for the believer is how to use these curse psalms in daily life or in a preaching context in light of Jesus's teaching to pray for one's enemies (Matt 5:44). Jesus's instruction during his Sermon on the Mount appears to teach something diametrically opposed to the message of the imprecatory psalms. Moreover, because these curse psalms are numerous in the Psalter, believers cannot ignore them (e.g., Pss 5; 10; 17; 28; 31; 35; 58; 59; 69; 70; 79; 83; 109; 129; 137; 140). Scholars and laypeople alike have struggled with how to use these texts. Some have suggested that the curses expressed in these psalms reflect evil emotions that should be suppressed or else expressed only in order to relinquish them. Others bifurcate the ethics of the OT and NT, suggesting that we have moved beyond this OT ethic. Yet one must also contend with the teaching of Paul in 2 Tim 3:16 that *all* Scripture is inspired and good for correction and teaching in *righteousness*! While space does not allow for a detailed discussion, some basic guidelines for using these psalms are worth considering.

First, those reading the Psalms are "eavesdropping" on the prayers of the psalmists. As such, much as we pray to God during our own struggles with those who oppress us, the psalmists are directing their prayers to God, not to people—God is the one passing judgment. Second, Jesus's teaching on praying for one's enemies does not preclude the possibility of "cursing" those who are recalcitrant, stand in the way of the progress of the gospel, and in the face of knowing what is good and right, still promote evil (cf. Matt 11:20-24; 21:19; 23:13-39; Mark 11:12-14, 20-21; John 2:17-20; Acts 8:20; 13:10-11; 1 Cor 16:22; Gal 1:8–9; 5:12; 2 Tim 4:14; 2 Peter 2:14; Rev 6:9-11; 14:19-20; 18:4-8, 20; 19:1-3, 15). Third, when Jesus says "You have heard that it was said, *You must love your neighbor and hate your enemy*" (Matt 5:43), Jesus was making a counterpoint against the teaching of his era (e.g., at Qumran 1QS 10:20-21 and Sirach 12:4-7), not against the general OT teaching (cf. Matt 5:17-18). Actually, in several places the OT law parallels Jesus's point (cf. Exod 23:4-5; Lev 19:18, 34). Fourth, the language of the imprecatory psalms, like that of the curse statements of the Mosaic covenant, is rooted in ANE curse language—a discourse that is foreign to us. What was done against an Israelite was done against YHWH. As such, for the Israelite, YHWH must act and repay equally. Finally, the imprecatory psalms are prayers that are offered to God in moments of distress and should be used as a last resort against one's enemies. When all the avenues of reconciliation and peace have been exhausted, these prayers allow the believer to hand their bitter emotions over to God, who is the righteous Judge.

Debated Issues (aka Great Paper Topics)

1) How do scholars reconcile the differing perspectives presented in Psalm 34 and 1 Sam 21:10-15?

2) How do scholars address the canonical status of Psalm 151, which is found in the LXX?

The Message of the Book

The life of God's people is marked by the study of God's law and the offering of worship to God through praises, songs, prayers, thanksgivings, and even laments. As God's creatures, we are to follow the psalmist's command to "let everything that has breath praise the LORD" (Ps 150:6 NASB).

Closing the Loop

Worship is Pentecostalism's most pronounced and prominently recognized area of distinction. The emotional intensity of Pentecostal worship has long caused many onlookers, both inside and outside Christianity, to dismiss Pentecostalism as nothing more than hyper-emotionalism. Such disparagement has often reminded Pentecostals of the Day of Pentecost in Acts 2, when spectators in the city of Jerusalem thought the disciples had been filled with too much wine rather than with the Holy Spirit (v. 13).

It has been common in Western Christianity, no doubt reflecting the Western scientific worldview's elevation of reason over emotion, to see worship as a place for only composed, solemn reflections with no place for extreme emotional expressions, whether of ecstatic shouts of joy or agonizing groans of sorrow. In this culture, the voicing of such intense passions is thought to belong to other venues, such as sports arenas or stadiums (in the case of ecstatic shouts) or the offices of psychiatrists, therapists, and counselors (in the case of heart-rending cries).

Yet surely one of the most striking and significant features of the book of Psalms, as Scripture's primary manual of worship, is that it makes room, even spacious room, for the full range of human expression, from shouts of ecstasy to cries of agony. This reveals something crucial about the God who stands at the center of this worship—this is a God who invites and receives into his presence the full expression of our humanness. God even affirms and facilitates this full expression by making poetry its essential form and music its frequent accompaniment. This God of poetry and song thus gives priority to the language of the heart, thereby giving voice to our deepest hurts and our highest joys.

In covering the full gamut of human emotions, the book of Psalms harks back to the twin roots of Hebrew worship found in the bitter cries of slaves in Egypt (Exod 2:23-25) and the joyous song of salvation at the Red Sea (Exod 15 KJV, or Reed Sea). At the same time, the book of Psalms also reaches forward to shape every spiritual renewal of God's people down through the ages, up to the Pentecostal movement of the present day. The Psalms continue to give voice to those who would worship God "in Spirit and in truth" (John 4:24 KJV), all the way from "sighs too deep for words" (Rom 8:26 NRSV) unto "joy [that's] unspeakable and full of glory" (1 Pet 1:8 KJV).

PROVERBS

The fear of the LORD is the beginning of wisdom, and the knowledge of the Holy One is understanding.
—*Proverbs 9:10 (NASB)*

When I think about the book of Proverbs,

I am reminded of the awesome responsibility I have as a father. Being a parent is more than providing a home, clothes, food, schooling, and general comfort for my children; it is about training my children "in the way they should go" (Prov 22:6). What is interesting about this verse is that some have argued that it can be translated in such a way as to give it a completely different meaning. Therefore, some render verse 6, "Train up a child according to his or her own way (i.e., wayward, selfish way), and when this child is old he or she will not depart from it." In a society where children are often viewed as an annoyance or merely as something you check off a list of "things" to acquire in life, it is important to remember the awesome responsibility God has placed upon parents to instruct and raise their children with a godly fear. This was so important to my wife and me that we decided *before* we were married that if we were blessed with children, one of us would stay at home and be with them so they would have godly influence 24/7. The author of Proverbs stresses the importance of godly instruction for children when they are young—instruction by both the father and the mother (1:8; 6:20; 23:22). As we will see, chapters 1–9 focus on parents' instructive words to their child. Yet instruction is more than practical knowledge; it is also spiritual for the author of Proverbs. Too often today parents focus on the former and leave the latter to the child—this ought not to be the case. In view of the parenting responsibilities that lie ahead for most of the readers of this text, it is important to realize that spiritual instruction must be a priority for your children *before* they are confronted with the evils of this world, for if we neglect this responsibility, children *will* go their *own* way.

Quick Facts

Title: The title comes from the LXX (*Parmoimiai*) and the Hebrew (*Mishlē*), both of which mean "Proverbs."

Date and Authorship: Traditionally authorship has been assigned to Solomon (cf. 1:1; 10:1; 25:1). This would place the date of composition sometime before the death of Solomon in 931 BCE. One stream

Cave 4 at Qumran where fragments of two scrolls of Proverbs were found (4QProv^a and 4QProv^b). Photo courtesy of Christine Curley.

of Jewish tradition assigns the authorship to Hezekiah (*Baba Bathra* 15a) in the late eighth or early seventh centuries BCE. This Jewish tradition no doubt arises from the notation in 25:1, which names Hezekiah as the one responsible for collecting a number of Solomon's proverbs. This indicates that the editing and collecting process, much like with the Psalms, transpired over a period of time. This helps to account for the inclusion of later sections attributed to "the wise" (22:17–24:34), Agur (30:1-33), and Lemuel (31:1-9).

Audience: While the original audience would have been Israelite, the wide appeal of wisdom sayings may have caused the book to have a wider audience, perhaps even in Egypt (cf. 1 Kgs 3).

Genre: Chapters 1–9 are composed of a series of instructional speeches. While 31:10-31 is presented as an acrostic poem, most of the material of Proverbs is in poetic verse written as aphorisms or wise sayings, usually in parallel bicola (10:1–31:9).

Purpose: As noted in the opening seven verses, Proverbs was written primarily to instruct young men (19:20; 23:19). Secondarily, it served as general wisdom instruction for those of all ages (1:5). It has often been called the "textbook" for instructing youth.

Structure

Proverbs is presented in seven clearly marked sections: parents' instruction to their child (1–9); miscellaneous proverbs of Solomon (10:1–22:16); the sayings of the wise (22:17–24:34); more proverbs of Solomon (25–29); the sayings of Agur (30); the words of Lemuel (31:1-9); the ideal woman (31:10-31).

Summary

Parents' Instruction to Their Child: Proverbs 1–9

Next to the ideal wife poem of 31:10-31, the most memorable portion of Proverbs is this opening section. This is mainly due to the speech format. The first seven verses set forth the purpose of book: to know wisdom and instruction (1:2a NASB). The leading theme is also noted in verse 7a: "the fear of the LORD is the beginning of knowledge" (KJV). From this point forward, the author addresses his comments to his "son" no fewer than 15 times (e.g., 1:8, 10, 15; 2:1; 3:1; etc.). This instruction could apply just as easily to a mother or father addressing a daughter. The first instruction to the son is to avoid the wrong crowd (1:8-19). The parents' warning is immediately followed by the introduction of the personified character, Woman Wisdom, who gives her own speech to the young person. Those who fail to listen to her voice will be destroyed by their own folly (1:20-33).

The parent goes on to note that Woman Wisdom is to be sought like silver or hidden treasure (2:4), or, as I tell my students, as you would pursue that significant other. When God grants wisdom to a young person, then the pitfalls of youthful folly will be avoided (2:6-21), especially the wiles of the "adulteress" (2:16-19 NASB).[42] The benefits of fearing God and pursuing wisdom include favor with God and humanity, long life, riches, honor, peace, and so on (3:2-26). Chapter 3 ends with a warning to the son that he should always try to help people when he can and to avoid envying the wicked (3:27-35). A choice is set forth: follow the way of the wise or suffer the consequences of the fool.

Chapter 4 returns to the importance of gaining wisdom and understanding by using the metaphor of Woman Wisdom as a spouse. By treasuring her and caring for her as one would his wife, the young man will not be lured aside by evil people (4:14-19). Throughout these next few chapters, the parents consistently warn their child to listen to their words (4:20-27; cf. 5:1-2, 7; 6:20-23; 7:1-4). The motif of the evil woman returns in chapters 5–7 with the parent offering stern warnings to avoid this pitfall (5:4-6; 6:24-25; 7:5-21; cf. 23:26-28). Those who indulge the adulteress will only suffer hardship (5:7-14, 20-23; 6:26-35; 7:22-27), whereas those who enjoy the "wife of [their] youth" will be blessed (5:15-19).

The speech portion ends in chapters 8 and 9 with a focus on Woman Wisdom as she calls to the young person to heed her call, to follow in her paths (8:1-11), and to experience blessing (8:12-21). The personification of Wisdom is carried one step further in the rest of this chapter; Wisdom here gives another first-person speech. This time it is about how she was created by YHWH "in the beginning" (KJV) and attended and assisted God in the creation of everything else (8:22-31). In chapter 9, Wisdom is likened to a well-built house full of fine foods (9:1-12), whereas Woman Folly's house is marked by death (9:13-18). The young person who chooses to "dwell" in the former will be well established and blessed with long life (9:11). Conversely, those who choose to dwell in the house of Woman Folly will reap death (9:18).

The importance of chapters 1–9 to the message of Proverbs cannot be overstated. The predominant area of concern for the father is who his son will be associated with in both a social and a sexual context. The stressing of sexual morals, especially as it relates to the adulteress, is central to the parents' instruction. It is during the sexually charged period of one's youth that sexual temptations can quickly lead a person astray. As part of the wisdom of this portion, the parents' instruction comes *before* their son actually is confronted with sexual temptation.

---

42. The dialogue here in Proverbs is between a father and a son; therefore the references are fitting to that context (i.e., avoid unfaithful/strange/foreign women). One could just as easily turn the tables and say to a girl, avoid an unfaithful/strange/foreign man.

One of the functions of wisdom literature in its original ANE context was to serve as instruction for how the individual could live successfully within the community. In this context, the unfaithful wife brought chaos to the patriarchal family structure and to the community as a whole. If the wife was unfaithful, then the possibility of an illegitimate son inheriting and ruling over another man's wealth was a dreaded possibility. In view of this, the adulteress and the adulterer could face the death penalty (Lev 20:10; Deut 22:22). As such, Proverbs presents the adulteress (rather than the prostitute) as a foil to Woman Wisdom (7:19). While associating with a prostitute would have been denounced, the prostitute's presence in society did not bring the chaos that an unfaithful wife would have generated in that culture. Finally, it is not a coincidence that the book begins and ends with female imagery. Whereas Woman Wisdom is a metaphor for wisdom cast in terms of an ideal "wife," the final poem of Proverbs (31:10-31) presents a picture of a real wife who fully lives up to the ideals of wisdom.

Miscellaneous Proverbs of Solomon: Proverbs 10:1–22:16

Short, pithy sayings compose this main portion of the book. Keep in mind when using the proverbs that they are *general principles only* and not hard-and-fast rules for life. In other words, the proverbs teach what will happen *most* of the time. In chapters 10–15 antithetic parallelism dominates these sayings. In fact, almost all of chapters 10–19 focus on the contrast between the righteous and the wicked (e.g., 10:6-7, 11, 20, 24-25, 28-32), and especially between the wise and the foolish (e.g., 10:1, 13-14, 21, 23; 12:15; 13:16; 14:7, 9, 16; 15:5; 17:7, 10, 12, 16, 21, 24, 28; 17:28; 18:2; cf. 20:3; 23:9). While by no means exhaustive, the array of specific topics throughout chapters 10:1–22:16 includes: the proper use of money (10:2, 16; 11:28; 14:4; 16:8; 18:11); treatment of the poor (17:5; 21:13; 22:9, 16; cf. 28:27; 29:7); the value of hard work (10:4-5, 26; 12:11, 27; 13:4, 11; 14:23-24; 18:9; 19:15; 20:4, 13; 21:17, 25; 22:29; cf. 28:19); friendship (17:17; 18:24; 22:11; cf. 27:6, 9); a good wife (12:4; 14:1; 18:22; 19:13-14); discipline (12:1; 13:1, 18, 24; 15:5, 10, 32; 19:18-20, 27; 22:15; 23:12-13; 22:6, 15; cf. 29:15, 17); the problems of pride or arrogance (11:2; 15:25; 16:5, 18-19; 18:12; 21:4, 24; cf. 29:23); gossip (18:8; 20:19; cf. 26:22); and the importance of honesty in business (11:1; 16:11; 20:10, 23; 21:6; cf. 28:6). Two central tenets of the wisdom tradition that appear in this section are the repeated motif of how one speaks (10:13, 18-21, 32; 12:13, 19, 22; 13:3; 14:3; 15:2, 7; 16:10, 13, 23, 30; 17:4, 7, 28; 18:4-7, 21; 19:1; 20:15; 21:23) and how one controls one's temper (14:29-30 NRSV; 15:1, 18; 16:24, 32; 17:13-14, 19, 27; 18:19; 20:3; cf. 29:11, 22).

The Sayings of the Wise: Proverbs 22:17–24:34

Two blocks of material, introduced as "sayings of the wise," compose this portion (22:17–24:22 and 24:23-34). The parallels between 22:17–23:14 and the Egyptian wisdom sayings of Amenemope (*ANET* 421–25) have caused many scholars to suggest a direct literary dependence. However, due to the fact that Solomon is said to have had a wide influence during his day (cf. 1 Kgs 3; 10), such interrelatedness should

The western retaining wall of the temple mount dating to the reign of Herod the Great. It is here that Jews come to pray at what is often called the "wailing wall." Photo by Brian Peterson.

not be surprising. In both groupings of the sayings of the wise, motifs similar to those noted for chapters 10:1–22:16 predominate.

More Proverbs of Solomon: Proverbs 25–29

A unique feature of this section is that it begins with a superscription that identifies the "men of Hezekiah" as playing a role in copying down these "proverbs of Solomon" (25:1). Much as in the two sections before it, we see motifs and topics here that appear earlier in the main body of the book. One section of interest is 25:6-7, an exhortation to avoid exalting oneself, which parallels Jesus's teaching in Luke 14:7-11. What makes this a point of special interest is the fact that Jesus obviously used the Proverbs in his parables as a means of teaching wisdom to his disciples.

The Sayings of Agur: Proverbs 30

The nationality of Agur is uncertain. His name may mean "I am a sojourner." Much like the way the book of Job ends, Agur begins his proverbial sayings by declaring his ignorance about the wisdom and power of God (30:1-6). The unique feature of this chapter is Agur's use of the poetic device known as the numerical saying (x, x+1; e.g., "three things . . . four that . . ."). Four stanzas utilize this pattern (30:15-17; 18-20; 21-23; 29-31). The sayings of Agur are perhaps the best example of biblical proverbial wisdom that requires more than a cursory reading. Most of the proverbs in the earlier chapters are easily understood; however, here one must slow down and ponder what Agur means when he makes statements such as, "Three things are too wonderful for me, four that I can't figure out: the way of an eagle in the sky, the way of a snake on the rock, the way of a ship out on the open sea, and the way of a man with a young woman" (30:18-19).

The Words of Lemuel: Proverbs 31:1-9

We cannot be certain about the identity of Lemuel. Most scholars now conclude that Lemuel is not another name for Solomon. His sayings *might* include the poem on the ideal wife in 31:10-31, although we cannot be certain. In the nine short verses attributed to Lemuel, one topic dominates: the dangers of using alcohol by those in positions of authority. Earlier proverbs also address the dangers of alcohol for the average person (20:1; 23:20-21, 30-35).

The Ideal Woman: Proverbs 31:10-31

Perhaps no passage has been used more for sermons preached on Mother's Day than the poem of the ideal wife. Written in an acrostic format, the ideal woman is defined as someone who: is trustworthy (31:11-12), provides for her family (31:13-15, 21-22, 27), is an entrepreneur (31:16, 24), is industrious (31:17-19), is compassionate (31:20), brings honor to her husband (31:23), is wise (31:26), is loved by her family (31:28), and most important, fears God (31:30). As an acrostic and in light of this list, one could say that the ideal woman described here has "it" from A to Z.

Debated Issues (aka Great Paper Topics)

1) How do scholars reconcile the apparent conflict between the two sayings found in Prov 26:4-5?

2) How do scholars understand the personification of Wisdom as a creature made by God "in the beginning" to assist in the creation of the world (Prov 8:22-31 KJV)?

The Message of the Book

The wise person fears the Lord and heeds the instruction of his or her parents and elders and the voice of Wisdom.

Closing the Loop

While most of the OT (especially the Torah and the Prophets) places primary emphasis upon supernatural revelation, Proverbs emphasizes what has often been described as "natural revelation," that is, truth gained through experiencing and observing the natural order of things or the normal course of things encountered by human beings as they live life in this world. This is the emphasis not only of Proverbs but also of all wisdom literature, whether it is found inside the Bible or outside. In fact, this kind of literature that focuses upon this kind of truth is common to all human cultures. As noted earlier (in the "Introduction to the Poetic Books"), one could even think of the wisdom that we are talking about here in terms of "*common* sense." Yet even though it is *common*, the book of Proverbs knows it is *urgent*.

Proverbs shows the pursuit of wisdom to be a matter of extreme urgency in at least three ways. First, Proverbs does this by making "the fear of YHWH" the starting point of this pursuit: "the beginning of wisdom is the fear of the Lord" (9:10; cf. 1:7). It is the same starting point as when Israel was given the Torah at Sinai (Exod 20:18-20; cf. Deut 5:23-29). Second, Proverbs commends wisdom to the young person by means of the urgent voice of parental instruction—a voice that clearly conveys the life-and-death stakes that are riding on this teaching. Third, Proverbs commends wisdom by means of still another urgent voice, namely the voice of Woman Wisdom as she speaks for herself. Proverbs seems to know how very important it will be for the young person to hear and to heed this voice, because, after all, one's parents will not always be around. And so Proverbs introduces the voice of Wisdom in the book *just as if it were the voice of a prophet*: "Wisdom shouts in the street; in the public square she raises her voice. Above the noisy crowd, she calls out. At the entrances of the city gates, she has her say: 'How long will you clueless people love your naiveté, mockers hold their mocking dear, and fools hate knowledge?'" (1:20-22).

Pentecostalism has been a tradition that has emphasized the voice of the prophet above, and even sometimes over against, the voice of wisdom. However, even as Scripture exhorts us to "despise not prophecies" (1 Thess 5:20 DRA), it also exhorts us to "get wisdom" (Prov 4:5, 7), and Proverbs presses this latter imperative in a voice that calls to everyone, including Pentecostals, with prophetic urgency and authority.

ECCLESIASTES

Vanity of vanities, says the Teacher; all is vanity.
          —Ecclesiastes 12:8 (NRSV)

When I think about the book of Ecclesiastes,

I am taken back to the night my mom passed away in December 2012. Because I lived more than 20 hours away, I was unable to be there in person, so I kept vigil via Skype. As the night wore on, I watched my mom's breathing become increasingly labored. At that moment I realized what Qoheleth (the author of Ecclesiastes) meant when he said, "*Remember Him* [your creator] before the silver cord is broken and the golden bowl is crushed" (12:6a NASB; cf. 12:1). This is a metaphor for the fragility of life. The "golden bowl" represents one's life whereas the "silver cord" is a metaphor for the tenuousness of life. A thin "cord" is all that holds aloft this valuable "golden bowl"; that is, death is only a heartbeat away. This is indeed the picture that I beheld that night. Here was the precious and valuable life of my mother hanging by a slender cord. I knew that at any moment that cord was going to break and my valued "golden bowl" was going to be "crushed." Having lived centuries before Jesus and the promise of resurrection that he brought, Qoheleth had a concept of an afterlife that was bleak at best. I was consoled knowing that my mom was a strong believer: I knew she would be with Jesus in a matter of minutes. The fresh realization of the precious value of life can stir one's desire to live it to the fullest in Christ.

Quick Facts

Title: The English title comes from the LXX title *Ekklesiastes*, which is a translation of the Hebrew title *Qoheleth*, meaning "Assembler"/"Gatherer" or "Preacher"/"Teacher." While Christians use "Ecclesiastes" to refer to the book, the Hebrew title "Qoheleth" is used to refer to the author as well as to the book.

Date: Dates for the book have ranged from the tenth century BCE (Solomon's day) to 200 BCE. References to Ecclesiastes in the apocryphal book of Sirach (ca. 180 BCE) and the discovery of manuscripts of Ecclesiastes at Qumran make a date later than 200 BCE untenable. Although a late date is preferred by most scholars, no consensus has been reached. Some conservative scholars posit that the book was written late in Solomon's life as he reflected back on his life.

Authorship: Jewish and church traditions assign the book to Solomon (1:1; 1 Kgs 4:34; cf. *Megillah* 7a; *Shabbat* 30) and some support is found for its having been edited by Hezekiah (*Baba Bathra* 15a). Today most scholars reject both of these views and propose an anonymous author usually from the Persian period. The main reason is that internal indicators seem to point to someone other than Solomon. A few of these include: the reference to the many kings in Jerusalem before the author (1:16); the fact that the author *was* king (Solomon died in office; cf. 1:12); the author sometimes speaks as if he is not in a position to address injustice, i.e., not a king (4:1; 5:8-9; 8:2-8; 10:16-17, 20; 12:9-14); and the apparent late Phoenician linguistic style. These arguments have been met by the following rebuttals: First, even though David was the only Israelite king to precede Solomon in Jerusalem, dozens of non-Israelite kings ruled there before its capture in 1000 BCE. Second, the Hebrew of 1:12 can be rendered "I *have been* king" instead of "I *was* king." Third, it is indeed possible that Solomon recognized injustice in other kingdoms, or perhaps even in portions of his own, but was still unable to do anything about it, especially late in his reign, when his power was dwindling. Finally, the language of Ecclesiastes may reflect how the book was updated in a subsequent editing process. Moreover, it is possible that Solomon used a Phoenician scribe to write the book.

Audience: The book was written for the wise person (Israelite) and the youth who could learn from Qoheleth's experiences.

Genre: The book fits into the broad category of wisdom literature with a mixture of poetry and prose. More specifically, it takes the form of wisdom reflections that look back on life's lessons from the vantage that comes with age. The book incorporates other genres, including aphorisms (7:1-14) and poems (3:2-8; 12:1-7). Although the book has been termed pessimistic wisdom literature, Ecclesiastes fits better under the category of exhortation. While taking account of the many futile aspects of life "under the sun" (e.g., 1:3, 9, 14; 2:11; et al.), the author encourages his readers to enjoy life and put God first (2:25; 3:14; 5:7; 7:18; 8:12-13; 11:9; 12:13).

Purpose: It appears that the author set out to challenge many of the wisdom concepts of his era. He also sought to show the futility of life without God. As one of the five *Megilloth* ("scrolls"), Ecclesiastes was read at the Feast of Booths to commemorate the wilderness wandering.

Structure

While there is no consensus on the structural outline of Ecclesiastes, the book can be divided into at least six blocks: introduction (1:1-18); Qoheleth's experiments with pleasure (2:1-26); Qoheleth's observations on the futility of life in general (3:1–6:12); Qoheleth's instructions for living (7:1–8:17); Qoheleth's conclusion: fear God and enjoy life (9:1–12:8); and an epilogue (12:9-14).

Summary

Introduction: Ecclesiastes 1:1-18

In the book's first two verses, a narrator introduces the reader to Qoheleth, who then introduces his reflections on the futility of life "under the sun" (i.e., perhaps, "apart from God above") by noting the monotonous cycles of the universe and the futility of human endeavors within this context. Verse 2b, "vanity of vanities; all is vanity" (KJV) or "perfectly pointless," forms a framing *inclusio* for the book (cf. 1:2; 12:8).

Qoheleth's Experiments with Pleasure: Ecclesiastes 2:1-26

Qoheleth decides to do an experiment (2:1-2): to experience the pleasures of life—wine (2:3), building projects (2:4-6), possessions (2:7-9), and wisdom (2:12-17)—to see if there is any fulfillment in them (2:10-11). His conclusion is that these things are meaningless in themselves (2:24-26).

Qoheleth's Observations on the Futility of Life in General: Ecclesiastes 3:1–6:12

After conveying to the reader that he found no fulfillment in the pleasures of his own personal life, Qoheleth next gives the reader examples from life in general that also show the futility of life. These include: injustice and the oppression of the poor (3:16-17; 4:1-3; 5:8); the inevitability of death for all (3:18-22); the futility of riches (4:4-8; 5:9-17; 6:1-2); the problems of foolish leadership (4:13-16); and the dangers in not being content with life (6:3-9). Even though some may read this as extremely pessimistic, Qoheleth actually prefaces these examples by noting both the good and bad in the perpetual cycles of life (3:1-8) and the importance of fearing God within this monotonous circle (3:9-15). Indeed, throughout this section Qoheleth gives clear examples of how to enjoy life and please God, namely, by finding a spouse (4:9-12), by honoring vows and watching how one speaks to God (5:1-7), and by enjoying the life God has given (5:18-20). He concludes his observations by noting that earthly existence "under the sun" is indeed "striving after wind" (6:9-12 NASB). However, his clear instruction to fear God speaks volumes. From the ANE perspective earthly existence was "under the sun" both literally and cosmologically. One could understand Qoheleth's implicit point to be that only when one focuses above that sphere, that is, on God, will the monotony of life become bearable.

Qoheleth's Instructions for Living: Ecclesiastes 7:1–8:17

This section makes a clear break with what has come before it. No longer do we find the phrase "chasing after wind" (cf. 1:14, 17; 2:11, 17, 26; 4:4, 6, 16; 6:9), which had earlier highlighted the futility of living life for "things" as opposed to living for God. Here Qoheleth seeks to give wisdom instruction on how to live a meaningful life despite the obvious futility of living in a broken world. Much like Proverbs 10–29, the aphorisms dealing with wisdom and folly in 7:1-14, along with the wisdom of obeying rulers

(8:1-9), reinforce Qoheleth's desire to give sound instruction for living. Even though evil men sometimes prosper and the righteous suffer (8:10-11, 14), Qoheleth still advises his reader to fear God (8:12-13) and enjoy the life God has given (8:15-17).

Qoheleth's Conclusion, Fear God and Enjoy Life: Ecclesiastes 9:1–12:8

The last verses of chapter 8 set the stage for Qoheleth's conclusion. Qoheleth gives an extended exhortation to the reader by noting that, because God is in control (9:1), a person should be happy that he or she is alive (9:2-6) and live life to the fullest, especially with one's spouse (9:7-9), for no one knows when she or he will die (9:10-12). Qoheleth points out the value of learning wisdom in the process of living life (9:13–10:20), investing wisely, and working hard (11:1-6). Qoheleth concludes by encouraging his readers once again to be happy they are alive (11:7-8) and to live life to the fullest while they are young (11:7-8) all the while keeping in mind that God will judge evil actions (11:9-10). For Qoheleth, the ideal life in a futile world is enjoying one's youth (11:7-8) but including God in it before becoming aged and decrepit as life itself slips away (12:1-7). It is here that Qoheleth repeats the phrase with which he began, "vanity of vanities; all is vanity" (cf. 1:2 ; 12:8, KJV both). In the light of Qoheleth's overall message, it is perhaps best not to translate the Hebrew word *hebel* as "vanity" but rather as "vapor." For indeed, by the time we reach these closing chapters, Qoheleth seems to be focused not so much on life's futility as on its brevity. Thus, his emphasis is to enjoy life while you are young and fear God, for, like a vapor, life soon passes.

Epilogue: Ecclesiastes 12:9-14

In this final paragraph of the book, we meet again the voice of the narrator who introduced Qoheleth at the beginning of the book (1:1-2). Here the narrator offers his concluding thoughts about Qoheleth. In keeping with the theme of the brevity of life, the narrator highlights Qoheleth's accomplishments as a sage; however, he addresses his "son" (KJV) with a warning to live a balanced life of study and enjoyment (12:9-12). And just in case the reader had missed the main thrust of Qoheleth's argument, the narrator closes his book by echoing

A rabbi studying the law at the Western Wall in Jerusalem. The author of Ecclesiastes encourages his reader to keep God's commandments (12:13). Photo by Brian Peterson.

Qoheleth's central imperatives: fear God, keep his commandments, and remember that God will judge all people (12:13-14).

Debated Issues (aka Great Paper Topics)

1) What does Qoheleth mean when he says, "Do not be overly righteous" (7:16 NKJV)?

2) What are the scholarly interpretations of Eccl 7:28?

3) What are the scholarly positions on the authorship and date of the epilogue?

The Message of the Book

Ecclesiastes could be viewed as a message about "journey versus destination." If we pursue anything "under the sun"—wisdom, a job, family, possessions, or what have you—as a *destination* or ultimate goal in life, then life will be a meaningless chase after vanity and futility. However, if such things play their part in a *journey* through life, a journey that has God as its ultimate destination, then life will find its true meaning and end.

Closing the Loop

Regardless of one's position on the Solomonic authorship of Ecclesiastes, it would be hard to deny that this wisdom book, just like the book of Proverbs, intends to project a Solomonic perspective. Yet whereas Proverbs presents the positive, optimistic side of the Solomonic wisdom tradition, Ecclesiastes shows its downside. As mentioned earlier, some have viewed this contrast in terms of Ecclesiastes reflecting the weariness, gloominess, regrets, and failings of Solomon in his old age, while Proverbs, on the other hand, is reflecting the optimism and success of Solomon in his younger years. Considering matters at the societal level and not just the personal level, some scholars have referred to the rise of Solomon's kingdom with all of its prosperity and cultural and intellectual advancements as the "Solomonic Enlightenment"—a term that is obviously drawing on the parallel to the Enlightenment of Western civilization. In light of this, one could think of Proverbs as reflecting the "Solomonic Enlightenment" and Ecclesiastes as reflecting what could be called the "Solomonic *Post*-Enlightenment"—the period in Israel's history after the lofty promise of Solomon's royal project finally began to deconstruct and tumble toward disillusionment (1 Kgs 11–12). Approaching Ecclesiastes from this angle allows us to appreciate that this book of the Bible offers a powerful reflection on life's meaning *in light of the end of life at the societal level as well as the individual level*. No wonder this ancient book rings so true and resonates so deeply in our own current post-Enlightenment age.

The *rise* of global Pentecostalism has taken place alongside what many have recognized as the *fall* of the Western Enlightenment. The grand project of the modern Western world, with its total faith in the

169

unlimited progress and promise of human knowledge, has given way, right before our Western eyes, to the crumbling worldview of postmodernism. At its best, Pentecostalism has been a herald that has borne fresh witness to Scripture's apocalyptic, end-of-the-world vision, which has seen this *fall of modernity* coming from a long way off—coming as a fulfillment of the divine judgment pronounced against *all* human kingdoms and constructions that are pursued apart from God (Dan 2; 7; cf. Gen 11:1-9).

Understandably, Pentecostalism's witness to such a *divine vision from above* found little hearing in the modern Enlightenment worldview and has found little more in the post-Enlightenment perspective that has followed. Yet this latter perspective, as it has pursued *human wisdom from below* to its logical conclusion, has come very close to Qoheleth's own conclusion "under the sun": "Vanity of vanities; all is vanity" (12:8 KJV). The narrator of Ecclesiastes, who speaks immediately after this and has the last word in the book, knows that this is not the final conclusion. Yet he knows it is one step closer, coming from below, to the conclusion that *is* final—the conclusion that opens at last to what Pentecostals have always known to be the vision coming from above: "The conclusion, when all has been heard, is: fear God and keep His commandments, because this applies to every person [or "all humankind," *ha-adam*]. For God will bring every act to judgment, everything which is hidden, whether it is good or evil" (12:13-14 NASB).

SONG OF SONGS

For love is as strong as death, passionate love unrelenting as the grave. Its darts are darts of fire—divine flame!
—*Song of Songs 8:6*

When I think about the book of Song of Songs,

I cannot help but ponder the admonitions of the author of the text concerning the proper time for "love." Three times, two of which are during the most sexually charged moments in the book, the author warns the reader, "Don't arouse love until it desires" (2:7; 3:5; cf. 8:4). Adherence to this wise advice is sorely lacking among many Christians today, especially those of the younger generation. The Song of Songs opens up a picture of romantic love within a proper biblical context—one that can inform the love relationship between a man and woman from the moment they first meet and fall in love until the day they get married and begin their lives of growing old together. The joys and fulfillment of sexual intimacy within the bonds of monogamous marriage form a beautiful part of God's greater plan for humanity. Sadly, God's plan for wholesome relationships has been mocked by society today, and as a result, family and relational chaos has ensued. It is time, once again, for Christians to return to the wisdom put forward in this book.

Quick Facts

Title: Both the LXX title, *Asma* ("Songs"), and the Hebrew title, *Shir HaShirim* ("The Song of Songs"), lie behind the English title. However, the English title adds the attribution to Solomon, which appears in 1:1. The Latin title is *Canticles*, meaning "hymns" or "songs."

Authorship and Date: Much as we saw with Ecclesiastes, dates for this book have ranged from the tenth century BCE (Solomon's day) to the Persian period or even later. Authorship traditionally has been assigned to Solomon, based on the superscription in 1:1. One Jewish tradition credits the book to Hezekiah (*Baba Bathra* 15a), perhaps more in terms of an editing role than one of authorship. A few biblical texts note Solomon's writing of songs and poetic literature (cf. 1 Kgs 4:32; Pss 72; 127). Certain details in the book correspond to the time of Solomon's reign before the division of the kingdom; for example, in the parallelism of 6:4 the northern city of Tirzah is mentioned alongside Jerusalem—an unlikely pairing after the kingdom divided. However, some think the language in the book (e.g., Persian and Greek loan words) might reflect a later period. On the latter point, scholars are divided on the importance of these proposed loan words to the dating process. Also, based on the dominant female voice (the book begins and ends with the Shulammite bride speaking), some suggest that the text was written by a woman. Others propose that, like Psalms, the book is an anthology of love poems that were collected over time. However, a strong case can be made for seeing the poem as a unity that fits within a Solomonic context.[43]

Audience and Purpose: The book served to teach Israelites, no doubt young people, the beauty, joy, and importance of courtship and marital love. As part of the five *Megilloth* ("scrolls"), the Song became a regular reading for the entire assembly at the annual Passover festival, and it was early on interpreted as an allegory depicting YHWH's love for Israel.

Genre: The book is a "song," constituted by love poetry, which finds parallels in Egyptian literature (ca. 1300–1000 BCE).

Structure

One possible way of understanding the book's structure, which will be followed in the summary that follows, is in terms of four phases in an unfolding intimate relationship: falling in love (1:1–2:7); the engagement period (2:8–3:5); the wedding and honeymoon period (3:6–7:13); and married life (ch. 8).

Summary

Before beginning a summary of the book, it is important to note the competing interpretive methods. Allegory has been the dominant means of interpretation by both the Christian and Jewish traditions. This method allowed interpreters to mute or downplay some of the more sexually explicit language within the book. Closely associated with this is the typological interpretation, which focuses more on the larger theme of love (as opposed to particular details) exemplified in the relationship between God and Israel or between Christ and the church. Other approaches include reading the book: as a cultic ritual depicting fertility rites; as a depiction of the events during a funerary ritual (closely associated with cultic-like fertility acts); as a poetic account of an actual event in the life of Solomon; as a text used in a week-long wedding celebration in which the bride and groom assumed the roles of a king and queen and performed dances and songs; or as a drama. In the latter case there is a debate as to whether the drama involves two or three characters (i.e., Solomon and the Shulammite, or Solomon, the Shulammite, and her young lover). The following content summary follows the approach of Duane Garrett. This approach interprets the book as a love song/poem.[44]

---

43. Duane A. Garrett, *Proverbs, Ecclesiastes, Song of Songs*, New American Commentary 14 (Nashville: Broadman Press, 1993).
44. Ibid.

Falling in Love: Song of Songs 1:1–2:7

The first verse is a superscription, which can be read either as ascribing authorship to Solomon or naming him as the one to whom the writing is dedicated. Then the Shulammite woman begins to speak. She expresses her wish that the man with whom she has become enamored would kiss her, for indeed all the young women find him attractive (1:2-4). Although she loathes her tanned skin (not considered a positive feature in the ANE), she looks beyond her insecurities and desires to know where her beloved is working so she can go and see him (1:5-7). The young man has obviously taken note of the Shulammite as well and tells her where he may be found (1:8). They both have been smitten with each other and praise each other's beauty (1:12-17). As the relationship develops, the language of love becomes more intense (2:1-6). At this point, when it seems they are getting close to "crossing the line" of propriety, the narrator interjects the warning not to arouse love before "it pleases" (2:7 NKJV).

The Engagement Period: Song of Songs 2:8–3:5

At this moment the scene changes as 2:8-16 depicts the two young lovers in the courting phase, frolicking in the fields, falling even deeper in love. By 2:16 it appears that the two have become engaged, as the Shulammite calls her lover "mine" (KJV), the first time she does so in the book (cf. 6:3). The interpretation of chapter 3 is one of the most debated within the book. The dreamlike state of the woman in 3:1-4 is actually the psychological musings of the young woman as she ponders (using metaphors) the idea of giving herself to her future husband and what it will mean for her status to change from a virgin in Israel to a married woman. The "watchmen" of the "city" in 3:3 (KJV) could be read as a metaphor for the guarding of her virginity and her body respectively (cf. 5:7; 8:9): "they" protect her from crossing inappropriate lines. Again, at the moment of intense sexual musing about her beloved, the narrator interjects the reminder not to arouse love before it pleases (3:5 NKJV).

Marriage and Honeymoon Period: Song of Songs 3:6–7:13

The next scene shifts from a nighttime setting to the actual wedding procession (3:6-11). The identification of Solomon by name may be a literary device whereby the groom is likened to the king. As soon as the groom sees his bride (4:8-12; 5:1) he extols her beauty using imagery and metaphors from ANE culture (4:1-6). The groom also praises his bride's chastity by using three metaphors: the "locked garden," the "locked rock garden," and the "sealed up spring" (4:12 ISV). Of course, the garden imagery both here and throughout the book recalls the original garden of Eden and the first couple. Chapter 5 moves ahead to what could be regarded as the honeymoon stage, where the marriage is consummated (5:1), using euphemisms and sensual metaphors for the act of sexual intercourse (5:2-5). The metaphors of the "watchmen" (KJV) and the "city" from chapter 3 are once again employed, but this time the action of the "watchmen" sounds violent (v. 7 KJV). This could be, here again, a metaphor; this time to register the bride's reaction to her loss of virginity and perhaps the emotional turmoil of her change of status from virgin to wife (5:8–6:1)—a struggle she undergoes alone even though her husband is by her side (6:2). Unlike those who are only out for sexual gratification driven by lust (e.g., Amnon; cf. 2 Sam 13), the husband, after consummating the marriage, turns to his new bride and again praises her beauty, twice (6:4-9; 7:1-9). The bride's response is to invite her husband to enjoy further the pleasures of married life (i.e., the honeymoon; cf. 7:10-13).

Life as a Married Couple: Song of Songs 8

The book concludes with the bride wishing her husband were like a "brother" so she could kiss him in public (8:1). She is so in love with her husband that she wants the entire world to know it! In the ANE, public displays of affection were not acceptable unless it was with the next of kin (i.e., a kiss of greeting and familial affection; cf. Gen 26:7-11). The final appearance of the injunction not to arouse love before it pleases (8:4 NKJV) perhaps serves as an appeal to others to wait for the proper time for love (i.e., within marriage), because the passions associated with love are intense (8:5-7). In this regard, in a patriarchal society it was the responsibility of brothers and fathers to guard the virgin status of their sisters and daughters (8:8-9). However, here in the book's final scene, the bride is no longer under their protection, but rather she is now her own woman under the protection of her husband (8:10-14).

Debated Issues (aka Great Paper Topics)

1) How do scholars interpret the mention of Tirzah in 6:4 in relation to the date of the book?

2) What are the scholarly perspectives concerning the meaning of the dream sequence in chapter 3?

3) How do scholars handle the comment in 8:1 where the woman likens her husband to her brother?

The Message of the Book

According to the original design in the garden of God's very good creation, romantic, sensuous love between a man and a woman is a beautiful, joyous, and powerful gift to be celebrated and pursued within the bounds and the bonds of monogamous marriage.

Closing the Loop

Song of Songs is a book of beautiful love poetry, which accounts for its placement in the Bible grouping we call "Poetic Books." Its more specific placement immediately after Proverbs and Ecclesiastes accords with its close identification with Solomon and wisdom literature. In the context of Old Testament wisdom, the Song of Songs is keenly focused on observing and even celebrating things found universally in human experience within God's good creation. In this context, then, it should not surprise us to find a book so intensely focused upon the ways and the wonders of romantic, erotic love between a man and a woman.

On the other hand, as the Song itself acknowledges, this kind of love is a powerful and even dangerous force, "a flame" that can quickly burn out of control (8:6-7). Thus, while the Song gives sensual love a place in Scripture, it is the only book in Scripture to give it such a wide-open place. And it is quite likely that even this place was not given apart from seeing such love poetry between humans as pointing at least indirectly to the passionate love between God and his people. We know this because the Song's placement in the *Megilloth* as a reading at the annual Passover observance indicates that it was seen to point to YHWH's romance with his people when he first brought them out of Egypt, such as Jer 2:2 explicitly names: "The Lᴏʀᴅ proclaims: I remember your first love, your devotion as a young bride, how you followed me in the wilderness."

As noted earlier, much of the history of Christian interpretation of the Song, spurred no doubt by embarrassment over the Song's sexually explicit nature, has seen the spiritual or allegorical meaning of the Song (i.e., love between God and his people) as the only possible meaning. It is more popular nowadays for Christian interpreters, prompted no doubt by embarrassment over Christianity's long discomfiture over sex, to see the Song only in terms of human sexual love without leaving any room for the additional spiritual application to God's love.

Yet throughout the history of God's people, one can trace a continual stream of individuals and groups who arise from time to time to bear witness to spiritual encounters with God that involve an intimacy, a passion, a pleasure, and even a rapturous ecstasy that invoke the language of the Song of Songs—from Old Testament prophets (Hos 1–2; Jer 15:16; 23:9; cf. Exod 34:34-35) to New Testament apostles (2 Cor 12:2; 1 Pet 1:8; 2 Pet 1:16-21) to Christian mystics through the ages[45] to the innumerable witnesses in Spirit movements up to the present day. The passionate language of the Song of Songs was especially prominent in the testimonies and texts of the early Pentecostal movement,[46] and it has become even more prominent, it seems, in the current teaching and practice of the charismatic network connected with the International House of Prayer.[47]

The place that the Song of Songs makes for human sexual love in Scripture is a holy place. One ancient rabbi even called the Song of Songs the Holy of Holies of Scripture.[48] The beauty, ecstasy, and mystery of human sexual love in the Song finally lead up to a climax that extols the wonder of love—not just the erotic love shared between the characters in the Song but love itself: "Love is as strong as death, passionate love

---

45. Dale M. Coulter, "The Spirit and the Bride Revisited: Pentecostalism, Renewal, and the Sense of History," *Journal of Pentecostal Theology* 21, no. 2 (2012): 298–319.

46. Ibid., 311–13.

47. Mike Bickle, "The Song of Songs: Introduction to the Song," MikeBickle.org, accessed November 8, 2016, http://mikebickle. org/resources/series/song-of-songs. See Caroline Redick, "'Let Me Hear Your Voice': Re-Hearing the Song of Songs through Pentecostal Hermeneutics," *Journal of Pentecostal Theology* 24, no. 2 (2015): 187–200.

48. Rabbi Akiba, Yadayim 3:5.

unrelenting as the grave. Its darts are darts of fire—divine flame!" (8:6b). The final phrase of that verse in the Hebrew can literally be rendered, "the flame of Yah," a shortened form of YHWH. Thus, the human love of the Song of Songs leads us at last to divine love because this is its ultimate source—the source that gives passionate, sensual love between a man and a woman its rightful and celebrated place in God's creation and in the very heart of Scripture.

INTRODUCTION TO THE PROPHETIC BOOKS

The final grouping of books in our Protestant Bible is the Prophetic Books, usually referred to in terms of two subdivisions: the *Major Prophets* (Isaiah, Jeremiah, Ezekiel, and Daniel) and the 12 *Minor Prophets* (Hosea, Joel, Amos, Obadiah, Jonah, Micah, Nahum, Habakkuk, Zephaniah, Haggai, Zechariah, and Malachi). This canonical arrangement, inherited from the Greek LXX, represents a substantial rearrangement of these materials from their original placement in the Hebrew canon (the *Tanak*).

First, the Hebrew canon placed the book of Daniel in the Writings rather than with the Prophets. Second, the Hebrew canon grouped the Minor Prophets together as one book (or scroll), calling it "The Book of the Twelve" (or simply "The Twelve"). This had the effect of accentuating the theological and literary unity of these prophetic writings, which was largely downplayed in favor of attention to their diverse historical contexts when the LXX divided them into 12 separate books. Third, and most consequentially, the LXX placed these Prophetic Books at the end of the OT canon, whereas the Hebrew Scriptures placed these books, calling them the Latter Prophets, immediately after the Former Prophets (Joshua, Judges, Samuel, and Kings)—the four "historical" books that continued the story of the Torah up to the Babylonian Exile. Thus, the original Hebrew placement of the Latter Prophets encouraged reading them against the background of the Babylonian Exile. By contrast, the Greek repositioning of these prophetic writings at the end of the OT encouraged reading them in light of the NT in the foreground. So, where the Hebrew canonical placement of the Latter Prophets highlights their *probing of the exile*, the Christian canonical rearrangement of these materials highlights their *prediction of the gospel*. Both emphases have merit, so we will try to appreciate both perspectives as we proceed with our survey of each prophetic book.

Hebrew prophecy existed in an ANE world that was populated by peoples who had their own prophetic intermediaries who were believed to bear revelations from the unseen world. The OT itself features appearances of such intermediaries on two dramatic occasions: when the Pharaoh of Egypt summons "his wise men and wizards, and [magicians]" to confront Moses in the Exodus story (Exod 7:10-13; see v. 11 note), and when Nebuchadnezzar, king of Babylon, summons his "dream interpreters, enchanters, [and] diviners" to unlock the mystery of his dream in the story of Daniel (Dan 2). Archaeologists have unearthed numerous ANE texts in the lands surrounding Israel that evidence the activities of such intermediaries, including Babylonian omen texts from the second millennium BCE and Akkadian texts from the first millennium BCE that predict future events. A number of ANE texts (from the 18th century BCE) found at Mari, an ancient city on the Euphrates River in northwest Mesopotamia (in what is now modern Syria), present what appear to be the closest ANE parallels to OT prophecy. Similarities include oracle-type messages, reports of visionary experiences, and predictions about the future. Yet Israelite prophecy stood apart from these and all other ANE parallels in substantial ways, as Israel's own law required (cf. Deut 18:9-22). These striking differences had everything to do with the vast differences between YHWH and the gods of the other nations.

In describing the Hebrew prophets, it is first helpful to realize that our term *prophet* comes from the Greek term *prophetes*, which literally means "one who speaks before, forth, or for." These three nuances of the prefix *pro* are all valid in relation to the OT prophet, for the prophet spoke: "before" as a *foreteller*, "forth" as a *proclaimer*, and "for" as a spokesperson *for* God. Yet even within this designation, a more nuanced distinction can be made. The prophet was both a *foreteller* and a *forth-teller* of the future. The former speaks directly to aspects of the distant future (e.g., Mic 5:2; Ezek 38–39) whereas the latter refers to prophecies related to the immediate future (e.g., Jer 20:4; Ezek 12). Most of the OT prophetic activity actually falls into the latter of these two categories.

The OT Hebrew term for "prophet" is *navi*, a noun derived from a verb meaning "to call." Thus, *navi* could mean "one who is called" or "one who calls out" or perhaps even both, "one who is called to call out." In other words, the *navi* is "one summoned by God to deliver a message." Indeed, while the prophets of ancient Israel exhibit much colorful individuality and variety, from this starting point it is possible to sketch a profile of the OT prophet in terms of the following four facets: the prophet as *messenger*, as *poet*, as *madman*, and as *martyr*.[49]

First of all, *the prophet is a messenger.* The most common phrase in OT prophetic literature is what scholars have long termed the messenger formula: "Thus says the Lord" (KJV). In the ANE world, when a king needed to communicate a message to his people or to another king or nation, he would summon a messenger to deliver a message that would begin with these words, "Thus says X" (as evidenced in many nonbiblical as well as biblical texts, e.g., 2 Kgs 18:19; Isa 36:4, 14 NASB). A particularly clear example of an OT prophet being called by YHWH on the model of the commissioning of a court messenger can be found in Isaiah 6, where Isaiah says, "I'm here; send me," to which YHWH responds, "Go and tell this people . . ." (vv. 8-9). The message entrusted to the OT prophet is usually designated as "the *word* of the Lord" (KJV). The Hebrew term for *word* is *davar*, and it can convey much more than just a simple relay of communication. It can signify an event or an extended experience that happens to and even overwhelms the prophet (e.g., Hos 1:2-8). This goes along with another term that is often used for the prophetic message, *massa*, which is translated as either "oracle" (NASB) or "burden" (KJV). This points to the fact that the message can be a heaviness that is carried before, and sometimes even after, it is delivered (cf. Isa 21:1-3). One other Hebrew term worth noting is *khazon*—that is, "vision"—for the prophets were not only messengers of words but also of visions (e.g., Ezek 1–3; 8–11; 37:1-14; 40–48). Thus, prophets are sometimes referred to as visionaries or seers (1 Sam 9:9; Hos 12:10; Isa 29:10; 30:10). This involved more than just the

49. Rickie D. Moore, *The Spirit of the Old Testament*, JPTS 35 (Blandford Forum, UK: Deo, 2011), 56–68.

fact that they had momentary visionary experiences. It entailed their being radically changed, in the light of such revelations, to see *everything* differently (e.g., Isa 6:5). Many times the prophet's message was rooted in God's covenantal law. Thus, the prophets are often regarded as covenant enforcers. They spoke for God and indicted the nation for covenant infractions (e.g., Mic 6; Amos 3; Isa 1; etc.), using a covenant lawsuit form (or *rîv* pattern, according to the Hebrew term). Because of this calling to point out wrongs perpetrated by the king and nation, the prophets were often rejected, as will be discussed further momentarily.

Second, *the prophet is a poet.* Poetry is the primary mode of OT prophetic speech.[50] This points to the fact that the prophets, in a way that departed from the ANE messenger role, were about more than conveying information and instructing the mind—their words aimed for transformation and moving the heart. Poetic language is well suited and perhaps even humanly necessary when it comes to trying to express visions of the future that move outside the confines of the presently experienced world. Such visions, infused by the power of inspired poetic rhetoric, often gave hope to the powerless while posing a threat to the powerful.[51] Kings were prone to think, *No news is good news,* for serious change is seldom welcomed by those on top. Yet the prophets represented the ultimate King who was all about news—indeed, breathtaking news that had everything to do with the inbreaking of his kingdom.

Third, *the prophet is a madman.* This is often how the prophet came to be regarded by those who could not permit themselves to take seriously the revelations to which the prophet bore witness. In Hos 9:7 the prophet appears to be quoting his detractors who held this perspective: "The prophet is a fool; the man of the spirit is mad!" This same opinion crops up in other places throughout the history of OT prophecy (e.g., Jer 29:26; 2 Kgs 9:11; cf. 1 Sam 10:11, 12; 19:23), for OT prophets were routinely rejected (e.g., Ezek 33:32; cf. Matt 5:12; Luke 11:47-49; 13:33-34; Acts 7:52). The *ruach,* the Spirit from YHWH coming upon the prophet, is prominent in these associations with madness. Perhaps that is because *ruach* is wind, and wind is the wild, untamable force controlled only by God (cf. John 3:8). This was all part of the inevitable clash between the otherworldly word that the prophet had to carry and the world to which the prophet was called to speak. The prophets found themselves in a situation that was much like speaking in an unknown tongue—a tongue that could be easily misunderstood and then quickly written off as madness (cf. Isa 6:9-10). Ironically, as they announced the unwelcomed message of the coming exile in which the Hebrews would become aliens in a foreign land, the prophets themselves became aliens in their own land. Thus, they were the first to enter the exile experience they prophesied. The prophets were not mad or drunk as some supposed, yet they nevertheless could have their own minds blown when they were lifted up into the reality and sanity of God (cf. Isa 6:5). Thus, Jeremiah exclaims, "My heart [or mind] inside me is broken [or shattered]; my body aches. I stagger like a drunk who has had too much wine to drink, because of the LORD and because of God's holy words" (Jer 23:9).

The previous three facets of the prophetic profile lead inevitably to the fourth: *the prophet is a martyr.* We associate this term with being put to death for a cause. The word's Greek root points to the idea of

---

50. Walter Brueggemann, *The Prophetic Imagination* (Philadelphia: Fortress Press, 1978), ch. 3.

51. Walter Brueggemann, *The Creative Word: Canon as a Model for Biblical Education* (Philadelphia: Fortress Press, 1982), 51–54.

being a witness. Indeed, prophets were regularly put to death because of their witness (cf. 1 Kgs 19:10; Neh 9:26). Yet this part of the prophet's "job description" involved not only what happened at the end of their prophetic mission but also what happened at the beginning. The prophets witnessed God, and in the overwhelming light of this theophany (appearance of God) the prophets seemed immediately to know that their lives, as they had known them, had utterly come to an end (Isa 6:5; Ezek 1–4; Mic 1:3-8; Hab 3:1-16, esp. v. 16). This accords with the oft-expressed OT conviction that seeing God meant death (cf. Gen 32:30; Exod 33:20; Deut 4:33; 5:23-26; Judg 6:22-23; 13:22). Martyrdom then was not just the culminating event of the prophetic role but its originating crisis. The prophets' readiness to face death in the physical sense undoubtedly found its generating source in the radical encounter with God that, at the outset in every sense that mattered, had already claimed their lives.

As we look at each prophetic book in the subsequent chapters, we will see how the prophetic role sketched above is played out in each individual case. We will also see how this role in the case of all of these prophets is, in one way or another, intensively focused on what God is trying to say to the people in the times before, during, and after the catastrophe of the exile. As the Exodus event is the pivotal focus of the Torah, the exile is the crucial focal point of the Prophets. The significance of this latter event for Israel and its prophets is understandable, for to them it represented nothing less than the end of their world.

This brings us to a consideration of that part of the prophetic message that directly focuses on the end of the world, *the apocalyptic tradition*. The meaning of the term *apocalyptic* has to do with "taking off the cover"; that is, "unveiling" or "revealing." Thus, apocalyptic is all about the revelation of the end-time and how the end-time will entail the revelation of all things. One of the leading scholars of OT apocalyptic, Paul Hanson, has identified five prominent features that characterize this tradition:

1. viewing all of human history in terms of two ages, specifically with a review of the decline of "this present age" and a preview of "the new age to come"

2. seeing a decisive cosmic conflict between two powers: God versus all the forces of evil

3. a pessimism as far as any hope arising from the present, decadent age

4. a hope seen to be entirely vested in the age to come through God's decisive end-time action

5. revelation entrusted to certain, privileged individuals, usually by means of angelic messengers, visions, and cryptic, symbolic communications[52]

With this in view, *apocalyptic* could be defined as a revelatory outlook that features a preview of the end that is given to God's people "in the middle" in order to expose the powers of the present as the temporary idols they are and to empower God's people to live in the light of the end.

The Intertestamental Period seems to have been the high time for apocalyptic spiritual and literary activity, generating a significant number of apocalyptic texts, including some among the deuterocanonical books and many more among texts outside the canon. Modern scholars point to the social alienation of

---

52. Paul D. Hanson, *The Dawn of Apocalyptic* (Philadelphia: Fortress Press, 1975).

societal groups as the key catalyst in the development of the apocalyptic perspective. With the collapse of hope in the present, the stage is set for a leap of faith in a final, radical intervention of God. These scholars see the Intertestamental Period, especially the time of the persecution of Jews in and around the Maccabean Revolt in the second century BCE, as the prime time for this.

The apocalyptic tradition is reflected in a number of passages throughout the OT prophetic books (e.g., Isa 24–27; Ezek 38–39; Joel 2–3; Hab 3; Zeph 1–3; Zech 9–14; Mal 4), but it is represented most fully in the book of Daniel. Modern academic scholarship has widely followed the view that the book of Daniel, at least its apocalyptic visions in chapters 7–12, and the apocalyptic portions of the major and minor prophets, were late additions to the canon of Scripture, even as late as the second century BCE. In this way, modern scholarship has driven a sizable wedge between the OT prophetic tradition and the apocalyptic tradition. As noted earlier, before the LXX placed Daniel among the Prophetic Books, the Hebrew canon placed Daniel among the Writings. Modern biblical scholarship has seen this original Hebrew placement of Daniel as a further indication of this book's late date in the second century BCE, even though Daniel's introduction as a sage or wise man (Dan 2:12-13) rather than a prophet could explain why the Hebrews did not place this book in the Prophets.

What all of this shows is modern scholarship's tendency to see the apocalyptic tradition as a marginal perspective in the OT—marginal because it is seen to come from a later time and also, as some scholars argue, from foreign influences (such as Persian dualism, the ANE royal cult, or the wisdom tradition). Yet one might wonder, is this only reflecting the tendency of modern scholars to marginalize apocalyptic thinking in the interest of modernity's own vision of the future—one that is not prepared to entertain any thought that its own worldview of the unending march of Enlightenment progress could ever come to an end? In any case, as modernity has increasingly given way to *post*-modernity in these last days, apocalyptic thinking does not seem nearly so marginal any more.

The OT apocalyptic tradition has certainly not been marginal to Pentecostalism, itself an apocalyptically oriented movement of the Spirit poured out *"in the last days"* (Acts 2:17). From the perspective of this movement, it is not so difficult to see how the seeds of the apocalyptic tradition grew directly out of the prophetic tradition from the outset, as the presence of apocalyptic passages in the major and minor prophets would already suggest. This is because the prophetic experience of encountering God, described earlier, is itself a revelation of the end. How could it be otherwise? For God is the Alpha *and the Omega* (so Rev 1:8). In this encounter the prophets suddenly come face-to-face with their own end (Isa 6:5 KJV—"Woe is me!") and are then able to see the end of their nation (Isa 6:11 NASB—"The land is utterly desolate") and even the end of the world (Isa 24:1—"The LORD will devastate the earth"). Yet in that revelation of the end, the prophets somehow know that it is only the beginning. How could it be otherwise? For God is the Omega *and the Alpha*. God makes all things new. So it is in Isa 6:13—"Its stump is a holy seed"—and in 66:22—"As the new heavens and the new earth that I'm making will endure before me, says the LORD, so your descendants [your seed] and your name will endure."

In the light of this panoramic view of the prophets, it's now time for us to take a closer look.

ISAIAH

"Holy, holy, holy is the LORD *of heavenly forces! All the earth is filled with God's glory!"*
    —Isaiah 6:3

When I think about the book of Isaiah,

I am reminded of a recent conversation I had with my wife concerning my final wishes in the event of my death. Not to be morbid, but she wanted to know what songs I would want sung at my funeral. After some thought, I concluded that the song "I Bowed on My Knees and Cried Holy" would have to be my first choice. The song, written by Nettie Dudley Washington in 1923, was made popular by Christian artist Michael English.[53] It is one of those songs that can cause you to stop in your tracks and seriously ponder not only the sacrifice of Jesus but also the holiness of God. The lyrics to the chorus are: "I bowed on my knees and cried, 'Holy, Holy, Holy.' I clapped my hands and sang, 'Glory! Glory to the Son of God!'" The famous threefold declaration of God's holiness comes from Isaiah's call narrative in 6:3. Both the song and Isaiah's call narrative are a glimpse into the heavenly sphere. The response of both the songwriter and Isaiah is to declare the holiness of God. For Isaiah this heavenly experience ended in his calling to speak to a people who would neither listen to his message nor see the error of their ways (Isa 6:9-10; cf. Matt 13:14-15; Mark 4:12; Luke 8:10; John 12:39-40). Isaiah ministered to the people of God, who had failed to recognize the need for personal holiness and in turn had thumbed their noses at God's holiness. In many ways, the status of the church in America is very similar to the people of God in Isaiah's day. Personal holiness is often seen as passé, due in part to people's failure to recognize the holiness of God. As a Pentecostal, I find it significant that our movement was birthed from the holiness movement of Methodism. My prayer is that we would once again recover this important part of our roots (cf. Isa 6:13) and rediscover the true holiness of the One we serve, for indeed, God is *holy, holy, holy*!

Quick Facts

Title: The title comes from the name of the prophet Isaiah, whose message comprises the book. It is the same in both the LXX and the Hebrew Scriptures. Isaiah's name means "YHWH is salvation."

---

53. Videos are available online if you search "Michael English I Bowed on My Knees and Cried Holy."

Authorship and Date: The discussion related to the authorship of the book of Isaiah is intricately connected to its date as well. Before the 19th century, there was universal acceptance of the traditional view that the book was a literary unity written by Isaiah. At this time, scholars such as Bernhard Duhm, applying historical-critical methods (especially source criticism) to the study of Isaiah, mounted a challenge against the traditional view of authorship and date. Duhm advanced an alternative view that credited the book to multiple authors writing over a lengthy period of time. His view soon gained widespread support in biblical scholarship—support that has prevailed to the present day, even currently among some conservative scholars. In the standard formulation of this view, chapters 1–39 are assigned to the prophet Isaiah (and referred to as "First Isaiah"), who lived in eighth-century BCE Judah, and ministered throughout the reigns of the kings of Judah from Uzziah to Hezekiah (see Isa 1:1). Thus, his dates would be approximately 740–681 BCE, a period covered in 2 Kgs 15–21. Chapters 40–55 are credited to an anonymous author, referred to as Second, or Deutero-, Isaiah, who is thought to have written this portion of the book during the later part of the Babylonian Exile. The final part of the book of Isaiah, chapters 56–66, is called Third, or Trito-, Isaiah and is seen to be the work of an author or group of authors writing in the postexilic period soon after the Jewish people returned from captivity to their homeland.

In addition to certain minor shifts in literary themes and styles, the major reason so many have found this view of the multiple authorship of the book of Isaiah so compelling is that chapters 40–55 and then chapters 56–66 seem to reflect shifts in the historical context from which the author is writing, with 40–55 reflecting an exilic perspective (sixth century BCE) and 56–66 reflecting a postexilic viewpoint (late sixth century BCE). It is not just that these sections of Isaiah are predicting or pointing *to* these two historical contexts; they appear to be assuming or looking *from* these contexts (both of which came long after Isaiah, who lived in the eighth century BCE).

Thus, if Isaiah wrote these latter two sections of the book, then it seems this would have required his being transferred forward through time somehow to occupy standpoints long after his own lifetime. While nothing quite like this seems to happen in any other prophetic book in the Old Testament, such a possibility would not be out of the question for people who believe in the supernatural experience of prophetic vision (cf. Isa 1:1). However, the historical critics who first developed and propagated the theory of the multiple authorship of Isaiah did so, of course, from a naturalistic perspective that ruled out the possibility of *any* supernatural phenomena. Not surprisingly, this led early on to a very polarized debate on Isaiah's authorship, which for many years completely dominated all academic study of Isaiah, with one side trying to defend unity of authorship and the other side trying to disprove it by looking *always and only* for differences between the so-called First, Second, and Third Isaiahs.

More recently the debate on authorship has moderated somewhat because of two developments. First, mainstream historical critics (no doubt influenced by literary criticism) have started paying much more attention to the thematic continuities and similarities between all three parts of Isaiah, rather than just trying to accentuate the differences. Second, advocates of Isaiah's unity have become less uptight about the possibility that later editors could have had a hand in shaping the final form of the book, even while they still view Isaiah as the primary author of all three sections. What all sides of the debate might do well to consider is this question: What is it about this prophetic writing—one that announces itself as "The vision of Isaiah" (1:1 KJV)—that has generated a prophetic book like no other, specifically in terms of its quality of reaching forward beyond a single generation to address a second and third generation of God's people? Regardless of one's view on multiple authorship, the book of Isaiah has *a unique, multigenerational aspect* to it that deserves some fresh focus.

Audience and Purpose: The general audience of the book is Israelite although Isaiah ministered specifically to the nation of Judah (1:1). The audience addressed in the book stretches forward over the span of three generations, whether one sees this in terms of separate authors arising from each of these separate contexts or in terms of Isaiah casting his singular vision forth in a way that ultimately aims to address all three. In any case, the book's purpose is to show God's people the way into, through, and then beyond the divine judgment of the exile.

Genre: The book's materials fall mostly into the broad category of prophetic oracles written in poetic form. Chapters 7–8 and 36–39 are historical narratives with a prophetic focus. Other genres incorporated at various points along the way include: prophetic indictment (*rîv* formula; ch. 1); a call narrative (ch. 6); and apocalyptic visions (chs. 24–27).

Structure

While any number of possible outlines could be given for the structure of Isaiah, we will follow the generally accepted fourfold division of the book: judgment from Assyria (1–35); the narrative transition to Babylon (36–39); the promise to those in exile (40–55); the promise to those returning from exile (56–66).

Summary

Judgment from Assyria: Isaiah 1–35

The tone with which Isaiah begins is not positive. He uses the prophetic indictment formula (also called the *rîv* formula, from the Hebrew verbal root meaning "to contend"; cf. 3:13 NASB) to show that the nation had broken the Mosaic covenant. The people had practiced sin (1:4, 16), vain worship (1:11-14), violence (1:15, 21), and social injustice (1:17, 23). Consequently, God promises to judge his people (1:24-25, 28-31). This indictment sets the stage for the first section of the book; judgment is coming! Indeed, chapters 2–5 highlight the sins of the people even further. They practiced idolatry (2:8, 18), materialistic excess (2:7; 5:11-12), pride (2:11-17; 3:16; 5:15), rebellion (3:8), oppression of the poor (3:14-15; 5:8), violence (5:7), injustice (5:7, 23), and drunkenness (5:22). Even though future hope is offered (2:1-4; cf. Mic 4:1-3; 4:2-6), judgment for the wicked is predicted (2:8-22; 3:10-13; 5:5-6) through famine (3:1), privation (5:10), the loss of Judah's army (3:2-3, 25), the removal of their wealth in which they trust (3:16-24), and through foreign invasion (5:25-30).

Isaiah 6 presents the story of how Isaiah was called and commissioned to be a prophet. Although it is not clear why this chapter comes after, rather than before, the first five chapters, this passage—probably the most famous in all of OT prophetic literature—serves as a preview to the rest of the book of Isaiah. It begins with Isaiah receiving an awesome vision of the glory of God on his throne (6:1-3), attended by angelic beings chanting, "Holy, holy, holy!" In the brilliant light of this vision, Isaiah sees his own uncleanness as well as that of his people (vv. 4-5). After he cries, "Woe is me! . . . I am a man of unclean lips" (KJV), an angel purifies his lips with the touch of a burning coal (vv. 6-7). Isaiah then hears God's own voice—"Who will go?" (v. 8a)—to which he responds "Here I am. Send me" (v. 8b HCSB). This results in his being commissioned to go speak to his people. However, he is told it will be a message that they will not hear—a message that will even *cause* them not to hear, not to see, and not to perceive (vv. 9-10). "For how long?" Isaiah asks (v. 11 ISV). The answer: until the land and the people are decimated, reduced to a tenth, and then this remnant will itself be devastated until nothing more than a stump, as it were, will remain (vv. 11-12). The final word of Isaiah's commission is one of hope: in the "stump is a holy seed" (v. 13)

We can see this commission play out in the subsequent sections of the book: we see Isaiah's own generation not heeding his message (chs. 7-8); and then his land and people being decimated by the Assyrians until only a "remnant . . . is left" (chs. 36–37; see 37:4 KJV); but then the remnant must look ahead to a further devastation that will result in its being cut down completely by the Babylonians (ch. 39); but after this, the book of Isaiah envisions a new generation, indeed *a holy "seed"* (53:10 KJV) rising up to new life out of and beyond the exile (chs. 40–66).

The historical narrative of chapters 7–8 further introduces how the first phase of Isaiah's mission will unfold, just as the second historical narrative of chapters 36–39 will introduce how the final phase of his mission will unfurl. The first narrative focuses on how God's judgment on his people through the Assyrian Empire comes about, beginning with a military crisis during the time of King Ahaz of Jerusalem. The second narrative focuses on how God's further judgment on the remnant of his people through the Babylonian Empire comes into view, beginning with a military crisis during the time of King Hezekiah, Ahaz's son. What adds to the comparison between these two historical narratives—the only two in the book—is that, in both stories, the military crisis is posed in a confrontation that takes place on the same geographical spot, namely, beside a water source just outside the walls of Jerusalem (see 7:3; 36:2). And in both cases the prophet Isaiah gives these two kings, who represent their respective generations, words and signs from YHWH on which the outcome of each of these two crises will turn.

The crisis for Ahaz in chapter 7 is an impending attack by Judah's northern neighbors, Syria and Ephraim (that is, the northern kingdom of Israel). Isaiah's word to Ahaz is "Trust in YHWH" rather than in other sources (7:9), but Ahaz rejects this word and an offer to choose a confirming sign. The story in 2

Kings 16 tells how Ahaz on this occasion ended up putting his trust in a security pact with the Assyrian Empire. Through Isaiah, God gives Ahaz a sign anyway, but it is a sign that is not perceived. The sign of a virgin (KJV) having a child named Immanuel, meaning "God with us" (7:14), would mean something to future followers of the Messiah (Matt 1:23), but its meaning here is lost on Ahaz—just the sort of thing Isaiah's commissioning word had predicted (6:9).

In chapter 8 God follows up this word delivered *through* Isaiah with a word spoken *to* Isaiah himself. Here God shows how the Immanuel prophecy refused by Ahaz will morph into another meaning. "God with us" will take the form of invasion by the Assyrian Empire (8:5-10). In light of this coming invasion, God now tells Isaiah to shift the focus of his ministry to "the children whom [YHWH] has given" him (8:18 ESV).[54] Everything in the rest of this section of Isaiah (chs. 8–35) can be seen as Isaiah's prophetic curriculum for that new generation of Hebrew children—the "teaching" (8:16) that will help get them ready for the coming crisis of the Assyrian invasion that will constitute their moment of truth, the defining test of their faith.

As a minister to children, Isaiah gives encouraging oracles about how God's kingdom plans will come through a promised child—a promise that points all the way to the Messiah ("Unto us a child is born . . ."—9:2-7 KJV; "A shoot will grow up from the stump of Jesse . . ."—11:1-10). In the meantime, judgment must first begin in the "house" of God. So Isaiah foretells the judgment of Israel due to their pervasive sin (9:8–10:4; 22:1-25). Yet, hope still remains for the survivors, or remnant (10:20-23; 11:11-16), as God promises to judge his *instrument of judgment*, Assyria (10:5-19, 24-34), an act of salvation for God's people that will inspire a joyful song of thanksgiving (12:1-6).

Chapters 13–23 record Isaiah's oracles against the nations. Isaiah's children need not make the same mistakes of Ahaz and his generation, fearing other nations or trusting in them for security. These oracles show God's dominion over all nations (14:24-27; 17:12-14; 18:7; 23:9), and that God judges sin wherever it is found, especially hubris (13:11; 14:11-16; 16:6; 22:16; 23:9; cf. 25:11). In turn, the punishment of the nations offers hope to God's people that God is just, and in some cases, God's judgment has redemptive implications for the nations (19:19-25). Not surprisingly, much like Amos 1–2, Isaiah pronounces judgment on all the nations that have in some way oppressed Israel and Judah or may have influenced them to commit spiritual adultery, that is, breaking their covenant with God. These nations include: Babylon (13:1-22; 14:4-24; 21:1-10); Assyria (14:25; cf. 31:8-9), Philistia (14:29-32); Moab (15:1–16:14; cf. 25:10-12), Syria/Damascus (17:1-3), Ethiopia/Cush (18:1-8; 20:3-6), Egypt (19:1-18; 20:3-6), Edom (Seir) and Arabia (21:11-17; cf. 34:5-15), and Tyre (23:1-18).

The "Little Apocalypse" of chapters 24–27 is so named due to its focus on the divine judgment of the entire earth (24:1-21; 25:8; 26:9, 21) in apocalyptic scenes (e.g., 24:1-6; 27:1) with cosmic upheaval (e.g., 24:18-20). Some scholars see these chapters as a much later addition, added during the Intertestamental Period, when apocalyptic thinking was especially prevalent. While this may be possible, it does not have to be the case, for in other sections one can find similar themes of judgment on the nations (e.g., 30:29-33;

---

54. Rickie D. Moore, *The Spirit of the Old Testament*, JPTS 35 (Blandford Forum, UK: Deo, 2011), 78–85.

34:1-4) and on Judah (chs. 13–23; 28–34). In preparation for the turbulent times ahead, Isaiah's children need to know this about YHWH: "He's got the whole world in his hands."

Chapters 28–35 switch to a series of woe oracles against Ephraim/Israel and Ariel/Jerusalem (cf. 28:1; 29:1; 30:1; 31:1; 33:1) followed by words of judgment, once again, for the nations (ch. 34) and hope for God's people (ch. 35). Isaiah points out four key areas in which God's people have sinned:

1) God's leaders are drunkards (28:1, 6-8; cf. 56:9-12);

2) his people pay lip service to him (29:13-14);

3) they have rebelled by making foreign alliances (30:1-7; 31:1-3); and

4) they have rejected God's prophets (30:8-17).

However, God's judgment is not forever (28:23-29; 30:18-26; 31:4-5; 32:15-20; 33:13-24; 35:1-4); it will bring about repentance in the end (29:23-24; 35:5-10).

The Narrative Transition to Babylon: Isaiah 36–39

The historical narrative of chapters 36–39 largely repeats 2 Kgs 18–20. In the book of Isaiah, this story serves to shift the focus from Assyria, which looms large in the first half of the book, to the Babylonians and the coming exile, which play such a dominant role in the second half. As seen earlier, in the same way that chapters 7–8 introduced Assyria as the world power in Ahaz's day, chapters 36–39 introduce Babylon's emergence in Hezekiah's day.

These chapters narrate three crises in the reign of Hezekiah. The first, in chapters 36–37, is the invasion of the Assyrian Empire (ca. 701 BCE), predicted in the aftermath of the Ahaz crisis in chapters 7–8 and taking place on the same spot of ground, beside the water source just outside the walls of Jerusalem (36:2; cf. 7:3). Thus, for Isaiah, this crisis of Hezekiah's day is obviously being presented to highlight comparison with the crisis of Ahaz's day. The significance of this episode in Israel's history is shown by the fact that it is recounted two other times in the OT (2 Kgs 18–19; 2 Chron 32), and what's more, it is referenced in some Assyrian records discovered by modern archaeologists. When Hezekiah is confronted by the Assyrian army encamped outside the gates of Jerusalem, Hezekiah, unlike his father, Ahaz, looks to the prophet Isaiah and heeds the word and the sign that God gives. And God, in response to Hezekiah's submission, works a dramatic and sudden deliverance of the city, involving a plague hitting the Assyrian camp, bringing death to thousands during the night (recalling the Passover night in Egypt), and causing the Assyrian army to lift its siege and return home (37:33-38).

Chapter 38 presents Hezekiah's second crisis, which actually dates three years before the Assyrian siege (ca. 704 BCE). Here Hezekiah is struck with a terminal illness. He responds similarly to how he responded during the siege. He seeks YHWH and receives an oracle of salvation (or deliverance) from the prophet Isaiah. God promises to extend Hezekiah's life another 15 years.

However, Hezekiah is tested by one final crisis in chapter 39. Babylonian officials come to Jerusalem, not to conquer but to court Hezekiah's favor. Hezekiah shows off all of his kingdom's treasures, even the treasures of the temple. The Babylonians leave, and then Isaiah comes to ask Hezekiah what he has shown these state visitors. "Everything," Hezekiah tells him, whereupon Isaiah gives him a word from YHWH that the Babylonians will come back at a later time to take everything, even Hezekiah's children. Hezekiah's response this time, unlike the two previous times, does not involve any appeal to the Lord. Earlier he had interceded for his city and for his own threatened life, but not here for his children. Chapter 39 ends with a telling comment in this regard: "Hezekiah said to Isaiah, 'The Lord's word that you delivered is good,' since he thought, That means there will be peace and security in my lifetime" (39:8).

Hezekiah had seen in his generation the salvation of YHWH that Ahaz had failed to see in his. However, both had failed the test of attending to the salvation of the generation that followed them. After Ahaz's failure in chapter 7, Isaiah is called to take up the cause of the children (cf. 8:16-18). Chapters 9–39 provide the proof that he did. After Hezekiah's failure in chapter 39, will Isaiah once again take up the cause of the children, indeed the children of the next generation? Perhaps chapters 40–66 should be seen as the proof that he did.

The Promise to Those in Exile: Isaiah 40–55

This part of Isaiah presents the longest, richest collection of salvation oracles in Scripture and is principally responsible for why Isaiah so regularly is called "the fifth gospel" in Christian tradition and why this biblical text became such a major source for the lyrics of Handel's *Messiah*. The salvation announced is all about YHWH's gracious, powerful, and unstoppable plan to rescue his people, to deliver them from—so it becomes increasingly clear—their captivity in Babylon (43:14; 45:13; 47:1-7; 48:20).

The section begins with words that immediately mark the dramatic shift beyond the impending judgment, which dominated chapters 1–39, to the promised salvation, which will dominate chapters 40–55: "Comfort, comfort my people! says your God" (40:1). As scholars often note, this verse together with the rest of chapter 40 is a bit like a second "call narrative," summoning someone to carry this glorious news (vv. 2-3) and even to enlist other voices in the effort (vv. 6, 9)—an emphasis that fits precisely with the idea that the book is now showing the passing of the torch of Isaiah's mission to the "voice" (vv. 3, 6) of another generation beyond Isaiah's own lifetime, regardless of how one views the question of authorship.

The primary thrust of the message is: "Behold your God!" (40:9 KJV). Whereas Isaiah was first called to a generation who would not "see . . . or hear" (6:10), this new section of Isaiah declares: "The Lord's glory will appear, and *all humanity will see it* together" (40:5, emphasis added). The same Lord, who appeared in Isaiah's vision as "holy, holy, holy!" (6:3) is "the holy one of Israel" (41:14; 43:3,14; 45:11; 47:4; 48:17; 49:7; 54:5; 55:5), who will now show himself in the act of saving his people (52:10), whereby Israel will become "a light to the nations" (42:6; 49:6; 51:4). The gods of the nations are "no-gods" (41:29; 43:10; 44:6) that the nations themselves have made and have to carry around (40:19-20; 46:6-7), but YHWH, "the creator of the ends of the earth" (40:28; cf. 45:12,18), has made Israel (43:1; 44:2) and now will carry

Israel out of captivity back to the promised land (40:11; 46:3-4) in a new exodus (43:16-21; 50:2; 51:9-10), a totally "new thing" in the earth (43:19; 48:6).

All of this will come from God alone, mediated especially by three divine means:

1) the "*word*" *of YHWH* (*davar*), which "endures forever" and "shall not return to me void, but it shall prosper in the thing for which I sent it" (40:8 NIV; 55:11 NKJV);

2) "*the spirit*" (*ruach*, wind or breath, KJV) *of YHWH*, by which "the flower withers when the Lord's breath blows on it" (40:7, 24) and yet which God promises "to pour out" like water "upon your descendants" to bring "blessing upon your offspring" (44:3); and

3) "*the glory of* [*YHWH*]" (God's *kavod*, i.e., his weighty, manifest presence), which will appear in a way that "all flesh will see it" (40:5 KJV).

YHWH is the sole source, but he will utilize human agency in three ways:

1) he will use a royal conqueror to execute the military defeat of Babylon (41:2; identified as Cyrus, king of Persia, in 44:28; 45:1, 13);

2) yet on the other end of the social spectrum, he will appoint and anoint a lowly servant, "the servant of YHWH," whose humble work, described in four passages (the so-called "Servant Songs" 42:1-9; 49:1-6; 50:4-6; 52:13–53:12), will bring about God's justice and salvation somehow through his sacrificial suffering and death, like a lamb, on behalf of God's people. This servant is first identified as Israel (41:8-9) but then identified as a remnant who will "bring back the survivors of Israel" (49:5-6)—a calling that, as we Christians have come to see, was fully and finally fulfilled only by the "Lamb of God who takes away the sin of the world" (John 1:29; cf. Isa 53; Matt 8:17; John 12:38; Acts 8:34-35).

3) And then finally God enlists his people, all of whom are "servants of [YHWH]" (54:17). They are all being summoned to take up the words of the entire message of chapters 40–55—these wondrous poems, oracles, and songs of salvation. God's people must believe and embrace these words enough to get up and to get out of Babylon and start heading home (48:20).

The amazing reality of it all is this: that is precisely and actually what happened in human history, in the sixth century BCE, when a nation that had, for all practical purposes, lost its life in Babylonian captivity, arose from the dead and sang its way back to its homeland on the wings of these words of Isaiah (cf. 40:31).

The Promise to Those Returning from Exile: Isaiah 56–66

The final block of Isaiah, often assigned to "Third-Isaiah," has clear indications of addressing the context that confronted the exiles who returned from Babylonian captivity in response to the Persian decree of Cyrus in 538 BCE. The background in view seems no longer to be that of Jews in exile but rather, Jews struggling to restore life in their homeland (e.g., 58:12). The returnees no doubt came back to Jerusalem with the high hopes inspired by Isaiah's visionary promises, but soon faced the hard task of rebuilding a city and a community in ruins (cf. Ezra and Nehemiah). The prophetic message for their situation came in the form of two types of material that characterize this section of the book: (1) oracles that address internal disputes and social divisions over matters of justice and community practice (esp. chs. 56–59) and (2) oracles of salvation similar to those in Isaiah 40–55 (esp. chs. 60–62; with 61:1-4 often being seen as a fifth "Servant Song"). Chapters 64–66 feature a mixture of these two types, with perhaps one additional type: a poignant communal lament asking God to intervene for his people (63:7–64:12). Even as chapters 40–55 deliver a message of God's "salvation *for all generations*" (51:8, emphasis added) and not just for the exiles in Babylon, chapters 56–66 present a message that speaks both to and well beyond the postexilic generation, even unto the most ultimate eschatological promises of God: "As the new heavens and the new earth that I'm making will endure before me, says the LORD, so your descendants [your seed] and your name will endure" (66:22).

Debated Issues (aka Great Paper Topics)

1) What are some of the explanations for the appearance of Cyrus's name in 44:28 and 45:1?

2) How do the "Servant Songs" of chapters 42–53 addressed to Israel relate to the life of Jesus?

3) What are some of the scholarly views on the authorship of the book of Isaiah?

The Message of the Book

In accord with the meaning of Isaiah's name, this book reveals YHWH's "salvation for all generations" (51:8). Unfolding through the generations of Israel's preexilic disobedience, exilic judgment, and postexilic restoration, it opens up God's ultimate plan of salvation for all humankind.

Closing the Loop

As the leading book of the Major Prophets, as well as the OT prophetic writings generally, Isaiah provides an overview of this important segment of Scripture. In a similar way, Isaiah's call narrative in chapter 6 presents an overview of his book. For several reasons, this most famous chapter has been especially important to Pentecostals. First, it features a dramatic encounter with God, involving visionary and spoken revelations—the kind of experience that Pentecostal spirituality has especially highlighted. Second, Isaiah 6 takes the form of a first-person report—what Pentecostals refer to as "testimony." Third, Isaiah's testimony is of the sort that focuses on a revelatory moment when a lifelong call from God is inaugurated—the kind that has been prominent in the history of Pentecostalism. Fourth, the altar context of such an experience, as depicted in Isaiah 6, powerfully resonates with the emphasis in Pentecostal worship on the "altar call" and "going down to the altar" in expectation of an encounter with God.[55] And of course there is the whole scene of heavenly worship, prefiguring the heavenly vision and angelic chorus of "Holy, holy, holy" in Revelation 4, which inspires so many songs and choruses in Pentecostal and charismatic worship. Finally, mention could be made of Isaiah's mouth being touched by a burning coal—a poignant detail that can quickly leap forward in Pentecostal imagination to the tongues of fire in Acts 2.

While Pentecostalism has been quick to identify closely with Isaiah 6, this chapter, in view of its connection to the whole book of Isaiah, has other things to offer this spiritual tradition—things that, like that coal of fire, may not be nearly so easy to embrace. Indeed, there is a painful paradox in how burned lips are somehow prepared to speak holy words that will not be understood by one's own generation. Yet these are the very words, Isaiah shows us, on which the salvation of future generations will depend.

---

55. Rickie D. Moore, "Altar Hermeneutics: Reflections on Pentecostal Biblical Interpretation," *Pneuma* 38 (2016): 1–12.

JEREMIAH

"This very day I appoint you over nations and empires, to dig up and pull down, to destroy and demolish, to build and plant."

—Jeremiah 1:10

When I think about the book of Jeremiah,

I recall the TV and Hollywood actor Patrick Dempsey. Why, you might ask? Because in 1998, Dempsey actually played the role of the prophet in the movie titled *Jeremiah*. An aspect of Jeremiah's character that is portrayed exquisitely by Dempsey in the film is his role as the "weeping prophet." While the film adds nonbiblical material to the story line (e.g., a love interest for Jeremiah, named Judith), the movie's portrayal of Jeremiah as a man who was rejected by his family, his people, and at times seemingly by his God, rings true to the scriptural text. At one point in the movie, after being beaten and imprisoned, Dempsey voices Jer 20:9, where the prophet declares that he will no longer speak in the name of God. Of course, in both the biblical account and the movie, Jeremiah could not fulfill that declaration before God because the prophetic word to the prophet was like "fire shut up in [his] bones," which the prophet could not contain (20:9b KJV; cf. 23:29).

On several occasions I have spoken to students who have what some Christians label as "the call of God" on their lives, and yet they attempt to walk away from it. In most cases these students have tried to avoid this call because of external pressures and internal struggles over what this call might entail. Indeed, trials, rejection, and weeping often accompany service for God. However, as these students have ventured into other areas of study and vocation, this calling became like "fire shut up in their bones." And in some cases, these students have surrendered to God and returned to their true calling to minister, willing to face whatever "weeping" and hardships may come their way. If you are presently feeling the weight of your "call," know for sure that you are not alone. God is with you. As Jeremiah clearly shows (and Dempsey, too), this pain is momentary in comparison to a lifetime *and* an eternity of regret.

Quick Facts

Title: The book is named after the prophet Jeremiah, whose message is conveyed in the book. It is the same in both the LXX and the Hebrew Bible. The meaning of Jeremiah's name is uncertain, but possibilities include "YHWH exalts" and "YHWH throws."

Authorship and Date: Several views on authorship have been proposed. The most prevalent view in both Jewish and conservative Christian circles is that Jeremiah, who came from a priestly family in a town near Jerusalem called Anathoth (1:1), wrote his book with the help of his scribe, Baruch (*Baba Bathra* 15a). Both OT and NT authors attribute the book, in whole or in part, to Jeremiah (cf. Dan 9:2; Matt 2:17; 27:9), as do the intertestamental Jewish writer Ben Sira (Sirach 49:6-7) and the first-century Jewish historian Josephus (cf. *Ant* 10:78-179; *Jwr* 5:391). Most of the book is a compilation of oracles delivered by Jeremiah throughout his ministry (ca. 627–580 BCE) during the reigns of Josiah to Zedekiah (1:3) and beyond (chs. 40–45; 52:31-34). Other parts of the book, often attributed to Baruch, are historical and biographical narratives, which focus on events in Jeremiah's life. Some scholars have argued that large portions of the book were later additions made in the exile or even later, in the Intertestamental Period, by some adherent of either the Deuteronomist tradition or the "school" of the prophet Jeremiah. Some of this debate centers on the two divergent text traditions of the book. The LXX translation of Jeremiah is approximately 13 percent shorter than the Hebrew MT text (which is followed in our English Bibles). Moreover, the chapters containing the oracles against the nations appear in a different order and location in the LXX (cf. chs. 46–51 in the MT versus 25:14–31:44 in the LXX). Interestingly, at Qumran six partial Jeremiah scrolls were found in caves 2 and 4 (i.e., 2QJer and 4QJer^{a-e} [4QJer^a dates ca. 200 BCE]), yielding support for both the LXX and MT text traditions of Jeremiah (e.g., 4QJer^b and 4QJer^d parallel the LXX). In light of this, two schools of thought on the authorship of Jeremiah have emerged. One camp argues that the two text traditions show that the book was in flux for a period of time and that those two separate traditions of the life and prophecies of Jeremiah existed side by side. The other camp posits that the shorter text tradition contains the earliest words of Jeremiah, which circulated independently, and that the longer tradition may reflect the added words of Jeremiah's amanuensis or secretary, Baruch (cf. 36:32; 45:1). The fact remains that while we cannot be certain of either hypothesis, most scholars agree that Jeremiah wrote at least some of the words contained in the book that bears his name. Based on the notation about Evilmerodach's rise to the throne of Babylon in 52:31 (cf. 2 Kgs 25:27-30), the book had to have been completed/edited no earlier than 562 BCE, the date of Nebuchadnezzar's death.

Audience and Purpose: Primarily, the book served to warn the nation of Judah to repent or else face the destruction of Jerusalem by Babylon. Secondarily, it was instructional for those who remained after the fall of the city in 586 BCE. At different junctures in the book, prophetic words were directed to Jews located in Judah, Babylon, and Egypt, respectively.

Genre: Most of the book falls into the category of prophetic oracles written in both prose and poetry. Other genres used include: covenant indictment (2:2-37); letters (29:1-27); and historical, biographical, and autobiographical narratives (e.g., 1:1-19; 26:1-24; 28:1-17; 35:1–39:18; 52:1-34).

Structure

Although not strictly chronological in its arrangement, the book of Jeremiah may be broken down into a series of divisions as follows: Jeremiah's early ministry (1–20); Jeremiah in the reigns of Josiah's sons and grandson (21–39); Jeremiah with the remnant in Judah (40–44); Jeremiah's prophecy to Baruch (45); oracles against the nations (46–51); historical epilogue on the fall of Jerusalem (52).

Summary

Jeremiah's Early Ministry: Chapters 1–20

The book of Jeremiah begins with a paragraph that sets the context of the book in Judah from the reign of Josiah to "when the people of Jerusalem were taken into exile" (i.e., 626–587 BCE; 1:1-3). Josiah came to the throne when he was eight years old and soon led the nation back to YHWH in a sweeping reform—a reform that was spurred by the finding of the book of the Torah in the Temple (2 Kgs 22–23). What makes this context so significant is that it represents the last days of the kingdom of Judah—the period that moves from the high hopes of Josiah's kingship to the catastrophic event of Jerusalem's destruction.

The rest of chapter 1 presents Jeremiah's call narrative—a first-person testimony of how he is called to be the prophet who would herald the hard news of God's coming judgment against Jerusalem (1:4-19). Like Josiah, Jeremiah is appointed to his role while "only a child" (1:7). Like Moses, Jeremiah shrinks back from the task, only to receive God's assurance that he must go unafraid wherever God sends him. The words God will put in his mouth will have the power "to dig up and pull down, to destroy and demolish, to build and plant" (v. 10). Like Isaiah, Jeremiah receives his prophetic call through word, vision, and a supernatural touch on his mouth. However, while Isaiah's encounter with God was heavenly, majestic, and awesome, the call of Jeremiah is a personal, intimate conversation with God reinforced by visions of ordinary things (a blooming branch and a boiling pot), which are given symbolic meanings: God's judgment against his people is about to blossom and spill out "from the north" (later to be identified as Babylon). As Jeremiah carries the unwelcomed message of the coming assault upon the chosen city of Jerusalem, Jeremiah is told that he himself will be attacked by Judah's "kings, its princes, its priests, and all its people" (v. 18). Yet not to worry; Jeremiah is given the promise that God will make him "a fortified city" and continue to be with him (vv. 18-19 NASB).

This call narrative in chapter 1 previews the entire book of Jeremiah, just as Isaiah 6 does for that prophetic book. Most of chapters 2–20 are oracles of Jeremiah that present God's case, his covenant lawsuit (*rîv*), against his people. The primary indictment is forsaking YHWH and turning to other gods (e.g., 2:5, 13), which Jeremiah depicts in the racy imagery of sexual promiscuity (e.g., 2:20-24), much as Hosea did for Israel a century earlier. Flowing from this main charge are various other charges, including social injustice (5:1, 28; 6:6), sexual sins (5:8), child sacrifice (7:31; 19:5; cf. 32:35), deception (9:3-8), Sabbath breaking (17:19-27), and general wickedness and rebellion (cf. 4:15-22; 5:3-4, 23; 6:7, 28; 7:8-10, 24; 16:12; 18:11-12).

Another prominent indictment alongside the worship of false gods is the false worship of the true God. In fact, chapter 7 presents a story about how God calls Jeremiah to go deliver a message on this issue beside the entrance to the temple—the so-called Temple Sermon of Jeremiah (ch. 26 shows how Jeremiah carried out this assignment soon after Josiah's death). The people are putting their trust in temple rites, while covering up their social wrongs. Jeremiah declares that God stands ready to forsake the temple and destroy it, just as God did with Shiloh (cf. 1 Sam 3–4; Ps 78:60). This idea that God would forsake and destroy the temple is considered a heresy by Jeremiah's audience.

Jeremiah not only elaborates the legal charges but also announces the legal sentence, using graphic, poetic depictions of military invasion (e.g., chs. 4 and 6). In these passages, divine judgment seems to be a done deal. Yet in other passages, Jeremiah seems to reflect God's struggle over the possibility of Israel's "turning around" so that God can "turn things around" (*shuv*; 3:1–4:4). What's more, some passages even show God's anguish and perhaps Jeremiah's, too, as their words seem to merge: "If only my head were a spring of water and my eyes a fountain of tears, I would weep day and night for the wounds of my people" (9:1; cf. 4:19; 8:18).

Thus, Jeremiah, like no other prophet, reveals *the pathos of YHWH*. And in a related way, Jeremiah exposes *his own pathos* and inner struggle, particularly in relation to the difficulties of his prophetic calling. He does this in a series of prayers, dispersed throughout chapters 11–20. Scholars have called these "the Confessions of Jeremiah" (11:18–12:6; 15:10-21; 17:14-18; 18:18-23; 20:7-18). Here the prophet talks back to God, pouring out cries to God for intervention, requests for God to punish his enemies, lamentations to the point of wishing he had never been born, and even strong complaints against God for leaving him hanging. Jeremiah wants to quit, but God refuses to accept his resignation (cf. 15:10-21). These passages add richly to the lament tradition seen elsewhere in the OT, such as in the books of Job and Psalms. These brutally honest prayers offer us important biblical resources for going through the depths of human trauma, and in so doing they prefigure Jesus's prayers in Gethsemane and ultimately reflect the passions of God.

Jeremiah in the Reigns of Josiah's Sons and Grandson: Chapters 21–39

The period immediately following the death of Josiah in 609 BCE betrays a spiritual milieu in Judah that was far from repentant. The general public and leadership appear to have given only lip service to Josiah's reforms. The rapid succession of Josiah's sons (Jehoahaz, Jehoiakim, and Zedekiah) and grandson (Jehoiachin) in a span of about 22 years is telling of the political volatility of the period. While Josiah may have been a true reformer (cf. 22:15-16), his children certainly did not have the wherewithal to continue those reforms. It was in this setting that Jeremiah delivered some of his most scathing indictments and warnings. At this point Jeremiah's ministry within Jerusalem in particular became extremely important for the spiritual well-being of the nation but dangerous for the prophet.

Chapter 21 jumps forward past the reigns of three kings and begins with Zedekiah's interaction with Jeremiah when Babylon was attacking Judah (21:2; ca. 589 BCE). Jeremiah's words from the Lord to the king are not encouraging: Jerusalem will fall to Nebuchadnezzar (21:10; cf. 22:7-9), and Zedekiah will be given into his hand (21:7). The only hope for the people is to go out to the Babylonians and surrender (21:9). Apart from the many sins mentioned in chapters 1–20, Jeremiah also highlights the injustice and unrighteousness of the kings and their cronies (21:12; 22:3). If only they would seek justice for the oppressed, then perhaps God's wrath could be averted (22:4). Instead, Judah's kings and the people continue to practice injustice and oppression (22:13-14, 17). Jehoiakim was particularly guilty of these atrocities and as such would suffer an ignominious death and no proper burial (22:18-19), a common motif in the book (cf. 7:33; 8:2; 9:22; 12:9; 16:4; 19:7; 25:33; 34:20). Because of their mistreatment of the people of God (23:1-2), throughout this section, Jeremiah delivers oracles against each one of the successors of Josiah: Shallum, or Jehoahaz (22:11-12), Jehoiakim (22:18-19), Coniah, or Jehoiachin (22:25-30), and Zedekiah (21:7; cf. 34:2-5). Moreover, as was common in an earlier era, there are prophets and priests who commit abominations (23:9-14) and speak in their own name, rather than God's (23:16, 21, 25, 32) thus receiving punishment as well (23:15-40). Although the current lineage of David is corrupt, God will raise up a "righteous Branch" from David's line who will execute justice and bring back God's scattered flock (23:3-8 KJV).

The next few chapters do not follow a chronological sequence. Chapters 24 and 27–29 address the period shortly after the deportation of 597 BCE (cf. 24:1; 27:1; 28:1), whereas chapters 25 and 26 go back to the early reign of Jehoiakim. In chapter 25, Jeremiah reminds the people of his prophecies against their idolatry and wickedness from the reign of Josiah until 605 (25:2-7; cf. chs. 1–20). Because they had rejected Jeremiah's message, judgment was coming upon them by the hand of Nebuchadnezzar: Judah will serve him for 70 years (25:8-11). However, God is eventually going to judge Babylon (25:12-14; cf. chs. 50–51) and all of the nations for their violence and bloodshed as well (25:15-38). Chapter 26 goes back further yet again to circa 609 BCE, when there appears to have been the possibility of averting the wrath of God if the people repented (26:1-3, 13; cf. ch. 7). Here we find a narrative account featuring leaders (i.e., the false prophets and priests) who withstood Jeremiah's words, even to the point of considering his execution. Nevertheless, certain officials and people delivered Jeremiah from their hands (26:16, 24) by recalling the testimony of earlier prophets, such as Micah, and King Hezekiah's humble response to Micah's prophecies (26:17-19). Jehoiakim's execution of a prophet named Uriah is noted, clearly showing that this king lacked this same level of humility (26:20-23).

Similar to the sign acts of earlier chapters, Jeremiah sees, in chapter 24, a vision of two baskets of figs: one good and one bad. The message is clear: those who have gone into exile are "good" and those remaining in Judah are "bad." God will restore the former and punish the latter. Chapters 27 and 28 appear to have happened at the same time (ca. 594/3 BCE). In chapter 27, Jeremiah wears an ox yoke as a sign act to inform Zedekiah and the surrounding nations that God has made Nebuchadnezzar their ruler (27:1-13); Zedekiah should not listen to the false prophets (27:14-17), for indeed, the remaining treasures of the temple will be taken to Babylon (27:18-22). Chapter 28 gives a specific example of the ongoing power struggle between Jeremiah and the false prophets. Here the false prophet Hananiah contradicts Jeremiah's prophecy concerning the destruction and exile of Jerusalem by declaring that God would bring back the exiles and the treasures of the temple within two years (28:1-4). Jeremiah's response is to affirm his original prophecy and to foretell the death of Hananiah because of his false prophecy (28:5-17). Continuing the themes of a long exile and false prophets, chapter 29 records how Jeremiah sent a letter to the Jews who had been exiled to Babylon in the earlier deportation of 597 BCE. The letter declares that the exile will last a long time, indeed 70 years (v. 10; cf. 25:11-12). He encourages these Jews to settle down and make a life in Babylon. They should not listen to the false prophets in Babylon who are prophesying a soon return, because, like Hananiah, these prophets will be judged by God (29:8-32).

Chapters 30–31 are often called the "Book of Consolation," a title based in God's instruction to Jeremiah in 30:2 to "write down in a scroll" words concerning God's promise "to restore the fortunes" (v. 3, note A in the CEB), or turn around the captivity of his people. These two chapters contain most of the oracles of hope in the entire book of Jeremiah. This collection of undated poetic oracles is framed by prose narratives whose historical context is clear: in chapter 29 there is Jeremiah's letter to the exiles in Babylon, sent soon after their deportation in 597 BCE; and in chapters 32–33 there is a story of Jeremiah following God's directive to buy back a piece of family property

Standing stones at Gezer. Most believe these types of stones were used in cultic practices. During the days of Isaiah, King Hezekiah removed sacred pillars as part of his reforms (2 Kgs 18:4). Photo courtesy of Christine Curley.

as a sign act of hope, right before the Babylonians take over the territory in 587 BCE. These prose narratives strike the same hopeful notes as the poetry they envelop, namely the promise that, after Judah's exile, God will turn around the captivity (29:14, 28; 30:2, 18; 31:23; 32:44; 33:7, 11, 26) so that there will again be building and planting (29:5; 30:18; 31:4-5, 28, 38-39; 33:7)—an echo of the hope-filled verbs in Jeremiah's initial call (1:10). Thus, the content of the poems that make up the "Book of Consolation" corresponds to how this collection is situated in the book of Jeremiah: the only place where hope can be found is right in the very midst of the inescapable judgment and grief of the exile. This is a tempered hope, yet it is a soaring hope that points all the way forward to far-future expectations of a coming messiah and a new covenant (30:9; 31:31-34).

Chapters 34–39, which oscillate between the period of Zedekiah and the earlier reign of Jehoiakim, are tied together by the themes of broken covenants and the rejection of the words of the prophet Jeremiah. Chapter 34 falls within the same time frame of chapters 32–33 (ca. 589–587 BCE). Zedekiah and the people added to their sins by re-enslaving their Israelite slaves after having released them according to a vow made to the Lord (34:8-22). Therefore, the message to Jerusalem and Zedekiah is the same as prophesied earlier: destruction and exile are coming (34:2, 22); even Zedekiah will not be able to escape (34:2-5). As part of the broken-covenant theme appearing first in chapter 34, chapter 35 returns to an undated period in the reign of Jehoiakim. Here Jeremiah lifts up the Rechabites as a sign against the people of Judah. The Rechabites honored their word/covenant with their forefathers not to drink wine, build or own houses, or plant vineyards (35:1-11), and they were blessed (35:18-19), but Judah had spurned their covenant with YHWH and the words of his prophets, and they will be cursed as a result (35:12-17). Similarly, chapter 36 (ca. 605/4 BCE) serves as a narrative example of Judah's rejection of YHWH's prophets and their words (36:24-25). Jehoiakim literally burns the words of God (36:20-23) written on a scroll by Baruch through the dictation of Jeremiah (36:4-5, 17-18, 27)—a book burning. However, this act will not stop the word of God from being declared. Jeremiah dictates to Baruch a second scroll and adds even more words of judgment to it (36:27-32).

The gravity of the sins of Judah and her kings comes to a head in chapters 37–39. Chronologically these chapters return to the reign of Zedekiah shortly before the final assault of Nebuchadnezzar on Jerusalem. These chapters also give a clear picture of the indecisive and tortured psychological state of Zedekiah before the city's fall (38:5, 14-26). The theme of rejecting the prophets' words (37:2; 38:4, 15) along with the mistreatment of Jeremiah plays a central role in the narrative (37:11-21; 38:5-7). So severe is the treatment of the prophet that a servant of Zedekiah, Ebed-melech, petitions the king to rescue Jeremiah from certain death (38:7-13)—a favor that is returned to Ebed-melech when the city fell (39:15-18). Jerusalem gets what they assume to be a reprieve when Babylon lifts their siege in order to confront Egypt's army, but Jeremiah assures his fellow citizens that Babylon will return to finish the job of destroying the city (37:5-10; cf. 38:2-3, 17-23)—a prediction that is realized in Zedekiah's 11th year, circa 587/6 BCE (39:1-2, 8). Even though Zedekiah attempts to escape from the hands of Nebuchadnezzar, he is captured, thus fulfilling the words of Jeremiah (39:4-5). As part of the punishment on the king, Nebuchadnezzar kills Zedekiah's sons and then blinds Zedekiah, leading him away to Babylon in chains along with many of the remaining inhabitants of the city (39:6-9). Conversely, Nebuchadnezzar sets Jeremiah free (39:11-15).

Jeremiah with the Remnant in Judah: Chapters 40–44

These chapters present an extended narrative of events after the fall of Jerusalem. When Jerusalem and many of Judah's cities lay in ruins after 586 BCE, there still was a large remnant of poorer people (39:10) remaining in Judah along with soldiers who had evaded capture. Even those who had fled to other places returned to Judah once Nebuchadnezzar left (40:11-12). Jeremiah is a part of that remnant, having been released by Nebuzaradan, the head of Nebuchadnezzar's bodyguard, to go wherever he pleased. He could go to Babylon or stay in Judah (40:1-4). Jeremiah decides to stay in Judah at Mizpah, which is put under the control of Gedaliah, Nebuchadnezzar's appointed leader of the remnant (40:7). Sadly, however, Jeremiah's troubles at the hands of his own people are not finished. Even after Babylon's conquest of Jerusalem, intrigue is far from over in Judah (40:13-16). Shortly after Nebuchadnezzar appoints Gedaliah, Ishmael, from the country of Ammon, comes and assassinates Gedaliah and several of his friends (41:1-10). After putting down the small rebellion (41:11-18), the remaining soldiers under the leadership of Johanan decide to round up as many of the remnant as possible and flee from the wrath of the Babylonians by going down to Egypt. However, before making a move, they seek out Jeremiah and ask him to inquire of the Lord, swearing that whatever God tells him, they will do (42:1-7). Jeremiah gives the people two options: stay in the land of Judah and be blessed (42:7-12) or go to Egypt and face God's wrath for disobeying (42:8-22). The people choose the latter and force the remnant, including Jeremiah and Baruch, to go to Egypt (43:1-7). No sooner do the people arrive in Egypt than Jeremiah delivers two more scathing oracles declaring that Nebuchadnezzar will soon arrive in Egypt to destroy both them and the land (43:8-13) because of their rebellion and idolatry (44:1-14). The people's response is once again to reject the words of Jeremiah and remain resolute in their idolatrous practices of worshipping the queen of heaven (44:15-19). In these final words of Jeremiah's biographical narrative, Jeremiah offers a final warning of judgment that the remnant will be subjected to violence and punishment: the sign that this will happen will be that Pharaoh Hophra will face defeat at the hands of his enemies (44:20-30).

Jeremiah's Prophecy to Baruch: Jeremiah 45

The prophetic oracles of Jeremiah to the people of Jerusalem and Judah before, during, and after the fall of the city culminate with Jeremiah's words of encouragement/warning to his longtime scribe and assistant, Baruch (45:1-5). Even though the words were written circa 605 BCE, they serve as a fitting end to the shared experience of the longtime ministry of Jeremiah and Baruch both before and after the destruction of Jerusalem.

The Oracles against the Nations: Jeremiah 46–51

Jeremiah's oracles against the nations begin with a denouncement of Egypt in 605 BCE, when Assyria and Egypt were defeated by Babylon at the battle of Carchemish (46:1-2), and this is followed by an oracle of judgment against the Philistines to the west (47:1-7). However, special attention is given to the desolation and judgment of Babylon for her treatment of God's covenant people (chs. 50–51 esp. 51:24, 34-36). What's more, the pride of Moab, Edom, and Babylon (48:29-30; 49:16; 50:29, 31-32) and the aggression of Ammon against Israel will be avenged (48:27; 49:1-2). By listing numerous Moabite cities set apart for judgment, Jeremiah's words to Moab, in particular, show that their punishment will be complete (e.g.,

48:21-24, 31-34). In keeping with Jeremiah's polemic against idols (51:17-18), Chemosh and Milcom (or Malcam), the gods of Moab and Ammon, will go into exile (48:7, 13, 46; 49:1, 3), and the gods Marduk and Bel of Babylon will be destroyed (50:2, 38; 51:44, 52). Judgment on these old enemies, along with Edom (49:7-22), Damascus (49:23-27), and Elam (49:34-39), offers hope to Israel (46:27-28). Yet in the midst of judgment, Jeremiah offers hope of restoration even to several of the nations God punished (cf. 48:47; 49:6; 49:39).

Historical Epilogue on the Fall of Jerusalem: Jeremiah 52

Chapter 52 is rightly labeled an epilogue, which again presents the fall of Jerusalem (cf. 39:1-10). It is the last event recorded in the book. Even though it is not last chronologically, it is last theologically, because it vindicates the message and mission of Jeremiah as seen from the beginning (cf. 1:3). Most of the chapter parallels and probably derives from 2 Kgs 24:18–25:30. As such, the account focuses on the loss of the temple and its furnishings (52:17-23), the judgment of Jerusalem's officials (52:24-27), and the number of people taken from Jerusalem to Babylon in 597, 587, and 582 BCE: 4,600 people altogether (52:28-30). Finally, as in the last paragraph of 2 Kgs 25, the book of Jeremiah ends with one closing glimmer of hope; the Babylonian king releases Judah's last king, Jehoiachin, from his prison cell so he can eat at the royal table (52:31-34; ca. 562/1 BCE)—a hint that God's promise to the Davidic dynasty is still alive.

Debated Issues (aka Great Paper Topics)

1) How do scholars interpret Jer 31:22?

2) What are the scholarly theories on the authorship of the historical epilogue of chapter 52?

3) According to scholars, what role does the putative Deuteronomist play in the authorship debate?

The Message of the Book

Breaking covenant with God finally leads to a broken people, and this brings about the breaking of the heart of God. Yet within this divine pathos lies the possibility of renewed hope for God's people, if they will but yield to the judgment and the relentless passions of YHWH.

Closing the Loop

Jeremiah's call to be a prophet came to him when he was "only a child" (1:6). This is one of its noteworthy characteristics—a feature that points back to Samuel, who also received his prophetic calling in childhood (1 Sam 3). Adding to the parallel between these two prophets is the divinely appointed beginning of both, even before they were in their mothers' wombs. In the case of Samuel, he comes as a promised child to a woman (Hannah) with a barren womb (1 Sam 1). In the case of Jeremiah, God informs him, "Before I created you in the womb I knew you; before you were born I set you apart; I made you a prophet to the nations" (Jer 1:5). What's more, these two prophets not only share the distinction of extraordinary beginnings; they also have prophetic calls that, from the start, point to dreadful endings. For Samuel, it is the end of the house of Eli, the priest, at Shiloh (1 Sam 3:11-14), and for Jeremiah, it is the end of the house of the Lord and Jerusalem (Jer 1:15-16). Jeremiah's famous "Temple Sermon" even draws attention to the parallel between these two endings: God says, "I will do to this temple that bears my name and on which you rely, the place that I gave to you and your ancestors, just as I did to Shiloh" (Jer 7:14). Obviously, much more is entailed here than the destruction of two buildings—these entail the endings of entire religious and cultural systems. In each case, this was quite a heavy burden to lay on a child.

The Day of Pentecost in Acts 2, which is the scriptural fountainhead for Pentecostalism, also brings together these same two things: the prophetic calling upon children and the weighty burden of dreaded endings coming with it. We see this in Peter's quotation of Joel's prophecy: "In the last days, God says, I will pour out my Spirit on all people. *Your sons and daughters* will prophesy. *Your young* will see visions. Your elders will dream dreams . . . The sun will be changed into darkness, and the moon will be changed into blood, before the great and spectacular day of the Lord comes" (Acts 2: 17, 20, emphasis added). Thus, the Day of Pentecost is not just about a new beginning, marked by sons and daughters prophesying; it is about "*last* days," indeed the coming "*day of the Lord.*" Losing sight of this connection between the Day of Pentecost and the day of the Lord will lead us to trivialize prophesy until it becomes nothing more than a spiritual gift serving to spice up our personal spiritual life.

The prophetic calling, from which Pentecostalism traces its lineage, is a heavy endowment that God gives to his people especially to prepare them for dark days and traumatic endings. The fact that God includes even children in this calling only sharpens the point. The book of Jeremiah, then, is particularly important for us in facing and going through the catastrophic times in human history, whether the catastrophe is international, national, local, or even personal in scope. Virtually all of the OT prophetic books share in this role, as they lead God's people into, through, and beyond their experience of the exile, but Jeremiah is especially significant, since he is the prophet who walks his people across the very threshold of the dreadful day. Thus, "the LORD proclaims," says Jeremiah, "I hear screams of panic and terror; no one is safe. Ask and see: Can men bear children? Then why do I see every man bent over in pain, as if he's in labor? Why have all turned pale? The day is awful, beyond words. A time of unspeakable pain for my people, Jacob. But they will be delivered from it" (30:5-7).

In the end, in these "last days," indeed in these times of terror, we need the prophetic words of Jeremiah, this prophet called from his mother's womb. Precisely because he gives full witness to the terror ahead of time; he bears what, in the end, proves to be the most timely and trustworthy words of hope.

LAMENTATIONS

Oh, no! She sits alone, the city that was once full of people. Once great among nations, she has become like a widow. Once a queen over provinces, she has become a slave.

—Lamentations 1:1

When I think about the book of Lamentations,

I remember the reaction of the people of New Orleans, Louisiana, after Hurricane Katrina devastated their city in late August 2005. More than 1,800 people perished during the storm, which leveled or flooded vast sections of the city. Tears and heartache were the common reaction of those who witnessed firsthand the devastation of the event. For those of us who recall the emotional displays of those who lost everything in 2005, we can easily imagine a similar scene for those surveying the razed city of Jerusalem in 586 BCE. While the phrase "act of God" has been used to describe natural disasters like Hurricane Katrina, scripture, in a much more intentional theological sense, presents the destruction of Jerusalem as an "act of God"—one brought about by God's judgment on Jerusalem for excessive sin and failure to heed his word. In the aftermath of the destruction of the city, the author of Lamentations puts pen to paper and writes down his raw emotions. The loss of the temple, king, and city was indeed heart-wrenching.

Quick Facts

Title: The English title comes from the meaning of the LXX title, *Thrēnoi* ("Lamentations"). In the Hebrew Bible the title is registered in the first word of the book, *'ēkah*, meaning "How?"

Authorship and Date: Jewish and LXX traditions attribute the book to Jeremiah. Although the Hebrew text is anonymous, verse 1 of the LXX (and Latin Vulgate) records the notation that Jeremiah wrote the book—a claim reinforced by the move, begun in the LXX, to place Lamentations immediately after Jeremiah. The book appears to have been written sometime after the destruction of Jerusalem circa 586 BCE (cf. 4:21-22; Edom is mentioned), but perhaps before 562 BCE when the hope of return began with the release of Jehoiachin (cf. 2 Kgs 25:27-30). Today, scholars are somewhat divided on who wrote the book. Those rejecting Jeremiah's authorship generally opt for an unknown author (or authors) living in Judah or the exile. There are a number of reasons to assign the text to Jeremiah or perhaps even Baruch, such as: (1) the author was clearly an eyewitness to the destruction of Jerusalem and its aftermath; (2) the weeping tone of the book matches Jeremiah; (3) the Chronicler notes Jeremiah's ability to write funeral songs (laments) (2 Chron 35:25); and (4) the language is similar to that found in several passages of Jeremiah (e.g., Lam 1:13//Jer 20:9; Lam 1:16//Jer 9:1; Lam 3:53, 55; Jer 38:6-13; etc.). However, others have posited that Jeremiah could not have been the author, in view of key motifs in Lamentations that are not present in Jeremiah's book. These include: the desire for the nations to help Judah (4:17); praise for Zedekiah (4:20); or the notation that Judah's prophets did not hear from YHWH (2:9). The truth is, we cannot be certain on the matter of the authorship of Lamentations.

Audience: The audience would have been those who survived the disaster of 586, both those in the exile in Babylon and those who remained in Judah.

Genre and Purpose: The book combines the genres of funeral dirge and lament. It features a dirge mourning the loss of Jerusalem, the temple, the Davidic kingdom, and its people. The book also reflects the ANE genre of city laments that were common in ancient Mesopotamia. In the ancient world when a nation's capital city was destroyed, authors would attempt to explain the reasons for the apparent inability of the patron god to protect the city. These city laments, such as the Lament for Sumer and Ur, and the Nippur, Eridu, and Uruk city laments, present a picture of the gods being upset with the people of their city for some mistreatment of the deity. The patron god is depicted as allowing other nations to come and punish the people of the city. In some cases the patron deity is seen joining in the devastation of their own city. These laments served the purpose of showing that one's gods were not weaker than the invaders' gods but rather that the patron deity was punishing his or her own people for malfeasance.

Historically, the book of Lamentations was originally placed in the Hebrew Scriptures as one of the five scrolls of the *Megilloth* and was assigned as a reading on the "Ninth of *Av*," the annual Jewish observance of the day that Jerusalem fell—an observance still practiced by Jews today.

Structure

The five chapters of the book present five poems, the first four of which are acrostics following the 22 letters of the Hebrew alphabet. In chapter 3 there are three verses for each letter of the Hebrew alphabet, yielding a total of 66 verses.

Summary

The five poems of Lamentations give varying perspectives relating to the loss of the city (1:1-4, 7-9; 2:9, 13; 3:48; 4:6, 22; 5:18), the temple (2:6-7), the people (1:5, 16, 18; 2:11-12, 19-21; 4:2-5, 7-10), and the Davidic king/princes/officials (1:6; 2:9; 4:20; 5:12). Chapter 1 presents the laments of Jerusalem, personified in the voice of a woman. Chapter 2, perhaps spoken by personified Judah, focuses on the Lord as the one who was responsible for the destruction (2:1-8, 17, 21-22; cf. 1:5b, 12-22; 3:43-45; 4:11; 5:19-22). Chapters 3–5 are formatted as personal laments by the author (e.g., 3:1-20, 52-56). Within these laments the author also bewails the fact that Judah's enemies now rule over the once-great city and people (1:5a, 10; 2:16; 3:45-46; 5:1-8). However, in the midst of these laments, the author breaks through to affirm that God's love endures forever (3:21-38) as he pleads for God finally to rescue his people (3:56-66).

Debated Issues (aka Great Paper Topics)

1) What are the theories on why chapter 5 is not an acrostic poem like the previous four chapters?

2) What are the differences between the Christian reading and the Jewish reading of this book?

The Message of the Book

When unthinkable disaster falls upon us, God's word provides the people of God with a way to lament. Sometimes it is only in the midst of the attempt at full expression of unspeakable grief that the glimpse of hope beyond that grief can be found, even when still more grieving lies ahead.

Closing the Loop

It is no secret that Jewish spirituality makes more room for lamentation than one usually finds in Christian faith and practice. It has been easy for Christians, living this side of Jesus's resurrection, to gravitate toward a triumphalism that sees the Christian life as all glory with no cross. The Pentecostal and charismatic streams of Christianity have been especially prone to this. The Apostle Paul found himself combatting this very tendency when writing his NT letters to the charismatically overcharged church at Corinth (cf. 1 Cor 1:18-25; 4:6-17; 2 Cor 12:6-11).

The Jews made room for Lamentations not only in Scripture but also in the annual observance of the anniversary of the temple's destruction on the "Ninth of *Av*," which nowadays also carries the burden of lingering grief over the Jewish Holocaust (*Shoah*) perpetrated by Nazi Germany. While the solemn national observance of 9/11 is a contemporary event that could perhaps offer a striking parallel for US citizens, there is little parallel to be found specifically in Christian worship practices. Even Christian readings of the book of Lamentations will almost invariably seek to ease the book's emphasis on lament by placing final stress on the book's affirmations of faith in 3:21-38. However, the book does not place this hopeful expression at the end and make it the last word, as Christian readers are inclined to do. Lamentations puts its brief burst of hope in the middle of the book, reinforcing that placement by the alphabetic order of the acrostic literary form. Like the message of hope in the book of Jeremiah (i.e., the "Book of Consolation"), the confession of hope in Lamentations is surrounded by texts that express the darkness and grief of the exile. Thus, we have been given a book that gives lament the first and last word, an entire book devoted to the full expression of lamentation, indeed, Lamentations from A to Z! Even as we Pentecostals believe we have been given the Holy Spirit to help us "with groans too deep for words" (Rom 8:26 ISV), we should be more open to the possibility that in Lamentations we have been given a holy word (as fundamental as our ABCs!) to help us find the words for, and literally come to terms with, our deepest griefs. Apparently, God knows that we will never get past our laments by suppressing them, but only by expressing them.

EZEKIEL

I was with the exiles at the Chebar River when the heavens opened and I saw visions of God.
   —*Ezekiel 1:1*

When I think about the book of Ezekiel,

a number of images come to mind. Having written my doctoral dissertation on this book, I am pulled in several directions as I ponder this spiritually weighty, exilic prophetic text. Despite this inner creative and expressive turmoil, one image still comes to the fore: Ezekiel's visionary experience of the defiled temple in chapter 8. Ezekiel, a priest, along with King Jehoiachin and many others, had been taken into exile to Babylon in 597 BCE. The exile events of 605/4 and 597 BCE were God's warning that judgment was coming on his people unless the nation repented. In 592 BCE, Ezekiel is taken by means of a vision to the temple in Jerusalem to view firsthand the wickedness of God's people. Here God pulls back the metaphorical curtain and lays bare the abominations of the people that were being practiced in God's very house! As Ezekiel views the idolatrous practices and the false worship, which is defiling the temple, he also sees the *kavod* ("glory") of YHWH as it departs the temple due to the sin of God's people. I cannot help but draw a direct connection to the situation in the worldwide church today. Sin, idolatry (not with wooden or golden images per se), and general wickedness pervade people's lives and churches. Faddish and worldly agendas have so engulfed many churches that there is no way of differentiating the message of the church from that of the world. What Ezekiel's vision makes clear is that sooner or later God will peel back and expose the wickedness of his people and wayward churches. Sin cannot, and will not, dwell side by side with a holy God. As the people of YHWH, Judah learned the hard way that this was so. As the people of God, the church too will learn that sin will not go unchecked. The Spirit's message to the church is similar to the message delivered through the Spirit to Ezekiel's audience: holiness, the truthfulness of God's Word, and the fear of God are required of God's people. Rejection of this reality means judgment is coming!

Quick Facts

Title: The title comes from the name of the prophet whose message forms the book. It is the same in both the LXX and Hebrew text traditions. Ezekiel's name means "God makes hard or strengthens."

Authorship and Date: According to Jewish tradition, the book of Ezekiel was compiled by the Great Assembly during the exile of the sixth century BCE (*Baba Bathra* 15a), after having been written by the prophet himself. With the exception of a few detractors (e.g., Baruch Spinoza 1632–1677 and G. L. Oeder ca. 1771), Ezekiel's authorship of the book was not challenged until the early 20th century in the wake of the continuing advance of the historical-critical method. Since then, the debate has come full circle, having moved from the perspective that virtually none of the book is Ezekielian (as propounded by Gustav Hölscher in 1924), to holistic approaches that argue for the unity and singularity of authorship and see the book as composed during the exile with varying degrees of editing—the view that is the majority position today. Some have suggested that the book should be divided between a "Palestinian Ezekiel" writing in Judah and a "Babylonian Ezekiel" writing in Babylon (possibly Ezekiel himself and/or an exilic redactor). Also, there are outliers who have argued for an unknown author writing much later during the postexilic period (ca. 500–450 BCE) or that the book is a pseudepigraph written as late as the Greek period. In a similar vein, the apocalyptic genre of chapters 38–39 and 40–48 has caused some to argue for a late date for these sections. However, many who approach the text in light of rhetorical and compositional considerations see these chapters as key to the unity of the book (cf. 37:1-14 and chs. 38–39; chs. 1–3; 8–11 and 40–43). Finally, while one cannot be certain when the book reached its final form, the absence of any mention of Nebuchadnezzar's death (562 BCE) or Cyrus's decree (539 BCE) suggests that the book reached its final form before these events transpired. Indeed, the dated oracles of the book place the book's content between 593 and 571 BCE.

Audience: Ezekiel's audience is made up of those already in exile in Babylon. However, his message before the fall of Jerusalem in 586 BCE would have resonated with Jeremiah's audience back in Jerusalem as well.

Genre: The book is a composite of prophetic oracles (e.g., chs. 6–7; 13–14; 25–36), visions (chs. 1–3; 8–11; 37:1-14; 40–48), extended metaphors (e.g., chs. 15; 16; 21; 23), sign acts (4:1–5:4; 12:1-20; 24:15-18, 24, 27; 37:15-28), laments (ch. 19), and proto-apocalyptic prophecies (chs. 38–39).

Purpose: The purpose of the book is twofold: (1) to call Judah to account for the broken covenant with their heavenly King and to warn the people of impending judgment and complete exile; (2) it also served as a message of hope by assuring a future return and the rebuilding of the temple.

Structure

A number of structural patterns have been proposed for the book based on chronology, themes, and genre. The chronological ordering is grounded upon the dated oracles in the book (1:1, 2; 3:16; 8:1; 20:1;

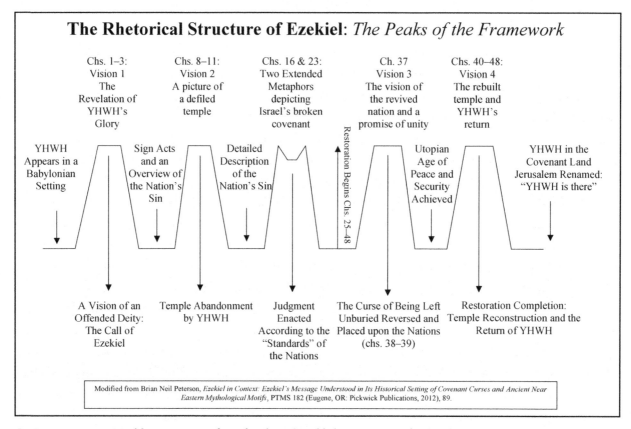

The Rhetorical Structure of Ezekiel: *The Peaks of the Framework*

Chs. 1–3: Vision 1 — The Revelation of YHWH's Glory

Chs. 8–11: Vision 2 — A picture of a defiled temple

Chs. 16 & 23: Two Extended Metaphors depicting Israel's broken covenant

Ch. 37: Vision 3 — The vision of the revived nation and a promise of unity

Chs. 40–48: Vision 4 — The rebuilt temple and YHWH's return

YHWH Appears in a Babylonian Setting

Sign Acts and an Overview of the Nation's Sin

Detailed Description of the Nation's Sin

Restoration Begins Chs. 25–48

Utopian Age of Peace and Security Achieved

YHWH in the Covenant Land Jerusalem Renamed: "YHWH is there"

A Vision of an Offended Deity: The Call of Ezekiel

Temple Abandonment by YHWH

Judgment Enacted According to the "Standards" of the Nations

The Curse of Being Left Unburied Reversed and Placed upon the Nations (chs. 38–39)

Restoration Completion: Temple Reconstruction and the Return of YHWH

Modified from Brian Neil Peterson, *Ezekiel in Context: Ezekiel's Message Understood in Its Historical Setting of Covenant Curses and Ancient Near Eastern Mythological Motifs*, PTMS 182 (Eugene, OR: Pickwick Publications, 2012), 89.

By Brian Peterson. Used by permission of Wipf and Stock Publishers. www.wipfandstock.com

24:1; 26:1; 29:1, 17; 30:20; 32:1, 17; 33:21; 40:1a, 1b). Only 29:17 does not follow a chronological sequence. The thematic structure has been variously arranged. One obvious arrangement is: judgment on the house of Israel (1–24); judgment on the nations (25–32); and restoration of the house of Israel (33–48). Another option is to see Ezekiel's main visions as the key to the book's arrangement. Four visions are strategically placed in the two halves of the book. The visions of YHWH's glory found in chapters 1–3 and 8–11 are a central focus of chapters 1–24 and the visions of chapters 37 and 40–48 highlight the oracles of hope in the second half in chapters 25–48. Still another very clear and useful view of the book's structure, and the one that will be observed in the following summary, is: the call of Ezekiel and the sin of Judah (1–12); oracles against Judah and her people (13–24); oracles against the nations (25–32); oracles of hope (33–39); and the new temple (40–48).

Summary

The Call of Ezekiel and the Sin of Judah: Ezekiel 1–12

Ezekiel's book is situated in the land of Babylon by the river Chebar (1:1). Ezekiel begins his ministry in the fifth year of Jehoiachin's exile (ca. 593 BCE) and in the thirtieth year. The latter chronological notation could either denote Ezekiel's age (the time when priests entered service in the temple; cf. 2 Chron 31:16) or how long it had been since the book of the law was found during Josiah's reforms (ca. 622 BCE). The former appears to be the more likely meaning.

Chapters 1–3 record the first of four visions. This first vision begins abruptly with Ezekiel seeing a foreboding theophany of YHWH's glory coming from the north (1:4; cf. 9:2). For those who had lived, or were presently living, in Jerusalem, the north bespeaks judgment and conquest from Judah's enemies (1:24; cf. Jer 1:12-15; 4:6; 6:1, 22; 10:22; 25:9). Adding to this picture is the fact that YHWH's presence is resting above a throne resembling the ark of the covenant, but, unlike the ark in Jerusalem, this throne has elaborate wheels and is being propelled along by four living beings, each with wings and four faces: that of a lion, an eagle, a bull, and a human (1:10). While these could denote the domains of creation, they may in fact represent the four main gods of the Babylonian pantheon: Marduk = bull; Nabu = a man; Ninib = an eagle; and Nergal = the lion. The message is clear: YHWH is coming against his own people and is bringing Babylon (represented by their gods) against the land of Judah (cf. 21:19-22 and the genre discussion of Lamentations in the previous chapter). What is more, Ezekiel is called to be a prophet (2:1–3:11) and a "watchman" (3:17-21 KJV; cf. 33:2-7 KJV) for the rebellious house (cf. 2:3, 5-8) of Judah in order to warn them of this impending disaster. However, like the audiences of Isaiah and Jeremiah (cf. Isa 6:9-12; Jer 1:17-19), Ezekiel's audience will refuse to listen even though YHWH has placed his words in Ezekiel's mouth (3:1-11). Realizing that this is a very hard message that will meet with hard opposition (2:3-4), God promises to make Ezekiel's head hard, as hard as the hardest stone, in the face of his opponents (3:7-9). All this accords with the meaning of Ezekiel's name: "God makes hard (or strengthens)." As a sign of God's commissioning of Ezekiel, Ezekiel will

Composite guardian cherubs from the Assyrian period. The composite nature of these statues have parallels with what Ezekiel saw in his first two visions. Photo courtesy of Michael Ludenni.

remain mute with the exception of the moments when God tells him to speak (3:26-27).

Closely connected to the motif of muteness are Ezekiel's sign acts, which begin in chapters 4 and 5. These include:

1) drawing Jerusalem on a brick and mimicking laying siege to the city (4:1-3);

2) lying on his side for 390 and then 40 days for the sins of Israel and Judah respectively (4:4-6);

3) eating rationed food cooked over dung as a sign of privation, siege, and exile to an "unclean" nation (4:9-17); and

4) cutting his hair to represent the destruction of the people by famine, war, and exile (5:1-12).

Here Ezekiel lays before the people the reason for YHWH's judgment: they have broken covenant with him (5:5-7) and because of this, YHWH is about to bring upon them the curses of the covenant (5:6-17). In fact, chapters 6 and 7 serve to highlight the sins of the people and this soon-coming judgment. Also, several of the motifs that will be covered in the ensuing chapters are introduced here. For example: idolatry (6:3-4, 13; 7:20; cf. chs. 8; 14; 18; 20); judgment by famine, plague, and the sword (6:3, 8, 11, 12; 7:15; cf. 12:16; 14:13, 19, 21; 21:1-32); judgment on the hills, in the ravines, and valleys (6:2; cf. 32:6; 35:8; 36:4, 6); the curse of non-burial (6:4-7, 13; cf. 37:1-14; 39:4-5, 12-20); and judgment on spiritual adultery (6:9; cf. chs. 16 and 23) and abominations (6:9, 11; 7:3, 4, 8, 9, 20; cf. 8:6, 9, 13, 15, 17; 9:4; 11:18 etc.) are highlighted.

Chapters 8–11 record the second vision, which is similar to the first only a year later. The difference is Ezekiel is taken by the Spirit to the temple in Jerusalem to see firsthand the sin that will cause YHWH's glory to depart the temple (8:3; see introduction above). Ezekiel sees all types of spiritual idolatry being performed in the very presence of YHWH. As a result, God orders the destruction of the city by the hand of seven destroyers (9:2; cf. Jer 22:7). Among them is one "man" who marks the righteous in order to deliver them from the coming judgment (9:4). These destroyers in many ways resemble the much-feared seven destroying gods of the Babylonians known as the *Sebetti*. The difference, however, is that YHWH is in control of these destroyers; they are at God's bidding. Also, as a result of the sinful actions of the people, YHWH departs his temple by first vacating the temple proper (10:1-22) and then moving out of the city to the Mount of Olives (11:22-24). From this vantage point YHWH will serve as the presiding Judge over the coming destruction of Jerusalem. Although Ezekiel is told to give a message of hope to those already in exile (11:16-20), the sign acts of chapter 12 (12:3-7, 17-20) show the nation that the exile of those remaining in Jerusalem is a foregone conclusion (12:8-28). Finally, the reiteration of the "rebellious house" motif serves as an *inclusio* to the first twelve chapters (12:2, 3, 9, 25; cf. 2:5, 6, 8; 3:9, 26, 27). The nation's rebellion had brought upon them the worst curse imaginable for a nation in the ancient world: temple abandonment. YHWH's departure from the temple assured certain destruction.

Oracles against Judah and Her People: Ezekiel 13–24

These chapters expand upon the previous section by highlighting the people's sins, which would cause the nation to go into exile. To begin, Ezekiel notes that the prophets and prophetesses reject the word of the Lord and practice divination and magic, declare false visions, and speak their own words, not God's

(13:1-10, 16-23; 14:9-11; cf. 22:25, 28). Moreover, the elders practice idolatry (14:1-8) and the nation is unfaithful (14:13). As rhetorical punctuation on the level of the nation's unfaithfulness, God says that even if Job, Noah, and Daniel were living there, their righteousness could save only themselves and not their families (14:12-23). As further elaboration on the sins of the nation and leadership, Ezekiel uses a series of metaphors to illustrate the debased spiritual state of the nation and God's assured judgment. The sinfulness of the nation had made them no better than a charred vine fit for the fire (15:1-8).

At the heart of the oracles against Judah are the two extended metaphors of chapters 16 and 23. Here Ezekiel depicts Jerusalem (alongside the previously destroyed city of Samaria) as an unfaithful wife who has "played the harlot" with her lovers (e.g., Egypt, Assyria, and Babylon; cf. 16:26-34 KJV; 23:1-21, 40-44 KJV). Ezekiel uses the marriage metaphor to relate how YHWH had entered into covenant with Israel in the wilderness (16:1-13). But they had broken that covenant (16:59) by their spiritual adultery, presented in metaphorical terms as lewd sexual acts (16:14-19, 22-25, 27, 36, 43-44, 58; 23:21, 27, 29, 35, 48-49; cf. 22:9-11; 24:13), which are described as even greater than the depravity of Sodom (16:46-56). Furthermore, Israel had committed child sacrifice, a direct affront to YHWH (16:20-21; 23:37-39). Therefore, Ezekiel prophesies the destruction of Jerusalem at the hands of her "lovers" (16:35-58; 23:9, 22-35). Jerusalem's punishment, metaphorically projected in terms of being stripped naked (16:39; 23:26), cut with swords (16:40; 23:47), and having her nose and ears cut off (23:25), is in keeping with Ezekiel's Babylonian context; these were the punishments meted out in a literal sense to unfaithful spouses in both ancient Assyria and Babylon.

Symptomatic of the rebellious nature of Judah (17:12) is the propensity of her kings to break covenant not only with YHWH, but also with others (17:13-19). Zedekiah's rebellion against Nebuchadnezzar, told in parabolic form (17:1-11; cf. 19:1-14), will be the undoing of the nation and his own family (17:19-21; cf. Jer 39:5-7). However, despite the actions of the king, every person is held accountable for his or her own sin. The righteous person can be saved by keeping the law and living righteously (18:1-9, 14-17, 19, 21-22, 27-28; 33:9, 14-16, 19); whereas those refusing to do so will perish (18:10-13, 18, 24, 26; 33:12-13, 18).

Sadly, the present situation of Judah's sinful ways (22:17-31) was not unique to Ezekiel's generation. Israel had a long history of rebellion that extended back to their time in Egypt (20:5-8). Ezekiel purposely passes over the memory of any period of divine blessing (e.g., the life of David) in an effort to paint the bleakest picture of Israel's past. When faced with a choice between the statutes and laws of God ("regulations and case laws" in the CEB), which would bring life, and the statutes and laws of the fathers, which would bring death, they had repeatedly chosen the latter (cf. 20:11, 13, 16, 19, 21 and 20:18, 24-25; cf. 33:16). As such, God gave them over to their own laws in order that they might defile themselves (20:25-26; cf. 36:31). God will use the sword to bring about the destruction of Judah (21:1-17); God will even use the divination of the Babylonians against Judah, as God predetermines the destruction of his own land (21:18-27). Indeed, because of the lewdness and wicked practices of the inhabitants of Jerusalem, Ezekiel likens the capital to a "bloody city" (22:1-16; 24:6, 9), which will become like a smelting furnace

(22:17-22) and a boiling cauldron of judgment (24:1-14). Yet, for the sake of his holy name (20:9, 14, 22, 39, 44; 36:21-23), God will deliver them from oppression and exile and return them to their land (20:40-44). Despite their rejection of God, he will be their king (20:34).

The oracles against Judah end with the death of Ezekiel's wife, which serves as a sign act foretelling the end of the temple and city (24:15-27). When the city and temple fall, God's wrath will be complete and Ezekiel's muteness will end (24:27; cf. 33:22). The oft-repeated phrase "and they will know that I am [YHWH]" (both here and elsewhere, e.g., 6:7, 10, 13, 14; 7:4, 27, etc.), also known as the divine "recognition formula," highlights the primary purpose of God through the words of the prophet. Thus the oracles against Judah and the promised destruction serve as a means of reeducating YHWH's people as to who he is and what is required of them.

Oracles against the Nations: Ezekiel 25–32

In the pattern of Isaiah, Jeremiah, and other Hebrew prophets, Ezekiel pronounces oracles against the nations who have mistreated Israel and gloated over Judah's demise (25:3, 6, 8, 12, 15; 26:2) or have practiced hubris before God (28:2-5; 29:3; 30:18; 31:10, 18; 32:2, 12). Curses that were previously pronounced upon Judah and Israel will now be turned upon those who have misused God's people (Deut 30:7; cf. Ezek 36:7, 15). While Ammon (25:1-7), Moab and Edom (25:8-14; cf. 35:1-15), Philistia (25:15-17), Tyre (26:1-28:19), Sidon (28:20-24), and Egypt (chs. 29–32) are all singled out for attention, it is Tyre and Egypt that are held up for special ridicule—Tyre no doubt due to its breach of covenant with Judah (1 Kgs 5:1, 12), and Egypt because of its oppression of Israel and its role as a rival of YHWH for Israel's affection (e.g., 29:6-7, 16). The devastation wrought against these nations by Babylon, God's instrument of judgment (26:7; 29:18-20; 30:10-11, 24-25; 32:11), functions as a message of hope to Israel that God's justice is even-handed—a fitting end for all the nations is punishment and ignominy in Sheol (32:17-32, notes d and g in the CEB).

Oracles of Hope: Ezekiel 33–39

Chapter 33 serves as a transition from the previous oracles to the oracles of hope. Here Ezekiel receives his second call to be a watchman for the nation (33:1-20). He also hears the news from an escapee from Jerusalem that "the city has fallen" (v. 21). This event marks the end of his muteness (v. 22). With the ability to speak freely, Ezekiel's first order of business is to issue a warning to those who had not gone into exile and had remained in the land of Judah: God would still pass judgment on them; they were not the elect (33:23-33). His second denunciation is for the wicked shepherds of Israel; hope for the future must be rooted in godly leadership. Whereas wicked leaders had brought hardship and privation for the flock (34:1-10), in the future, YHWH would take over the role as Shepherd (34:11-22) and appoint his servant David as leader (34:23-31; cf. 37:24-25). This declaration is one of the clearest messianic prophecies in the book, a message of hope that is ultimately fulfilled in the person and work of the ultimate Shepherd, Jesus (cf. John 10). Indeed, Ezekiel's covenant of peace bespeaks the new covenant initiated by Jesus (cf. 34:25; 37:26; Luke 22:20; 1 Cor 11:25).

With the changed tone of the book from cursing to hope, in chapters 35 and 36 Ezekiel uses Edom, Israel's brother, as paradigmatic of God's punishment on the nations due to their mistreatment of Israel (36:1-6). Edom, as a blood relative, should have known better than to abuse his brother (cf. Obadiah). In light of this broken family covenant, the intentions of Edom will be thwarted (35:1-15) and Judah will be elevated at the expense of Edom and the nations (36:8-38). Moreover, God will place his Spirit upon his people (36:25-28).

Within these two chapters, which highlight curse reversal (Deut 30:7), we also see the motif of non-burial (35:8). Ezekiel's third vision—the valley of dry bones—is a visual presentation of this curse (37:1-14). In the ANE the most feared curse that could befall an individual was the curse of non-burial. Proper burial was needed in order for a person to have a connection with his or her ancestors and his or her progeny. This curse, which was once the plight of Judah, will be removed from God's people and placed upon the nations (39:4-5, 12-20). The message of the vision includes both spiritual renewal and a physical return to the land (37:11-14). While the return from captivity in 538 BCE serves as a foretaste of the fulfillment of the vision, it still has an eschatological aspect, as seen in Ezekiel's references to the unified nation (37:15-23), God's servant David (37:24-25; cf. 34:23-24), and the new covenant (37:24-28; 39:29). The eschatological dimension is also made evident by the later use of chapters 38–39 in Revelation 19–20. What's more, God's people who are living securely in their own land (38:8, 11-14; 39:26; cf. 34:25, 28), will be attacked by the surrounding nations. God's involvement in this final judgment on the nations (38:1-6, 16-23; 39:1-2, 21) is required for the eschatological age of peace to unfold, a picture that is expanded upon in chapters 40–48.

The New Temple: Ezekiel 40–48

The second vision (chs. 8–11) depicting the curse of temple abandonment—the curse most feared by a nation in the ANE—is reversed in the final vision of chapters 40–48. For Ezekiel, this curse had to be remedied in order for Israel to be at peace with its God and at rest in the land. Not surprisingly, the vision begins with a detailed description of the eschatological temple (40:3–42:20) and YHWH's return (43:1-5), and it ends with the affirmation that the name of the city will be "[YHWH] is there" (48:35). The vision of the return of YHWH's glory reverses the departure of his glory in chapter 11 (cf. 43:1-5; 10:1-22; 11:22-23). As is typical of ancient Near Eastern motifs, once the glory of YHWH returns to the land, blessings flow. These envisioned blessings include a reconstituted priesthood (44:1-31), reestablished laws and sacrifice (45:10–46:24), and a revitalized land (45:1-9; 47:13–48:35; cf. Rev 21). The blessings are so great that even the Dead Sea will come to life with fish, and a land that once knew scarcity of water will have abundance (47:1-12; cf. Rev 22:1-2).

Debated Issues (aka Great Paper Topics)

1) According to scholars, what does the reference to Ezekiel's "thirtieth year" in 1:1 designate?

2) What are the different interpretations of the meaning of the faces of the living creatures in chapter 1?

3) How do scholars interpret Ezekiel's muteness (3:26; 33:22): was it real or figurative?

4) Do scholars see Ezekiel's temple in 40:1–42:20 as real or figurative?

The Message of the Book

God takes covenant very seriously. Those who break covenant will be punished. However, God's desire is that no person perishes but that all come to repentance (18:23, 32; 33:11).

Closing the Loop

Ezekiel was a priest who was called to be a prophet. In Ezekiel's 30th year, when he would have been expected to begin fulfilling the role of representing God in a priestly way, Ezekiel is suddenly called and compelled to represent God *in a prophetic way*. He has the first of a series of prophetic visions in which God brings forth a new and unprecedented revelation of himself.[56] This fresh self-revelation of God first blows Ezekiel's priestly mind (ch. 1) and then blows away the entire religious and theological system of the Jerusalem temple (chs. 8-10). Accordingly, Ezekiel focuses upon *God's wind* (Heb *ruach*), indeed, *the Spirit of YHWH*, more than any other prophet before him. It is for good reason that Ezekiel has been called "the prophet of the Spirit."[57] Ezekiel's first vision of God begins with the approach of "*a storm wind*" (*ruach sa'arah*; 1:4 NASB)—a wind that turns out to be nothing less than a theophany, an appearance of God. This is similar to what Job encountered when the Lord approached him "*from the whirlwind*" (so Job 38:1 and 40:6, where the same Hebrew term, *sa'arah*, is used). In Ezekiel's initial vision, the Spirit is seen to be the force behind all the movement within the living creatures and the wheels (1:12, 20), but then the Spirit comes upon Ezekiel himself, raising him up on his feet to hear God's word (2:1-2) after the vision had caused him to fall on his face (1:28).

We see a similar emphasis on the *ruach*, the Spirit, in the other three major visions of Ezekiel. The *ruach* lifts Ezekiel up and brings him to Jerusalem (8:3) and back again (11:24) in the divine vision of chapters 8–11, when Ezekiel sees the glory of God, energized by the *ruach* (10:17), departing from the temple. The

---

56. Rickie D. Moore, "'Then They Will Know That a Prophet Has Been Among Them': The Source and End of the Call of Ezekiel" in *Passover, Pentecost & Parousia: Studies in Celebration of the Life & Ministry of R. Hollis Gause*, ed. Steven J. Land, Rickie D. Moore, and John Christopher Thomas (Leiderdorp, NL: Deo, 2010), 53–65.

57. Daniel I. Block, "The Prophet of the Spirit: The Use of RWH in the Book of Ezekiel," *Journal of the Evangelical Theological Society* 32, no.1 (March 1989): 27–49.

ruach shows up similarly in chapters 40–48 in the vision where Ezekiel is once again transported to the temple precincts to witness the return of God's glory to the restored temple (43:5). Yet the most spectacular manifestation of the *ruach* appears in chapter 37 in Ezekiel's vision of the valley of dry bones. "In the spirit [*ruach*] of [YHWH]" Ezekiel is brought to this valley (37:1 KJV), and when the moment of truth comes, the prophet is directed to speak to the wind (or breath, i.e., *ruach*) (v. 9), whereupon the *ruach* enters the dead corpses and brings them to life (v. 10).

All of this emphasis upon the Spirit, the *ruach* of YHWH, in the visions of Ezekiel forms the background of God's signal promise to the people in this book: "I will give you a new heart and put a new spirit [*ruach*] within you. I will remove your stony heart from your body and replace it with a living one, and I will give you my spirit [*ruach*]" (36:26-27; cf. 11:19). While this promise of God's Spirit obviously points forward to the fulfillment of Pentecost, the portrayal of God's Spirit in all the visions of Ezekiel provides powerful witness to how very awesome and holy this promised *ruach* is. The book of Ezekiel, then, is a sobering warning to all people of the Spirit that God's *ruach* is not a familiar spirit that we can capture in our religious boxes. God's Spirit is the *Holy* Spirit, who will not be confined within our boundaries or abide in unclean temples. Here we find the vision of God's Spirit that will take our breath away . . . and yet, for God's sake and for God's sake alone (36:26, 32), will give it back again.

DANIEL

The king declared to Daniel . . . "Your God is God of gods, Lord of kings, and a revealer of mysteries."
—Daniel 2:47

When I think about the book of Daniel,

I am reminded of the importance of committing one's life to God at a young age. I have often heard the slogan that people need to "sow their wild oats" when they are young, especially in a world full of temptation. This belief is then used to justify any number of sinful actions: the proverbial sex, drugs, and rock 'n' roll, both metaphorical, and sadly, literal. In all reality, this slogan is actually more spiritually dangerous than most realize. When I teach the book of Daniel, I often remind my students that sooner or later Jesus will return for his church and there will be a generation of youth "sowing their wild oats." The question I then ask is, "Do you think this will be an acceptable excuse for blatant sin?" Daniel, who was perhaps no more than 16 when he went into exile, was faced with a world of temptation in Babylon. There he was put into a place where spiritual and cultural assimilation was expected. Failure to conform would bring not only opposition, but also possible death. Yet in the face of such a challenge, the youthful Daniel chose to follow his God and not conform to the ways of Babylon. Although Daniel's choices were honored by God, he and his friends were still subjected to trials, such as the fiery furnace and the lions' den. My prayer for this generation of college students is that they too will have the spiritual fortitude to stand firm in the faith when a corrupt culture seeks to twist and stifle their Christian witness. May they, as the old hymn states, "dare to be a Daniel, dare to stand alone! Dare to have a purpose firm! Dare to make it known."[58]

Quick Facts

Title: The title comes from the name of the person whose message forms the book. It is the same in both the LXX and Hebrew text traditions. Daniel's name means "God is my Judge" or "God rules."

Authorship and Date: As with the book of Isaiah, the authorship and the date of the book of Daniel are among the most debated issues within biblical studies. Three positions are held: (1) that Daniel is

---

58. "Dare to Be a Daniel," words and music by Philip P. Bliss, 1873.

written in the sixth century BCE by Daniel; (2) that Daniel is a second-century BCE pseudepigraph (i.e., false or falsely attributed writing) written in the period of the Maccabees as *vaticinium ex-eventu* ("prophecy after the event"); or (3) that the first six chapters are written by Daniel in the sixth century BCE and the last six chapters are written in the second century BCE by an unknown author. While the scholarly debate is too complex to handle in detail here, we can still point out that several premises lie behind positions 2 and 3.

First, the material handled in chapters 7–12 (especially chapter 11) is thought to be too detailed about the Greek period to be from the sixth century BCE. Second, the apocalyptic nature of these chapters is believed to fit best within this later period. Third, the book of Daniel appears in the third division (the Writings) of the Hebrew canon, material often dated to a later period. Fourth, a large portion of the book of Daniel, 2:4b–7:28, is in Aramaic rather than the Hebrew language, and this is seen to be an indication of the later date. There are several arguments used to counter these claims. First, if one grants the metaphysical possibility of predictive prophecy, then nothing would rule out the possibility of Daniel's being given detailed insights into the future of Israel's interactions with the Greek Empire. What's more, portions of Daniel (e.g., the "Son of man" motif in ch. 7 [KJV] and "the abomination of desolation" motif in chs. 9 and 11 [NASB]) would appear to have a future fulfillment beyond the Greek period, as indicated in Jesus's later allusions to the prophecies of Daniel (cf. Dan 7:13-14; Matt 24:30; 26:64; Mark 13:26; 14:62; and Dan 9:27; 11:31; Matt 24:15). Second, the fact that Daniel uses an apocalyptic genre does not mean that the book had to have been written in the second century BCE. Proto-apocalyptic texts appear in Isaiah and Ezekiel long before the second century BCE. Third, the modern threefold ordering of the Hebrew canon came from a much later period than the second century BCE. Josephus lists Daniel among the prophets (*Against Apion* 1:40), not the Writings, as did the Qumran community (cf. the *Florilegium* 4Q174). Even if one does follow the later ordering, Daniel's placement in the Writings does not mean the book is late; other books from the Writings have valid claims for being written earlier than the second century BCE (e.g., many of the Psalms, Ruth, etc.). Also, Daniel's links with the wisdom tradition and his explicit vocational identity as a wise man, or sage, rather than a prophet (Dan 2:12-13) could have accounted for the book's placement in the Writings, where the wisdom books were placed. Fourth, the use of Aramaic in 2:4b–7:28, which cuts across the proposed division at chapter 6, features a form of Aramaic that is closer to the sixth century BCE than the second. Fifth, one of the eight copies of Daniel found among the Dead Sea Scrolls (i.e., 4QDanª ca. 125 BCE) dates to within 40 years of the date espoused by the late-date theorists (ca. 165 BCE). Despite scholarly arguments to the contrary, this seems to be too short of a period for the book to have been written, copied, and accepted among the Hebrew canonical books. Sixth, the positive relations that the book depicts between Daniel and the kings of Babylon and Persia do not correspond very well with the antagonistic relations between the Hebrews and their Greek rulers in the Maccabean period of the second century BCE. Finally, an ancient Jewish tradition makes the claim that the book of Daniel was used to thwart Alexander the Great's attack of Jerusalem in 332 BCE (cf. Josephus *Ant* 11:337), which would have been almost 170 years *before* the proposed second century BCE date for the book.

Audience and Purpose: Daniel's original audience, as implied by the book itself, is the Hebrew people during their captivity in the sixth century BCE, with the book's final verses indicating that its eschatological message will have relevance to God's people in a much later period (12:8-13). In accord with the meaning of Daniel's name, "God rules," the book's obvious purpose is to show the sovereign hand of God over the affairs and history of both Israel and the nations. Those who see the book as a second-century pseudepigraph would see this same purpose but would see it as more narrowly focused on encouraging a Jewish audience in the midst of persecution from the Greek/Seleucid Empire.

Genre: Daniel is a mixture of historical narrative in the form of court tales (chs. 1–6), which includes two dream reports (in chs. 2 and 4), and apocalyptic visions (chs. 7–12).

Structure

The book divides evenly with chapters 1–6 presenting six stories that each feature the interaction of Daniel and his three friends with respective Babylonian and Persian kings, and chapters 7–12 presenting a series of apocalyptic visions that Daniel has concerning the future of Israel within the context of world empires.

Summary

Court Tales and Faithfulness in a Foreign Land: Daniel 1–6

The book opens with a historical notation that places the setting of chapter 1 in the "third year of . . . Jehoiakim" (1:1). Based on chronological records from Babylon (cf. Jer 25:1; 46:2 for the Jewish chronology), where Daniel was living, this would equate to 605 BCE. Thus, the first exile of Judah took place immediately after Nebuchadnezzar's defeat of Assyria and Egypt at the battle of Carchemish in 605 BC (cf. 2 Kgs 24:1-2). Nebuchadnezzar traveled south from Carchemish and subjugated the former vassal states of Assyria. Typical of the practices of the period, kings would take the children of the upper class of the vassal state as political hostages in order to keep the vassal in compliance with the ruler's wishes (1:3-4).

Following the introductory paragraph, chapter 1 tells the story of how the four Hebrew youths, Daniel, Hananiah, Mishael, and Azariah, are chosen from among the Hebrew exiles to be groomed as servants for the Babylonian court. The goal of complete assimilation is registered in that, along with their Babylonian training, Babylonian names are given to these youths (Belteshazzar, Shadrach, Meshach, and Abednego). However, their refusal to fully partake of all they were presented results in God giving them special favor (1:9) to surpass their Babylonian peers in physical health (1:8-16) and attainment of wisdom (1:17-20).

Chapters 2–7 form a chiastic structure whereby pairs of chapters (i.e., 2 and 7; 3 and 6; and 4 and 5) present similar messages and motifs. To begin, chapter 2 relates the dream of Nebuchadnezzar and his demand that his sages and diviners not only give the interpretation, but also tell him the dream (2:1-13)!

Failure to carry out this order subjected these men to an execution sentence (2:5, 12-13). It is in this context that God reveals to Daniel and his friends the dream's content (viz., a giant statue made of four types of materials of descending quality) and its interpretation (2:14-23). Nebuchadnezzar's dream in chapter 2 is paralleled by Daniel's vision of the four beasts in chapter 7. Both of these revelations envision a succession of four world empires beginning with Babylon. The specific identification of all four empires is a matter of much debate. For those holding to a second-century BCE date for the book, the head of gold is Babylon; the chest and arms of silver is Media; the bronze belly and thighs are Persia; and the legs of iron and the feet of mingled clay and iron represent Greece. Those holding a sixth-century BCE date interpret the head of gold as Babylon (2:37-38); the silver chest and arms as Media-Persia; the bronze belly and thighs as Greece; and the legs of iron as Rome, with the feet possibly representing a future empire that somehow extends from Rome (2:40-43). This latter scheme makes room for a more futuristic prophetic interpretation of the text. The dream concludes with the destruction of the statue by a "stone" made without hands. This is often interpreted as pointing to the kingdom established by Jesus (perhaps at his first and/or second coming; cf. 2:34-35, 44-45; Rev 19:15). Many see the scheme based

Reconstruction of the Ishtar Gate from ancient Babylon during the period of Nebuchadnezzar II. Daniel no doubt would have seen this gate. Photo courtesy of Michael Luddeni.

on a sixth-century date forming a better parallel when applied to the four beasts of chapter 7. The winged lion would represent Babylon; the lopsided bear would represent the uneven power between the Media-Persian Empire (cf. 11:2); the winged leopard with four heads would be a particularly apt representation of the Greek Empire (for after the death of Alexander the Great, his kingdom was divided among his four generals: Seleucus, Ptolemy, Philip, and Antigonus, the latter two being replaced by Lysimachus and Cassander; cf. 11:2-4); and the iron-toothed beast with ten horns would represent Rome and the ensuing political systems of the world. Parallel to the stone made without hands at the conclusion of chapter 2 is the description at the end of chapter 7 of the "Ancient of Days" bestowing all dominion and kingship to one called the "Son of man" (7:9-14 KJV, 19-22 KJV). The ultimate message of chapters 2 and 7 is clear: God (and his kingdom) will at last reign supreme (2:20-23, 46-47; 7:14, 27).

Chapters 3 and 6 present stories that are similar. In both, an imperial edict is issued that, on threat of death, demands everyone to worship/pray to false gods—a demand that comes to a focus on Daniel's three friends in the first instance and on Daniel in the second. In chapter 3, Shadrach, Meshach, and Abednego refuse to adhere to the human decree to bow to Nebuchadnezzar's great image/idol. Their lack of compliance is told to the king (3:8-12) and he has them thrown into a fiery furnace. God sends a deliverer, one like "a son of the gods" (3:25 NASB), and all three are unharmed by the fire. In chapter 6, Daniel refuses to adhere to the human decree to pray only to King Darius (6:7, 12). Daniel's lack of compliance is told to the king (6:10-13), and as a result he is thrown into a pit of lions (6:16-18). God again sends a deliverer, an angel, and rescues his servant Daniel (6:22). These chapters again reveal that God is sovereign (3:28-29; 6:26-27) over the destructive power of fire and wild animals. As a result of their faithfulness to God, Daniel and his friends prosper in the kingdom (3:30; 6:28).

Chapters 4 and 5 parallel each other by focusing on God's humbling of two foreign rulers due to their hubris. In chapter 4 Nebuchadnezzar sees a vision of a tall tree (representing the king), which is cut down (4:10-18). In chapter 5, after using the utensils looted from the Jerusalem temple for a drinking feast (5:1-4), Belshazzar sees handwriting on the wall, foretelling his downfall (5:5-9). In both cases Daniel is called to interpret the meanings of these miraculous revelations (4:19-26; 5:25-28). For Nebuchadnezzar it is a warning that he will be humbled like an animal (4:25, 32-33) if he does not repent (4:27). For Belshazzar it is a solemn denunciation because he did not learn from Nebuchadnezzar's humbling experience (cf. 5:17-23) and a warning that judgment is coming (5:26-28). While God's judgment falls upon both rulers, Nebuchadnezzar repents, survives, and has his kingdom restored (4:34), but Belshazzar dies and his kingdom falls to his enemy (5:30). The central message again is that God is sovereign over the lives of all rulers and their kingdoms (4:1-3, 32-37; 5:30-31).

The Cyrus Cylinder records the conquest of Babylon by the Persian, Cyrus the Great, in 539 BCE and has parallels with the events noted in Daniel 5. Photo courtesy of Michael Luddeni.

Whereas chapters 2, 4, and 5 depict Daniel interpreting the dreams or visions of kings, chapters 7–12 depict Daniel's dreams and their interpretation by a heavenly figure (7:16-27; 8:15-16; 9:21-27; 10:11-21; 11:1–12:13). Another contrast is that the third-person narrative form in chapters 1–6 shifts to the form of first-person report in chapters 7–12. One could argue that the opening six chapters serve as proof that Daniel is a man of God, thus bringing validity to his visions in the second half of the book. Finally, the use of the dating formula using the reigns of a particular king helps to show the unity of both halves of the book (cf. 1:1; 2:1; 7:1; 8:1; 9:1; 10:1; 11:1).

Apocalyptic Visions: Daniel 7–12

Chapter 8 narrows the focus from the four beasts of chapter 7 (see discussion above), to the battles between the Media-Persian (8:3-4, 20; cf. 7:5) and Greek empires (8:5-8, 21-22; cf. 7:6). After the death of Alexander the Great (8:8), his four generals took over (8:22; see above), with Antiochus Epiphanes IV (175–164 BCE) of the Seleucid Empire taking a primary role in oppressing Israel (8:9-14, 23-25). However, there is a major debate as to what time period the remaining portion of chapter 8 is referencing: is it referring only to Antiochus's oppression or is it referring to a still later event (8:15-19, 26)? This poses an issue that is similar to what one meets in the last portion of chapter 11 and in the passage in chapter 9 on the 70 weeks (9:22-27)—a message concerning the duration of the captivity of the Hebrews that Daniel receives while he is interceding for his people (9:4-21).

Chapter 10, though brief, highlights the truth noted by Paul in Eph 6:12: "For we do not wrestle against flesh and blood, but against principalities, against powers, against the rulers of the darkness of this age, against spiritual *hosts* of wickedness in the heavenly *places*" (NKJV, emphasis added). Daniel's vision of Gabriel and Gabriel's revelation that the "prince of . . . Persia" had withstood him for 21 days until Michael came to his aid (10:13 KJV) reveals that God is sovereign even over the forces of darkness in the heavenly places. Also, the declaration that Daniel's insight concerning Israel's future is of heavenly origin (10:14) sets the stage for chapter 11.

Chapter 11 is one of the most debated chapters in the entire OT, especially as it relates to eschatology—we will certainly not be able to handle all the issues here. There is virtually unanimous scholarly agreement that Daniel's final prophetic vision here is pointing to the wars for dominance, especially over the land of Israel, between the Ptolemies ("the kings of the South") and the Seleucids ("the kings of the North") during the Greek period (11:5-20). From verse 21 onward the question arises as to whether the account refers only to Antiochus Epiphanes IV or whether there is a secondary, still future, fulfillment. To be sure, Antiochus's two successive invasions of Egypt (ca. 169–168 BCE), the latter of which was thwarted by Rome ("Kittim," v. 30), appears to be what Daniel is referring to in 11:21-30. Historians point to this humiliating setback, loss of loot, and the rebellion of Jewish leadership in Jerusalem as triggering Antiochus's policy to loot and desecrate the Jewish temple (v. 31)—he had to pay his army some way. What's more, this was the impetus for outlawing Judaism in his realm (11:30-32) and the resulting Jewish revolt led by the Maccabeans (11:32-34). The cleansing of the temple by Judas Maccabaeus in 165 BCE inaugurated the observance of the Jewish holiday of Hanukkah. The final portion of chapter 11 (vv. 35-45) has been variously understood based upon one's presuppositions: is it referring to Antiochus IV, or his future, end-time counterpart, the Antichrist? The major problem is that, whereas this paragraph predicts this leader's death in Israel (v. 45), Antiochus Epiphanes IV did not die in Israel but rather in a military campaign in Persia (ca. 164 BCE; cf.

1 Macc 6:1-16; 2 Macc 1:14-16). For this reason many believe the book was written just before this event, when the author knew the course of history up to this point but did not yet know how Antiochus would die. Others believe that the chapter makes a shift at verse 35 with its reference to the "end time," so that the verses from this point on point beyond Antiochus to eschatological events when a future Antichrist ruler will arise to pose the ultimate threat to God's people before being brought down to his death in Israel. This end-time interpretation is reinforced by the eschatological language of chapter 12 (e.g., 12:1; Rev 12:7) and the stunning promise of a final resurrection for God's people (12:2-3). However, the fact remains that certainty about what is in view here is elusive, as the final paragraph of the book itself indicates (12:5-13).

Debated Issues (aka Great Paper Topics)

1) How do scholars explain the close parallels between the experiences of Nebuchadnezzar described in Daniel 4 and experiences that ancient historical records ascribe to the Babylonian king Nabonidus?

2) How do scholars reconcile the discrepancy between Belshazzar's identification as the "son" of Nebuchadnezzar in Dan 5:11 and ancient historical records that indicate otherwise?

3) How do scholars understand the identity of Darius the Mede (Dan 5:31) in relation to ANE records?

4) How do scholars understand the reference to the "prince of . . . Persia" in 10:13 (KJV)?

The Message of the Book

When God's people face the dark threat of being brought to their end by the powerful who presume to rule this world, God's vision of the end reveals to the faithful that "God rules"—a message conveyed in the meaning of Daniel's name. Indeed, God rules over all and unto the very end, enabling us to live in the light of the end.

Closing the Loop

The book of Daniel is the prime example of apocalyptic literature in the OT, and Pentecostalism is a prime example of a contemporary movement born in a burst of apocalyptic vision and expectancy. This emphasis is understandable for people bearing special witness to the outpouring of God's Spirit *"in the last days"* (Acts 2:17; cf. Joel 2:28). This has made the book of Daniel, together with the NT book of Revelation, an area of special scriptural focus for Pentecostals. Yet with this scriptural emphasis has come much difficulty, for apocalyptic literature, with all of its eerie and otherworldly symbolism, is not easy to interpret.

Pentecostals over the last century have been particularly vulnerable to approaches to this literature that come up with elaborate schemes for interpreting all the symbolism of Daniel and Revelation in order to arrive at precise and dogmatic predictions of when and how the world will come to an end. At times, such approaches have generated detailed timetables that chart (even with actual full-color charts!) how current events, nations, and leaders fit into end-time scenarios—scenarios that have often been discredited by the eventual unfolding of contemporary world events.

The best guide to the most valid approach to interpreting the apocalyptic literature of the Bible, and Daniel in particular, is no doubt to be found within the book of Daniel itself. This is indicated by the fact that the book not only presents a number of visionary apocalyptic revelations but also draws attention in each case to Daniel's own challenge and struggle to grasp the proper interpretation of them. In the first case in chapter 2, Nebuchadnezzar is altogether rattled when he cannot interpret his own dream, but its content and meaning are supernaturally revealed to Daniel in "a night vision" after he and his three friends seek the Lord (v. 19 KJV). This suggests that apocalyptic revelations may require further revelations in order for their meaning to be understood. Furthermore, prayer in the face of mortal threat might be an important precondition for God's granting such further revelations.

In the case of the visions in chapters 7–12, it is Daniel who receives the apocalyptic revelations, and he is as mystified and upset by them as Nebuchadnezzar was in chapter 2. What's more, Daniel expresses his lack of understanding and upset not only after receiving each vision (7:15; 8:15; 10:7-17) but also after receiving the further revelation in each case that purports to give Daniel the vision's explanation or interpretation (7:28; 8:27; 12:8). What finally comes in the last paragraph of the book, after Daniel confesses that he is not able to understand the apocalyptic revelation he had been given (12:8—"I heard it, but I didn't understand it"), is a divine messenger's statement to Daniel that "these words must remain secret and sealed up until the end time" (12:9). The messenger even pronounces a blessing on "the one who waits" (12:12).

All of this, it would seem, could suggest to us that the proper approach to the interpretation of apocalyptic revelations is not to seek and to presume to be able to wrestle the understanding of these revelations to the ground, but rather, to see that *these revelations are meant to wrestle us to the ground* (cf. Daniel who falls facedown in 10:9). They are meant to make us know that we are not saved by our own knowledge—which is shown to shrivel and melt before such awesome divine revelations. In the end we are saved by knowing the One who alone knows the end . . . the One who knows us.

HOSEA

"My people are destroyed from lack of knowledge."
—Hosea 4:6a

When I think about the book of Hosea,

the movie *Pretty Woman* (1990), starring Richard Gere and Julia Roberts, immediately comes to mind. In the movie, Richard Gere's character, Edward Lewis, who is a very wealthy Wall Street type, hires the services of a "lady of the evening," Vivian Ward, played by Julia Roberts. Mr. Lewis, a romantically aloof guy, enters into a "business arrangement" with Vivian so he will not be alone at a series of social events. In the course of these events, along with a whole lot of awkwardness, both fall in love and live happily ever after. The message of the movie is summed up in the last vignette as a man walking along the street says, "Welcome to Hollywood! What's your dream? . . . Some dreams come true, some don't."[59] Of course, only in Hollywood would one find such a movie topic that would garner such world-wide acclaim.

Most people living outside of the United States would have a hard time resonating with this message. This is no less true of the biblical period. In the book of Hosea, God tells Hosea not just to date, but to marry a "promiscuous woman" named Gomer (1:2 NIV). Sadly, Hosea's and Gomer's "dreams" of a blissful marriage are far from the starry-eyed outcome of the lead characters of *Pretty Woman*. What unfolds in the opening three chapters of the book shows a broken marriage of emotional pain and turmoil that spills over into their family life. Unfaithfulness, possibly an illegitimate child (or two), a wife who runs away, and a troubled reconciliation serves as a real-life picture for the ancient reader of how Israel had acted within her "marriage" (i.e., covenant) with God.

Quick Facts

Title: The title comes from the name of the prophet whose message forms the book. It is the same in both the LXX and the Hebrew text. Hosea's name means "Yahweh saves."

---

59. *Pretty Woman*, dir. Garry Marshall, perf. Julia Roberts and Richard Gere (USA: Touchstone Pictures/Silver Screen Partners, 1990), film.

Date: Based on the superscription in Hosea 1:1, the date of the final form of Hosea must be after 720 BCE. The only northern king to be mentioned in the superscription is Jeroboam II, who ruled from 793 to 753 BCE, and the first and last of the Judahite kings mentioned are Uzziah/Azariah (792–740 BCE) and Hezekiah (729–686 BCE; Hezekiah had a co-regency with his father, Ahaz, from 729 to 715 BCE). A beginning date of 760 BCE would allow for an overlap of the reigns of Jeroboam II and Uzziah, and an end date of 710 BCE would allow Hosea to experience Hezekiah's independent rule for at least five years. Nevertheless, it is possible to stretch these dates on both ends, allowing for Hosea's ministry to extend to 60 or even 70 years!

Authorship: Most ascribe the majority of the book to Hosea the son of Beeri. At certain points in Hosea's long ministry, he would have been a contemporary with Amos, Micah, and Isaiah.

Audience: The frequent mentioning of Samaria (7:1; 8:5-6; 10:5, 7; 13:16) and the lack of reference to Jerusalem indicates that Hosea's message is directed primarily to the people of the northern kingdom before their exile by Assyria in 722 BCE (cf. 9:3; 10:6; 11:5, 11; 12:1). However, Hosea's message includes oracles against Judah (cf. 1:7, 11; 4:15; 5:5, 10, 12-14; 6:4, 11; 8:14; 10:11; 11:12; 12:2) and would have been theologically important for a Judahite audience. This would explain why Hosea mentions the Judahite king Hezekiah (1:1), and why the book survived beyond the destruction and exile of the northern kingdom of Israel.

Genre: While the book falls mostly into the broad category of prophetic oracles written in poetic form, chapters 1–3 feature the genre of historical narrative with a prophetic thrust.

Purpose: Hosea's message is delivered to the northern kingdom as a warning against the dangers of broken covenant, especially through Baal worship.

Structure

Hosea can be divided into two blocks: Hosea's marriage and its use as a spiritual example for Israel and Judah (1–3); and oracles of doom and warnings against Israel and Judah. with a concluding oracle of hope (4–14).

Summary

Hosea's Marriage and Its Use as a Spiritual Example for Israel and Judah: Hosea 1–3

The first three chapters of the book of Hosea are perhaps the best known by the average believer. This is due in part to the narrative genre used to frame these chapters. Much as the parables of Jesus relate a greater truth, these chapters interpret the rest of the book through the marriage relationship of Hosea and Gomer (e.g., 9:15). These opening chapters relate how Hosea is told to marry an unfaithful woman. Hosea has a son by her, but she then goes on to have two more children, apparently born from her adulterous relations with other men, thus forming what would be classified in today's terms as a "blended family" (2:1). Hosea gives the three children names that represent some aspect of God's relationship with and/or judgment upon Israel: a son, Jezreel ("God sows/scatters"); a daughter, Lo-ruhamah ("no mercy" or "not cared for"); and a son, Lo-Ammi ("not my people"). The latter two names appear to reveal that Hosea was not actually the father. Chapter 2 switches focus to that of the nation and their sins, which have caused God to enter into judgment against them; to offer them no mercy and to no longer call them God's people—playing, obviously, on the names of Hosea's children. Chapter 3 resumes and brings to a close the narrative of chapter 1 with Hosea, at God's command, buying back his estranged wife after she had left him for other men. Hosea then renews the marriage agreement—a picture of God's renewed love for Israel (cf. 3:1-5; 14:1-9).

Pillar figurines, which were often connected to cultic functions. Hosea railed against such idolatry. Photo courtesy of Michael Luddeni.

Oracles of Doom and Warnings against Israel and Judah: Hosea 4–14

Chapters 4–14 serve as a series of covenant indictments in the form of a covenant lawsuit. Chapter 4 verse 1 sets the stage for what is to follow: "Hear the LORD's word, people of Israel, for the LORD has a dispute with the inhabitants of the land" (also called a *rîv* pattern or form; cf. 12:3; and 2:4, see "Introduction to the Prophets"). These indictments focus on Israel's spiritual infidelity with their idols (4:12, 17; 8:4-6; 10:1, 2, 5; 11:2; 13:2; 14:8), especially the Canaanite storm god, Baal (2:13, 17; 11:2; 13:1). The failure of the priests (4:4, 6, 9; 5:1; 6:9; 10:5) to teach the law and instruct the people about God (4:1; 8:12) is the main reason Israel (and Judah) has broken covenant with their God (6:7; 8:1). Hosea 4:6a highlights this well, "My people are destroyed from lack of knowledge" (cf. 6:6). God no longer delights in their rituals or sacrifices (8:13; 9:4) and will punish them with exile to Assyria (9:3; 10:6; 11:5, 11; 12:1). Nevertheless, the prophet ends his message on a note of hope that, if the people repent, God will forgive them and restore them—a similar picture depicted in Hosea's marriage to Gomer (14:1-9; cf. chs. 2-3).

Debated Issues (aka Great Paper Topics)

1) Why would God ask a prophet of God to marry an adulterous woman (1:2)?

2) Did Hosea actually marry a prostitute, or is this merely an allegory?

3) Is the "woman" in 3:1 Gomer?

The Message of the Book

The marriage metaphor (cf. Jer 2; Ezek 16; 23) in Hosea is a fitting display of how God feels when people reject God's love. Constant rejection of God's love and wooing will bring about judgment; yet even then God still desires reconciliation.

Closing the Loop

Knowledge of God is clearly Hosea's primary concern. It rings out loudly in what is probably the most quoted line of the book: "My people are destroyed," says God, "from lack of knowledge" (4:6a). However, this is not about intellectual knowledge, as many have assumed, but rather relational knowledge, knowing God in an experiential way, indeed in terms of faithful and intimate covenant relationship. "For I desire steadfast love and not sacrifice," God goes on to say, "the knowledge of God rather than burnt offerings" (6:6 ESV). The Hebrew term "knowledge" or "to know," *yada*, used here and repeatedly throughout the book of Hosea (4:6; 5:4; 6:6; 11:3), points to the intimate experience of relationship, as it so clearly does in one of the Bible's first uses of the term in Genesis: "The man Adam *knew* his wife Eve intimately. She became pregnant and gave birth to Cain" (Gen 4:1). Thus, the term *yada* in Hosea is being employed in relation to the marital symbolism of the first three chapters of this biblical book, where the dramatic parallel between Hosea's broken marriage with Gomer and God's broken marriage with Israel is laid bare, where promiscuous carnal knowledge has taken the place of pure conjugal knowledge. Yet more is going on here than mere symbolism, because in Hosea's very experience of hearing and carrying out this outrageously difficult and even scandalous prophetic assignment, this prophet is himself drawn into the experience of knowing God intimately, knowing not just the words of God but *knowing the very passions and pains of God's own broken marriage and broken heart.*

Yet God's prophetic call in the book of Hosea to know God does not stop with knowing only God's heartbreak over our broken covenant with him that produces all the broken covenants and the resulting heartbreaks that lie almost everywhere beneath the surface of our lives. Hosea's call moves him (and aims to move us) deeper and further than this, until it finally breaks through to the *knowledge of God's passions and power and promise to restore all that has been broken*—to restore God's broken home with Israel and Hosea's broken home with Gomer and our broken homes with all their dissention, division, and divorce, which, if we are honest, lie all too close to home for every single one of us. So Hosea calls us and leads us all the way through the brokenness to the restoring wholeness of the knowledge of God. It is precisely the same call that the apostle Paul holds out to us in his words in Philippians 3:10, "that I may know Him and the power of His resurrection, and the fellowship of His sufferings" (NKJV).

The movement of the Spirit throughout global Christianity over the last century has once again posed this powerful and passionate call for us to know God in an experiential way—a way that goes beyond merely subscribing to a set of beliefs or submitting to a set of practices, indeed calling us to know God in the kind of way that Hosea was called and in the kind of way that the disciples at Pentecost in Acts 2 were called—called by a God who breaks into our lives in a personal and passionate and powerful way and indeed calls us, calls us by name, calls us to know God and thereby to make him known through living lives of intimate spiritual experience that bears the fruit—indeed, the covenant offspring—of God's Holy Spirit.

JOEL

"Afterward I will pour out my spirit on all flesh; your sons and your daughters shall prophesy, your old men shall dream dreams, and your young men shall see visions."

—*Joel 2:28 (NRSV)*

When I think about the book of Joel,

I am reminded of General William Tecumseh Sherman's "March to the Sea" from Atlanta to Savannah in late 1864 and early 1865 during the American Civil War. The attack was meant to demonstrate to the average person living in the heart of the Confederate states the devastating effects of war. Sherman sought to break the morale of the common folk by pillaging or destroying Southern supplies. According to a traditional saying, the devastation wrought by Sherman's 62,000-man advance was so complete that a crow had to pack a lunch when flying across the wake of Sherman's swath of destruction. The image depicted in Joel is no less poignant. The invasion of locust swarms (or a literal army) brought similar devastation for the average person. Thankfully, it is in the midst of this utter devastation that Joel prophesies that God will pour out the Spirit upon all flesh (2:28-29) and revive the people. Indeed, the promise of Pentecost and spiritual renewal is often most deeply linked to the anguish of the human spirit.

Quick Facts

Title: The title comes from the name of the prophet whose message comprises the book. It is the same in both the LXX and Hebrew texts. Joel's name means "YHWH is God."

Date: No clearly datable event appears in the book. Theories on Joel's date have been offered ranging from the ninth to second centuries BCE. For example, because elders and priests are mentioned (1:2, 13; 2:16) with no reference to a king, the book could fall within the ninth-century reign of the boy-king Jehoash, or Joash (2 Kgs 11–12). Also, if the locust plague is taken figuratively, then the book depicts an invasion by a foreign army, which could refer to any of the invasion forces beginning as early as the Assyrian onslaught in the eighth century to the Babylonian invasions in the late seventh and early sixth centuries. However, the absence of direct references to Assyria and Babylon may reflect a period either before their ascendancy (ca. ninth century BCE) or long after (i.e., postexilic period). The reality is, we just cannot be certain of the date.

Authorship: The text is assigned to the prophet Joel, the son of Pethuel (1:1). Nothing beyond this is known of either him or his father.

Audience: The audience could be pre- or postexilic from the land of Judah (cf. 3:1, 6, 8, 18-20).

Genre: The book presents a series of prophetic oracles of the following three types: a call to lament, a promise of salvation, and an announcement of judgment.

Purpose: Joel offers hope to his nation in the midst of severe suffering due to calamities described in terms of a locust plague and an enemy invasion. In the midst of these calamities, Joel announces the coming of the day of the Lord—an event marked by judgment on both Judah and the nations (cf. 2:19–3:21).

Structure

While the book of Joel has been divided in several ways (the Hebrew text even divides the book into four chapters instead of three), the three genre types mentioned earlier form a sequential structure: a call for God's people to lament (1:1–2:17), a promise for the restoration of God's people (2:18-32), and an announcement of judgment upon the nations (3:1-21).[60]

Summary

A Call for God's People to Lament: Joel 1:2–2:17

After a brief introduction of the prophet (1:1), the book launches into a call to lament—the longest such call for communal lamentation in all of Scripture. The precipitating cause is a locust plague, the devastating effects of which are elaborated with poignant, poetic detail (1:7-12). Scholars debate whether this should be understood literally as an actual locust plague or figuratively as a metaphorical description of an invading foreign army (2:1-9) or even as apocalyptic imagery of otherworldly forces that are being turned loose by God against the people (2:10-11). Whether one argues for one of these options or for a combination of all of them, the poetic picture that Joel is drawing points to one thing above all else. The focus is not just the day of the locust or the day of military invasion; it is the coming of the day of the Lord (1:15; 2:11). This advent entails devastation so complete that it will live in the memory of God's people for generations to come (1:2-3). Joel addresses his call to lament first to the elders (1:2) but finally to the priests (1:13; 2:17), who are exhorted to call everyone in the land to gather in God's house for "a solemn assembly" and cry out to the Lord (1:13-14; 2:15-17 KJV). Joel uses a variety of Hebrew terms to call his people to weep, mourn, sigh, grieve, groan, and lament. He finally pushes the call to the breaking point

---

60. Larry R. McQueen, *Joel and the Spirit: The Cry of a Prophetic Hermeneutic* (Cleveland, TN: CPT Press, 2009), 21–43.

with the famous words, "Yet even now, says the LORD, return to me with all your hearts, with fasting, with weeping, and with sorrow; tear your hearts and not your clothing . . . Who knows whether he will have a change of heart and leave a blessing behind him" (2:12-14a).

A Promise for the Restoration of God's People: Joel 2:18-32

While the previous section culminates with an intense call for God's people to experience a radical change of heart, this section begins announcing a dramatic change of heart on God's part: "Then the LORD became passionate about this land, and had pity on his people" (2:18). This is the turning point from which a divine promise of restoration bursts forth, announcing a total reversal of the agricultural and military devastations previously described (2:19-24). Indeed, God promises "to restore . . . the years that the . . . locust has eaten" (2:25 NKJV). Yet there is still more: "After that I will pour out my spirit," God says, "on everyone" (lit. 'all flesh'; 2:28a). Crossing gender barriers, the promise includes, "your sons and your daughters will prophesy" (2:28b), and then crossing the generation gap, "your old men will dream dreams, and your young men will see visions" (2:28c). Even social and ethnic divisions are overcome in God's following statement: "In those days, I will also pour out my spirit on the male and female slaves" (2:29; slaves in the ancient world were commonly foreigners). This overflowing promise is connected to the day of the Lord, which will be prefaced by cosmic upheavals affecting the whole world (2:30-31), not unlike what was earlier envisioned for God's people and land (2:1-2). Yet in the face of these dreadful events comes God's promise that "everyone who calls on the LORD's name will be saved" (2:32)—a promise, here again, that seems to transcend all national and even international boundaries.

An Announcement of Judgment upon the Nations: Joel 3:1-21

Again using the imagery and terminology of "the Day of the Lord" (3:14-15), the book concludes with an announcement to Judah that God will summon all nations into a great valley by raising a battle cry (3:9-11). Yet the nations will assemble (like a solemn assembly of all nations) only to meet God sitting there to judge them (3:2, 12-13; cf. Ezek 38–39; Rev 19–20). The final scene shifts from "the valley of judgment" to the mountain of Zion, from which "the LORD roars" (3:16). It is God's declaration of both the lasting restoration of the land, the holy city, and God's people and the desolation of those who have done violence to them (3:16-21).

Debated Issues (aka Great Paper Topics)

1) How do scholars understand the relationship between Joel 3:10 and the two prophetic texts of Isa 2:4 and Mic 4:3?

2) What are the different views of the locusts mentioned in the first two chapters of Joel?

The Message of the Book

When God's children stop living their days in the light of the day of the Lord, his day will come as night. Yet there can still be hope in that day for all who call on the name of Lord, for all who would tear open their hearts to receive God's Spirit outpoured.

Closing the Loop

God's promise through the prophet Joel to pour out his Spirit on all flesh (2:28) becomes the signal text of the Day of Pentecost in Acts 2 (Acts 2:16-21). Consequently, it has become a golden text of the modern Pentecostal movement. In striking accordance with this text, this movement over the past century bears witness to a move of God's Spirit that has overflowed all boundaries, including those between genders, social stations, generations, nations, and denominations. Yet while Pentecostalism can point to the vast fruit of its movement, it does not everywhere show the deep root of prophetic witness revealed in the book of Joel. The prophet Joel would remind us that the day of Pentecost will be fully understood only in the light of the day of the Lord. And the promise of the Spirit outpoured will be fully realized only by those whose hearts have been torn open and poured out.

AMOS

*A lion has roared; who will not fear? The L*ORD *God has spoken; who can but prophesy?*
—Amos 3:8

When I think about the book of Amos,

I immediately envision a preacher from rural Alabama being asked by God to drive to Wall Street in lower Manhattan in New York City and stand on a street corner with a sandwich sign that reads, "Turn or burn: Repent of your excess and greed!" I am sure that, as the preacher spoke with a Southern drawl, those from Manhattan would quickly notice. Furthermore, a message that cuts to the heart of America's excess and greed would no doubt evoke a bitter response and jeers for the preacher to go back from whence he came. To a degree this was a similar scenario Amos found himself experiencing. God asked him, a farmer from Tekoa in rural Judah, to go north and prophesy in the cult city of Bethel, which happened to be a royal city of King Jeroboam II (7:13). Once there, Amos delivered a scathing indictment of the people's excesses and ethical shortcomings. The incredulous and indignant response of the religious elite, the priest Amaziah in particular, called for Amos to return to his own region and prophesy there (7:12). When one considers the social injustices practiced by Israel, it does not take too much of an imagination to draw parallels with Western culture today.

Quick Facts

Title: The title comes from the name of the prophet whose message forms the book. It is the same in both the LXX and Hebrew texts. Amos's name means "burden-bearer."

Date: Amos 1:1 places the time frame for the book during the reigns of Uzziah (792–740 BCE) in Judah and Jeroboam II (793–753 BCE) in Israel. More specifically, the prophet delivered his message "two years before the earthquake" (understood by scholars to be circa 755 BCE; cf. Zech 14:5).

Authorship: Most agree that the eighth-century prophet Amos wrote much of his book. Some argue that the oracle against Judah (2:4-5) and the prophecy of hope with which the book ends (9:8b-15) are possible instances of later additions to the text.

Audience: The audience is predominantly the people of the northern kingdom, with special focus on the priests at Bethel. The inclusion of the oracle against Judah in chapter 2 makes the book instructional for the people of the southern kingdom as well.

Genre: The book is constituted primarily with prophetic oracles in chapters 1–6 and vision reports in 7–9, with a short section of historical narrative in 7:10-17.

Purpose: The book of Amos served as a warning to the northern kingdom, on the threshold of their demise, to turn from their social injustice and to care for the poor by practicing justice and righteousness (5:24).

Structure

While scholars have proposed a number of structures, a three-part structure is widely observed and seems most fitting: oracles against the nations (1:1–2:5); the indictment of Israel (2:6–9:10) using calls to "hear" the word of YHWH (3:1–6:14) and to see visions from YHWH (7:1–9:10); and a message of hope (9:11-15).

Summary

Oracles against the Nations: Amos 1:1–2:5

The book of Amos opens with a series of oracles against the nations surrounding Israel and Judah. These messages focus on war crimes—atrocities perpetrated in the time of war. God requires, both then and now, that nations show mercy and practice a level of social justice for those they conquer. The indicted nations include: Damascus/Syria, Gaza/Philistia, Tyre/Phoenicia, Edom, Ammon, and Moab. Using the common poetic device of the numerical saying or "x, x+1" pattern (i.e., "for three transgressions . . . and for four . . ."; cf. 1:3, 6, 9, 11, 13; 2:1, 4, 6 in KJV), Amos denounces the injustices of these nations and pronounces God's judgment upon them in the form of fire (1:4, 7, 10, 12, 14; 2:2; cf.

Excavated ruins at the site of ancient Samaria. Amos prophesied the destruction of Samaria and the northern kingdom in chapter 6, a prophecy that came to pass in 722 BCE. Photo courtesy of Michael Luddeni.

2:5; 5:6; 7:4). These injustices include: threshing the captives of war with iron sledges (1:3); population displacement and enslavement (vv. 6, 9); relentless aggression (v. 11); gratuitous violence against the innocent (v. 13); and desecration of the dead (2:1). Amos then shifts to indictments against Judah and Israel using the same prophetic formulae. Judah had rejected God's laws (2:4), and many of the leaders and wealthy people in Israel had committed social injustices against their own people (2:6-8). The most sustained indictment falls upon Israel, the nation to which Amos is called to prophesy. This will remain Amos's focus through the rest of the book.

The Indictment of Israel: Amos 2:6–9:10

Using a prophetic covenant lawsuit, Amos indicts Israel. The lawsuit format included: an address to the defendant (2:6a), the pronouncement of guilt (2:6b-8, 12), and the declaration of the sentence (3:1–9:10). In some cases, as we see here in Amos, Israelite prophets included the identification of the plaintiff (i.e., God 2:6a) and a brief historical overview (2:9-11), which paralleled the covenant formulary (see discussion on chapter 24 in Joshua). This portion of Amos also has two pairs of statements that function to frame the section: one focused on selling the poor for a pair of sandals (cf. 2:6b; 8:6) and the other served to remind Israel of God's role in bringing them out of Egypt (2:10; 9:7a; cf. also 3:1). While not all-inclusive, Amos highlights Israel's sin, which centered on social injustice and sexual deviance (2:6-8). In the sentencing phase, Amos uses oracles introduced by the call to "hear" (3:1; 4:1; 5:1), and oracles conveyed through a series of visions, which included a locust swarm (7:1-2); a fire (7:4); a plumb line (7:7-9); a basket of summer fruit (8:1-14); and YHWH standing by the altar (9:1-10). Throughout both of these subsections, the declaration of judgment predominates (3:11-15; 4:6-12; 5:1-3, 9, 16-27; 6:1-14; 7:1-9; 8:2-3, 7-14; 9:1-4, 8a). In the case of the first two visions, Amos's intercession causes God to relent from sending the envisioned locust swarm and fire (7:3, 6). However, in the latter three visions God reaffirms the punishment on Israel that will no longer be turned back. Tucked in the midst of the visions Amos makes it clear why Israel was in this predicament—her priests had ceased teaching the people about God. This is graphically shown in the narrative that presents Amos's encounter with Amaziah, the priest in Bethel (7:10-17). Indeed, throughout his book Amos rails against the false worship at Bethel (3:14; 4:4-5; 5:5-6; 7:10-17). Because of this, Amos pronounces judgment on the house of Amaziah, while assuring him that Israel would indeed go into exile—a reality that came to pass when the Assyrians exiled Israel in 722 BCE.

At the heart of Amos's message is his concern for ethical living and the practice of social justice. This driving conviction is famously expressed in 5:24: "But let justice roll down like waters, and righteousness like an ever-flowing stream." Israel's sins in this area are legion: they abused the needy and humble (2:6-8; 4:1; 5:10, 12; 8:4); they practiced defiling sexual acts (2:7); they encouraged their nazirites and priests to sin (2:12); they pursued violence (3:10) and self-indulgence (4:1; 6:4-6); they hated those who were just and honest (5:10, 12, 24); and they used dishonest business practices (8:5). In all of these acts they did not fear their Sovereign and revere the creator of the earth (4:13; 5:8; 9:5-6).

Despite these egregious sins and the certainty of divine punishment, Amos finally announces God's promise that a remnant will be saved. After a period of judgment, God will bring them back to the land (9:15) and make them flourish once again. Not surprisingly, Amos the herdsman and vinedresser (7:14-15) uses agrarian imagery as a means of showing God's restoration of Israel (9:13-14). It is a restoration that intimates reconciliation, for this prophet from the south, who had pronounced the downfall of the altar at Bethel (3:14; cf. 7:17; 9:1) in the north, now declares God's promise to "raise up the meeting tent of David" in the south (9:11)—a picture of Israel made whole again in every way.

Debated Issues (aka Great Paper Topics)

1) What are the scholarly theories concerning the inclusion of Amos 2:4-5 in the book?

2) According to scholars, what time period best fits the situation described in 9:11-15?

The Message of the Book

God will not allow social injustice to go unpunished in any context, especially among his own people. Yet his punishment, though harsh, is enacted with a view to the promise of making us whole at last.

Closing the Loop

Amos is a prophet best known for confronting the rich and powerful for their social injustices against the poor. While many OT prophets take up this message, Amos's laser focus on this issue has caused this prophet to be widely regarded as Scripture's leading voice on the subject—uttering words that have reverberated down through history and that have been taken up again and again, most notably in Martin Luther King Jr.'s "I Have a Dream" speech, which echoes Amos's call to "let justice roll down like waters."

This mighty message and cause of social justice is one of the chief contributions of the OT prophets to the history of the human race, and any group of people who would claim to be heirs of the prophetic tradition, as Pentecostals have done, should feel the solemn weight and responsibility of carrying this cause. Where Pentecostalism has emerged among the poor and oppressed, especially in the Global South, the movement has done better with this but much less so as its adherents have climbed the ladder of social standing, especially in North America.[61]

Yet there is another important cause in Amos that should not be missed. Although Amos had an extremely confrontational message and approach, it was ultimately in the service of a vision of reconciliation.

---

61. Cheryl Bridges Johns, *Pentecostal Formation: A Pedagogy Among the Oppressed*, JPTSup Series (Eugene, OR: Wipf & Stock, 2010), 138–40. See also Donald E. Miller and Tetsunao Yamamori, *Global Pentecostalism: The New Face of Christian Social Engagement* (Oakland, CA: University of California Press, 2007), 1–38.

He was raised up during the time of the divided kingdoms of Judah and Israel (cf. Elijah's prophetic action in 1 Kgs 18:30-32). The book itself, as if to refuse the finality of this division, is dated in terms of the dating systems of both kingdoms (1:1). Amos was from the south, but he was called to the north. The priest of Bethel told Amos to go back home "to the land of Judah, eat your bread there, and prophesy there" (7:12). Amos not only was willing to endure such rejection from the northern Israelites, but he was even twice moved to intercede on their behalf when God showed him visions of their destruction: "'LORD God, I beg you, stop! How can Jacob survive? He is so small!'" And then we are told, "The LORD relented concerning this" (7:2-3, 5-6). Surely this is an indication to us that God can entrust his messages of harsh judgment only to those who are not judgmental. Perhaps this is what qualifies Amos in the end to glimpse and to share a message of hope for Israel beyond the judgment—one that does not stop with the northern kingdom of Israel. It includes the promise of a coming day when God will raise up the fallen "tabernacle of David" where "*all the nations* [*goyim*/Gentiles]" can be called by the name of the Lord (9:11-12).

In Acts 15 the Jewish followers of Jesus gather in Jerusalem and bear witness to the fulfillment of this prophecy when they quote these words of Amos (vv. 16-17) and then declare that "it seemed good to the Holy Spirit, and to us" (v. 28 KJV) to receive into fellowship the Gentiles who had received the Spirit (vv. 7-8). It is a fulfillment that has extended from the church of the first century to the present day—one that surely should continue to confront us and inspire us, across all of our lines of division, with a world-shaking vision of reconciliation and unity.

OBADIAH

"Because of the slaughter and violence done to your brother Jacob, shame will cover you, and you will be destroyed forever."
—Obadiah 10

When I think about the book of Obadiah,

I find myself turning to recollections of my childhood. Having grown up as the seventh of eight children, I am all too familiar with sibling rivalry. Within this often-chaotic setting, on more than one occasion, one of us would call out to Mom or Dad, usually accompanied by a bloodcurdling scream, to bring "justice" to what we assured them was an "unfair" situation. After all, the "oppressor" should have known better, being a family member and all! Although the shortest book in the OT, Obadiah is a paradigmatic statement on the topic of sibling rivalry (cf. Gen 25:22-34; 27:39-40). Obadiah, an Israelite prophet, delivers an oracle against Edom, the brother of Jacob/Israel, because of their unfair treatment of Israel. When Israel found itself in the dire situation of being attacked by an outside force, his brother Edom did not do what brothers are supposed to do, instead, Edom joined in the oppression of Israel.

Quick Facts

Title: The title comes from the name of the prophet whose message comprises the book. It is the same in both the LXX and Hebrew texts. Obadiah's name means "servant of YHWH."

Date: As with the book of Joel, no definitive date can be assigned to this book. Scholarly perspectives range from the ninth to fifth centuries BCE. Second Kgs 8:20-22 and 2 Chron 21:8-17 (cf. Amos 1:6-8, 11-12) give a clear reference to Edom's part in a coalition with the Philistines and Arabs against Judah during the days of Jehoram (848–841 BCE), and 2 Chron 28:16-18 recalls Edom's attack during the reign of Ahaz (735–715 BCE). Thus, a preexilic date fits well. However, there are many who think the situation surrounding the destruction of Jerusalem by the Babylonians in 586 BCE is the most likely context for the book (cf. Ps 137:7 and Lam 4:21-22).

Authorship: The text is assigned to the prophet Obadiah, with no references even to his family connections (v. 1). Some posit that this is Ahab's servant, Obadiah (1 Kgs 18:3-16), but there is no basis for certainty for this or for identifying this minor prophet with any of a number of other individuals named Obadiah in Hebrew Scripture.

Audience: The audience could be pre- or postexilic from the land of Judah.

Genre: The book is constituted by a prophetic oracle that represents the common category of oracles against foreign nations.

Purpose: Obadiah serves as a message of hope and justice for Judah in light of God's retribution on Edom for their treatment of God's people.

Nabatean remains at Petra, the region of ancient Edom. Obadiah's prophecy is directed against the Edomites. Photo courtesy of Michael Luddeni.

Structure

The single chapter of Obadiah has a three-part structure: Edom's destruction foretold (vv. 1-9); the reason for Edom's destruction (vv. 10-14); Judah's blessing foretold (vv. 15-21).

Summary

Edom's Destruction Foretold: Verses 1-9

At the pinnacle of Edom's hubris (1:3-4), Obadiah declares the complete destruction of Edom (vv. 8-9) at the hands of the nations (vv. 1, 5-6) and their allies (v. 7).

The Reason for Edom's Destruction: Verses 10-16

What was the reason for God's judgment? Edom did not help his brother Israel in the time of his despair (v. 10). Instead Edom gloated over Judah's distress (vv. 12-13) and even joined, indirectly, in the attacks of the enemy against him (v. 11), profiting from Judah's hardships and killing some of the fugitives while taking others as prisoners of war (vv. 13-14).

Judah's Blessing Foretold: Verses 15-21

As part of the restoration of Judah, the day of the Lord will fall not only upon Edom but also upon all the nations (vv. 15-16). It is as if Edom, in its opposition to God's plan and God's people, ultimately represents all peoples. Reinforcing this idea is the fact that the names Edom and Adam (i.e., "humankind") are very similar in Hebrew, sharing the very same consonants. Thus, the book concludes with an ultimate global vision of the triumph of Judah judging and possessing the wealth of Edom and the nations so that "the kingdom will be the LORD's" (vv. 17-21; cf. Ezek 35).

Debated Issues (aka Great Paper Topics)

1) What are the different scholarly views and arguments on the historical context of Obadiah?

2) What is the history of relations between Edom and Israel that forms the background of the book of Obadiah?

The Message of the Book

God's judgment is reserved for those who oppose God's plan and oppress God's people, especially when it involves the betrayal of a covenant between siblings.

Closing the Loop

Strife between brothers is a pervasive and tragic theme in the Bible, starting with Scripture's first brothers, Cain and Abel, and then moving on to Isaac and Ishmael and then to Jacob and Esau—a struggle that begins for these two twin brothers while they are still in their mother's womb. This struggle becomes a defining one for Jacob, because in the midst of it is where God gives him his new name, Israel. Thus, the very identity of Israel as a person and as a people is forged in the heat of his conflict and accompanying desire for reconciliation with his brother, Esau.

Even as this conflict marks the beginning of Israel, the book of Obadiah would indicate that it marks the end of Esau. Indeed, Obadiah declares the end of Esau's descendants, the people of Edom together finally with all people and nations of the earth who follow in the lineage of this sibling, who, like Cain in the beginning, refused to be his "brother's keeper" (cf. Gen 4:9 KJV).

The flip side of the message of Obadiah is declared in Psalm 133: "How good and pleasant it is when brothers dwell [together] in unity!" (v. 1 ESV). This psalm, with beautiful poetic imagery, compares this sibling unity to two things: first to the anointing oil that flows down from the head of Aaron to the hem of his garments, and then to the dew of Hermon falling down upon Zion, that most crucial high place in Jerusalem. These powerful images can easily point forward to the Day of Pentecost in Acts 2, when the fire of God falls down upon and anoints 120 believers in "one accord" in an upper room in Jerusalem (v. 1 KJV). This scene is truly one of Scripture's clearest pictures of where "the LORD command[s] his blessing, even life for evermore" (Ps 133:3 KJV). And the book of Obadiah is also one of Scripture's most representative pictures of where the Lord directs his curse. This is surely enough to urge every one of us who sooner or later must contend with estranged siblings, "to make every effort to keep the unity of the Spirit through the bond of peace" (Eph 4:3 NIV).

JONAH

"I know that you are a merciful and compassionate God, very patient, full of faithful love, and willing not to destroy."

     —Jonah 4:2

When I think about the book of Jonah,

I am reminded of Jesus's words to the Pharisees when they asked him for a sign. Jonah's three-day ordeal in the belly of the fish was the only sign Jesus gave to them (Matt 12:39-41; 16:4; Luke 11:29-30, 32). While most scholars today reject the historicity of the book of Jonah, seeing it more in terms of a parable, Jesus's use of Jonah's experience as a sign of his death, burial, and resurrection has often been seen as his affirmation of the historicity of the book. There are those who would ask, would Jesus use a parable to *prove* his resurrection, especially in light of future skepticism related to this very event?

Quick Facts

Title: The title comes from the name of the prophet whose message forms the book. It is the same in both the LXX and Hebrew texts. Jonah's name means "dove."

Date: As with many books of the OT, there are two ways to date Jonah: according to the time period of Jonah or in terms of when the account was written (which could be a time long after the narrated events). As far as the first approach, 2 Kgs 14:25 makes reference to "Jonah, the son of Amittai" (KJV) during the reign of Jeroboam II (ca. 793–753 BCE; cf. 1:1), which provides a basis for dating the book of Jonah in this period. Taking the second approach, scholars have proposed dates ranging from the time of Jeroboam II to well into the Intertestamental Period. Some who have favored the possibility of the earlier date have noted the political events going on in Assyria during the eighth century BCE, particularly during the tumultuous reign of Ashur-Dan III (772–755 BCE) as fitting the historical context for the book. According to Assyrian and astronomical records, there was a solar eclipse in 763 BCE—an event that the ancients would have seen as a harbinger of disaster. Accordingly, it appears that this eclipse was attended by a series of plagues and uprisings that ravaged the land of Assyria, likely contributing to the waning power of Ashur-Dan III.

It is conceivable that all of this could have been the foreboding background that prepared the Assyrian city of Nineveh for Jonah's message of judgment. Interestingly, one of the Assyrian gods, Dagon, was often depicted as a fish. Could all of this have contributed to Nineveh's readiness to listen and to respond to a messenger who had come their way from the mouth of a great fish?

Authorship: No clear attribution of authorship is given. Some have read 1:1 as an attribution that names the author as Jonah, the son of Amittai.

Audience and Purpose: The population of Nineveh, one of Assyria's great cities, is the audience of Jonah within the story line of the book. Jonah's prophecy pronounces their coming judgment. The book serves as a message to God's own people about his love and saving power, reaching forward to all times and outward to all nations.

Genre: Chapters 1 and 3 are in the form of historical narrative, while chapter 2 is a psalm-like prayer in poetic form. Chapter 4 narrates an interaction that features prayerful dialogue between Jonah and YHWH. Alternately, some scholars assert that the entire book is to be categorized as a parable or allegory.

Structure

Jonah has a four-part structure corresponding to the four chapters of the book: YHWH's call and Jonah's rebellion (1); Jonah's prayer inside the fish (2); YHWH's re-call and Jonah's obedience (3); Jonah's prayer outside Nineveh (4).

Summary

YHWH's Call and Jonah's Rebellion: Chapter 1

YHWH's commissioning of Jonah to go to Nineveh and preach was not well received by Jonah (1:2). His response is somewhat understandable. After all, Nineveh was part of the Assyrian Empire, which had long oppressed Israel and the entire region. Jonah no doubt saw judgment on Nineveh as well deserved. What's more, if the Assyrians were to be judged, Israel would be free of their oppressive policies. Jonah decides to run from the call of God by going down to Joppa and boarding a boat to Tarshish (1:3). This is most likely the Tarshish in Spain. Thus, Jonah is running as far away from God as possible. Once out to sea, God sends a great storm against the boat (1:4). The sailors throw the cargo overboard to keep the ship from sinking. Meanwhile, Jonah is fast asleep in the hold of the ship (1:5). After being confronted by the captain of the ship, and after being singled out by casting lots as the cause of the trouble that had come their way, Jonah reveals to his shipmates that the storm came upon them because of his rebellion. Once they realize that he is a servant of the God who made the sea and dry land (1:6-9; cf. Ps 95:5), they fear for their lives (1:10). Jonah assures them that if they cast him into the sea, the storm will cease. While at first they reject this option, in the end they feel compelled to throw Jonah into the sea to save their lives and the ship (1:11-16). Although Jonah may have thought his death would release him from his calling, God had other plans by preparing a great fish to swallow him (1:17).

Jonah's Prayer inside the Fish: Chapter 2

In the brief ten verses of chapter 2, Jonah acknowledges God's deliverance, even though he is still inside the fish (cf. 2:6, 9). The language, while poetic, reflects ancient cosmology, i.e., the waters of "the deep," the "bars" of the earth, the "roots of the mountains" (NASB), and Sheol (NASB). While it is possible that Jonah thought he was dying as he descended into the depths of the sea, he could also be describing his descent into the belly of the fish. God responds by making the fish expel Jonah onto "dry land," the same term used when God delivered his people through the Red Sea (2:10; cf. Exod 14:22 NASB).

YHWH's Re-Call and Jonah's Obedience: Chapter 3

Jonah listens to God's second call and goes to Nineveh. The statement that Nineveh was a great city of three days' walk no doubt refers to the amount of time it normally took a person to see all the main sites of the city. Jonah's declaration that judgment was coming within 40 days ("three days" in the LXX) caused the people to repent in sackcloth including the king. The king calls for a citywide fast, including the animals, in hopes that God would spare them (3:7-9)—an outcome that in fact happens when God relents (3:10). While the notation about the "king" of Nineveh in verse 6 has caused many to doubt the historicity of the text (Assyria's capital, where the king resided, was not in Nineveh at this time), there are at least two factors to offset this argument. First, the Hebrew term for "king" (*melek*) can also mean "ruler" or "governor." Second, it is very likely that the actual king of Assyria visited Nineveh on a regular basis, because it was the main city of that region of the Assyrian Empire.

Jonah's Prayer outside Nineveh: Chapter 4

God's mercy to Nineveh in response to their repentance is so frustrating for Jonah that, after departing the city and waiting to no avail for its destruction, Jonah expresses his desire to die (4:1-3). In an effort to teach Jonah about divine mercy, God sets up a teaching moment for Jonah. First he causes a gourd plant (KJV) to grow up to shade Jonah from the sun. Then he sends a worm to kill the plant (4:6-7). When the sun beats down on Jonah, he returns to his death wish. In a final exchange, God asks Jonah how he can have more concern for the plant than for the 120,000 Ninevites, "who cannot discern between their right . . . and . . . left," as well as their animals (NKJV). The story ends with this unanswered question.

Debated Issues (aka Great Paper Topics)

1) How do scholars explain the discrepancy between the time spans in the Hebrew text and the LXX in Jonah 3:4 ("forty days" in the Hebrew text and "three days" in the LXX)?

2) How do scholars correlate the details about Nineveh in the book of Jonah with archaeological discoveries related to this ancient Assyrian city?

3) What are the main scholarly views on the meaning and purpose of the book of Jonah?

The Message of the Book

God's mercy is wider than the people of God and even a prophet of God might be prepared to accept, extending even to those we have known as our mortal enemies.

Closing the Loop

Jonah is unique among the OT prophetic books, for it is not primarily a collection of prophetic messages like all the rest. It is a story about a prophet. What's more, it is a story that is brief enough, wonder-filled enough, and simple enough to readily connect with children. Indeed, Jonah is the only book in the Latter Prophets that young children grow up knowing. Could it be that this is one of the key purposes of this book's uniqueness?

C. S. Lewis once wrote, "A book worth reading only in childhood is not worth reading even then."[62] The significance of the book of Jonah is that beneath its charming, child-friendly surface, there is a profound depth to the story—enough to probe even the most mature human heart. The story line itself seems to hint at this by means of the theme of "going down." When Jonah ran away from God's call, he "went down" to Joppa (1:3), then "had gone down" into the lowest parts of the ship (1:5), and then, when he was cast overboard, he "went down" to "the bottoms of the mountains" at the bottom of the sea (2:6), even into, as he put it, "the belly of the underworld [*Sheol*]" (2:2).

Yet the deepest point in the story of Jonah comes in the final chapter, when God probes Jonah in order to uncover the deep passions that lie hidden in his heart. After God reverses his decision to destroy Nineveh, Jonah divulges why he had run away from his call in the first place: "This is why I fled to Tarshish earlier! I know that you are a merciful and compassionate God" (4:2). Like a skillful therapist, God asks Jonah, "Is your anger a good thing?" (4:4). Jonah's response is much like his initial response to God's call: he walks away (4:5). Yet God presses in on Jonah even more deeply by questioning his anger a second time from another angle. He uses a shade plant, a cutworm, and then a hot wind to make Jonah even hotter before asking him, "Is your anger about the shrub a good thing?" Good "to the point of death!" is Jonah's reply (4:9). This is the breaking point of Jonah's suppressed passions that sets up the final point about God's expressed passions. This final point could be posed this way: *Is your passion to see divine judgment greater than your passion to see divine mercy?* In the end, this is the deep, unanswered question posed

---

62. C. S. Lewis, *Of Other Worlds: Essays and Stories*, ed. Walter Hooper (New York: Harcourt, Brace, Jovanovich, 1966), 38.

to Jonah and to everyone who has ears to hear Jonah's story.[63] In the first chapter, God uses a violent wind (*ruach*—1:4) to stop Jonah from running away from this question, and in the last chapter he uses a hot wind (*ruach*—4:8) to force Jonah to see what a burning question this is. And surely this is meant to help all of God's people, encountered by Holy Wind, to see that "the Spirit searches all things, even the deep things of God" (1 Cor 2:10 NIV).

---

63. Rickie D. Moore, *The Spirit of the Old Testament*, JPTS 35 (Blandford Forum, UK: Deo, 2011), 101–13.

MICAH

"He has told you, human one, what is good and what the LORD requires from you: to do justice, embrace faithful love, and walk humbly with your God.

—*Micah 6:8*

When I think about the book of Micah,

the verse quoted above stands out. This verse has often been considered the heart of prophetic ethics. When one considers the overall message of the prophets, sacrifices and rituals are not at the top of their list of the things that please God. On the contrary, the timeless message of Micah and the prophets has always focused on right motives and holy living. In a 21st-century context, Micah's message is no less relevant. One can go through the motions of attending church and singing the songs; one might even tithe regularly and serve in some position in the church; yet, if one's heart is not right with God, does not seek justice for those without a voice, and is full of pride, then such a person is basically a clanging gong and a clashing cymbal (1 Cor 13:1). Sadly, the prophetic indictment that Micah levels against Israel and Judah is just as valid for those fitting this description in the church today.

Quick Facts

Title: The title comes from the name of the prophet whose message forms the book. It is the same in both the LXX and the Hebrew text. Micah's name means "who is like YHWH."

Date: According to Mic 1:1, Micah ministered during the reigns of Jotham (750–731 BCE), Ahaz (731–715 BCE), and Hezekiah (715–686 BCE). In light of the indictments within the book, most of Micah's prophecies best fit between 750 BCE and the early part of Hezekiah's reign before he began his reforms. The wicked reign of Ahaz is an even likelier context for the book (cf. 2 Kgs 16; 2 Chron 28; 29:19; Isa 7). Micah was a contemporary of Isaiah, Amos, and Hosea.

Authorship: Although a number of theories have been proposed for the authorship and editing of Micah, there is no reason to rule out the attribution of authorship to Micah of Moresheth, a town located in the Shephelah region of Judah.

Audience and Purpose: The original audience was those living in preexilic Judah. During the reigns of Jeroboam II and Uzziah, Judah and Israel had experienced a period of unprecedented wealth and ease with territorial expansion almost equivalent to that of the period of Solomon. In this context Judah and Israel slipped into a spiritual lukewarmness that had fostered abuses, both spiritual and social, especially against the poorest and most underprivileged in the nation. Micah set out to warn the people of impending judgment: first Israel would receive punishment at the hands of Assyria in 722 BCE, and Judah eventually received her punishment from Babylon in 586 BCE.

Genre: Prophetic oracles written in poetic style comprise the main genre form. Within this broad genre, the covenant lawsuit is an important form that appears in the book (e.g., 6:1-8).

An excavated section of Hezekiah's wall, which he extended prior to the invasion of Sennacherib in 701 BCE. Micah ministered during the reign of Hezekiah (Micah 1:1). Photo courtesy of Christine Curley.

Structure

Micah consists of three oracles: an oracle against Israel and Judah and a future hope (1–2); an oracle of judgment for the leaders and hope for the nation (3–5); an indictment against Judah and final word of hope (6–7). These three oracles may have been delivered over a period of time before being assembled into one book.

Summary

An Oracle against Israel and Judah and a Future Hope: Micah 1–2

After the superscription of 1:1, Micah sets an ominous tone for the book by employing the Divine Warrior motif for YHWH (1:3-4). The prophet then launches into an oracle against both Israel/Samaria and Judah/Jerusalem (1:5). The warning against Israel for idolatry (1:7) indicates a context before the fall of Samaria in 722 BCE. Because Judah did not turn from committing the shameful acts practiced by Israel, she too will end up in exile (1:16). The reason for this judgment rests in the social evils of the people. They covet and devise evil plans to rob fellow citizens of their belongings and inheritance while oppressing widows and poor people (2:1-2, 8-9), actions directly contrary to God's commandments (Exod 20:15, 17). Even though restoration is promised in the future (2:12-13), at this moment in history, God is against this people (2:3-5). A future hope is given in 2:12-13 that is cast in terms of Messianic expectation and shepherd imagery, as can be seen quite often throughout both the Old and New Testaments (cf. 5:2-5; 7:14; Ps 23; Ezek 34; John 10).

An Oracle of Judgment for the Leaders and Hope for the Nation: Micah 3–5

The second oracle focuses even more attention on the wickedness of the rulers and leaders (e.g., prophets and priests). Because the leaders of God's people pervert the law (3:2-3, 9-10), accept bribes (3:5, 11), and deny justice to those of low status (3:11), God will judge them harshly (3:6-7, 12; 4:10). Following this judgment, Micah once again offers hope for the future of the nation and even people from other nations, who will come to Mount Zion, will learn the ways of YHWH, "beat their swords into plowshares," and experience God's lasting peace (4:1-5 KJV; a version of this same oracle appears in Isa 2:2-4). In that day, those of lowest status in the nation will find prosperity (4:6-8), and the defiant nations will be judged (4:11-13; 5:7-9, 15). Moreover, the Messiah will bring forth justice and righteous leadership for his people (5:2-6) and purge the land of idolatrous practices and the false security of military might (5:10-14).

An Indictment against Judah and Final Word of Hope: Micah 6–7

The final oracle begins with a covenant indictment formula, also known as the *rîv* ("dispute") formula (6:1-8). Micah calls the mountains as witnesses to the indictment (6:1-2) and then rehearses a brief history of how YHWH had delivered his people in Egypt and the wilderness (6:4-5). After a series of four rhetorical questions centered on hyperbolic acts of sacrifice that ask whether these will please God (all requiring a "no" answer), the prophet declares what God truly requires: justice, mercy, and humility. The negation of these three virtues is shown in the people's use of false scales in business, general violence (6:12; 7:2), lying lips (6:12), following the statutes of the house of Omri and Ahab (6:9-12, 16), bribery (7:3), and communal and familial discord (7:5-6). For all this, God will judge his people (6:13-15; 7:1). Nevertheless, for a third time Micah issues a word of hope for future restoration. Here he projects that it will be marked by miracles and acts of kindness for Israel parallel to the days of the exodus from Egypt (7:7-20).

Debated Issues (aka Great Paper Topics)

1) What are the scholarly theories regarding the inclusion of the historical notations in 6:4-5?

2) What are the scholarly views on the relationship between the very similar oracles that begin Micah 4 and Isaiah 2?

The Message of the Book

God requires for his followers a life of heartfelt obedience marked by justice, mercy, and humility.

Closing the Loop

Like the prophets who were his contemporaries in the eighth century BCE (Isaiah, Amos, and Hosea), Micah is known as a champion of social justice. This is the first priority Micah voices in his signature verse: "what the LORD requires from you," he says, is "to do justice" (6:8). Micah's role in carrying this message stands especially close to that of Isaiah, not only by taking place during the same time but also by its special focus upon the same place: the city of Jerusalem (cf. Isa 1:1; Mic 1:1). These two prophets even share an almost-identical oracle of Jerusalem's final destiny as the place where many nations will one day "go up to the mountain of the LORD, to the house of the God of Jacob" and learn God's ways of justice and peace— like a United Nations that truly works! (Mic 4:1-5 KJV; cf. Isa 2:1-5). Yet Micah delivers this message of justice with a special touch all his own—one that no doubt reflects his humble background from the rural region of Moresheth from which he comes. To the shared oracle of Jerusalem's future role as the center of global peace he adds his special word on peace at the domestic level—an ideal pastoral scene of everyone sitting under his or her own vine and fig tree (4:4). Yet Micah's word against Jerusalem for its people's present injustices is especially blunt and harsh: "Zion will be plowed like a field, Jerusalem will become piles of rubble" (3:12). Micah is still being remembered for this daring prediction over a century later when Jeremiah takes up this word at great cost on the threshold of its fulfillment (Jer 26:16-19).

Micah's capacity to come to Jerusalem and confront those in power there was surely informed by the critical perspective of his social background from rural Judah. Yet this prophet was well aware that there was more to it than this. "But [as for] me," he says, "I am filled with power, with the spirit [*ruach*] of the LORD, with justice and might, to declare to Jacob his wrongdoing and to Israel his sin!" (3:8). In Micah's day the Spirit of the Lord empowered the cause of social justice in the face of the powerful, and this is still the case today.

NAHUM

The LORD is very patient but great in power; the LORD punishes. His way is in whirlwind and storm.
—Nahum 1:3

When I think about the book of Nahum,

I actually think about the baseball fans of the Boston Red Sox. For me, a longtime Red Sox fan, the connection is obvious. For others, it may not be so clear. Let me explain. From 1918 until 2004 the Red Sox failed to win a World Series title. For 86 years Red Sox fans were patient and, you could say, long-suffering, as their team time and again failed to live up to expectations. (I am sure Chicago Cubs fans felt the same way until the year 2016, too!) When one considers the long-suffering nature of God toward Nineveh, the connection is evident. Both Jonah and Nahum prophesied destruction to Nineveh; in Jonah's day (ca. 763 BCE) Nineveh had repented and was spared. From that time until Nineveh finally was destroyed in 612 BCE, as prophesied by Nahum, God exhibited long-suffering patience toward Nineveh/Assyria, waiting nearly 150 years for the people of Nineveh to cease from their wicked ways. I do not know how long Red Sox fans would have been patient with their team had they not won in 2004. What I do know is that the long-suffering nature of God is evident throughout the OT, toward both Israel and foreign nations—the city of Nineveh represents just one of those nations.

Quick Facts

Title: The title comes from the name of the prophet whose message constitutes the book. It is the same in both the LXX and Hebrew text traditions. Nahum's name means "consolation" or "comfort" (cf. 3:7).

Date: No exact date can be given for Nahum's ministry. Based on the reference to the destruction of Thebes, or No (KJV)/No-amon (NASB; "city of Amun") in 3:8-10, it must be after Ashurbanipal's destruction of the city in 664/63 BCE and before the sacking of Nineveh by the Medes and Babylon in 612 BCE.

Authorship: The book is attributed to Nahum the Elkoshite. Scholars are uncertain as to where he lived. Some postulate that he was from the Galilee in or near Capernaum ("town of Nahum"), mentioned several times in the New Testament Gospels.

Audience and Purpose: Like Jonah's, the prophetic message of Nahum is addressed to the foreign nation of Assyria (i.e., Nineveh). However, similar to the way the oracles against the nations in many of the prophetic texts served to offer hope to God's people, Nahum's message would have been received by the people of Judah as a message offering hope to them (2:2), especially after the northern kingdom was exiled by Assyria in 722 BCE. Nahum is assuring the people that God's justice extends even to Israel's enemies (cf. Ps 137).

Genre: According to 1:1, the three chapters of Nahum are both an oracle and a vision.

Structure

Nahum has a two-part structure: YHWH's wrath revealed (chapter 1), and Nineveh's fall foretold (2–3).

Summary

YHWH's Wrath Revealed: Nahum 1

Nahum begins by acknowledging the just nature of God (1:2-3a), depicting God as a cosmic Divine Warrior, which we also see in Micah (1:3b-7). When YHWH's anger is aroused against the wicked (1:8-14), in this case Nineveh/Assyria (2:8), Judah will be liberated (1:15).

Nineveh's Fall Foretold: Nahum 2–3

In the last two chapters, Nahum describes the frenetic pace of the battle (2:3-6; 3:1-3) and the plundering of Nineveh (2:7-10). God's judgment on Nineveh is the consequence of her spiritual infidelities practiced on the nations (3:4). In keeping with the punishments for prostitutes noted in Hosea (Hos 2:3) and Ezekiel (cf. Ezek 16:39; 23:26; 26:16), Nahum metaphorically describes how Nineveh will be stripped naked (3:5-7). God's judgment will bring utter destruction upon Nineveh and her nobles (2:13; 3:11-19) like that brought upon Thebes (3:8-10).

Debated Issues (aka Great Paper Topics)

1) How does Nahum's message of destruction align with the historical facts of Nineveh's fall?

2) Both Nahum and Jonah are Old Testament books that focus on Nineveh and end with a question; what does a comparison of these two questions reveal to us about God and his people?

The Message of the Book

Sooner or later God's long-suffering comes to an end and God's judgment falls upon the wicked.

Closing the Loop

The books of Nahum and Jonah are closely linked together in several ways. Both feature prophetic words of judgment against Nineveh. Whereas Jonah sees God's mercy overrule his word of judgment after Nineveh's repentance, Nahum sees God's eventual and final judgment of Nineveh in response to its persistent practice of imperial evil. These two aspects of God's dealings with the Assyrian Empire are both grounded in a scripture passage from Exod 34:6-7, which is quoted by both Nahum and Jonah. It reads, "The Lord! The Lord! a God who is compassionate and merciful, very patient [literally, slow to anger], full of great loyalty and faithfulness, showing great loyalty to a thousand generations, forgiving every kind of sin and rebellion, yet by no means clearing the guilty, punishing for their parents' sins their children and the grandchildren, as well as the third and the fourth generation." Jonah recalls the first part of this text when he says, "This is why I fled to Tarshish earlier! I know that you are a merciful and compassionate God, very patient [slow to anger], full of faithful love, and willing not to destroy" (Jon 4:3). Nahum recalls both parts when he says, "The Lord is very patient [slow to anger] but great in power; the Lord punishes. His way is in whirlwind and storm; clouds are the dust of his feet" (Nah 1:3). In this statement by Nahum, we once again see the wind (*ruach*) of God that plays such a pivotal role in confronting Jonah and changing his course (cf. Jon 1:4; 4:8). Now Nahum sees this same wind, indeed the Spirit of the Lord, finally turning the tables on Nineveh.

Yet the book of Nahum is not about only the fall of Nineveh. The acrostic psalm in the first eight verses of the book is about God's way throughout the whole world and all of time. This sets the following prophetic oracle against Nineveh in a much larger framework and shows it to be but one example of God's eventual judgment against every evil empire that marches across the stage of human history. Thus, Nahum represents a very important revelation about the Spirit of God. God's Holy Spirit is not only the enlivening breath that inspires God's people at an individual and personal level but also the Holy Whirlwind that brings about the massive transitions in world history at the geopolitical level. This is Nahum's added contribution to Exod 34:6-7 and its oft-quoted revelation of the defining passions of God: "His way is in whirlwind and storm."

HABAKKUK

Write a vision, make it plain upon a tablet so that a runner can read it.
    —Habakkuk 2:2

When I think about the book of Habakkuk,

I think of his petitions to God and the similar prayers that I have prayed concerning both Canada and the United States. Habakkuk asked God how long God would allow evil and injustice to go unpunished in Judah. Much to Habakkuk's chagrin, God's response was that he was aware of the evil of his people and that he was sending the Babylonians to judge Judah. While I understand that Western countries are not theocracies, as Israel was, we are nonetheless responsible before God for our actions and policies (see the books of Jonah and Nahum). I have often looked at the wickedness of the West as it relates to the values of pop culture and "info-tainment," the cheapening of life through the blight of abortion, institutionalized racism, oppressive business practices, exploitive international relations, and asked God: "How long will you allow this to continue?" My only hope is that we repent before God sends "Babylon" against us in judgment; for we can be assured that what a nation sows is what a nation will reap (see Gal 6:7).

Quick Facts

Title: The title comes from the name of the prophet whose message is featured in the book. It is the same in both the LXX and Hebrew text traditions. Habakkuk's name means to "embrace/wrestle."

Date: While no specific date is given in the book, based on the references to the forthcoming onslaught of the Chaldeans (Babylonians), most scholars conclude that Habakkuk ministered before the rise of Babylon and the Babylonian invasion of Judah in 605–586 BCE. A date between 626 BCE (the year of Nabopolassar's rise to the Babylonian throne) and 605 BCE (the first invasion of Judah) seems appropriate.

Authorship: The book is attributed to Habakkuk, a Judean prophet. His identity is uncertain, but he may have also been a priest (cf. 3:19). Some argue that chapter 3 is by a later author (see below).

Audience and Purpose: The audience appears to be the people of Judah. The purpose of the short book is to draw attention to God's displeasure with the nation for their wickedness. It also serves as a warning that the Babylonians are coming to bring about God's judgment on his people.

Genre: The book's genres include prophetic oracles framed in a dialogue with God that has elements of lament (1:1–2:5), a taunt song (2:6-20), and a prayer psalm with a vision report (ch. 3).

Structure

The three genres used in the book generate its threefold structure: a dialogue (1:1–2:5); a taunt (2:6-20); a prayer psalm (3:1-19).

Summary

A Dialogue: Habakkuk 1:1–2:5

The opening section records a dialogue between Habakkuk and God concerning violations of covenant "law" among his fellow citizens of Judah. Habakkuk complains to God about divine inaction in response to sins of injustice (i.e., unrighteousness) and violence (1:2-4). God responds to this complaint by announcing that he is bringing against Judah the Chaldeans (i.e., Babylonians), who are both fierce warriors and experts in pillaging and conquering (1:5-11). In response to this shocking revelation, Habakkuk asks the Lord how a holy God could use a nation more wicked than Judah to judge them (1:12–2:1). God responds again by directing Habakkuk to write down "a vision," the content of which is not immediately described. While the reader must wait to learn more about the vision itself, the prophet is encouraged to wait for the vision's fulfillment that will not be delayed (2:2-3). In this light, we are given the most famous words of Habakkuk: "the just [i.e. those who are righteous] shall live by . . . faith [or faithfulness]" (2:4 KJV).

A Taunt: Habakkuk 2:6-20

This section takes the form of a taunt song, which most interpreters assume to be aimed at Babylon, but Babylon is not explicitly mentioned here. Thus, another way to understand this section is to see it pointing to the final end of everyone who lives a life of greedy exploitation and violence against others, whether they are the Babylonians or those from Judah, such as those about whom Habakkuk first began his complaint in chapter 1. What is altogether clear is that the last word of this section mutes all us-versus-them distinctions by declaring, "The LORD is in his holy temple. Let all the earth be silent before him" (2:20).

A Prayer Psalm: Habakkuk 3:1-19

Chapter 3 begins and ends with notations typical of the Psalms. This psalm is to be accompanied with stringed instruments (3:19) set to the tempo of Shigionoth (3:1; cf. Ps 7), a term about which scholars are uncertain. While chapter 3 is often seen as a later addition or an afterthought to the two previous sections, it seems reasonable to see this chapter as the prophet's follow-through on God's earlier direction to write down the vision he is given. Furthermore, in view of the world-shattering impact of what Habakkuk here reports having envisioned ("I have seen your work," 3:2), it makes sense for the prophet to begin with a prayer of intercession to God in the face of the impending doom (3:2). The essence of what Habakkuk sees is something far greater than the coming of the Babylonians. He sees *the coming of the Lord*. In keeping with the Divine Warrior motif accompanied by cosmic imagery used also by both Micah and Nahum, Habakkuk presents YHWH coming from Teman (out of the southern region of Edom) to execute judgment on the nations (3:3-12). YHWH as warrior also brings deliverance and salvation for his people (3:13). Habakkuk completes his song by expressing his trembling submission before such an awesome revelation and his readiness to wait (cf. his "How long?" of 1:2) with full trust in his God (3:18-19), even though God will soon bring judgment on the nation of Judah (3:14-17). Thus, Habakkuk seems to have come at last to exemplify the pivotal truth declared in 2:4, "the righteous shall live by . . . faith" (RSV).

Debated Issues (aka Great Paper Topics)

1) How does the Divine Warrior motif bring an element of unity to the Book of the Twelve?

2) How are the famous words of Hab 2:4 taken up and applied in passages in the NT?

The Message of the Book

Two messages are central: (1) God will judge sin by whatever means necessary; (2) "the righteous shall live by their faith [or faithfulness]" (2:4b; cf. Rom 1:17; Gal 3:11; Heb 10:38).

Closing the Loop

Habakkuk begins with a prayer of lament and ends with a prayer of praise. The book's three brief chapters track the movement from the one to the other.[64] The transition hinges upon Habakkuk's receiving a vision from the Lord (2:2). Chapter 3 can be seen as a report of what the prophet saw in this vision (or, at the very least, what he saw in the light of this vision). Prophetic visions and vision reports do not have much of a place in many ecclesial and theological traditions in the world today, but they have always had a special place in Pentecostal and charismatic theology and practice. The book of Habakkuk serves as an especially powerful example of the pivotal role that prophetic vision can have for the people of God, especially in troublesome times.

A few summary remarks on Habakkuk with an eye toward our own troublesome times might help us more clearly to see the significance of his vision for us. First, the prophet sees injustices among his people and presses God to do something about it. God then responds by declaring that he most certainly will do so: he will raise up a Middle Eastern nation to spread acts of terrorism across the world (cf. 1:7, which

---

64. Rickie D. Moore, *The Spirit of the Old Testament*, JPTS 35 (Blandford Forum, UK: Deo, 2011), 114–17.

emphasizes the "terror" factor). The prophet then responds by insisting that God surely would not use such a terrorist nation to come against his own exceptional ("more righteous"—1:13) people. At this point, Habakkuk pledges to wait as long as it takes for God to answer. The answer comes: the prophet must write down a vision and wait for it. Such waiting requires faith, which is no doubt why we are here told, "the righteous shall live by . . . faith" (2:4 RSV). We ourselves must wait until the final chapter to see what the prophet had seen: his eyes had seen the glory of the coming of the Lord—nothing less and nothing more than this. Yet what could be more?! And will anything less than this provide an adequate answer to the threat of the terrorism in our times? A prophetic vision of the coming of the Lord in all of its terrifying glory (cf. 3:16—"I hear and my insides tremble . . .") might be the only thing left that can take us beyond the terrifying prospects of the future we now face in our world today.

ZEPHANIAH

Then I will change the speech of the peoples into pure speech, that all of them will call on the name of the LORD and will serve him [in one accord].
  —*Zephaniah 3:9*

When I think about the book of Zephaniah,

I am reminded of my visits to several of the ancient ruins of the Philistine Pentapolis (Ashdod, Ekron, Gaza, Ashkelon, and Gath). Zephaniah mentions all of these cities (except Gath) in 2:4-7. Here he points out that God will cause these cities to be abandoned (i.e., destroyed). In my visits to Ashdod, Ashkelon, and Ekron, the one common thread I noticed was the total destruction and abandonment of the cities. Now, while it is true that these cities were destroyed and rebuilt multiple times even into the Muslim period, as of today, they are mere ruins. The connection between the modern sites and the period of Zephaniah is that the word spoken by Zephaniah did indeed come to pass.

Quick Facts

Title: The title comes from the name of the prophetic figure whose message forms the book. It is the same in both the LXX and Hebrew text traditions. Zephaniah's name means "YHWH hides/conceals."

Date: Scholars have dated the book, in whole or in part, from the seventh century to as late as 200 BCE. According to 1:1, Zephaniah ministered during the reign of Josiah (ca. 640–609 BCE). Based on his prophecy concerning Nineveh's destruction in 2:13, this portion of Zephaniah appears to have been written before 612 BCE. While one cannot rule out the possibility that he ministered also during the last half of Josiah's reign when the people appear to have served YHWH only superficially (cf. 1:4-6, 8-9; 3:1-4, 7), it is likely that Zephaniah prophesied predominantly during the period of 640–630 BCE (2 Kgs 22:1), before the full effects of Josiah's reforms (2 Kgs 22:3; 2 Chron 34:8). This would be before Jeremiah's call in 626 BCE. Zephaniah was a contemporary of Jeremiah and perhaps Obadiah.

Authorship: According to 1:1, Zephaniah is the author of the oracles in his book. Because the book's introduction takes the unusual step of tracing Zephaniah's lineage back four generations to Hezekiah, some assert that he was a descendant of King Hezekiah. If this is so, then Zephaniah was of royal lineage.

Audience: The audience is preexilic Judah.

Genre: Prophetic oracles written in poetic style comprise the main genre form.

Purpose: Although one-third of his book is focused on oracles against the nations, Zephaniah's words serve to warn the people of Judah of the coming destruction due to their sin. Zephaniah may be referring to sins carried over from the reigns of Manasseh and Amon (ca. 695–640 BCE for both).

Structure

The book can be seen in terms of a fivefold structure: introduction and warning of judgment (1:1-4); judgment against Judah (1:5–2:3); judgment against the nations (2:4-16); judgment against Jerusalem (3:1-8); and a promise of future restoration (3:9-20).

Summary

Introduction and Warning of Judgment: Zephaniah 1:1-4

After the introduction of the prophet in verse 1, verses 2-4 warn of a coming Noah-like divine judgment when all the world, including humankind, animals, birds, and even fish, will be swept away.

Judgment on Judah: Zephaniah 1:5–2:3

Zephaniah focuses this judgment first on Judah because of their worship of Baal, Molech, Dagon (1:9; cf. 1 Sam 5:5), and the celestial hosts (1:4-5). Moreover, those of royalty and the merchants will lose their wealth (1:8, 10-13). Zephaniah, more than any other OT prophet, speaks of this day in terms of the day of the Lord—a time of great wrath and distress on earth and in the heavens (1:14-15) and a time when death will come to those who oppose God (1:16-18). There is acknowledgment that those who truly seek God and repent will perhaps be spared (2:1-3).

Judgment on the Nations: Zephaniah 2:4-16

As is typical of the prophets, Zephaniah indicts all of Judah's neighbors for wrongdoing. Philistia (2:4-7), Moab and Ammon (2:8-11), Cush (i.e., Ethiopia, 2:12), and Assyria (2:13-15) will all feel the wrath of God for their hubris and mistreatment of God's people.

Judgment on Jerusalem: Zephaniah 3:1-8

Serving as an *inclusio* for the judgment oracles, there is a special, second oracle of judgment for Jerusalem (cf. 1:4; 3:1). Despite the Lord's presence in the city (3:5), every segment of the population is wicked (3:1-4). Indeed, Jerusalem refused to learn from God's judgment on the nations (3:6-8).

A Promise of Future Restoration: Zephaniah 3:9-20

Even as Zephaniah's message of judgment begins with all peoples before shifting to a focus on God's people, so does his message of restoration. First God promises to restore to "the peoples" a pure language so they may "call on the name of the Lord" and serve him in unity (3:9). Then, turning to his own people who have been scattered among the nations, God will remove the proud and bring back those who are humble before God (3:9-12, 19-20). In that day God will remove their reproach and dwell in their midst, causing those who have returned to Zion to rejoice (3:14-18).

Debated Issues (aka Great Paper Topics)

1) What are the theories related to the identification of the Hezekiah noted in 1:1?

2) How does Zephaniah's perspective on the day of the Lord compare to that of other OT prophets?

The Message of the Book

The prophetic word on the "day of the Lord" calls all God's people and ultimately all the peoples of the world to see the end and goal of life in the light of this day.

Closing the Loop

Most every theme of the book of Zephaniah can be found in other OT prophetic books: the movement from judgment to restoration, the day of the Lord, oracles against the nations, and the final exaltation of Zion. Zephaniah is nevertheless distinct in the way it emphasizes the global and cosmic scope of God's judgments in the coming day of the Lord. Yet on one point, Zephaniah presents a word that is completely new and unprecedented. It comes at the very beginning of his prophecy of restoration with these remarkable words of divine promise in 3:9, "Then I will change the speech of the peoples into pure speech [or "a pure language"], that all of them will call on the name of the Lord and will serve him as one" or "with one accord," as many English translations render the phrase.

Obviously, this promise points forward to the Day of Pentecost in Acts 2, where speech inspired by the Holy Spirit (v. 4) is given to the followers of Jesus who are gathered together "with one accord" (v. 1 KJV), so that bystanders who are there "from every nation under heaven" can hear praises to God being spoken in their own languages (vv. 5-8). All of this sets the stage for Peter's message on the prophecy of Joel that declares, "Everyone who calls on the name of the Lord will be saved" (vv. 16-21).

While the prophecy of Joel (2:28-32) is clearly important for illuminating the Day of Pentecost, Zephaniah 3:9 has its own special ray of light to give. This single verse helps us to see God's special Pentecost desire to touch our language—the very thing that so deeply divides us (cf. the Babel story of Gen 11:1-9) and so often defiles us (cf. Isa 6:5)—so that we can at last become one people, brought together in one accord "from every tribe, language, people, and nation" to be "a kingdom and priests to our God, and . . . rule on earth" (Rev 5:9-10).

HAGGAI

Is it time for you to dwell in your own paneled houses while this [temple] lies in ruins?
    —Haggai 1:4

When I think about the book of Haggai,

I am reminded of my visit to the Gambia, West Africa, a few years ago. As a carpenter, I noticed a common phenomenon in their building practices. Once a Gambian purchases a piece of land, it is a common practice to build a wall around the new property before actually building a house. Apparently this is a means of defining one's property lines while offering a level of privacy and protection. The problem I noticed, however, was that people would often build the wall and then, because of either lack of funds or some other problem, actually fail to follow through on building the house or building. I saw house after house sitting half-constructed. This is something close to the picture of the Jewish community after returning from the Babylonian captivity in the period of Haggai (and Zechariah). The people had laid the foundations of the temple in 537 BCE (cf. Ezra 3:8-10; 4:4-24), but due to a number of hindering factors, they had failed, over the course of 17 years, to complete the project. This was the context in which Haggai ministered. Haggai delivers four dated oracles strongly encouraging the people to rebuild the temple and live holy lives. The temple was finally completed in 516 BCE.

Quick Facts

Title: The title comes from the name of the prophet whose messages comprise the book. It is the same in both the LXX and Hebrew text traditions. Haggai's name means "festal" or "feast of YHWH."

Date: Based on the precisely dated oracles, the book of Haggai can be dated to a four-month period in 520 BCE (late August to late December) in the second year of the Persian king Darius I.

Authorship: According to 1:1, 12; 2:1, 20, Haggai, a contemporary of the prophet Zechariah (cf. Zech 8:9), wrote the book. Nothing beyond this can be known with certainty about the prophet.

Audience: The original audience consisted of the roughly 50,000 Jewish returnees of 538 BCE who lived in and around Jerusalem (Ezra 1, 8).

Genre: The book is constituted of prophetic oracles, delivered in both prose and poetry.

Purpose: The book aims to encourage the people to rebuild the temple, live righteous lives, and receive God's blessings.

Structure

The two chapters of Haggai follow a fourfold division based on the dated oracles: the first oracle (1:1-15); the second oracle (2:1-9); the third oracle (2:10-19); and the fourth oracle (2:20-23).

Summary

The First Oracle: Haggai 1:1-15

Haggai's first oracle is delivered on the first day of the sixth month (i.e., Elul = Aug–Sept) in the fall of 520 in the second year of Darius Hystaspes (522–486 BCE). The primary addressees are Zerubbabel (grandson of Jehoiachin; cf. Matt 1:12), who is the administrative leader of the Jewish community, and the high priest, Joshua. In dialogic fashion, Haggai declares that despite popular opinion to the contrary, now is the time to rebuild the temple. The people, while living in comfortable homes (1:4), were experiencing privation (1:6, 9) because of God's judgment on them (1:10-11) for their failure to honor God by rebuilding the temple. Haggai tells the people to go to the mountains and cut trees to use to build the temple (1:8). In a rare instance of positive response to the prophetic voice, Zerubbabel and the people, stirred by the Spirit of God (1:12-14), obey the word brought by Haggai. The work commences on the 24th day of the same month in which Haggai delivers this first oracle.

The Second Oracle: Haggai 2:1-9

Delivered on the 21st day of the seventh month (i.e., Tishri = Sept–Oct), the second oracle is given to Zerubbabel, Joshua, and the people. It serves as a word of encouragement to any who might be disappointed over the apparent inferiority of their "new" temple as compared to Solomon's temple (2:3). Haggai assures the people that God will bring the wealth of the nations into the temple so that it will indeed be greater than the first temple (2:4-9). While it is possible that Haggai is foreseeing the much-improved Herodian temple of much later times, or perhaps even the eschatological temple, the reference to God's peace upon the temple in verse 9 has messianic overtones and pushes one in the direction of Jesus's inauguration of the new covenant; the covenant of peace (cf. Ezek 34:25; 37:26; Mal 2:5). Jesus eventually presents himself as the new "temple" (John 2:19-21).

The Third Oracle: Haggai 2:10-19

On the 24th day of the ninth month (i.e., Chisleu = Nov–Dec) Haggai delivers his third oracle, using a priestly analogy of unclean and holy objects. Up to this point, the people had brought defilement upon all that they touched, but from now on, in response to their obedient follow-through in rebuilding God's house, God would bless them. Life would no longer be as it had been in the past when privation was the order of the day (2:16-19).

The Fourth Oracle: Haggai 2:20-23

Haggai delivers the final oracle, an oracle of hope, on the same day as the third oracle. Directed at Zerubbabel, this apocalyptic-oriented oracle appears to have eschatological significance and the hope of a resumption of the Davidic dynasty (cf. 2 Kgs 25:27-30). Haggai tells of a time when the nations would be subjugated and Zerubbabel, the "servant" of God (v. 23), would be like a signet ring in God's hands. This word to Zerubbabel can be understood to have a messianic fulfillment through Zerubbabel's future descendant, Jesus (Matt 1:12-13), the ultimate Shepherd and King of Israel.

Debated Issues (aka Great Paper Topics)

1) Based on Ezra 3:6, 8; 5:16 and Hag 2:15, when was the foundation of the temple laid?

2) Where do the dates of Haggai's oracles fall in relation to the agricultural seasons, and what bearing might this have had on the specific impact of any of these oracles?

The Message of the Book

God blesses those who make God's house and spiritual things their foundational priorities in life.

Closing the Loop

The book of Haggai shows the vital significance of the temple of the Lord, particularly in relation to Haggai's specific historical context, which is especially emphasized by the book's precisely dated oracles. Before the exile, prophets such as Jeremiah and Ezekiel prophesied the destruction of the temple (cf. Jer 7 and Ezek 24), but this did not keep the temple from reemerging in the postexilic period as a vital center of Jewish life and faith and a cause worthy of prophetic support. In fact, the book of Haggai is significant for showing the crucial role of the prophet in the reestablishment of the temple and the priestly ministry that came with it. In the Jews' postexilic struggle for physical survival, they had lost sight of the spiritual center and foundation (2:18) on which they depended. It took a prophet with the word of the Lord to help them see how much their present survival and future flourishing depended on them rebuilding the house of the Lord. Physically this rebuilt house might have appeared in their eyes "as nothing" (2:3), but the prophetic word is there to reveal, "My Spirit [is] in your midst" (2:5). Nothing more is needed to make this the center of the renewal of God's people and the epicenter of the shaking of "all the nations" of the earth (2:6-7). This is the prophetic word of Haggai that reverberates all the way from his day to our own.

ZECHARIAH

"Not by might nor by power, but by My Spirit," says the LORD of hosts.
    —*Zechariah 4:6 (NKJV)*

When I think about the book of Zechariah,

one phrase in the book stands out: "they will look to me concerning the one whom they pierced; they will mourn over him" (12:10). Zechariah's message, directed to a Jewish audience, is delivered more than 500 years before Jesus's crucifixion (cf. John 19:37; Rev 1:7). This stirring prophecy, which appears to have an eschatological fulfillment, is at once declaring the triumphant return of Jesus, and yet delivering a poignantly somber commentary to those who have rejected Messiah. It envisions a moment when they will realize their tragic mistake. Verses like these not only give me faith in the prophetic voice, but also cause me to pray for Israel.

Quick Facts

Title: The book's title comes from the name of the prophet whose message constitutes the book. It is the same in both the LXX and Hebrew text traditions. Zechariah's name means "YHWH has remembered."

Date: Based on Zech 1:1, chapters 1–8 take place around 520 BCE during the reign of the Persian king Darius I. Chapters 9–14 have been variously dated, ranging from the preexilic period to the third century BCE. Zechariah appears to be the younger contemporary of Haggai (Zech 2:4).

Authorship: According to 1:1 and 1:7, the author is Zechariah, the grandson of the priest Iddo (Neh 12:4). Scholars debate how much of the book is actually from the hand of the sixth-century prophet. Many suggest a "Deutero-Zechariah" for chapters 9–14 based on stylistic changes and historical references (e.g., Zech 9:13). However, others have offered a variety of responses to address these issues while holding to the unity of the book and its authorship.

Audience: The original audience of the book is the roughly 50,000 Jewish returnees of 538 BCE who lived in and around Jerusalem (Ezra 2:64-65).

Purpose: Like Haggai, Zechariah encourages the people to rebuild the temple and seek spiritual renewal. He also offers a visionary preview of the messianic future promised to God's people.

Genre: The book contains both apocalyptic visions (1:7–6:8) and prophetic oracles (6:9–14:21).

Structure

The book divides naturally into two parts: chapters 1–8, which are dominated by eight apocalyptic-type visions, and chapters 9–14, presented as two prophetic oracles (9–11; 12–14).

Summary

The Eight Visions: Zechariah 1–8

After a brief historical introduction (1:1), Zechariah encourages his audience not to be obstinate like their ancestors, but rather to return to God (1:2-6). The presence of an interpreting angel signals the apocalyptic nature of the visions (cf. Ezek 40:3-4; Dan 8:16). Similar to the abrupt visionary opening of the book of Ezekiel, Zechariah's first vision (ca. 520 BCE) reveals riders on red and white horses patrolling the earth, declaring that the whole earth is at peace (1:11; cf. 6:1-8; Rev 6:1-8). Zechariah asks how long God will be angry with his people; God promises that he will avenge his people by striking the nations and rebuilding Jerusalem and the temple (1:7-17). The motif of the nations' oppression of Israel and Judah is carried forward in the second vision (1:18-21) where four horns (i.e., nations; cf. Dan 7–8; Rev 12:3; 13:1, 11; 17:3-18) are overthrown by four "craftsmen" (v. 20 ESV). The third vision blends the motifs of the restoration of Jerusalem and the judgment on the nations (2:1-13). Here a surveying angel goes forth and measures the city (cf. Ezek 40–42; Rev 11; 21) and God promises to place his protection on his people, the "apple of his eye" (2:8 KJV). While many nations will join God's people (2:11), those who oppress his people will be judged (2:9). The fourth vision shifts focus to Joshua the high priest—representing all Israel—standing in dirty garments before God and being accused by Satan. God rebukes Satan, gives Joshua new garments (3:3-5), and promises that he will be blessed with position and authority in the temple if he is obedient (3:7). The vision closes with a messianic promise of the coming Branch (3:6-10; cf. 6:12; Isa 4:2; Jer 23:5; 33:15). The fifth vision is of a golden lampstand and two olive trees (4:1-14). Within this vision God promises Zerubbabel that he will indeed finish the temple through the power of the Spirit (4:6-10). The sixth vision features a flying scroll that symbolically represents God's judgment on all people who are thieves and swear falsely by the name of God (5:1-4). The scroll is open and large (20 × 10 cubits = 30 × 15 feet) so all can see it. On both sides are written curses for those who break the third and eighth commandments (cf. Exod 20:7, 15). The seventh vision (5:5-11) reveals a woman sitting in "an ephah" (KJV; i.e., a measuring basket that holds an ephah). The woman represents the wickedness/idolatry of the people (5:7-8; cf. Ezek 8). Fittingly, God will purge their wickedness by symbolically removing their sin and returning it to Babylon, the land where the people had "acquired" it (5:9-11; cf. Gen 10:10; 11:2). The final vision of four chariots being drawn by horses of four different colors (red, black, white, and spotted) represents God's judgment (6:1-8; cf. Rev 6:1-8). The chariots pulled by black horses and white horses going to the north represent God's appeased wrath brought about by the exile (6:6-8).

The last two and a half chapters of this section return to the genre of prophetic oracle. Zechariah is told to crown Joshua as a symbol of the coming priest-king rule of the Messiah/Branch (cf. 6:12; John 4:19-26; Rev 19:12). Another dated oracle (ca. 518 BCE) appears in 7:1. Here Zechariah reminds the people of what God expects from them: justice, kindness, and mercy, the rejection of which had brought about the earlier fall of Jerusalem (7:8-14; cf. 8:16; Mic 6:8). However, in typical prophetic style, Zechariah offers a word of hope as God proclaims that he will restore Jerusalem (8:1-6), bring his people from exile (8:7-8), make prosperity and justice the hallmarks of the new era (8:9-17), and cause the nations to seek the Lord (8:18-23).

The Two Prophetic Oracles: Zechariah 9–14

The last two oracles of Zechariah contain a number of messianic prophecies. The first of the oracles (chs. 9–11) begins with words of judgment against the surrounding nations: Syria, Tyre and Sidon, and the Philistines (9:1-7). Zechariah foretells the coming defeat of Tyre (fulfilled at the hands of Alexander the Great) and events that correspond to the overthrow of the Seleucids by the Maccabees (9:2-4, 12-17). Woven into these prophetic words is the messianic promise that is cited at Jesus's entrance into Jerusalem to present himself as Israel's King and Shepherd (9:9; cf. Matt 21:5; John 10:11-13; 12:15); there is the further messianic prophecy concerning how the people will reject their Messiah and sell him for 30 pieces of silver (11:11-12; cf. Matt 27:3-10). Zechariah then sees even further into the future to a time when blessings will abound (10:1), but not before the false diviners, idols, and wicked shepherds have been judged by God (10:2-3; 11:1-6, 14-17), perhaps reflective of the recurring ineffective "shepherds" of Israel's history (e.g., during both revolts BCE 66–70 and 132–135; cf. Ezek 34). Yet, from their midst will come God-ordained leadership (10:4-5). Moreover, God will bring back his scattered people and they will serve him (10:6-12).

Chapters 12–14 record the last of Zechariah's oracles—prophecies featuring apocalyptic motifs in which Christian interpreters find mingled references to the first and second advents of Jesus. Here the reader is told about God's plan to make the nations drunk with the "cup" of Jerusalem (12:2-3; cf. Ezek 38–39). Even though the nations' attack of the city will at first be successful (14:1-2), God will then come with his armies in an apocalyptic scene (14:5; cf. Matt 16:27; 25:31; Rev 19:11-15), split the Mount of Olives (14:4-8), and fight for his people, defeating the nations (12:4-9; 14:3) with a "plague" that sounds eerily similar to modern nuclear or chemical warfare (14:12-15). At that time God's people will recognize the "One whom they have pierced" (12:10 NRSV) and mourn their past actions (12:10-14).

A view of Jerusalem and the temple mount from the Mount of Olives. Photo by Brian Peterson.

Indeed, Messiah will end idolatry and false prophecy (13:1-6). Within these words of prophecy, Zechariah describes scenes that are taken up by NT writers as predictions of moments in the first coming of Jesus: the scattering of the disciples, the crucifixion of Jesus, and the fall of many in Israel (13:6-9; cf. Matt 26:31; Mark 14:27). Nevertheless, in the final outcome Zechariah envisions how God will rule supreme (14:9), renew peace upon the land (14:10-11), and cause the nations to worship him in Jerusalem at the Festival of Booths (14:16-19). Those failing to comply will suffer famine (14:17-19). In that day, holiness will be the hallmark of Jerusalem and its temple (14:20-21; cf. Ezek 43–48).

Debated Issues (aka Great Paper Topics)

1) How do scholars handle the attribution of authorship of Zech 11:12-13 to Jeremiah in Matt 27:9?

2) What are the authorship and dating concerns of 9:2-4 and 9:12-17?

The Message of the Book

Do not despise the day of "small beginnings" (Zech 4:10 MSG), for the future of God's people, in light of the coming of Messiah, will be greater than anyone can imagine.

Closing the Loop

A common way of speaking of the exile of God's people in the OT is in terms of *scattering*. The people were scattered among the nations. The stones of their capital city of Jerusalem, its walls, its royal buildings, and its temple, were scattered upon the ground. Yet perhaps most devastatingly of all, the very worldview of the Jewish people was shattered to pieces in the exile and blown in all directions like chaff in the wind (cf. Hos 13:3).

The writer of Ecclesiastes observes that there is a time for scattering stones (as in NIV) and a time for gathering stones (Eccl 3:5). Haggai and Zechariah are two prophets who were clearly raised up during the latter kind of time. Together they form a quite complementary pair. Haggai's prophetic oracles are the most straightforward and practical of all the OT prophets. Zechariah's oracles are the most mystifying and visionary. Haggai's words are especially geared to help a depleted postexilic community, quite literally, to start picking up the pieces of their broken-down city and temple and putting everything back together again. And Zechariah's vision reports and visionary oracles are especially designed to help a dispirited people recover the one thing that is perhaps most difficult to restore once it has been shattered, namely, a sense of hope and vision for the future. Thus, Zechariah's mission is all about remembering (cf. Zechariah's name, "YHWH remembers"), regathering, and reassembling the fragments of the faith that have been scattered far and wide by the upheaval of the exile experience. This is a mission that requires vision—sweeping supernatural vision that ranges as far and wide as all the gaping spaces between the fragments of a shattered faith. Thus, this is a mission that can be accomplished only by the Spirit of the Lord, who fills all the gaps and spaces. A broken temple might be restored with enough manpower, but when it comes to restoring a broken people, the prophet Zechariah would have us to know that it's "not by might, nor by power, but by my spirit, says the LORD of hosts" (Zech 4:6 NRSV).

MALACHI

Turn the hearts of the parents to the children and the hearts of the children to their parents.
    —*Malachi 4:6*

When I think about the book of Malachi,

the Jewish Seder (Passover) meal comes to mind. Anyone who has taken part in a true Seder meal knows that as the meal comes to a close, a cup of wine is poured for the prophet Elijah, and someone goes to the door to see if he is there so he or she can invite him in. Based on the prophet Malachi, and according to Jewish tradition, Elijah will be the forerunner of Messiah (4:5). This is why those of the NT era were looking for Elijah before the coming of Christ (cf. Matt 17:10-12; Mark 9:11-13; Luke 1:17; John 1:21). The NT declares John the Baptist to be the forerunner spoken of by Malachi (Matt 17:13). While the Protestant canon closes with Malachi and the promise of the forerunner, the very last words are a warning to those who reject the words of Elijah. God will come and smite the land with a curse. To this day the Jewish people await the coming of their Messiah. Those who accept Jesus as the promised Messiah receive the blessings of the fulfillment of Jesus's work on the cross.

Quick Facts

Title: The title comes from the name of the prophet whose message forms the book. It is the same in both the LXX and Hebrew text traditions. Malachi's name means either "my messenger" or "messenger of YHWH."

Date: The exact date for the book is unknown. Most scholars place it between 460 and 420 BCE. Some date Malachi to the 430s between Nehemiah's two periods as governor of Judea, while others see his ministry fitting just before Ezra, circa 460 BCE.

Authorship: Some argue that the authorship of the book is unknown because the word "Malachi" is to be read as a regular noun, meaning "my messenger," rather than as a proper name. Most scholars, however, attribute the book to a prophet by the name of Malachi. Two Jewish traditions have competing authorship ascriptions: the Targum of Jonathan attributes the book to Ezra and the Babylonian Talmud assigns it to either Mordecai or Ezra (*Megillah* 15a).

Audience: The original audience of the book is most likely those in Judah roughly 100 years after the first return in 538 BCE.

Purpose: The book serves to indict those living in Judea for laxness in their spiritual lives.

Genre: The book's main genre, aside from its superscription (1:1) and brief conclusion (4:4-6), is best categorized as disputation speeches framed as a series of questions/indictments, much like a court case.

Structure

The most common way of outlining the book is in terms of its series of disputations, where God responds to questions of complaint that are being posed by his people. The following summary takes up the seven major questions raised in the book's four chapters (three chapters in the Hebrew text).

Summary

After a terse introduction (1:1) Malachi begins his book by assuring the people of Judah that God loves them. To this they respond with their first question: how has God loved us? (1:2). Malachi reminds them to look at Edom as an example. Even though Edom may try to succeed, they will fail (1:2-5). God's divine election of Judah and cursing of Edom should be evidence enough of his love; yet the people and priests have despised the name of their Master. This elicits a second question from the people: how have we despised God's name? (1:6-7). Through the prophet God responds: by offering blemished sacrifices and lame animals to God, something you would not do for an earthly ruler (1:8-14). The priests are particularly guilty of unfaithfulness to their office. They should know better, because their forebears, Levi and his sons, respected God (2:5-7). Because the priests have not followed the ways of Levi but rather have perverted instruction for the people, have shown partiality, and have profaned the sanctuary with idolatry (2:9-11), God will cut off the wicked from his people (2:12).

This gives way to a third question: why does the Lord not respond to our prayers and weeping? (2:13-14). Malachi says that God is not responding to the people's prayers because they have been unfaithful to their wives: I hate divorce, says the Lord, so take heed of your actions (2:14-16) and do not weary the Lord with your words. The people respond with a fourth question: how have we wearied the Lord with our words? (2:17). To this Malachi rejoins: because you say that the ones doing evil in the sight of the Lord are good and God delights in them, a fact that is patently false. In light of these indictments, the Lord declares that he will come to his temple (cf. John 2:13-22) and refine the priests, set things in order, and effect judgment on all sorcerers, adulterers, those who swear falsely, and those who oppress the weak and poor (3:1-5). God's coming will be preceded by his messenger who will prepare the way before him (3:1; cf. 4:5, the sending of Elijah before the coming of the day of the LORD). God pleads with his people to return to him and he will turn to them (3:7).

Questions five and six are evoked in tandem in response to God's pleas for the people to return to him and to stop robbing him. The people retort: how can we return to God and how have we robbed God? (3:7-8). To this Malachi says: you have robbed God by not paying your tithes and offerings; because of this God is cursing you (3:9). Malachi goes on to use a cosmological image for blessings: bring in your tithes and God will open the windows of heaven to bless you with excess (3:10-12). Indeed, the oppressor will no longer touch you, and the nations will call you blessed! Therefore, cease speaking arrogant words against God, and these things will take place. God's promise of blessing is met with the seventh and final question from the people when they ask: how have we spoken against God? (3:13). Malachi offers one last indictment. He says: you have been arrogant and said it does not pay to serve God (3:14-15); God's judgment is coming against those who persist in this course of covenant unfaithfulness (4:1). However, those who fear God will be saved and triumph over the wicked (3:16-18; 4:2-4). The coming day of judgment and blessing will be signaled by the sending of Elijah as a forerunner who will begin the restoration (4:5-6). This serves as a fitting end to the OT and a point of transition to the book of Matthew.

Debated Issues (aka Great Paper Topics)

1) What are the scholarly theories related to the identity of Malachi?

2) What are the major views on the return of Elijah mentioned in Mal 4:5-6?

The Message of the Book

The God who restores his people from exile continues to struggle with them and dispute with them when their faith begins to falter, holding forth stern warnings of the prospect of divine judgment, but also bright promises of blessing for those who will fear the Lord and turn to him.

Closing the Loop

As the last prophet of the Old Testament, Malachi well represents the prime role of the prophet, namely, to serve as a messenger.[65] As noted above, Malachi's name means "my messenger." This prophet serves as God's messenger, of course, through the very means of the book that bears his name. Yet Malachi also recognizes others who serve God in the messenger role: in the prophet's own day, the priest who takes up the law (*torah*) "in his mouth" is "the messenger of the LORD of hosts" (2:6-7 KJV); and before the great day of the Lord's coming, God promises to send a special messenger to prepare the way before him (3:1)—one finally specified as the prophet Elijah, who will accomplish this task by turning the hearts of elders to their children and the hearts of children to their elders (4:5-6).

---

65. Rickie D. Moore, *The Spirit of the Old Testament*, JPTS 35 (Blandford Forum, UK: Deo, 2011), 56–68.

Clearly, this messenger role is a mediating role. Not only does the prophet mediate God's message to his people but also, at times, mediates this people's questions and complaints back to God. Nowhere is this better shown than in the book of Malachi. The prophet here plays something like the role of a marriage counselor who facilitates communication between the parties of a troubled marriage—all in hopes of restoring the covenant relationship to wholeness.

Yet Malachi shows us how the mediating role of the prophet can go even one step further. The prophet can also be called upon to mediate divisions that have set people against one another. This becomes urgent in light of the fact that what divides us from one another often divides us from God. Nowhere is this more evident than in the divisions between generations, whether in Malachi's day or in our own. Accordingly, this is the final issue addressed in the book of Malachi, in the prophetic books of the OT generally, and in the OT as a whole (in our Protestant canonical arrangement). Here we come to the "grand finale" promise of the OT: God will send the prophet, the prophet will turn divided hearts, generations will be reconciled, and blessing will reverse the curse. For Christians it is a promise once fulfilled when God raised up John the Baptist "in the spirit and power of Elijah" (Luke 1:17 ESV). And it is a promise still embraced with expectancy today by heirs of this same prophetic Spirit—by those whose hearts are still being turned by Peter's Pentecost words: "This promise is for you, your children, and for all who are far away—as many as the Lord our God shall call" (Acts 2:39).

Origin of the Patriarchs   Date: c. 2100–1950 BCE

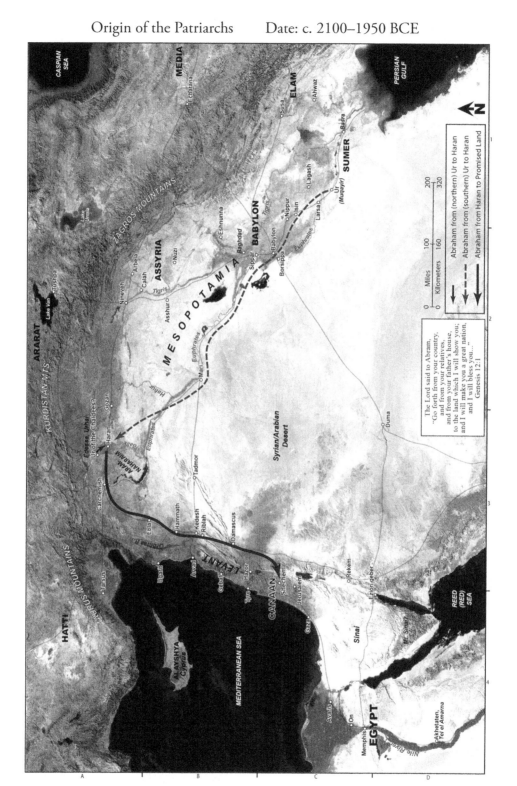

Courtesy of W. Schlegel, Satellite Bible Atlas. Base map courtesy of NASA and US Geological Survey.

3-D Views of Israel

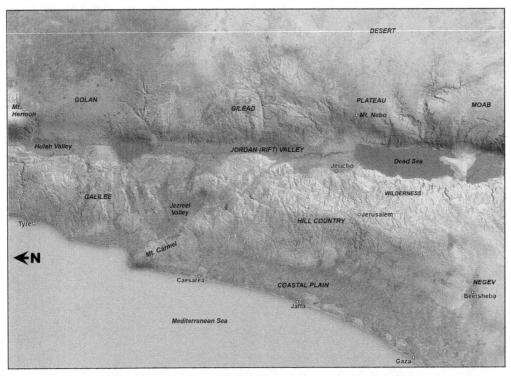

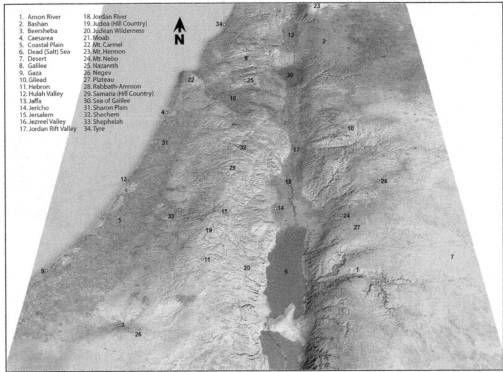

1. Arnon River
2. Bashan
3. Beersheba
4. Caesarea
5. Coastal Plain
6. Dead (Salt) Sea
7. Desert
8. Galilee
9. Gaza
10. Gilead
11. Hebron
12. Hulah Valley
13. Jaffa
14. Jericho
15. Jersalem
16. Jezreel Valley
17. Jordan Rift Valley
18. Jordan River
19. Judea (Hill Country)
20. Judean Wilderness
21. Moab
22. Mt. Carmel
23. Mt. Hermon
24. Mt. Nebo
25. Nazareth
26. Negev
27. Plateau
28. Rabbath-Ammon
29. Samaria (Hill Country)
30. Sea of Galilee
31. Sharon Plain
32. Shechem
33. Shephelah
34. Tyre

Courtesy of W. Schlegel, Satellite Bible Atlas. Base map courtesy of NASA and US Geological Survey.

Exodus and Journey through Sinai   Date: c. 1446 BCE

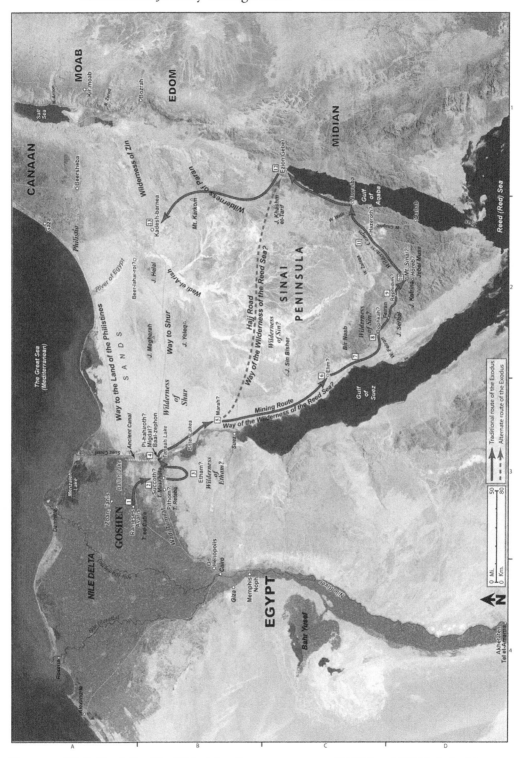

Courtesy of W. Schlegel, Satellite Bible Atlas. Base map courtesy of NASA and US Geological Survey.

Israelite Tribal Allotments   Date: c. 1400 BCE and following

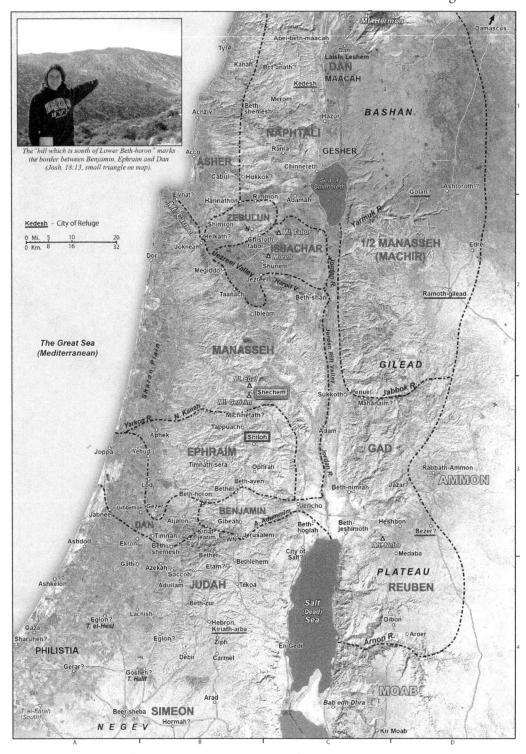

The "hill which is south of Lower Beth-horon" marks
the border between Benjamin, Ephraim and Dan
(Josh. 18:13, small triangle on map).

Courtesy of W. Schlegel, Satellite Bible Atlas. Base map courtesy of NASA and US Geological Survey.

Division of the Kingdom and Shishak Campaign   Date: 931–925 BCE

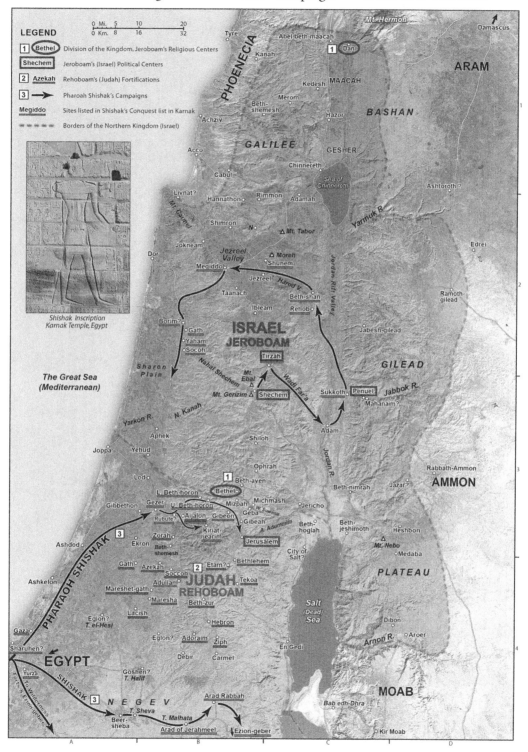

Courtesy of W. Schlegel, Satellite Bible Atlas. Base map courtesy of NASA and US Geological Survey.

Return and Restoration   Date: 538–400 BCE

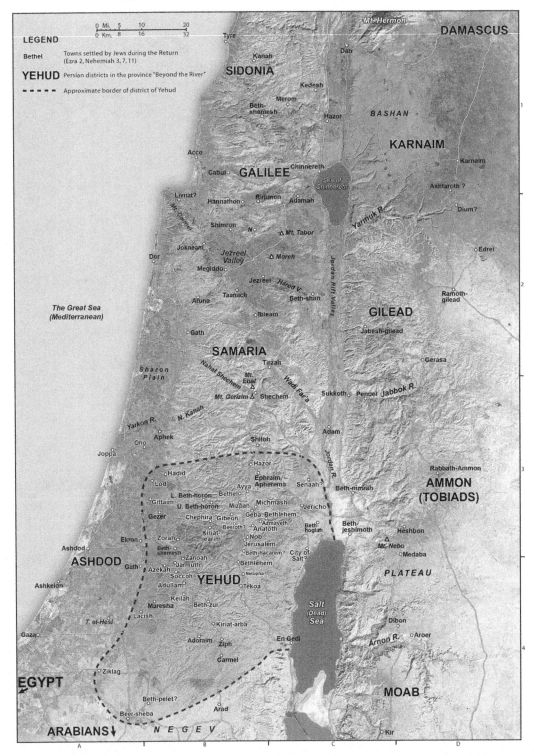

Babylonian Empire   Date: 626–529 BCE

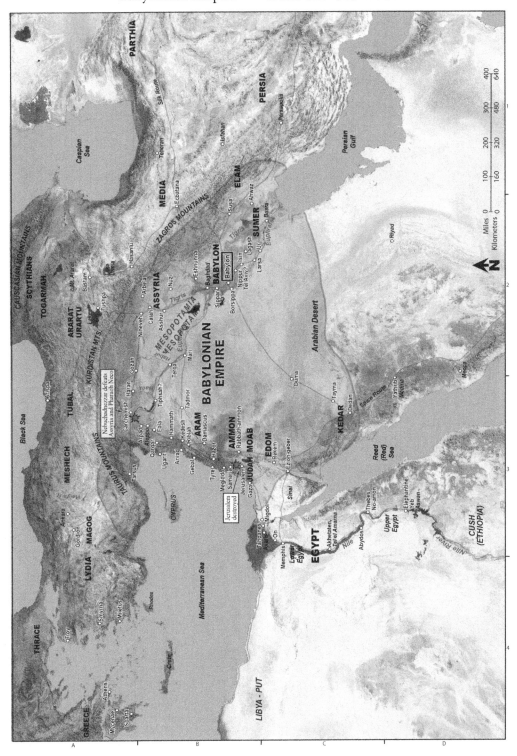

Courtesy of W. Schlegel, Satellite Bible Atlas. Base map courtesy of NASA and US Geological Survey.

Assyrian Empre   Date: 9th–7th centuries BCE

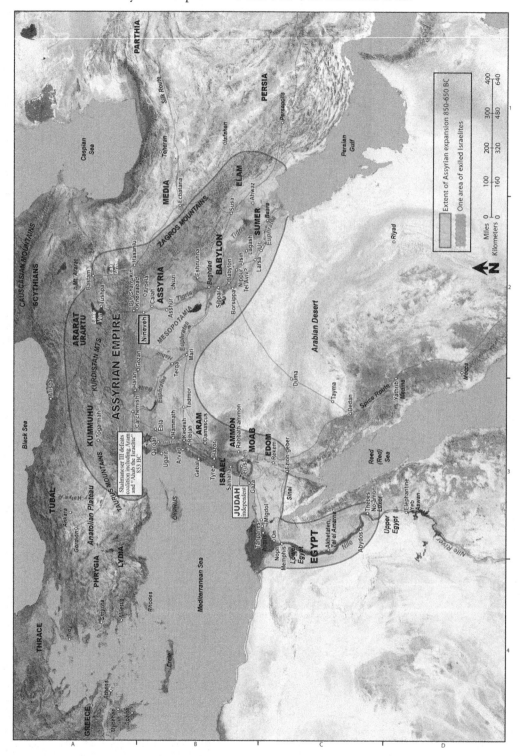

Courtesy of W. Schlegel, Satellite Bible Atlas. Base map courtesy of NASA and US Geological Survey.

Jerusalem: First Temple Period   Date: 1010–586 BCE

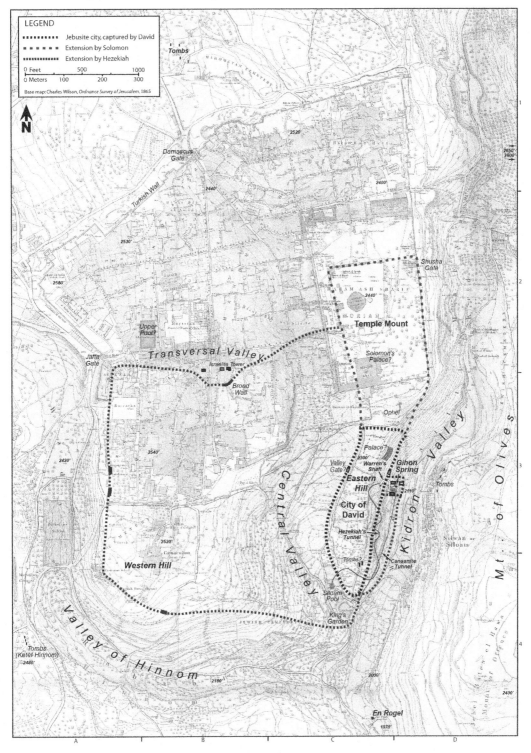

Courtesy of W. Schlegel, Satellite Bible Atlas. Base map courtesy of NASA and US Geological Survey.

Persian Empire   Date: 538–332 BCE

Courtesy of W. Schlegel, Satellite Bible Atlas. Base map courtesy of NASA and US Geological Survey.

BIBLIOGRAPHY

Abegg, Martin, Jr., Peter Flint, and Eugene Ulrich. *The Dead Sea Scrolls Bible*. New York: HarperSanFrancisco, 1999.

Alden, Robert L. *Malachi*. Vol. 7 of *The Expositor's Bible Commentary*, edited by Frank E. Gaebelein. Grand Rapids: Zondervan, 1985.

Anderson, R. Dean, Jr. "The Division and Order of the Psalms." *Westminster Theological Journal* 56 (1994): 219–41.

Arnold, Bill, and Bryan Beyer. *Reading from the Ancient Near East: Primary Sources for Old Testament Study*. Encountering Biblical Studies. Grand Rapids: Baker Academic, 2002.

Bickle, Mike. "The Song of Songs: Introduction to the Song." http://mikebickle.org/resources/series/song-of-songs.

Block, Daniel I. "The Prophet of the Spirit: The Use of RWH in the Book of Ezekiel." *Journal of the Evangelical Theological Society* 32, no. 1 (March 1989): 27–49.

Brueggemann, Walter. *1 Kings*. Knox Preaching Guides. Atlanta: John Knox Press, 1983.

———. "Elisha as the Original Pentecost Guy: Ten Theses." *Journal for Preachers* 32, no. 4 (Pentecost 2009): 41–47.

———. *The Prophetic Imagination*. Philadelphia: Fortress Press, 1978.

Clines, David J. A. *The Theme of the Pentateuch*. 2nd ed. JSOTSup 10. Sheffield, UK: JSOT Press, 1997.

Copan, Paul. *Is God a Moral Monster? Making Sense of the Old Testament God*. Grand Rapids: Baker, 2011.

Copan, Paul, and Matthew Flannagan. *Did God Really Command Genocide? Coming to Terms with the Justice of God*. Grand Rapids: Baker, 2014.

Coulter, Dale M. "The Spirit and the Bride Revisited: Pentecostalism, Renewal, and the Sense of History." *Journal of Pentecostal Theology* 21, no. 2 (2012): 298–319.

Cox, Harvey. *Fire from Heaven: The Rise of Pentecostal Spirituality and the Reshaping of Religion in the Twenty-First Century*. Reading, MA: Addison-Wesley, 1995.

Cross, Frank Moore. *Canaanite Myth and Hebrew Epic*. Cambridge, MA: Harvard Press, 1973.

Curley, Christine, and Brian Peterson. "Eve's Curse Revisited: An Increase of 'Sorrowful Conceptions.'" *Bulletin of Biblical Research* 26, no. 2 (2016): 1–16.

Day, John N. "The Imprecatory Psalms and Christian Ethics." *Bibliotheca Sacra* 159 (April–June 2002): 166–86.

Estes, Daniel J. *Handbook on the Wisdom Books and Psalms*. Grand Rapids: Baker, 2005.

Garrett, Duane A. *Proverbs, Ecclesiastes, Song of Songs*. Vol. 14 in *The New American Commentary*. Nashville: Broadman Press, 1993.

Geisler, Norman L. *A Popular Survey of the Old Testament*. Grand Rapids: Baker, 1977.

Hanson, Paul D. *The Dawn of Apocalyptic*. Philadelphia: Fortress Press, 1975.

Hill, A. and J. Walton. *A Survey of the Old Testament*. Grand Rapids: Zondervan, 2009.

Hillers, Delbert R. *Lamentations*. Vol. 7A in *The Anchor Bible*. New York: Doubleday, 1972.

Johns, Cheryl Bridges. *Pentecostal Formation: A Pedagogy Among the Oppressed*. JPTSup Series, Eugene, OR: Wipf & Stock, 2010.

Kitchen, Kenneth. *On the Reliability of the Old Testament*. Grand Rapids: Eerdmans, 2006.

Lasor, William Sanford, David Allan Hubbard, Frederic William Bush. *Old Testament Survey: The Message, Form, and Background of the Old Testament*. 2nd ed. Grand Rapids: Eerdmans, 1996.

Lewis, C. S. *Of Other Worlds: Essays and Stories*. Edited by Walter Hooper. New York: Harcourt, Brace, Jovanovich, 1966.

Longman, Tremper, III. *Introducing the Old Testament*. Grand Rapids: Zondervan, 2012.

Lucas, Ernest C. *Exploring the Old Testament: A Guide to the Psalms & Wisdom Literature*. Downers Grove, IL: InterVarsity Press, 2003.

Martin, Lee Roy. "Delighting in the Torah: The Affective Dimension of Psalm 1." *Old Testament Essays* 23, no. 3 (2010): 707–27.

———. "Where Are the Descendants of Abraham? Finding the Source of a Missing Link in Genesis." In *The Spirit and the Mind: Essays in Informed Pentecostalism*, edited by Terry L. Cross and Emerson Powery, 23–34. Lanham, MD: University Press of America, 2000.

McCarter, P. Kyle, Jr. "The Apology of David." *Journal of Biblical Literature* 99, no. 4 (1980): 489–504.

McQueen, Larry R. *Joel and the Spirit: The Cry of a Prophetic Hermeneutic*. Cleveland, TN: CPT Press, 2009.

Merrill, Eugene. *Kingdom of Priests: A History of Old Testament Israel*. 2nd ed. Grand Rapids: Baker, 2008.

Miller, Donald E., and Tetsunao Yamamori. *Global Pentecostalism: The New Face of Christian Social Engagement*. Oakland, CA: University of California Press, 2007.

Moore, Rickie D. "Altar Hermeneutics: Reflections on Pentecostal Biblical Interpretation." *Pneuma* 38 (2016): 1–12.

———. *The Spirit of the Old Testament*. JPTSup 35. Blandford Forum, UK: Deo, 2011.

———. "'Then They Will Know That a Prophet Has Been Among Them': The Source and End of the Call of Ezekiel." In *Passover, Pentecost & Parousia: Studies in Celebration of the Life & Ministry of R. Hollis Gause*, edited by Steven J. Land, Rickie D. Moore, and John Christopher Thomas. Leiderdorp, NL: Deo, 2010.

Nida, Eugene A., and Charles R. Taber. *The Theory and Practice of Translation*. Leiden, NL: E. J. Brill, 1982.

Niehaus, Jeffrey. "Obadiah." In Vol. 2 of *An Exegetical & Expository Commentary: The Minor Prophets*, edited by Thomas Edward McComiskey, 495–541. Grand Rapids: Baker, 2006.

Olson, Dennis T. *Deuteronomy and the Death of Moses: A Theological Reading*. Eugene, OR: Wipf & Stock, 2005.

Payne, J. Barton. *1 & 2 Chronicles*. Vol. 4 in *The Expositor's Bible Commentary*, edited by Frank E. Gaebelein. Grand Rapids: Zondervan, 1988.

Peterson, Brian. *The Authors of the Deuteronomistic History: Locating a Tradition in Ancient Israel*. Minneapolis: Fortress Press, 2014.

———. "The Authorship of Samuel: 70 Years after Noth." *Bibliotheca Sacra* 172, no. 688 (2015): 416–32.

———. "Could Abiathar, the Priest, Be the Author of Judges?" *Bibliotheca Sacra* 170, no. 680 (October–December 2013): 432–52.

———. *Ezekiel in Context: Ezekiel's Message Understood in Its Historical Setting of Covenant Curses and Ancient Near Eastern Mythological Motifs*. Princeton Theological Monograph Series 182. Eugene, OR: Pickwick, 2012.

———. "Ezekiel's Rhetoric: ANE Building Protocol and Shame and Honor as the Keys in Identifying the Builder of the Eschatological Temple." *Journal of the Evangelical Theological Society* 56, no. 4 (2013): 707–31.

———. "The Gibeonite Revenge of 2 Sam 21:1–14: Another Example of David's Darker Side or a Picture of a Shrewd Monarch?" *Journal for the Evangelical Study of the Old Testament* 1, no. 2 (2012): 201–22.

———. *John's Use of Ezekiel: Understanding the Unique Perspective of the Fourth Gospel*. Minneapolis: Fortress Press, 2015.

———. "Judges: An Apologia for Davidic Kingship: An Inductive Approach." *McMaster Journal of Theology and Ministry* 17 (2016–2017): 3-46.

———. "Samson: Hero or Villain? Reading the Samson Narrative in Light of David and Saul." *Bibliotheca Sacra* (forthcoming).

———. "The Sin of Sodom Revisited: Reading Genesis 19 in Light of Torah." *Journal of the Evangelical Theological Society* 59, no. 1 (2016): 17–31.

———. *What Was the Sin of Sodom: Homosexuality, Inhospitality, or Something Else? Reading Genesis 19 as Torah.* Eugene, OR: Resource, 2016.

Polzin, Robert. *Samuel and the Deuteronomist: A Literary Study of the Deteronomistic History II: 1 Samuel.* San Francisco: Harper & Row, 1989.

Redick, Caroline. "'Let Me Hear Your Voice': Re-Hearing the Song of Songs through Pentecostal Hermeneutics." *Journal of Pentecostal Theology* 24, no. 2 (2015): 187–200.

Schlegel, William. *Satellite Bible Atlas: Historical Geography of the Bible.* Jerusalem: Master's College, 2013.

Smick, Elmer B. J. *Job.* Vol. 4 in *The Expositor's Bible Commentary*, edited by Frank E. Gaebelein. Grand Rapids: Zondervan, 1988.

Stuart, Douglas. "Malachi." In Vol. 3 of *An Exegetical & Expository Commentary: The Minor Prophets: Zephaniah to Malachi*, edited by Thomas E. McComiskey, 1245–1396. Grand Rapids: Baker, 1998.

Thomas, John Christopher. "Pentecostal Biblical Interpretation." In Vol. 2 of the *Oxford Encyclopedia of Biblical Interpretation*, edited by S. L. McKenzie, 89–97. Oxford: Oxford University Press, 2013.

———. "Where the Spirit Leads: The Development of Pentecostal Hermeneutics." *Journal of Beliefs & Values: Studies in Religion & Education* 30, no. 3 (December 2009): 289–302.

Walvoord, John F. *Daniel: The Key to Prophetic Revelation.* Chicago: Moody Press, 1989.

Wilson, Gerald. *The Editing of the Hebrew Psalter.* SBL Dissertation Series 76. Chico, CA: Scholars Press, 1985.

Wood, Bryant. "Did the Israelites Conquer Jericho? A New Look at the Archaeological Evidence." *Biblical Archaeology Review* 16, no. 2 (1990): 44–58.

———. "The Rise and Fall of the 13th Century Exodus-Conquest Theory." *Journal of the Evangelical Theological Society* 48, no. 3 (2005): 475–89.

———. "The Search for Joshua's Ai." In *Critical Issues in Early Israelite History*, edited by R. S. Hess, G. A. Klingbeil, and P. J. Ray Jr., 205–40. Winona Lake, IN: Eisenbrauns, 2008.

Yamauchi, Edwin. *Ezra, Nehemiah.* Vol. 4 in *The Expositor's Bible Commentary*, edited by Frank E. Gaebelein. Grand Rapids: Zondervan, 1988.

Yancey, Philip. *The Bible Jesus Read.* Grand Rapids: Zondervan, 2002.

GLOSSARY OF IMPORTANT TERMS

acrostic: a poetic device in which the consecutive lines or sets of lines (stanzas) of a poem begin with the consecutive letters of the Hebrew alphabet (e.g., Ps 119).

Akedah: the Hebrew term for the "binding" of Isaac, used to refer to the entire story of Genesis 22, where Abraham is called to offer his son as a sacrifice to God on Mount Moriah.

Amenemope: an Egyptian sage whose wise sayings in a text discovered by archaeologists show a striking similarity to wise sayings in Prov 22:17–23:14.

ancient Near East (ANE): the term used to identify the region of the world that was the center of the ancient world of Bible times and before. It includes, for example, Egypt, Babylon (modern Iraq), Persia (modern Iran), Israel, Syria, Lebanon, Amon and Moab (modern Jordan), and Assyria (modern northeast Syria and northern Iraq).

Apocalyptic: (from the Greek meaning to "reveal") a genre of literature focused on the end of the world and characterized by symbolism, numerology, and elaborate imagery made popular by Jewish authors from about the 3rd century BCE to the 2nd century CE.

Apocrypha: a term meaning "hidden writings" that refers to books included in the Greek Septuagint, accepted as part of the Catholic canon of the OT but not included in the Protestant OT.

Arabah: a term used for the regions to the north and south of the Dead Sea but most typically used to identify the arid region to the south of the Dead Sea, which ends at the Gulf of Aqabah of the Red Sea.

ark of the covenant: the covenant chest that kept the Ten Commandments and also served as a footstool for the presence of God in the tabernacle in the wilderness and then in the temple in Jerusalem.

Assur: the chief god of the Assyrians. Also the name given to the region of Assyria (Ezra 4:2 KJV).

autobiographical saying: a form of wisdom literature where a sage in first-person voice presents a personal experience that is intended to stand as an observation about the way things are in universal human experience (e.g., Eccl 2).

Azuza Street: the location in Los Angeles, California, where the historic revival of 1906 took place that marked the beginning of the modern Pentecostal movement.

Baal: the storm god of the ancient Canaanites, often associated specifically with the region of Phoenicia. Elijah challenged Baal on Mount Carmel as recorded in 1 Kings 18.

Babel: the place where people proposed to build a tower to reach heaven, before God stopped them by causing them to speak in different languages (Gen 11:1-9).

Babylonian Exile: the 70-year captivity of the Jewish people that began with the destruction of Jerusalem by the Babylonians in 587/586 BCE.

Baruch: the scribe who served Jeremiah and produced scrolls that recorded Jeremiah's messages.

biblical historical criticism: the approach to biblical study that emerged with the Western Enlightenment. It focuses on "the history behind the text," especially its compositional development, by using a number of scholarly methods including source criticism, form criticism, and redaction criticism.

biblical literary criticism: the approach to biblical study that rose to prominence in the last quarter of the 20th century. It focuses on the rhetorical features and literary artistry of the final form of the biblical text by means of a number of specific methods, including canonical criticism, rhetorical criticism, narrative criticism, and aesthetic criticism.

canon: Greek term meaning "measuring stick," which was adopted by the church to designate which books were to be included in the Bible.

canonical criticism: the literary approach championed by Brevard Childs that focused on the final form of a book and its placement in the canon.

canonization: the process of determining if a book is divinely inspired, which would allow for its inclusion in the canon of Scripture.

Chemosh: the god of the ancient Moabites. He was often associated with child sacrifice.

chiasm: a literary pattern where the parts of the literary unit are presented in a symmetrical structure (e.g., ABCCBA) or X pattern.

Chronicler's History: the term scholars use for 1 and 2 Chronicles, Ezra, and Nehemiah, viewed as a unified collection and believed to be composed or compiled by a post-exilic author, known as the Chronicler.

Confessions of Jeremiah: a series of prayers by Jeremiah dispersed throughout Jeremiah 11–20 where the prophet laments, complains, and confronts God over the difficulties and demands of his prophetic calling.

cosmogony: the term used to describe the study of the origins of the universe.

cosmology: the study of how the universe is structured.

Council of Jamnia: a hypothesized meeting of the Jews gathered at Jamnia, a town west of Jerusalem close to the Mediterranean coast, near the end of the 1st century CE, where some scholars believe the contents of Hebrew Scriptures were determined and the canon was closed.

Cyrus's decree: the edict issued by the Persian ruler Cyrus in 538 BCE that permitted the Jewish exiles to leave Babylon and return to their homeland.

Davidic covenant: the covenant established with David in 2 Samuel 7, which entailed God's promise that David's dynasty would endure forever.

Day of Atonement (or Reconciliation): the holiest day of the year for the Hebrews, who call it Yom Kippur. It is set forth in Leviticus 16 and provides atonement for Israel's sins for the entire year.

Day of the Lord: a futuristic concept put forward by a number of OT prophets (e.g., Joel, Amos, Zephaniah, Malachi) that focused on God's end-time intervention to set things right for God's people and for the entire world.

Dead Sea Scrolls: the body of literature discovered between 1947 and 1956 in caves along the northwest side of the Dead Sea in what is modern-day Israel. In addition to numerous noncanonical scrolls, these texts included portions of all the books of Hebrew Scripture except Esther, providing the oldest available biblical manuscripts.

Decalogue: the "ten words." The term used to describe the Ten Commandments as found in Exodus 20 and Deuteronomy 5. The only portion of the OT law said to have been written by the finger of God (Exod 31:18; Deut 9:10). Most believe it was the earliest of Israel's written law.

deuterocanonical books: intertestamental writings that came to be regarded as having secondary canonical status and incorporated into the early Greek canon as the Apocrypha.

Deutero-Isaiah (or Second Isaiah): the name scholars give to the supposed author of Isaiah 40–55, which they date near the end of the Babylonian Exile.

Deuteronomistic History (DtrH): Martin Noth's theory that the book of Deuteronomy and the Former Prophets (Josh, Judg, Sam, and Kgs) were compiled as a single literary work in order to explain how Israel came to suffer the fate of the Babylonian Exile.

diachronic: a term that refers to the study of how something (e.g., a text or book) developed over time.

Diaspora: the scattering of the Jewish people throughout the world as a consequence of their displacement by the military and political intrusions of other nations.

documentary hypothesis: the source critical theory of the authorship of the Pentateuch; also called the Wellhausen hypothesis, after its leading proponent, and the JEDP hypothesis, after the four source writers thought to have produced it.

Enuma Elish: the Babylonian creation story.

etiology: a narrative written to account for the origin of something.

exilic: generally speaking, it refers to the time of Israel's exile in Babylon from 586 to 539 BCE.

Fertile Crescent: the region of fertile land stretching in an arch from the Persian Gulf up the Euphrates River and back down through ancient Canaan to include the upper Nile River/delta in Egypt.

form criticism: the method of biblical historical criticism that attempts to determine the forms and patterned literary units used to compose the biblical text and to determine their original "setting in life" (*Sitz im Leben*).

Former Prophets: the first four books of the Prophets or *Nevi'im* (Josh, Judg, Sam, Kgs) in the Hebrew canon of scriptures.

Gunkel, Hermann: the German OT scholar known for pioneering the use of form criticism in OT study, especially the study of Psalms.

Hammurabi: a Babylonian ruler from the 18th century BCE who is known for a famous law code ("Code of Hammurabi"), which provides significant insight into ANE legal traditions and the laws found in Exodus.

Hasmonean: the dynastic name adopted by the Maccabees. The Hasmoneans ruled Israel from approximately 164–63 BCE.

henotheism: the belief in one god without denying the existence of other gods.

hermeneutics: the art and science of biblical interpretation that utilizes a defined set of rules (hence a "science") and yet requires a measure of acquired skill and understanding to apply these rules (hence there is an "art" to the process).

Holiness Code: the term scholars use for Leviticus 17–26, a legal corpus that gives priestly regulations for maintaining holiness in the communal life of ancient Israel.

Horeb: another name for Sinai, the mountain where Moses encountered God in a burning bush and where God revealed the covenant law to the people of Israel.

inclusio **(or inclusion):** a literary framing device where a literary passage or unit begins and ends with the same term or motif.

International Coastal Highway: (*Via Maris*—the way of the Sea) the important trade route extending from the northeastern delta of the Nile all the way to Mesopotamia.

Intertestamental Period: the term used to designate the roughly 400-year period between the last OT prophet Malachi and the birth of Jesus.

Iron Age: generally assigned to the period of 1200–333 BCE. Some break this into subcategories of Iron 1–3 with the Babylonian (605–539 BCE) and Persian (539–333 BCE) periods being categorized separately. Iron was the dominant metal used in warfare.

JEDP: the abbreviation for the four documentary sources believed to have comprised the Pentateuch in the Wellhausen/documentary/JEDP hypothesis: J referring to the Jahwist (or Yahwist) source; E referring to the Elohist source; D referring to the Deuteronomist source; and P referring to the Priestly source.

Jordan: the river that flows from the northern part of Israel to the southern part, where it empties into the Dead Sea.

Josiah's reforms: the efforts of King Josiah in the 7th century BCE to lead Judah back from its religious decline under the reign of his wicked predecessors, Manasseh and Amon.

Ketuvim: Hebrew for "Writings," the third division of the Hebrew Scriptures.

King's Highway: the ancient road running along the Transjordan plateau from the Gulf of Aqabah to Damascus.

Late Bronze Age: generally assigned to the period of 1550–1200 BCE, the time period associated with the exodus and conquest of Canaan.

Latter Prophets: the last four books of the Prophets or *Nevi'im* (Isa, Jer, Ezek, the Twelve) in the Hebrew canon of scriptures.

levirite marriage: an Israelite legal provision that obligated the brother of a deceased man to marry the widowed wife in order to provide for the widow and to continue the lineage of the deceased brother (cf. Ruth 4).

LXX: abbreviation for Septuagint (*see* "Septuagint").

Maccabees: the second-century Jewish family that dominated the political scene of Israel during the Intertestamental Period. The father, Mattathias, was followed by his five sons, the most famous of which was Judas Maccabeus, who led the Maccabean Revolt of the Jews against Greek persecution.

Masoretic Text (MT): the term that refers to the Hebrew text of Scripture as standardized by the Masoretes, the scribal guild who meticulously copied and transmitted the Hebrew Scriptures for many generations (6th–10th centuries CE). The Masoretes carried forward the work of the Sopherim (lit. "book men" or scribes; 400 BCE—200 CE) and the Talmudists (200–500 CE) who came before them.

Marduk: one of the chief deities of the Babylonian pantheon.

Megilloth: the Hebrew word meaning "scrolls" that's used in reference to the collection of five scrolls in the Writings (Song, Ruth, Lam, Eccl, Esth), which became the assigned scripture readings respectively for the five Jewish holidays of Passover, Pentecost, Ninth of Av, Tabernacles, and Purim.

Mesopotamia: (literally "between the rivers") the name given to the land/region between and around the Euphrates and the Tigris rivers in ancient Babylon and Assyria stretching from the Persian Gulf to ancient Haran.

Middle Bronze Age: generally assigned to the period of 2200–1550 BCE, the time period associated with the Patriarchs and Matriarchs. Bronze was the dominant metal for warfare.

Molech: the god of the ancient Ammonites. Like Chemosh, Molech was associated with child sacrifice (Lev 18:21; 2 Kgs 23:10).

monotheism: the belief in one god.

Mosaic covenant: the covenant established between God and Israel at Mount Sinai, mediated by Moses and recorded in the book of Exodus.

Nebo: the mountain on the east side of the Jordan River where Moses surveyed the promised land before he died.

Nabopolassar: the father of Nebuchadnezzar II, who was responsible for defeating the Assyrian Empire. He was the founder of the Neo-Babylonian Empire.

Nebuchadnezzar: the Babylonian king who conquered and destroyed Jerusalem and presided over the Babylonian captivity in 587/586 BCE.

Negev: the semi-arid region to the south of ancient Judah. It is a term still used today to identify the region.

Nevi'im: the Hebrew term for "Prophets," which designates the second part of the Hebrew Scriptures.

Ninth of Av: the day and month that the Jerusalem temple was destroyed. It became an annual solemn observance on which the book of Lamentations is read.

Noth, Martin: the German OT scholar who advanced the theory of the Deuteronomistic History (DtrH).

numerical saying: a common form of ancient Israelite wisdom literature that identifies a given number of things (in a pattern of x, x+1) that fall in a certain category (e.g., Prov 30:18-31).

onomasticon: a form of wisdom literature common in the ANE that consists in simply listing natural phenomena that fall in given category (e.g., Job 38–41).

Palestine: the region between the Jordan River valley to the east of Israel and the Mediterranean Sea on the west. The name is derived from the ancient Philistine people, who lived in the southwestern region of ancient Israel. The term was used by the Emperor Hadrian to remove any association of Israel with the land. Many Jewish people today see it as a pejorative term.

parallelism: the most prominent feature of Hebrew poetry. It typically involves two poetic lines that parallel each other in some artistic way.

Passover: the Hebrew feast (*Pesach*) that commemorates the Exodus deliverance of Israel from Egypt on the night when death overtook the firstborn of Egypt but passed over the homes of the Hebrews who sprinkled their doorposts with the blood of a sacrificed lamb.

patriarchal (or ancestral) history: the term used by scholars to refer to Genesis 12–50.

patriarchy: a social system in which males have primary power and predominate in leadership roles, moral authority, social privilege, inheritance rights, and property ownership.

Pentecost: feast that is observed 50 days (seven weeks) after Passover; also called the Feast of Weeks; it commemorates the giving of the law at Mount Sinai.

Pentecostal: the term used to identify the movement associated with the outpouring of the Holy Spirit at Azusa Street in Los Angeles, California, beginning in 1906 and spreading to all continents by the end of the 20th century.

Pentateuch: the title favored in the Christian tradition for the first five books of the OT.

postexilic: the time period after the end of the Babylonian Exile of 605–538 BCE until the Roman Period in 63 BCE.

postmodern biblical criticism: an approach that represents the most recent wave of academic biblical study, emerging with the larger cultural shift from modernity to postmodernity. It focuses on "the reader in front of the text," that is, what the reader brings to the text as being decisive for interpretation. The numerous terms associated with this approach include reader-response criticism, contextual hermeneutics, post-critical hermeneutics, and deconstruction.

preexilic: the period of Israel's history before the last major exile of 586 BCE.

primeval history: the term used by scholars to refer to Genesis 1–11.

proverb: a wise saying, aphorism, or maxim; the most common form of ancient Israelite wisdom literature.

pseudepigraph: a term that means "false writing"; a prominent form of writing in the Intertestamental Period where a writing was fictitiously ascribed to a famous figure from the past in order to give it a sense of antiquity and authority.

293

Ptolemy: one of Alexander the Great's four generals who took over the region of Egypt after the death of Alexander. Daniel 11 appears to address the wars between the Seleucids and the Ptolemies.

Purim: the holiday established in the book of Esther to commemorate the intervention enabling the Jewish people living in Persia to escape a plot to exterminate them.

Qoheleth: the Hebrew name for Ecclesiastes, the preacher (or teacher) whose wise reflections are presented in the book of Ecclesiastes in a voice sounding like Solomon's.

Qumran: the proposed location of the monastic-like settlement on the northwest shore of the Dead Sea. It is believed that a group of Essenes who lived here were responsible for copying and hiding the Dead Sea Scrolls.

Red Sea (or Reed Sea): the body of water between Egypt and the Sinai Peninsula where the people of Israel were miraculously delivered from the Egyptian army when God parted the waters, allowing the Israelites to cross over on dry land (Exod 14).

redaction criticism: the method of biblical historical criticism that attempts to determine the editorial stages by which the biblical text was developed.

rhetorical criticism: the literary approach that focuses on the use of words and concepts that develop an author's argument within a book.

Rimmon: one of the chief gods of ancient Syria (2 Kgs 5:18).

rîv: the Hebrew term designating a covenant lawsuit; a literary form commonly used by OT prophets when presenting an oracle of divine judgment.

Seleucids: the dynasty named after Seleucus, one of Alexander the Great's four generals who took over the region of Syria and Israel after the death of Alexander. Daniel 11 appears to relate the wars between the Seleucids and the Ptolemies.

Septuagint: (abbreviated LXX) the Greek Old Testament written in Alexandria, Egypt, during the third century BCE (ca. 285 BCE), which was used by the Greek-speaking Jewish people and by the NT church.

Servant Songs: the term scholars use to designate a series of passages dispersed throughout Isaiah 42–53 that describe the special calling of a "servant of the LORD" whose saving work culminates in an act of vicarious suffering, which the NT identifies as pointing to the crucifixion of Christ.

Seymour, William J.: the African American preacher often credited with the beginnings of the Pentecostal movement at Azusa Street in Los Angeles, California, beginning in 1906.

Shema: the Hebrew term for "hear" that presents "The Great Commandment" recorded in Deut 6:4-5, which says, "Hear O Israel: The Lord our God, the Lord is one. You shall love the Lord your God with all your heart and with all your soul and with all your might" (ESV).

Sheol: the Hebrew term for the underworld or the grave.

Shephelah: the lowlands consisting of low, rolling hills located on Judah's western frontier next to the region controlled by the Philistines.

Sinai: the mountain where Moses encountered God in the burning bush and where God gave his people the law; also called Mount Horeb.

Sitz im Leben: the German phrase meaning "setting in life" that is used in the context of form criticism.

sola scriptura: a Latin phrase meaning "Scripture alone" that emerged in the Protestant Reformation to emphasize the primacy of scriptural authority.

Solomonic Enlightenment: a term used by OT scholars to describe Solomon's era as a time of major cultural advancement, drawing a parallel with the modern Western Enlightenment.

source criticism: the method of biblical historical criticism that attempts to determine the human sources/authors of biblical books and the time of their writing.

synchronic: the study of something (e.g., a text or book of the Bible) in terms of its final form rather than in terms of its stages of development over time.

Tabernacles: the feast commemorating the time Israel spent in the wilderness living in tents; also called the Feast of Booths.

Talmud: The body of Jewish literature that consists of the Mishnah (the recorded Jewish oral tradition) and the Gemara (the explanation of the traditions).

Tanak: the term for the Hebrew Scriptures, formed from the initial letters of the three parts of the Hebrew canon: Torah, *Nevi'im, Kethuvim*.

Tiamat: the Babylonian goddess of the sea.

Targum: the Aramaic paraphrase of the Hebrew Scriptures that came into use after the classical form of the Hebrew language died out.

Temple Sermon: the famous message that Jeremiah was directed to deliver at the entrance of the Jerusalem temple that announced the prospect of God's destruction of the temple (Jer 7; 26).

Ten Commandments: the "ten words," or Decalogue, that present the core commands of the law written on stone tablets by God and brought down by Moses at Mount Sinai.

text criticism: the study of the textual transmission process in order to determine the most likely original wording of the text as supported by the ancient manuscript evidence.

theocracy: a nation that understands itself to be governed by a god and set of religious rules or laws established by that deity (e.g., ancient Israel and certain sectors of modern Iran or Saudi Arabia).

theophany: the appearance of God or a heavenly being (such as an angel) to a human.

toledoth: the Hebrew term for "generations," used in the phrase "these are the generations," which Genesis uses as a recurring heading to introduce most of its main sections.

Torah: the Hebrew term for "law" or "Instruction" that became the primary title of the first part of the Hebrew canon of scripture (i.e., the five books also known as the Pentateuch).

Trito-Isaiah (or Third Isaiah): the name scholars give to the supposed author(s) of Isaiah 56–66, which they date to the time of the post-exilic restoration of the Jewish people upon their return from Babylon.

Wellhausen, Julius: the German OT scholar known for being the leading proponent of the JEDP/documentary hypothesis for the authorship of the Pentateuch.

YHWH: the personal name of God in Hebrew Scripture, often written as "Yahweh" but represented here by its four consonants (often called the Tetragrammaton, which simply means "four letters") out of respect for the Jewish aversion to pronouncing it in reverence of its extreme holy nature. Often represented in English translation by "Lord" spelled with with a capital "L" and "ord" in small caps.

ziggurat: a human-made mountain constructed by ANE people as a high place for meeting with their gods.

11044549R00171

Made in the USA
Monee, IL
05 September 2019